GCSE

GERMAN

David Rogers

LONGMAN
REVISE
GUIDES

Longman

LONGMAN GCSE REVISE GUIDES

Series Editors: Geoff Black and Stuart Wall

TITLES AVAILABLE:
Art and Design
Biology
Business Studies
C.D.T. - Design and Realisation
C.D.T. - Technology
Chemistry
Computer Studies
Economics
English*
English Literature*
French
Geography
German
Home Economics
Mathematics*
Mathematics: Higher Level and Extension
Music
Physics
Religious Studies
Science*
World History

* New editions for Key Stage 4

Longman Group UK Limited,
Longman House, Burnt Mill, Harlow,
Essex CM20 2JE, England
and Associated Companies throughout the world.

© Longman Group UK Limited 1988

First published 1988
Eighth impression 1994

British Library Cataloguing in Publication Data

Rogers, David
German. – (Longman GCSE revise guides).
1. German language – For schools
I. Title
438

ISBN 0-582-02430-7

Set in 10/12pt Century Old Style

Produced by Longman Singapore Publishers Pte Ltd
Printed in Singapore

enter for the other elements of the examination, but they cannot enter for the **Higher** level in a particular skill unless they also enter for the **Basic** level in that skill. Also, as we shall see below, a candidate will be unable to score more than a grade D unless **Basic Writing** is chosen.

66 Take care with choices 99

The examination scheme is designed to allow candidates to enter for what they can do, and to allow for maximum flexibility. In this way a candidate should not be faced with an impossible task on the day of the examination.

Table 1.1 shows, in grid form, the requirements laid down by the different examining groups. If it looks complicated, remember two things. First, you are only involved with **one** examining group. Find out which one that is, and then ignore the others in the table. Second, there is a key at the bottom of the table to help you understand it.

At the end of the chapter you can find the addresses of all the examining groups. You can ask your teacher for more information on your examination syllabus, or write directly to your examining group for your own copy.

Table 1.1: Grid showing GCSE Exam Group Requirements

EXAMINING GROUP	ULEAC		MEG			NEAB		SEG		NISEAC		WJEC	
Level	B	H	B	H1	H2	B	H	GL	EL	B	H	B	H
Listening													
Time allowed (minutes)	30	30	20	20	20	30	30	30	35	30	30	30	40
Stimulus	RT	RT	RT	RT	RT	RT	RT	RT	RT	RT	RT	RT	RT
Questions & answers in E/W	E	E	E	E	E	E	E	E	E	E	E	E/W	E/W
Reading													
Time allowed (minutes)	30	30	25	25	25	25	40	30	40	45	40	30	40
Questions & answers in E/W	E	E	E	E	E	E	E	E	E	E	E	E/W	E/W
Speaking													
Time allowed (minutes)	10	20	10	12	15	5–10	10–15	10	12	10	15	10	15
Rôle-plays	2	3	2	3	3	2/VS	4/VS	2	2	2	2	2	4
Conversation	√	√	√	√	√	√	√	√	√	√	√	√	√
Writing													
Time allowed (minutes)	45	60	25	30	35	25	50	30	60	45	50	30	70
Lists/Forms	O		C							*		*	
Messages	O		C			*C		*C		*		*	
Postcards	O		C			*C		*C		*		*	
Letters	CO	O		CO		C	C	C		*		*	C
Visuals/Pictures		O					*C				*		CO
Narrative/Topic/Report		O			CO		*C			*	*		CO

Key:

B	= Basic	E	= English
H	= Higher	W	= Welsh
H1	= Higher Part One	VS	= Visual Stimulus
H2	= Higher Part Two	O	= Option
GL	= General Level	C	= Compulsory
EL	= Extended Level	CO	= Compulsory but with an Option
RT	= Recording on Tape	*	= Could appear

The scheme for the Midland Examining Group (MEG) is somewhat different because the Higher Level is divided into 2 parts: Higher Part One and Higher Part Two. The idea is to extend further the range of choices the candidate has. You could, for example, do only Higher Part One Listening if that was the best you could be expected to do. However, if you have done Higher Part One in a skill, you can always **attempt** Higher Part Two, as you have nothing to lose by doing so.

The Southern Examining Group (SEG) calls its papers 'General Level' (= Basic) and 'Extended Level' (= Higher).

IGCSE

The International GCSE is an examination developed by the University of Cambridge Local Examinations Syndicate in co-operation with International Schools and Education Officials from different parts of the world. If you live in the United Kingdom and do not attend an international school, you will not be able to follow a course leading to the IGCSE.

The IGCSE follows the same aims as the GCSE and there are many areas which are common to GCSE and IGCSE. Although this book concentrates on the GCSE, it will also help you if you are studying for the IGCSE.

There are some important differences, however, which relate to the options, the grades and the type of questions.

As with GCSE, there are 7 Grades (A–G) and there are sections of the examination to test Listening, Reading, Speaking and Writing. The examination has two levels – Core and Extended – and you have to decide before the examination which level to enter. There are then only two possibilities:

1 **Core**
   Students opting for the Core can gain Grades C–G only. They must sit the following papers:

Paper 1 Listening – sections 1 and 2 (30 minutes)	$33^{1}/3$
Paper 2 Reading and directed Writing – sections 1 and 2 ($1^{3}/4$ hours)	$33^{1}/3$
Paper 3 or Paper 5 Speaking (15 minutes)	$33^{1}/3$

2 **Extended**
   Students opting for the Extended can gain Grades A–E only. They must sit the following papers:

Paper 1 Listening – sections 1, 2 and 3 (45 minutes)	25%
Paper 2 Reading and directed writing ($2^{1}/4$ hours)	25%
Paper 4 Continuous writing ($1^{1}/4$ hours)	25%
Paper 3 or Paper 5 Speaking (15 minutes)	25%

Papers 1 & 2 and 4 & 5 have some common sections, and Paper 6 is identical for Core and Extended. Paper 7 includes elements for Core and additional tests for Extended Level.

In general, the Core is like the GCSE Basic and the first part of the GCSE Higher Level, and the Extended covers all of the GCSE Higher Level.

Note that all questions are written in German and all answers are to be written in German; but as with the GCSE, the emphasis is very much on **communication**.

GRADES

Table 1.2 sets out the MINIMUM entry requirements for the different grades as stated in the national criteria. It must be stressed that candidates will have to perform very well across the full range of elements if they are to gain the MAXIMUM grade available on the basis of the minimum entry only. It is sensible to attempt an **additional** element beyond the minimum requirement for any particular grade.

Table 1.2: Minimum Entry Requirements

ELEMENTS ENTERED	MAXIMUM GRADE ATTAINABLE
Basic Listening, Basic Reading and Basic Speaking	E
Basic Listening, Basic Reading, Basic Speaking + one other element	D
Basic Listening, Basic Reading, Basic Speaking + Basic Writing + one other element	C
Basic Listening, Basic Reading, Basic Speaking + Basic Writing + Higher Writing + one other element	B
Basic Listening, Basic Reading, Basic Speaking + Basic Writing + Higher Writing + two other elements	A

Notice that you cannot gain a grade C or above unless you enter for **Basic Writing**, and you cannot obtain a grade B or above unless you also enter for **Higher Writing**.

THE MODES OF EXAMINATION

There are **three** different 'modes' or ways in which you can be examined. These are described below. Make sure you know which one applies to you.

Mode 1: Examinations conducted by an examining group on syllabuses set and published by the examining group.

Mode 2: Examinations conducted by an examining group on syllabuses devised by individual schools or groups of schools and approved by the examining group.

Mode 3: Examinations set and marked internally by individual schools or groups of schools, but moderated by an examining group, on syllabuses devised by individual schools or groups of schools.

There are also **'Mixed Mode'** examinations with both Mode 1 and Mode 3 features.

It is perhaps more helpful to define individual parts of an examination as being:

■ 'internally set and/or internally assessed', i.e. school based, or

■ 'externally set and/or externally assessed', i.e. examining group based.

For GCSE German most schools will follow Mode 1 courses. However, the oral tests (Basic Speaking and Higher Speaking), which will be set by the examining group, will be conducted by the candidate's teacher. The teacher will either mark the tests, or record them and send the recording to the examining group for marking. Some schools will devise their own **oral** tests, as under Mode 3 procedures, and follow the Mode 1 course for the **other** parts of the examination. On the other hand some schools or groups of schools will follow Mode 3 courses throughout.

Many students ask whether their German GCSE syllabus includes coursework, in the same way as other GCSE subjects. The simple answer to this is **no**, but some schools using a Mode 2 or Mode 3 examination **may** include some coursework. Find out!

ADDRESSES OF THE EXAM BOARDS

ULEAC **University of London Examinations and Assessment Council**
Stewart House, 32 Russell Square, London, WC1B 5DN
Tel: 071 331 4000
Fax: 071 631 3369

MEG **Midland Examining Group**
1 Hills Road, Cambridge, CB1 2EU
Tel: 0223 61111
Fax: 0223 460278

NEAB **Northern Examinations and Assessment Group**
Devas Street, Manchester, M15 6EX
Tel: 061 953 1180
Fax: 061 273 7572

NISEAC **Northern Ireland Schools Examinations and Assessment Council**
Beechill House, 42 Beechill Road, Belfast, BT8 4RS
Tel: 0232 704666
Fax: 0232 799913

SEG	**Southern Examining Group** Stag Hill House, Guildford, GU2 5XJ Tel: 0483 506506 Fax: 0483 300152
WJEC	**Welsh Joint Education Committee** 245 Western Road, Cardiff, CF5 2YX Tel: 0222 561231 Fax: 0222 571234
IGCSE	**International General Certificate of Secondary Education** University of Cambridge Local Examinations Syndicate 1 Hills Road, Cambridge, CB1 2EU Tel: 0223 61111 Fax: 0223 460278

CHAPTER 2

EXAMINATION TECHNIQUES

PREPARATION

LISTENING

READING

SPEAKING

WRITING

IN THE EXAMINATION

GETTING STARTED

As we have already established in Chapter 1, the GCSE examinations in German test the four language skills separately. In this section we look at ways of preparing yourself for tests in these skills. Here we shall concentrate on the more **general** techniques you can apply to each skill, leaving more detailed consideration to later chapters. We also look at a few techniques which are important in the **exam room** itself.

ESSENTIAL PRINCIPLES

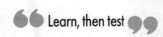

66 Learn, then test 99

Although the four skills are tested separately, they are very closely linked in real life. This means that any work you do to improve **one**, such as listening techniques, will also have a positive 'spin-off' effect on the other three.

Vocabulary-learning is a chore, but it is a necessary part of your preparation. Make sure you begin early and learn gradually, remembering to test yourself as you learn. Chapter 3 will help you to work your way through the topic areas you have to study in depth.

Grammar is an integral part of any language. Although the emphasis in the GCSE examination is less academic than in previous examinations, the more accurate you are, the higher the marks you will gain. Again, be methodical:

■ go over exercises you have done in class, do them again and see if you can improve on your earlier performances,

■ use the grammar section in Chapter 13 of this book,

■ draw up a practical checklist for use before and during the examination (see Chapter 14).

Working with a friend can often be a helpful change from working on your own. This is especially important for speaking and vocabulary work.

LISTENING

At first sight **Listening** is a difficult skill to practise on your own, but there is still plenty you can do. In the chapters on listening (Chapters 4 and 5) we go into detail about some of the things you can do, but here are some brief points as an introduction:

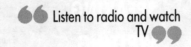

66 Listen to radio and watch TV 99

■ There is an increasing number of language programmes on radio and television. Watch them whenever you can. Make recordings, where that is possible, so that you can listen to them again, but check copyright procedures. Series worth trying are 'Get by in German', 'Deutsch direkt' and 'The German Programme'. You will need to check details yourself, because the series and times of transmission are constantly changing.

■ Most courses now have cassettes to accompany them, so make sure you hear them at school. You may be able to borrow listening material from your teacher. The cassette that goes with this book will also give you valuable practice in listening.

■ Depending on where you live, you may be able to pick up **German** radio stations. It's a good idea to tune in occasionally – even if only for the English football results in German, which are broadcast on German stations about an hour after they have been broadcast here. Again, you will be familiar with the news headlines in English, so when you hear them in German, at regular intervals during programmes, you will already have a good background. Similarly, you will know many of the music groups whose records are played on German radio, so this will help you understand some of the German spoken about them.

The 'Step Further' section at the end of Chapter 5 gives you a range of practical ways in which you can develop your listening skills.

READING

Reading is probably the easiest skill to revise, because there is plenty of material available. At GCSE you are required to read a wide range of texts in different styles, so the more you read, the better. Chapters 6 and 7 cover reading in detail, but here are some introductory points:

■ Make full use of your school textbook. It will no doubt contain much reading material, and the more modern courses provide an excellent range of texts suitable for GCSE. Re-read articles you have read and note down any vocabulary you do not know, without looking it up. This is an invaluable step on the way to learning vocabulary.

■ There are some interesting readers in schools and libraries. Find out what there is

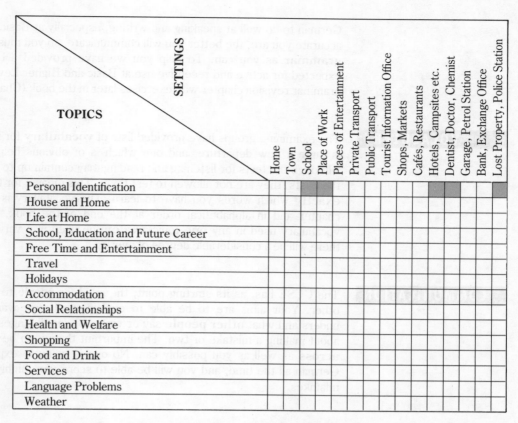

Table 3.1: Settings and Topic Areas

You should shade or colour in the squares where the topics and settings are most likely to coincide. **Personal Identification**, for instance, is most likely to be required at school, at your place of work, at a hotel (etc.), at the dentist (etc.) and at the Lost Property Office (etc.). So these squares have been shaded in for you. Now you consider the others.

LANGUAGE TASKS

A comprehensive list of the things you will be expected to do is provided on pages 14 to 21, broken down by topic area. It may appear somewhat off-putting at first, but you will soon see that there are many things that you can already do quite well. The list will also show you clearly what else you need to learn! Keep referring back to it.

You need to work your way through the list systematically and check that you can perform all the tasks relevant to you and the level of your examination entry. Towards the end of the book (Chapter 14) is a checklist on which you can record your progress. Note that there are two columns to show that you have tested yourself on two different occasions (it's no good learning something and then forgetting all about it!).

ACTIVE AND RECEPTIVE USE

In the same way that the examination is divided into Basic and Higher Levels, what you are required to do is also divided into two sections: Active and Receptive. **Active use** means what you will be expected to use, i.e. say or write. **Receptive use** refers to what you are expected to understand (when listening or reading). There are some differences in the requirements of the individual examining groups on this point, so in the lists under topic areas we have listed the most common words and expressions without indicating whether they are for active or receptive use. The vast majority are for **active** use, so you should learn to **use** as many as possible and ensure that you **understand** the rest. Do remember that you are free to use words which do **not** appear as long as they are relevant – indeed their use is encouraged. This is of course still more important at Higher Level.

GRAMMAR

One of the main aims of the GCSE course is to equip you to use language effectively for purposes of **practical communication**. This means that you do not have to use perfect

German to do well at speaking and writing, especially at Basic Level. However, the more accurate you are, the better you will communicate, so you must revise (or learn?) as much **grammar** as you can. To help you we have provided a breakdown of the grammar expected for active and receptive use at Basic and Higher Level. There is also a separate grammar revision chapter with exercises later in the book (Chapter 13).

VOCABULARY

The examining groups have provided lists of **vocabulary** for inclusion in their tests. This is quite a new departure, and one which is of obvious help to you and your teacher. Although the tests for listening and reading may contain up to 5% of words not included in their lists, they are not allowed to test them. This means, for the first time, that you know **exactly** which words you have to learn. The vocabulary is listed by topic area in this chapter and in alphabetical order at the end of the book. Please remember that the vocabulary used in any **one** topic area can be used in a variety of different settings, so there will be a considerable degree of overlap.

COMMUNICATION

The GCSE has, as its starting point, the need for people to be able to understand each other. Your aims are to be able to explain what **you** want to say or write, and to understand what **other people** say or write. So, at all stages, you should not be worried about making a mistake or two. The important thing is to be able to **get your message across** as well as you possibly can. No one is going to expect you to produce perfect German all the time, and you will be able to score very highly even if you do make some mistakes.

LANGUAGE TASKS BY TOPIC AREA

Tasks required at Higher Level **only** are marked with an H.

PERSONAL IDENTIFICATION

You should be able to give information about yourself and others (e.g. members of your family or host family) and seek information from others on the following points:

- Names (including spelling out your own name)
- Home Address (including spelling out the name of your home town)
- Telephone Numbers
- Ages and Birthdays
- Nationality

- General Descriptions (including sex, marital status, physical appearance, character or disposition of yourself and others.
- H ■ Religion
- H ■ Likes and Dislikes (with regard to people and other topics in the syllabus).

HOUSE AND HOME

GENERAL

You should be able to discuss where and under what conditions you and others live. In particular you should be able to do the following:

- Say whether you live in a house, flat etc., and ask others the same.
- Describe your house, flat etc. and its location.
- Find out about, and give details of, rooms, garage, garden etc. as appropriate.

- Mention or enquire about the availability of the most essential pieces of furniture, the various amenities, services etc.
- Say whether you have a room of your own and describe your room or the room where you sleep.

- Say what jobs you do around the home.
- Ask where places and things are in a house.
- Say you need soap, toothpaste or a towel.
- Invite someone to come in, sit down, etc.

- Thank someone for hospitality.
- H ■ Offer and ask for help to do something about the house
- H ■ Ask permission to use or do things when a guest of a **German-speaking** family.

GEOGRAPHICAL SURROUNDINGS

You should be able to give information about your home town or village and surrounding areas, and seek information from others, with respect to:

- Location
- Character
- Amenities, attractions, features of interest, entertainment.

- what is good about it
- what is not so good about it
- how long you have been living there
- how you would improve it.

You should be able to name parts of Germany/Austria/Switzerland or the UK you know, and to talk about them.

LIFE AT HOME

You should be able to give and seek information about:

- members of the family, including a description of members of the family and their occupations
- family pets
- your daily routine
- the time you usually get up, go to bed and have meals, and how you spend your evenings and weekends

- what you do to help at home
- whether you have a spare-time job, and if so, what working hours and how much you earn
- how much pocket money you get and what you do with it.

SCHOOL

You should be able to exchange information and opinions about:

- your school/college and its facilities
- the type, size and location of your school and its buildings
- daily routines:
  when school begins and ends
  how many lessons there are and how long they last
  break times and lunch times
  homework

- how you travel to and from school
- your school year and holidays
- the subjects studied and your preferences
- clubs, sports, trips and other activities.

EDUCATION AND FUTURE CAREER

You should be able to discuss the following:

- H ■ the sort of education you have had or propose to continue with, mentioning the types of educational institution
- H ■ examinations
- H ■ special events in the school year, e.g. plays, sports day, visits

- H ■ your plans and hopes for the future, giving reasons as appropriate, including:
  immediate plans for the coming months and plans for the time after the completion of compulsory education
- where you would like to work.

FREE TIME AND ENTERTAINMENT

GENERAL

- State your hobbies and interests.
- Ask about the hobbies and interests of other people.
- Discuss your evening, weekend and holiday activities, and those of other people.
- Discuss your interest and involvement in:
  sport and sporting events
  intellectual and artistic pursuits
  youth clubs or societies.
- Give and seek information about leisure facilities.
- Express simple opinions about:
  radio and TV, films, and performances.

- Agree or disagree with **other people's** opinions.
- Ask if someone agrees with **your** opinions.
- Describe and comment on the leisure and entertainment facilities of the area you live in.
- H Discuss in more detail your interests and activities.
- H Discuss films/plays/concerts etc. in greater detail.
- H Describe how you spent a period of free time, e.g. an evening, a weekend.
- H Describe what you would like to do if opportunities and finance permitted.

PLACES OF ENTERTAINMENT

- Buy entry tickets for cinema or theatre, concert, swimming pool, football match, sports centre.
- Find out the cost of seats or entry.
- Find out or state the starting/finishing times.
- State or ask what sort of film or play it is.

- Ask if the film or event is/was good.
- Express an opinion (about the film or event).
- Agree or disagree with **other people's** opinions.
- Ask if someone agrees with **your** opinion.

TRAVEL

GENERAL

- Say how you get to your school/place of work (means of transport, if any; duration of journey).

- Understand and give information about other journeys.

FINDING THE WAY

- Attract the attention of a passer-by.
- Ask where a place is.
- Ask the way (to a place).
- Ask if it is a long way (to a place).
- Ask if a place is nearby.
- Ask if there is a place or an amenity nearby.
- Understand directions.
- Ask if there is a bus, train, tram or coach.

- Ask someone to repeat what he or she has said.
- Say you do not understand.
- Thank someone for his or her help.
- H Give directions to strangers.
- H State and enquire about distances.

TRAVEL BY PUBLIC TRANSPORT

- Ask if there is a bus, train, tram, tube or coach to a particular place.
- Buy tickets, stating:
  destination
  single or return
  class of travel
  day of travel.
- Ask about the cost of tickets.
- Ask about times of departure and arrival.

- Tell someone about proposed times of departure and arrival.
- Ask and check whether it is:
  the right platform
  the right station
  the right line or bus, tram, coach or stop.

- Ask about the location of facilities, e.g. bus stop, waiting room, information office, toilets.
- Ask if and/or where it is necessary to change buses, trains, trams or coaches.
- Ask or state whether a seat is free.
- Understand information given in brochures and tables.
- Write a letter about requirements for travel arrangements.
- Give travel information to others.
- Say what you have lost at the lost property office.

H ■ Ask how to get to a place by bus, train, tram, tube or coach.
H ■ Give the same information to others.
H ■ Reserve a seat.
H ■ Ask for information, timetables or a plan.
H ■ Ask about price reductions and supplements.
H ■ Make arrangements for taking, leaving or sending luggage.
H ■ Deal with an element of the unexpected in travel arrangements, e.g. delayed or cancelled departures, mislaid tickets, documents, lost luggage.

PRIVATE TRANSPORT

- Buy petrol by grade, volume or price.
- Ask for the tank to be filled up.
- Ask the cost.
- Ask someone to check oil, water and tyres.
- Ask where facilities are.
- Ask about the availability of facilities nearby.
- Check on your route.

H ■ Obtain and give information about routes, types of roads, traffic rules, parking facilities.
H ■ Report a breakdown, giving location and other relevant information.
H ■ Ask for technical help.
H ■ Pay and ask for a receipt.

TRAVEL BY AIR OR SEA

H ■ Buy a ticket.
H ■ Ask about the cost of a flight or crossing.
H ■ Say where you would like to sit.
H ■ Ask about times of departure and arrival.
H ■ Inform someone about your proposed times of arrival and departure.

H ■ Check which is the right flight, ferry or hovercraft.
H ■ Ask about the location of facilities.
H ■ State whether you wish to declare anything at the customs.

HOLIDAYS GENERAL

- Talk about holidays in general, saying: where you normally spend your holidays how long they last with whom you go on holiday what you normally do.
- Understand others giving the above information.
- Describe a previous holiday, saying: where you went how you went with whom you went for how long where you stayed what the weather was like what you saw and did what your general impressions were.

- Understand others giving information.
- Describe your holiday plans.
- Say whether you have been abroad, e.g. to Germany/Austria/Switzerland, and give details if applicable.
- Understand others giving above information.

H ■ Supply information about travel documents.

TOURIST INFORMATION

- Ask for and understand information about a town or region (maps, brochures of hotels and campsites).
- Ask for and understand details of excursions, shows, places of interest (location, costs, times).
- Give tourist information to others, e.g. prospective tourists, about your own area or one you have visited.

- React to (i.e. welcome or reject) suggestions about activities and places of interest.
- Write a short letter asking for information and brochures about a town or region and its tourist facilities or attractions.

ACCOMMODATION

GENERAL

- Describe accommodation you use or have used.
- Write a short letter asking about the availability and price of accommodation at a hotel, campsite or youth hostel and about amenities available.

- Write a short letter booking such accommodation.
- Read and understand relevant information about accommodation, e.g. brochures.
- H ■ Make complaints.

HOTEL

- Ask if there are rooms available.
- State when you require a room/rooms and for how long.
- Say what sort of room is required.
- Ask the cost (per night, per person, per room).
- Say it is too expensive.
- Ask to see the room(s).
- Accept or reject a room.
- Check in.
- Say that you have (not) reserved accommodation.

- Identify yourself.
- Ask if there is a particular facility (e.g. restaurant) in or near the hotel.
- Ask where facilities are, e.g. telephone, car park, lift, lounge.
- Ask if meals are included.
- Ask what meals are available.
- Ask the times of meals.
- Ask for your key.
- Say you would like to pay.
- Thank someone for his or her help.

YOUTH HOSTEL

- Ask if there is any room.
- State when you wish to stay and for how long.
- State how many males and females require accommodation.
- Say whether you have reserved or not.
- Identify yourself.
- Ask the cost (e.g. per night or per person).

- Ask where facilities are.
- Say you would like to pay.
- Ask about meal times.
- Ask about opening and closing times.
- H ■ Ask about rules and regulations.
- H ■ Say you have a sleeping bag.
- H ■ Say you wish to hire a sleeping bag.

CAMPSITE

- Ask if there is any room.
- State when you wish to stay and for how long.
- Say whether you have reserved a place or not.
- Identify yourself.
- Say how many tents, caravans, people or vehicles there are.
- Say how many children and adults are in the group.

- Ask the cost (per night, per person, per tent, caravan, vehicle or facility).
- Say it is too expensive.
- Ask if there is a particular facility on or near the site.
- Ask where the facilities are.
- Buy essential supplies.
- H ■ Ask about rules and regulations.

SOCIAL RELATIONSHIPS

RELATIONS WITH OTHERS (GENERAL)

- Say whether you are a member of any clubs or groups; if so, which clubs and what activities are involved.
- Give information about your friends.
- Say if you have any friends in Austria/Germany/Switzerland.

MAKING ACQUAINTANCES

- Greet someone and respond to greetings.
- Ask how someone is and reply to similar enquiries.
- Say that you are pleased to meet someone.
- Introduce yourself (see also Personal Identification).
- Introduce an acquaintance to someone else.
- Give, receive and exchange gifts.
- Make a telephone call.

ARRANGING A MEETING OR AN ACTIVITY

- Find out what a friend wants to do.
- Ask what is on TV or at the cinema.
- Express a preference for an activity (e.g. watching TV, going out, visiting a friend).
- Invite someone to go out (stating when and where).
- Invite someone or suggest going to a particular place or event, or on a visit.
- Accept or decline invitations.
- State that something is possible, impossible, probable or certain.
- Say thank you and apologise.
- Express pleasure.
- Ask about, suggest or confirm a time and place to meet.
- Ask about and state the cost (of entry, etc).
- Express surprise, pleasure, regret, doubt, certainty.
- Apologise for late arrival.
- State likes and dislikes.

CURRENT AFFAIRS

- You should be able to follow the recounting or discussion of current issues and events of general news value, and of interest to 16-year-old students,

H - and to express your reaction to such items.

HEALTH AND WELFARE

GENERAL

- State how you feel (well, ill, better, hot, cold, hungry, thirsty, tired).
- Ask others how they feel.
- Ask about taking a bath or shower.
- Ask for soap, toothpaste, towel.
- Refer to parts of the body where you are in pain or discomfort.
- Call for help.
- Warn about danger.

H - Say you would like to rest or go to bed.

ILLNESS AND INJURY

H - Report minor ailments (e.g. temperature, cold, sunburn).
H - Ask for items in a chemist's and ask if they have anything for particular ailments.
H - Say you would like to lie down.
H - Respond to an enquiry about how long an ailment or symptom has persisted.
H - Say you would like to see a doctor or dentist.

H - Report injuries.
H - Deal with contact with the medical services.
H - Say whether you take medicine regularly and, if so, what.
H - Say whether or not you are insured.
H - Tell others about medical facilities and surgery hours.

ACCIDENT

H - Ask or advise someone to phone (doctor, police, fire brigade, ambulance, consulate, acquaintance).
H - Ask for someone's name and address.
H - Suggest filling in a road accident form.

H - Describe an accident.
H - Report that there has been an accident.
H - Ask or say whether it is serious.
H - Deny responsibility and say whose fault it was.

SHOPPING

GENERAL

- Ask for information about supermarkets, shopping centres, markets, shops.

- Ask where specific shops and departments are.

H ■ Discuss shopping habits.

SHOPS AND MARKETS

- Ask whether particular goods are available.
- Ask for particular items (mentioning e.g. colour, size, who it is for, etc.).
- Find out how much things cost.
- Say an item is (not) satisfactory or too expensive, small, big, etc.
- Say you (do not) prefer or want to take something.
- Express quantity required (including weights, volumes, containers).
- Find out opening and closing times.
- Say that is all you require.

- Say thank you.
- Enquire about costs and prices.
- Pay for items.
- Say whether things are too expensive.
- State whether you have enough money.
- Understand currencies used in German-speaking countries, including written and printed prices.

H ■ Ask for small change.

H ■ Return unsatisfactory goods and ask for a refund or replacement.

FOOD AND DRINK

GENERAL

- Discuss your likes, dislikes and preferences and those of others.
- Discuss your typical meals, meal times and eating habits.

- Buy food and drink (see Shops and Markets).

H ■ Explain to a visitor what a dish is or what it contains.

CAFÉ, RESTAURANT AND OTHER PUBLIC PLACES

- Attract the attention of the waiter/waitress.
- Order a drink or snack.
- Order a meal.
- Ask for a particular fixed-price menu.
- Say how many there are in your group.
- Ask for a table (for a certain number).
- Ask about availability of certain dishes and drinks.

- Ask the cost of dishes and drinks.
- Ask for an explanation or description of something on the menu.
- Express opinions about a meal or dish.
- Accept or reject suggestions.
- Ask if the service charge is included.
- Ask about the location of facilities (e.g. toilets, telephone).

AT HOME

- Express hunger and thirst.
- Ask about time and place of meals.
- Ask for food and table articles (including asking for more, a little, a lot).
- React to offers of food (accept, decline, apologise, express pleasure).

- Express likes, dislikes and preferences.
- Express appreciation and pay compliments.
- Respond to a toast, e.g. *Prost*.

SERVICES

POST OFFICE

- Ask where a post office or letter box is.
- Ask how much it costs to send letters, postcards or parcels to a particular country or within Germany/Austria/Switzerland.
- Say whether you would like to send letters, postcards or parcels.
- Buy stamps of a particular value.
- Find out opening and closing times.

- Say that is all you require.
- Give and seek information about where phone calls can be made.
- Ask if you can make a phone call.
- Ask for a phone number and give your own phone number.
- Answer a phone call, stating who you are.

- Make a phone call and ask to speak to someone.
- H ■ Ask someone to ring you up.
- H ■ Find out if others can be contacted by phone.

H ■ Tell others you will ring up.
H ■ Ask for coins.
H ■ Ask for a reversed charge call.
H ■ Send a telegram.

BANK OR EXCHANGE OFFICE

H ■ Say you would like to change travellers' cheques or money (including sterling).
H ■ Ask for coins or notes of a particular denomination.
H ■ Give proof of identify (e.g. show passport).

H ■ Cope with any likely eventuality that may arise while using a bank or foreign exchange office to change currency or cheques.

LOST PROPERTY

H ■ Report a loss or theft, stating what you have lost saying when and where it was lost or left, describing the item (size, shape, colour, make, contents).

H ■ Express surprise, pleasure, disappointment, anger.

HAVING THINGS REPAIRED AND CLEANED

H ■ Report an accident, damage done or breakdown.
H ■ Ask if shoes, clothes, camera, etc. can be repaired.
H ■ Explain what is wrong and ask if shoes, etc can be repaired.
H ■ Ask for, and offer, advice about getting something cleaned or repaired.
H ■ Ask for an item of clothing to be cleaned.

H ■ Arrange for clothing to be washed.
H ■ Find out how long it will take, what it will cost, when an item will be ready.
H ■ Thank, complain, express disappointment or pleasure.
H ■ Suggest the need for repair or cleaning and report or comment on any action taken.

LANGUAGE PROBLEMS

- State whether or not you understand.
- Ask someone to repeat what he or she has said.
- Ask for and understand the spelling out of names, place-names, etc.
- Ask if someone speaks English or German.
- State how well or how little you speak and understand German.
- Ask what things are called in German or English.
- Ask what words or phrases mean.

- Say you do not know (something).
- Say that you have forgotten (something).
- Apologise.
- Ask whether, or state that, something is correct.
- H ■ Say for how long you have been learning German and any other languages you know.
- H ■ Ask someone to explain something or to correct mistakes.
- H ■ Ask how something is pronounced.

WEATHER

- Describe or comment on current weather conditions.
- Ask about weather conditions in Germany/Austria/Switzerland.
- Describe the climate of your own country and ask about the climate in Germany/Austria/Switzerland.

- Understand simple predictions about the weather.
- H ■ Understand spoken and written weather forecasts.

VOCABULARY BY TOPIC AREAS

Here the vocabulary required by the examining groups is broken down by **topic area**. This should help you in preparing for **all four skills** in German. The lists within each topic area are often alphabetical, **but not always**. Especially with shorter lists, it sometimes makes more sense to arrange the words in clusters of related items. You can of course find a **full** alphabetical listing of vocabulary in Chapter 15.

PERSONAL IDENTIFICATION

NAME

Basic

der Name (-n)   *name*
der Nachname/Familienname (-n)   *surname*
der Vorname (-n)   *first name*
　　heißen   *to be called*
　　nennen   *to call*
　　schreiben   *to write*
　　in Ordnung   *all right*
　　Herr, Frau, Fräulein   *Mr, Mrs, Miss*
　　(e.g. Herr Kaupsch)   *(e.g. Mr Kaupsch)*
die Unterschrift (-en)   *signature*

Higher

der Mädchenname (-n)   *maiden name*
　　buchstabieren   *to spell*
　　sich schreiben   *to write one's name*
　　unterschreiben   *to sign*

　　letters of the alphabet (see Chapter 15)

ADDRESS AND TELEPHONE

Basic

die Adresse (-n)   *address*
die Allee (-n)   *avenue*
die Anschrift (-en)   *address*
der Wohnort (-e)   *place of residence*
die Straße (Str.) (-n)   *street*
die (Haus)Nummer (Nr.) (-n)   *(house) number*
das Dorf (-̈er)   *village*
die Stadt (-̈e)   *town*
das Land (-̈er)   *country, state (of Germany)*
der Park (-s)   *park*
die Parkanlage (-n)   *park*
der Platz (-̈e)   *place, square*
die Postleitzahl (-en)   *postal code*
der Weg (-e)   *way, path*

der Brief (-e)   *letter*
der Briefumschlag (-̈e)   *envelope*
der Umschlag (-̈e)   *envelope*
das Telefon   *telephone*
das Telefonbuch (-̈er)   *telephone directory*
die Telefonnummer (-n)   *telephone number*
die Vorwahlnummer (-n)   *dialling (STD) code*

　　wohnen   *to live*

NATIONALITY

Basic

der Ausweis (-e)   *identity card*
der Paß (-̈e)   *passport*
der Staat (-en)   *state*
die Postleitzahl (-en)   *postcode*

　　England/Deutschland/Österreich
　　　England/Germany/Austria

die BRD   *the FRG*
die DDR   *the GDR*
die Schweiz   *Switzerland*
die Bundesrepublik   *the Federal Republic (and other countries as appropriate)*
　　Belgien – Belgier/-in – belgisch   *Belgium – Belgian (person)–Belgian*
　　Frankreich – Franzose/Französin – französisch   *France – Frenchman/woman – French*
　　Holland (die Niederlande) – Holländer/-in – holländisch   *Holland (The Netherlands) – Dutchman/woman – Dutch*
　　Italien – Italiener/-in – italienisch   *Italy – Italian (person) – Italian*
　　Spanien – Spanier/-in – spanisch   *Spain – Spaniard – Spanish*
die (Vereinigten) Staaten/Amerika – Amerikaner/-in – amerikanisch   *the (United) States/America – American – American*

Higher

das Ausland   *abroad*
der Ausländer (-)   *foreigner (male)*
die Ausländerin (-nen)   *foreigner (female)*
　　names of other major countries, nationalities, adjectives

AGE

Basic

　　geboren am . . .   *born on*
　　(e.g. ich bin am zweiten Juni geboren)   *(e.g. I was born on the 2nd of June)*
　　geboren in . . .   *born in*
　　(e.g. ich bin in London geboren)   *(e.g. I was born in London)*
der Geburtstag (-e)   *birthday*
das Geburtsdatum (Geburtsdaten)   *date of birth*
der Geburtsort (-e)   *place of birth*
das Alter (-)   *age*
das Jahr (-e)   *year*
der Monat (-e)   *month*
　　(e.g. 4 Monate alt)   *(e.g. 4 months old)*
das Kind (-er)   *child*
der/die Erwachsene (-n)   *adult*

　　jung   *young*
　　alt   *old*

PEOPLE

Basic

der Mann (-̈er)   *man*

	Herren (H)	*Gentlemen (on toilet door)*
der	Junge (-n)	*boy*
die	Dame (-n)	*lady*
	Damen (D)	*Ladies (on toilet door)*
die	Frau (-en)	*woman*
das	Mädchen (-)	*girl*
die	Staatsangehörigkeit	*nationality*
der	Engländer (-)/die Engländerin (-nen)	
	Englishman/woman, Englander	
	englisch *English*	
der } die }	Deutsche (-n)	*German (person)*
ein	Deutscher/eine Deutsche	*a German*
	deutsch *German*	
	(and other nationalities as appropriate)	
	von wo	*where from, from where*
das	Land (¨er)	*country, state (of Germany)*

Higher

der } die }	Jugendliche (-n)	*young person, youth*
ein	Jugendlicher/eine Jugendliche	*a youth*
das	Geschlecht (-er)	*sex*
	männlich *male*	
	weiblich *female*	
	verlobt *engaged*	
der } die }	Verlobte	*fiancé(e)*
	verheiratet *married*	
	ledig *single*	
	geschieden *separated, divorced*	
die	Witwe (-n)	*widow*
der	Witwer (-)	*widower*
der	Österreicher (-)/die Österreicherin (-nen)	
	Austrian (person)	
	österreichisch *Austrian*	
der	Schweizer (-)/die Schweizerin (-nen)	
	Swiss (person)	
der	Ausländer (-)/die Ausländerin (-nen)	
	foreigner	
die	Heimat (-en)	*home country*

DESCRIBING PEOPLE

Basic

	was für (ein/eine) . . .?	*what kind of (a) . . .?*
	wie (*e.g.* Wie ist dein Bruder?)	*how, what, what is . . . like (e.g. what is your brother like?)*
	freundlich *friendly*	
	unfreundlich *unfriendly*	
	lustig *happy, cheerful, funny*	
	faul *lazy*	
	fleißig *hard-working*	
	intelligent *intelligent*	
	dumm *stupid*	
	dick *fat*	
	schlank *slim*	
der	Bart *beard*	
der	Schnurrbart (¨e) *moustache*	
die	Brille (-n) *glasses*	
das	Auge (-n) *eye*	
das	Haar (-e) *hair*	
	ähnlich *similar, like*	
	reich *rich*	
	arm *poor*	
	allein *alone*	
	böse *angry, naughty*	
	glücklich *happy*	
	aussehen (*sep.*) *to look (like)*	
	lachen *to laugh*	
	erkennen *to recognise*	
die	Angst (¨e) *worry*	

Higher

	sympathisch *friendly, nice*	
	ehrlich *sincere, honest*	
	nervös *nervous*	
	gut/schlecht gelaunt *good/bad tempered*	
	neugierig *inquisitive*	
	blöd *stupid*	
	doof *stupid*	
	dünn *thin*	
	(sich) erinnern *to remind (remember)*	
	lebhaft *lively*	
	frech *cheeky*	
	schüchtern *shy*	
	leiden können *to like*	
	sich vertragen *to get on with each other*	
die	Religion *religion*	
	katholisch *Catholic*	
	evangelisch *Protestant*	
	(and other religions as appropriate)	

THE FAMILY AND RELATIVES

Basic

die	Familie (-n)	*family*
die	Eltern	*parents*
der	Vater (¨)	*father*
	Vati	*dad*
die	Mutter (¨)	*mother*
	Mutti	*mum*
der	Mann (¨er)	*man, husband*
die	Frau (-en)	*woman, wife*
das	Kind (-er)	*child*
das	Einzelkind (-er)	*only child*
das	Baby (-s)	*baby*
der	Junge (-n)	*boy*
das	Mädchen (-)	*girl*
der	Sohn (¨e)	*son*
die	Tochter (¨)	*daughter*
	Geschwister	*brothers and sisters*
der	Bruder (¨)	*brother*
die	Schwester (-n)	*sister*
die	Großeltern	*grandparents*
der	Großvater (¨)	*grandfather*
der	Opa/Opi	*grandad*
die	Großmutter (¨)	*grandmother*
	Oma/Omi	*granny*
der	Onkel (-)	*uncle*
die	Tante (-n)	*aunt*
der	Neffe (-n)	*nephew*
die	Nichte (-n)	*niece*
der } die }	Verwandte (-n)	*relative*
der	Vetter (-)	*cousin (male)*
die	Kusine (-n)	*cousin (female)*
der } die }	Älteste (-n)	*the eldest*
der	Freund (-e)	*friend (male)*
die	Freundin (-nen)	*friend (female)*
der	Mensch (-en)	*person*
die	Person (-en)	*person*
die	Leute	*people*
	heiraten	*to marry, get married*

Higher

der	Cousin (-s)/die Cousine (-n)	*cousin*
der	Ehemann (¨er)	*husband*
die	Ehefrau (-en)	*wife*
das	Ehepaar (-e)	*married couple*
der	Schwager (¨)	*brother-in-law*
die	Schwägerin (-nen)	*sister-in-law*
	Schwieger-	*-in-law*
der	Schwiegersohn (¨e)	*son-in-law*

HOUSE AND HOME – LIFE AT HOME

HOUSE

Basic
das Haus (¨er) *house*
das Doppelhaus (¨er) *semi-detached house*
das Einfamilienhaus (¨er) *detached house*
das Reihenhaus (¨er) *terraced house*
das Bungalow (-s) *bungalow*
der Bauernhof (¨e) *farm*
die Wohnung (-en) *home, flat*
der Block (-s) *block (of flats)*
das Gebäude *building*
die (Haus)Tür (-en) *(front) door*
der Schlüssel (-) *key*
klingeln *to ring*
klopfen *to knock*
schellen *to ring*
der Garten (¨) *garden*
der Hof (¨e) *yard, courtyard*
die Garage (-n) *garage*
die Scheune (-n) *barn, shed*
die Mauer (-n) *wall*
die Etage (-n) *floor, storey*
der Stock (¨e) *floor, storey*
das Stockwerk (-e) *floor, storey*
die Terrasse (-n) *terrace*

alt *old*
bequem *comfortable*
groß *big, large*
klein *small, little*
modern *modern*
nett *nice, pleasant*
neu *new*
oben *upstairs, above*
unten *downstairs, below*

bauen *to build*
anbauen *(sep.)* *to extend*
kaufen *to buy*
verkaufen *to sell*
mieten *to rent*
wechseln *to change*
wohnen *to live*

ROOMS

General
das Badezimmer (-) *bathroom*
das Eßzimmer (-) *dining room*
die Küche (-n) *kitchen*
das Schlafzimmer (-) *bedroom*
das Wohnzimmer (-) *living room*
der Raum (¨e) *room*
das Zimmer (-) *room*
der Flur (-e) *hall*
der Keller (-) *cellar*
die Toilette (-n) *toilet*
das Klo/WC *toilet*
die Treppe (-n) *stairs, staircase*
der Lift (-e *or* -s) *lift*
die Decke (-n) *ceiling*
der Fahrstuhl (¨e) *lift*
der (Fuß)Boden (¨) *floor*
die Wand (¨e) *wall*
das Fenster (-) *window*

Higher
das Dach (¨er) *roof*
der Dachboden (¨) *attic, loft*
das Erdgeschoß (-sse) *ground floor*
das Obergeschoß (-sse) *upper floor*
das Hochhaus (¨er) *block of flats*
die Aussicht (-en) *view*

die Lage (-n) *situation, location*
die (Zentral)Heizung *(central) heating*

gemütlich *cosy*
möbliert *furnished*
(an)streichen *to paint*
tapezieren *to wallpaper*
heizen *to heat*
umziehen *(sep.)* *to move*

BEDROOM

Basic
das Schlafzimmer (-) *bedroom*

das Bett (-en) *bed*
das Bettzeug (-e) *bedclothes, bedding*
die Kleiderbürste (-n) *clothes, brush*
der Kleiderschrank (¨e) *wardrobe*
die Kommode (-n) *chest of drawers*
die Lampe (-n) *lamp*
der Sessel (-) *armchair*
der Stuhl (¨e) *chair*
der Tisch (-e) *table*
der Wecker (-) *alarm clock*

eigen *own*
teilen *to share*

Higher
die (Bett)Decke (-n) *bedcover, bedspread, quilt*
das Bettlaken (-) *sheet*
das Bettuch (¨er) *sheet*
die Bettwäsche *bedding, bed linen*
das Federbett (-en) *quilt, duvet*
die Gardine (-n) *curtain*
der Vorhang (¨e) *curtain*
das Rollo (-s) *blind, roller blind*
das Kopfkissen (-) *pillow*
der Nachttisch (-e) *bedside table*
der Spiegel (-) *mirror*
die Steppdecke (-n) *down quilt*
der Teppich (-e) *carpet*

KITCHEN

Basic
die Küche (-n) *kitchen*

die Gabel (-n) *fork*
der Löffel (-) *spoon*
das Messer (-) *knife*
das Glas (¨er) *glass*
die Tasse (-n) *cup*
der Teller (-) *plate*
der Apparat (-e) *electrical appliance, machine*
der Herd (-e) *cooker, stove*
der Kühlschrank (¨e) *refrigerator*
die Waschmaschine (-n) *washing machine*
die Kaffeekanne (-n) *coffee pot*
die Teekanne (-n) *teapot*
das Licht (-er) *light*
das Wasser *water*
der (Wasser)Hahn (¨e) *tap*
der Knopf (¨e) *button, knob*

drücken *to press*
anmachen *(sep.)* *to turn/switch on*
ausmachen *(sep.)* *to turn/switch off*
ziehen *to pull*

Higher
das Geschirr (-e) *crockery*
der (Koch)Topf (¨e) *saucepan*

der Ofen (-) *oven, stove*
die Schale (-n) *bowl, dish; scales*
die Schüssel (-n) *container, dish*
der (Abfall)Eimer (-) *(rubbish) bin*
    Elektro- *electric-*
    elektrisch *electric*
die Spülmaschine (-n) *dishwasher*
der Staubsauger (-) *vacuum cleaner*
die Tiefkühltruhe (-n) *deep-freeze*
das Spülmittel (-) *washing-up liquid*
das Waschpulver (-) *washing powder*

an sein (das Licht ist an) *to be on (the light is on)*
ausschalten (*sep.*) *to switch/turn off*
einschalten (*sep.*) *to switch/turn on*
wegwerfen (*sep.*) *to throw away*

BATHROOM

Basic
das Badezimmer (-) *bathroom*

das Bad (-̈er) *bath, bathroom*
die Badewanne (-n) *bath (tub)*
die Dusche (-n) *shower*
das (Haar)Shampoo *shampoo*
das Toilettenpapier (-e) *toilet paper*
das Wasser *water*
die Zahnbürste (-n) *toothbrush*
die Zahnpasta *toothpaste*

Higher
das Handtuch (-̈er) *hand towel*
der Rasierapparat (-e) *electric shaver*
das Waschbecken (-) *washbasin, sink*
der (Wasch)Lappen (-) *flannel, cloth*

DINING ROOM, LIVING ROOM

Basic
das Eßzimmer (-) *dining room*
das Wohnzimmer (-) *living room*

der Aschenbecher (-) *ashtray*
das Bild (-er) *picture*
das Foto (-s) *photo*
der Fernsehapparat (-e) *TV set*
der Fernseher (-) *TV set*
der Kamin *fireplace*
die Stereo(anlage) (-n) *stereo*
die Uhr (-en) *clock*
die Pflanze (-n) *plant*
die Möbel (*plural*) *furniture*
das Sofa (-s) *sofa*
der Tisch (-e) *table*
die Elektrizität *electricity*
das Gas *gas*
das Holz (-̈er) *wood, log*
der Knopf (-̈e) *button, knob*
das Öl *oil*
die Steckdose (-n) *electric socket*
das Wasser *water*

Higher
das Kissen (-) *cushion*
das Regal (-e) *shelf*
das Tablett (-e) *tray*
die Tischdecke (-n) *table-cloth*
die Birne (-n) *(light) bulb*
die Kerze (-n) *candle*
die Kohle (-n) *coal*
der Schalter (-) *switch*
der Stecker (-) *(electric) plug*
der Strom *current, electricity*

DAILY ROUTINE

Basic
abräumen (*sep.*) *to clear up/away*
anhaben (*sep.*) *to wear, have on*
aufmachen (*sep.*) *to open*
aufräumen (*sep.*) *to tidy (up), clear up*
aufstehen (*sep.*) *to get up*
aufwachen (*sep.*) *to wake up*
bringen *to bring*
decken *to cover, lay (table)*
duschen *to shower*
essen *to eat*
fernsehen (*sep.*) *to watch television*
frühstücken *to have breakfast*
kochen *to cook*
lassen *to leave, let*
machen *to do, make*
nähen *to sew*
nehmen *to take*
öffnen *to open*
schlafen *to sleep*
schließen *to close, shut*
sich (hin)setzen *to sit down*
sitzen *to sit*
sprechen *to speak, talk*
stehen *to stand*
tragen *to carry, wear*
trinken *to drink*
tun *to do, make*
verlassen *to leave*
vorbereiten *to prepare*
(sich) waschen *to wash*
zumachen (*sep.*) *to close, shut*

das Frühstück (-e) *breakfast*
das Mittagessen (-) *lunch*
das Abendbrot (-e) *tea, evening meal (cold)*
das Abendessen (-) *tea, evening meal (hot)*
zu Abend/Mittag essen *to have tea/lunch*
auf die Toilette gehen *to go to the toilet*
Platz nehmen *to sit down*
sauber machen *to clean*

Higher
abspülen (*sep.*) *to wash up*
(ab)trocknen (*sep.*) *to dry (up)*
abwaschen (*sep.*) *to wash up*
(sich) anziehen (*sep.*) *to put on/get dressed*
(sich) ausziehen (*sep.*) *to take off/get undressed*
benutzen *to use*
betreten *to enter*
(sich) bewegen *to move*
bügeln *to iron*
einschlafen (*sep.*) *to go to sleep*
erwachen *to wake up (yourself)*
fallen (lassen) *to fall/drop*
füllen *to fill*
leeren *to empty*
plaudern *to chat, talk*
putzen *to clean*
reden *to talk*
stricken *to knit*
sich umziehen (*sep.*) *to change (clothes)*
wecken *to wake up (someone else)*
die Wäsche *washing (clothes)*

GARDEN

Basic
der Garten (-̈) *garden*
die Gartenarbeit *gardening*
die Blume (-n) *flower*

der (Obst) Baum (¨e) *(fruit) tree*
das Gemüse (-) *vegetables*
das Gras (¨er) *grass*
die Pflanze (-n) *plant*

Higher

begießen *to water (flowers)*
mähen *to mow*
wachsen *to grow*
die Gartengeräte (*plural*) *garden tools*
der Rasen (-) *lawn*

ANIMALS AND PETS

Basic
das (Haus)Tier (-e) *animal/(pet)*
der (Gold)Fisch (-e) *(gold)fish*
der Hamster (-) *hamster*
der Hund (-e) *dog*
die Katze (-n) *cat*
die Maus (¨e) *mouse*
das Kaninchen (-) *rabbit*

das Meerschweinchen (-) *guinea pig*
die Schildkröte (-n) *tortoise*
das Pferd (-e) *horse*
das Insekt (-en) *insect*
die Kuh (¨e) *cow*
das Schaf (-e) *sheep*
das Schwein (-e) *pig*
der Vogel (¨) *bird*
der Wellensittich (-e) *budgerigar*

Higher
die Ente (-n) *duck*
die Fliege (-n) *fly*
die Gans (¨e) *goose*
das Huhn (¨er) *chicken*
das Vieh *cattle*
das Futter *food (for animals)*
der Käfig (-e) *cage*
die Hütte (-n) *hut, shed*
der Stall (¨e) *stable*
bellen *to bark*
fressen *to eat (of animals)*
füttern *to feed (animals)*

GEOGRAPHICAL SURROUNDINGS

URBAN/TOWN

Basic
die Stadt (¨e) *town*

die Altstadt (¨e) *old town*
die Ampel (-n) *traffic lights*
die Autobahn (-en) *motorway*
der Bahnhof (¨e) *station*
die Bank (-en) *bank*
die Baustelle(-n) *building site*
die Brücke (-n) *bridge*
die Bundesstraße (-n) *A road*
die Burg (-en) *castle*
der Bürgersteig (-e) *pavement*
das Büro (-s) *office*
die Bushaltestelle (-n) *bus stop*
der Dom (-e) *cathedral*
die Fabrik (-en) *factory*
der Fernsprecher (-) *telephone*
der Flughafen (¨) *airport*
der Fluß (¨sse) *river*
das Freibad (¨er) *open-air swimming pool*
der Fußgänger (-) *pedestrian*
die Fußgängerzone (-n) *pedestrian zone*
die Gefahr (-en) *danger*
das Hallenbad (¨er) *indoor swimming pool*
die Hauptstadt (¨e) *capital*
die Industrie (-n) *industry*
das Kino (-s) *cinema*
die Kirche (-n) *church*
die Klinik (-en) *clinic*
das Krankenhaus (¨er) *hospital*
die Kreuzung (-en) *crossing, junction*
der Lärm (*no plural*) *noise, din*
der Markt (¨e) *market*
der Marktplatz (¨e) *market square, market place*
das Museum (Museen) *museum*
in der Nähe (von) *near, nearby*
die Neustadt (¨e) *new town*
der Park (-s) *park*
die Parkanlage (-n) *park*
das Parkhaus (¨er) *multi-storey car park*
der Parkplatz (¨e) *car park, parking space*
die Polizei *police*
die Polizeiwache (-n) *police station*

die Post *post office*
das Postamt (¨er) *post office*
das Rathaus (¨er) *town hall*
das Schloß (¨sser) *castle*
das Schwimmbad (¨er) *indoor swimming pool*
das Stadion (Stadien) *stadium*
die Stadtmauer (-n) *town/city wall*
die Stadtmitte (-n) *town centre*
das Stadtzentrum (-tren) *town centre*
der Stein (-e) *stone*
die Stelle (-n) *place*
die Tankstelle (-n) *petrol station*
das Theater (-) *theatre*
die Treppe (-n) *stairs, staircase, steps*
der Turm (¨e) *tower*
der Verkehr (*no plural*) *traffic*
das Verkehrsamt (¨er) *tourist office*

Higher
der Bahnübergang (¨e) *level crossing*
der Bezirk (-e) *area, district*
die Bibliothek (-en) *library*
der Briefkasten (-) *letter box*
das Denkmal (¨er) *monument*
der Einwohner (-) *inhabitant*
das Gebiet (-e) *area, region*
die Gegend (-en) *region, neighbourhood*
der Kreis (-e) *district, ward, constituency*
der Ort (-e) *place*
das Reisebüro (-s) *travel agent's*
die Rolltreppe (-n) *escalator*
der Stadtbummel (-) *town walk, wander in town*
der Stadtteil (-e) *part of town*
der Vorort (-e) *suburb*
der Wegweiser (-) *traffic sign*
der Zebrastreifen (-) *zebra crossing*

frisch gestrichen *wet paint*
irgendwo *somewhere or other*
bummeln *to wander (e.g. when window-shopping)*
schützen *to protect*

RURAL/COUNTRYSIDE

Basic

das Land *the country*
    auf dem Lande *in the country*

der Berg (-e) *mountain*
das Dorf (¨er) *village*
das Feld (-er) *field*
der Fluß (¨sse) *river*
der Hügel (-) *hill*
die Insel (-n) *island*
die Landstraße (-n) *country road*
das Meer (-e) *sea*
    in der Nähe (von) *near, nearby*
die Natur (-en) *nature*
der Sand (*no plural*) *sand*
der See (-n) *lake*
die See (-n) *sea*
der Strand (¨e) *beach*
das Tal (¨er) *valley*
der Wald (¨er) *wood, forest*
die Wiese (-n) *field, meadow*

Higher

der Bach (¨e) *stream*
der Bahnübergang (¨e) *level crossing*
der Forst (-e) *forest*
das Gebirge (-) *mountains, mountain range*
der Gipfel (-) *summit*
die Küste (-n) *coast*
die Landschaft (-en) *scenery, countryside*

die Natur *Nature*
die Talsperre (-n) *dam*
die Überfahrt (-en) *crossing (of sea)*
das Ufer (-) *bank (of river)*

DESCRIBING SURROUNDINGS

Useful adjectives and other words.

Basic

angenehm *pleasant, attractive*
freundlich *friendly*
gefährlich *dangerous*
hoch *high, tall*
nett *nice, pleasant*
ruhig *quiet, peaceful*
sauber *clean*
schmutzig *dirty*
still *quiet, peaceful*
tief *deep*
unfreundlich *unfriendly*

gegenüber *opposite*
links *left, on the left*
rechts *right, on the right*
fließen *to flow*

Higher

flach *flat*
steil *steep*

SCHOOL BUILDINGS

Basic

die Gesamtschule (-n) *comprehensive school*
die Grundschule (-n) *primary school*
das Gymnasium (-ien) *grammar school*
die Hauptschule (-n) *secondary modern school*
der Kindergarten (¨) *kindergarten, nursery*
die Realschule (-n) *type of secondary school between Gymnasium and Hauptschule*
die Schule (-n) *school*

das Klassenzimmer (-) *classroom*
das Lehrerzimmer (-) *staffroom*
die Werkstatt (¨e) *workshop, studio*
der Hof (¨e) *yard, playground*
der Schulhof (¨e) *schoolyard, playground*

Higher

die Aula (Aulen) *hall*
die Bibliothek (-en) *library*
das (Sprach)Labor (-s) *(language) laboratory*
die Turnhalle (-n) *sports hall, gym*

SCHOOL ROUTINE

Basic

die Antwort (-en) *answer*
die Aufgabe (-n) *exercise*
das Beispiel (-e) *example*
der Bleistift (-e) *pencil*
das Buch (¨er) *book*
der Direktor (-en) *headmaster*
die Ferien *holidays*
die Frage (-n) *question*
    eine Frage stellen *to ask a question*
der Füller (-) *fountain pen*
die Hausaufgabe (-n) *homework*
der Hausmeister (-) *caretaker*

das Heft (-e) *exercise book*
die Klasse (-n) *class*
die Klassenarbeit (-en) *class test*
der Klassenlehrer (-) *class teacher (male)*
die Klassenlehrerin (-nen) *class teacher (female)*
der Kugelschreiber (-) *ball-point pen*
der Kuli (-s) *biro, pen*
der Lehrer (-)/die Lehrerin (-nen) *teacher*
die Mappe (-n) *briefcase, schoolbag*
die Mittagspause (-n) *lunch/midday break*
die Morgenpause (-n) *morning break*
die Pause (-n) *break*
Oster- *Easter . . .*
das Papier (-e) *paper*
das Schulbuch (¨er) *school book*
der Schulfreund (-e) *schoolfriend (male)*
die Schulfreundin (-nen) *schoolfriend (female)*
die Schultasche (-n) *schoolbag*
der Schüler (-)/die Schülerin (-nen) *(school) pupil*
der Semester (-) *term*
Sommer- *Summer . . .*
die Stunde (-n) *lesson, hour*
der Stundenplan (¨e) *timetable*
Weihnachts- *Christmas . . .*

streng *strict*
sehen *to see*
ansehen (*sep.*) *to look at*
antworten *to answer*
aufpassen (*sep.*) *to pay attention*
beantworten *to answer (someone or something)*
besuchen *to visit, attend*
fehlen *to be away/missing*
fragen *to ask*
lernen *to learn*
lesen *to read*

studieren *to study*
vergessen *to forget*
zuhören (*sep.*) *to listen*

Higher
das Blatt (¨er) *piece/sheet of paper*
der Filzstift (-e) *felt-tip pen*
das Klassenbuch (¨er) *class book/form book*
der Klassensprecher (-) *class representative (male)*
die Klassensprecherin (-nen) *class representative (female)*
die Kreide (-n) *chalk*
der Lappen (-) *cloth*
das Lineal (-e) *ruler*
das Pult (-e) *desk*
der Radiergummi (-s) *rubber, eraser*
der Schwamm (¨e) *sponge*
die Strafarbeit (-en) *punishment*
die Tafel (-n) *blackboard*
der Unterricht (*no plural*) *lessons*
der Zettel (-) *note*
das Zeugnis (-sse) *report*

hitzefrei *day off because of heat*
schulfrei *day off school*
abschreiben (*sep.*) *to copy*
ausfallen (*sep.*) *to be cancelled (e.g. due to teacher absence)*
bestrafen *to punish*
erfahren *to learn, experience*
loben *to praise*
nachsitzen (*sep.*) *to stay in/behind*
rechnen *to calculate*
schwänzen *to skip, skive, play truant*
versetzen *to transfer*

SUBJECTS, MARKS, EXAMINATIONS, FUTURE PLANS

Basic
Biologie *Biology*
Chemie *Chemistry*
der Computer (-) *computer*
Deutsch *German*
Englisch *English*
Erdkunde *Geography*
das Fach (¨er) *school subject*
Französisch *French*
die Fremdsprache (-n) *foreign language*
Geographie *Geography*
Geschichte *History*
Handarbeit *Handiwork (eg. Sewing, Needlework)*
Handelswissenschaft *Commerce*
Holzarbeit *Woodwork*
Informatik *Technology/IT/Computer Studies*
Kochen *Cookery, Domestic Science*
Kunst *Art*
Latein *Latin*
Maschineschreiben *Typing*
Mathe(matik) *Maths, Mathematics*
Metallarbeit *Metalwork*
Musik *Music*
Nähen *Sewing/Needlework*
Naturwissenschaft (-en) *Science*
Physik *Physics*
Religion *Religion*
Spanisch *Spanish*
Sport *Sport/Games*
Sport treiben *to do sport*
Technik *Technical Studies*
technisches Zeichnen *Technical Drawing*

Turnen *PE/PT/Gym*

ausgezeichnet *excellent*
gut *good*
interessant *interesting*
langweilig *boring*
leicht *easy*
mangelhaft *weak, lacking, unsatisfactory*
schwierig *difficult*
sehr gut *very good*
ziemlich gut *quite good*
das Lieblingsfach (¨er) *favourite subject*
die Note (-n) *mark*
Eins (bis) Sechs *1 to 6 (German school grades)*
die Abschlußprüfung (-en) *school-leaving examination*
die Prüfung (-en) *examination*
bestehen *to pass (an examination)*
durchfallen (*sep.*) *to fail (an examination)*

Higher
das Pflichtfach (¨er) *compulsory subject*
das Wahlfach (¨er) *optional subject*
das Abitur *Advanced Level examination*
die Oberstufe (-n) *sixth form*
die Leistung (-en) *performance, achievement*
die Berufsberatung (-en) *career guidance/advice*
die Fach(hoch)schule (-n) *technical college*
die technische Hochschule (-n) *technical high school*
der Lehrling (-e) *apprentice*
der Student (-en) *student*
die Universität (-en) *university*
die Uni *university*

mündlich *oral*
schriftlich *written*
mogeln *to cheat*
sitzenbleiben (*sep.*) *to repeat a year, stay in the same class*

OCCUPATIONS

Basic
der Apotheker (-) *chemist, pharmacist*
die Arbeit (-en) *work*
der Arbeiter (-) *worker*
die Arbeitsstelle (-n) *job; place of work*
der Arzt (¨e) *doctor*
der Bäcker (-) *baker*
der Bauarbeiter (-) *builder, building worker*
beim Bau arbeiten *to work in the building*
auf dem Bau arbeiten *trade*
der Bauer (-n) *farmer*
der Beamte (-n) *official, civil servant*
der Beruf (-e) *profession*
der Briefträger (-) *postman*
das Büro (-s) *office*
der Busfahrer (-) *bus-driver*
der Chef (-s) *chef*
der Computer (-) *computer*
der Direktor (-en) *director, manager*
der Drogist (-en) *chemist*
der Elektriker (-) *electrician*
die Fabrik (-en) *factory*
der Fabrikarbeiter (-) *factory worker*
der Fahrer (-) *driver*
der Fleischer (-) *butcher*
der Friseur (-)/der Frisör (-e) *hairdresser*
der Fußballspieler (-) *footballer*
die Industrie (-n) *industry*
der Kaufmann (¨er)/(die Kaufleute) *businessman*

der Kellner (-)   *waiter*
der Koch (ᵈe)   *cook*
die Konditorei (-en)   *cake shop, confectioner's*
die Krankenschwester (-n)   *nurse*
der Lehrer (-)   *teacher*
der Lkw-Fahrer (-)   *lorry-driver*
der Mechaniker (-)   *mechanic*
der Metzger (-)   *butcher*
der Musiker (-)   *musician*
das Orchester (-)   *orchestra*
der Pilot (-en)   *pilot*
der Plan (ᵈe)   *plan*
der Polizist (-en)   *policeman*
das Postamt (ᵈer)   *post office*
der Sekretär (-e)   *secretary*
der Staatsbeamte (-n)   *government official, civil servant*
die Stewardeß (-essen)   *stewardess*
der Sport (Sportarten)   *sport*
das Theater (-)   *theatre*
das Verkehrsamt (ᵈer)   *tourist office*
der Zahnarzt (ᵈe)   *dentist*
das Zimmermädchen (-)   *chambermaid*

vielleicht   *perhaps*
werden   *to become*

Higher
der Angestellte (-n)   *clerk*

der Arbeitgeber (-)   *employer*
der Arbeitnehmer (-)   *employee*
das Arbeitsamt (ᵈer)   *employment office*
der Betrieb (-e)   *large business, firm*
die Bundesbahn (-en)   *(Federal) Railway*
bei der Bahn arbeiten   *to work on the railways*
der Feuerwehrmann (ᵈer *or* -leute)   *fireman*
die Firma (-en)   *firm*
das Gehalt (ᵈer)   *salary*
der Geschäftsmann (ᵈer *or* -leute)   *businessman*
der Ingenieur (-e)   *engineer*
der Lohn (ᵈe)   *wage*
der Matrose (-n)   *sailor*
das Reisebüro (-s)   *travel agency*
der Rentner (-)   *pensioner*
der Schaffner (-)   *ticket collector*
der Schauspieler (-)   *actor*
der Schiedsrichter (-)   *referee*
der Soldat (-en)   *soldier*
der Tierarzt (ᵈe)   *vet*
der Verkäufer (-)   *salesman*
das Werk (-e)   *work*

arbeitslos   *unemployed*
berufstätig   *employed*
selbständig   *independent, self-employed*

FREE TIME AND ENTERTAINMENT

FREE TIME AND HOBBIES

Basic
der Ausflug (ᵈe)   *excursion, trip*
der Badeanzug (ᵈe)   *swimsuit*
die Badehose (-n)   *swimming trunks*
die Bademütze (-n)   *swimming hat*
das Badetuch (ᵈer)   *bath towel*
das Badminton   *badminton*
der Besuch (-e)   *visit*
das Boot (-e)   *boat*
der Computer (-)   *computer*
der Federball   *badminton*
das Fernsehen   *television*
im Fernsehen   *on television*
die Flöte (-n)   *flute*
der (Foto)Apparat (-e)   *camera*
die Freizeit   *free time*
der Fußball (ᵈe)   *football*
die Geige (-n)   *violin*
die Gitarre (-n)   *guitar*
der Handball (ᵈe)   *handball*
die Hit(parade)   *hit (parade)*
der Hobby (-s)   *hobby*
das Instrument (-e)   *instrument*
das Interesse (-n)   *interest*
das Jogging   *jogging*
die Karten (*plural*)   *cards*
die Kassette (-n)   *cassette*
der Kassettenrecorder (-)   *cassette recorder*
das Klavier (-e)   *piano*
die Langspielplatte (-n)   *long-playing record, LP*
das Magazin (-e)   *magazine*
die Mannschaft (-en)   *team*
das Orchester (-)   *orchestra*
das Picknick (-s *or* -e)   *picnic*
die Platte (-n)   *record*
der Plattenspieler (-)   *record player*
die Popmusik   *pop music*
das Programm (-e)   *(TV) channel, (radio) station*

das Radio   *radio*
im Radio   *on the radio*
der Rucksack (ᵈe)   *rucksack*
die Schallplatte (-n)   *record*
der Schild (-e)   *badge*
der Schlager (-)   *hit song*
das Schlagzeug (*no plural*)   *drums*
die Sendung (-en)   *(TV/radio) programme*
der Skilift (-e)   *ski lift*
der Ski (-s *or* -er)   *ski*
der Skistock (ᵈe)   *ski stick*
der Spaziergang (ᵈe)   *walk*
der Sport   *sport*
die Sportart (-en)   *kind of/type of sport*
der Sportplatz (ᵈe)   *sports field*
das Tennis   *tennis*
das Tischtennis   *table-tennis*
das Transistorradio (-s)   *transistor radio*
die Trompete (-n)   *trumpet*
der Verein (-e)   *club*
der Volleyball   *volleyball*
die Wanderung (-en)   *hike*
der Wasserball   *water polo*
das Windsurfen   *windsurfing*
die Zeitschrift (-en)   *magazine*
die Zeitung (-en)   *newspaper*

anfangen (*sep.*)   *to begin, start*
angeln   *to fish*
aufhören (*sep.*)   *to stop (doing something)*
ausgehen (*sep.*)   *to go out*
baden   *to swim*
beginnen   *to begin, start*
fahren   *to go, drive*
fernsehen (*sep.*)   *to watch television*
gucken   *to look, watch*
hören   *to hear, listen to*
joggen   *to jog*
kleben   *to stick*
knipsen   *to take photographs*
laufen   *to run*
nähen   *to sew*

radfahren (*sep.*)   *to bike, cycle*
reiten   *to ride (horse)*
sammeln   *to collect*
schauen   *to watch*
schwimmen   *to swim*
skifahren (*sep.*)   *to ski*
spazierengehen (*sep.*)   *to go for a walk*
spielen   *to play*
springen   *to jump, dive*
(sich) treffen   *to meet*
treiben   *to do (sport)*
wandern   *to hike*
werfen   *to throw*

fertig   *ready, finished*
klassisch   *classical*
laut   *loud*
leise   *quiet*

Higher

der Ansager (-)/die Ansagerin (-nen)   *(TV/radio) announcer*
die Aufnahme (-n)   *recording, photograph*
die Blaskapelle (-n)   *brass band*
das Brett (-er)   *board, stage (slang)*
das Dia (-s)   *slide (photographic)*
im Freien   *in the open (air)*
die Freizeitsbeschäftigung (-en)   *hobby, leisure activity*
die Illustrierte (-n)   *magazine*
die Kapelle (-n)   *band*
die Leichtathletik   *gymnastics, athletics*
die Messe (-n)   *fair*
das Mitglied (-er)   *member*
die Nachrichten (*plural*)   *news*
die Nadel (-n)   *needle*
das Netz (-e)   *net*
der Pfadfinder (-)   *scout*
die Reklame (-n)   *advertisement*
der Rollschuh (-e)   *roller skate*
der Roman (-e)   *novel (book)*
das Ruderboot (-e)   *rowing boat*
der Rundfunk (*no plural*)   *radio*
die Sammlung (-en)   *collection*
das Schach (*no plural*)   *chess*
der Schläger (-)   *bat, raquet (tennis, cricket etc.)*
Schlittschuh laufen   *to ice skate*
das Segelboot (-e)   *yacht*
die Seilbahn (-en)   *cable car*
die Sendefolge (-n)   *eposide (of series)*
die Sendereihe (-n)   *series*
das Taschenbuch (¨er)   *paperback book*
das Tonbandgerät (-e)   *tape recorder*
das Tor (-e)   *goal*
das Training (*no plural*)   *training*
der Trainingsanzug (¨e)   *tracksuit*
der Umkleideraum (¨e)   *changing room*
das Videogerät (-e)   *video recorder*
der Wegweiser (-)   *signpost*

basteln   *to make things with your hands (e.g. models)*
(sich) erkundigen   *to enquire*
fangen   *to catch (fish/ball)*
fotografieren   *to photograph*
kegeln   *to bowl (e.g. tenpin)*
klettern   *to climb*
malen   *to paint*
rennen   *to run*
rudern   *to row*
segeln   *to sail*
senden   *to send, broadcast*
stricken   *to knit*
tauchen   *to dive*

(sich) trainieren   *to train*
(sich) trimmen   *to get fit*

ENTERTAINMENT

Basic

der Ausgang (¨e)   *exit, way out*
die Ausstellung (-en)   *exhibition*
die Burg (-en)   *castle*
der Club (-s)   *club*
die Disco (-s)   *disco*
die Diskothek (-en)   *discotheque*
der Dokumentarfilm (-e)   *documentary (film)*
der Eingang (¨e)   *entrance*
der Eintritt (-e)   *entrance ticket*
das Eintrittsgeld (-er)   *entry cost/fee/price/money*
die Eintrittskarte (-n)   *(entrance) ticket*
zu Ende sein   *to be over/finished, to end*
das Endspiel (-e)   *final*
der Fan (-s)   *fan, supporter*
der Fanatiker (-)   *fan, supporter*
der Film (-e)   *film*
die Gruppe (-n)   *group*
der Jugendklub (-s)   *youth club*
die Karte (-n)   *card*
die Kasse (-n)   *cash desk, box office*
das Kino (-s)   *cinema*
der Klub (-s)   *club*
das Konzert (-e)   *concert*
der Krimi (-s)   *thriller (TV/book), detective story*
der Kriminalfilm (-e)   *thriller, detective story (TV/cinema)*
das Museum (Museen)   *museum*
der Notausgang (¨e)   *emergency exit*
der Platz (¨e)   *place, seat*
der Rang (¨e)   *row (in cinema, etc.)*
die Reihe (-n)   *row (in cinema, etc.)*
die Rundfahrt (-en)   *tour, round trip*
der Sänger (-)   *singer (male)*
die Sängerin (-nen)   *singer (female)*
das Schauspiel (-e)   *play (in theatre)*
das Schloß (¨sser)   *castle*
das Spiel (-e)   *play, game*
das Stadion (Stadien)   *stadium*
das Theater (-)   *theatre*
das Theaterstück (-e)   *stage play*
der Trickfilm (-e)   *cartoon*
die Vorstellung (-en)   *performance, show*
der Wildwestfilm (-e)   *western (film)*
der Zoo (-s)   *zoo*

besichtigen   *to visit*
gewinnen   *to win*
singen   *to sing*
tanzen   *to dance*
verlieren   *to lose*

frei   *free (not engaged)*

Higher

der Affe (-n)   *monkey, ape*
die Aufführung (-en)   *performance*
der Balkon (-s)   *balcony*
die Besichtigung (-en)   *visit*
die Bühne (-n)   *stage*
die Bundesliga (-gen)   *German Football League*
der Elefant (-en)   *elephant*
das Ergebnis (-se)   *result*
die Führung (-en)   *guided tour*
die Garderobe (-n)   *cloakroom*
der Jahrmarkt (-e)   *fair*

die Kirmes (-sen) *fair*
die Komödie (-n) *comedy*
der Löwe (-n) *lion*
die Meisterschaft (-en) *championship*
das Parkett (-e) *stalls (cinema/theatre)*
der Pokal (-e) *cup (for sporting event)*
der Profi (-s) *professional*
der Punkt (-e) *point*
der Reiseführer (-) *guide (male)*
die Reiseführerin (-nen) *guide (female)*
der Reiseleiter (-) *guide (male)*
die Reiseleiterin (-nen) *guide (female)*
der Saal (Säle) *hall*
die Saison (-s) *season*
die Schlange (-n) *snake, queue*
　　Schlange stehen *to queue*

der Tiger (-) *tiger*
der Treffpunkt (-e) *place to meet, meeting-place, rendezvous*
die Weltmeisterschaft (-en) *World Championship*
der Zuschauer (-) *spectator*

ausverkauft *sold out*
berühmt *famous*
eins zu null (*etc.*) *one–nil (etc.) (score)*
unentschieden *drawn (match)*
beschließen *to decide*
besorgen *to obtain*
schießen *to shoot*

TRAVEL FINDING YOUR WAY

Basic
die Ampel (-n) *traffic lights*
das Auto (-s) *car*
die Autobahn (-en) *motorway*
die Brücke (-n) *bridge*
die Bundesstraße (-n) *A road*
der Bus (-se) *bus*
das Dorf ("er) *village*
die Ecke (-n) *corner*
　　am/zum Ende *at the/to the end*
　　entschuldigen Sie bitte! *excuse me please!*
das Fahrrad ("er) *bicycle*
die Fahrt (-en) *journey, trip*
der Fluß ("sse) *river*
　　zu Fuß *on foot*
der Fußgänger (-) *pedestrian (male)*
die Fußgängerin (-nen) *pedestrian (female)*
die Hauptstraße (-n) *main street*
die Innenstadt ("e) *inner city*
die Klassenfahrt (-en) *class trip, excursion*
das Krankenhaus ("er) *hospital*
die Kreuzung (-en) *crossing*
die Landkarte (-n) *map*
die Landstraße (-n) *country road*
das Mofa (-s) *moped*
　　in der Nähe (von) *near*
der Platz ("e) *place, square*
die Post *post office*
das Postamt ("er) *post office*
das Rad ("er) *wheel, bicycle*
das Rathaus ("er) *town hall*
der Reisebus (-se) *coach*
die Richtung (-en) *direction*
die Seite (-n) *side*
die Stadt ("e) *town*
der Stadtplan ("e) *town plan*
die Straße (-n) *street, road*
die Toiletten (*plural*) *toilets*
der Wagen (-) *car*
der Weg (-e) *way, path*
der Zug ("e) *train*

ander *other*
breit *broad, wide*
dieser *this*
eng *narrow*
fremd (sein) *(be a) stranger, (be) foreign*
immer *always*
nächst *next*
spät *late*
(nicht) weit (von) *(not) far (from)*
erste/zweite/dritte (etc) *first/second/third (etc.)*

links *left, on the left*
rechts *right, on the right*
geradeaus *straight on*
da *there*
dahin *(to) there*
dann *then*
dort *there*
dorthin *(to) there*
drüben *over there*
gleich *straight away, immediately*
hier *here*
hinauf *up*
hinten *behind*
hinüber *over*
hinunter *down*
an . . . vorbei *past*
auf *on*
außer *apart from, besides*
bis zu . . . *as far as . . .*
entlang *along*
gegenüber *opposite*
hinter *behind*
neben *next to, by*
über *over, above*
um *around*
unter *under, below*
vor *in front of*
zu *to*
zwischen *between*
wie komme ich (am besten) . . .? *what's the (best) way . . .?*

abbiegen (*sep.*) *to turn off*
fahren *to travel, go*
finden *to find*
folgen *to follow*
gehen *to go (on foot)*
kommen *to come*
mitfahren (*sep.*) *to accompany, travel with (someone)*
nehmen *to take*

Higher
die Nebenstraße (-n) *side road, minor road*
die Querstraße (-n) *junction road*
der Schülerlotse (-n) *lollipop person*
das Ufer (-) *bank (of river)*

pünktlich *punctual*
weg *away*

dauern *to last*
sich erkundigen *to enquire*
überqueren *to cross*
sich verfahren *to get lost (by car)*

sich verirren   *to get lost (on foot)*
sich verlaufen   *to get lost (on foot)*
verpassen   *to miss (e.g. bus)*

TRAVEL BY BOAT, BUS, PLANE

Basic
die Abfahrt (-en)   *departure*
die Ankunft (¨e)   *arrival*
der Ausgang (¨e)   *exit*
die Auskunft (¨e)   *information*
der Ausstieg (-e)   *exit (on bus/tram)*
die Bahn (-en)   *railway*
der Bahnhof (¨e)   *railway station*
 Bhf   *abbreviation of 'Bahnhof'*
der Bahnsteig (-e)   *platform*
der Bus (-se)   *bus*
der Dampfer (-)   *steam (boat)*
die Deutsche Bundesbahn   *German Railways*
 DB   *abbreviation for 'Deutsche Bundesbahn'*
der D-Zug (¨e)   *express, fast train*
der Eilzug (¨e)   *express, fast train*
der Einstieg (-e)   *entrance, way in (on bus/ tram)*
der Fahrer (-)   *driver*
der Fahrgast (¨e)   *passenger*
die Fahrkarte (-n)   *ticket*
der Fahrkartenschalter (-)   *ticket office*
der Fahrplan (¨e)   *timetable*
der Fahrschein (-e)   *ticket*
der Flughafen (¨)   *airport*
das Flugzeug (-e)   *aeroplane*
das Gleis (-e)   *platform*
die Haltestelle (-n)   *stop (e.g. bus stop)*
der Hauptbahnhof (¨e)   *main railway station*
 Hbf   *abbreviation of 'Hauptbahnhof'*
der Inter-City-Zug (¨e)   *Inter-City train*
der Kofferkuli (-s)   *luggage trolley*
der Krankenwagen (-)   *ambulance*
die Maschine (-n)   *machine, locomotive*
der Nahverkehrszug (¨e)   *local train*
der (Nicht)Raucher (-)   *(non) smoker*
die Nummer (-n)   *number*
der Passagier (-e)   *passenger*
die Reise (-n)   *journey*
der/die} Reisende (-n)   *traveller*
die Richtung (-en)   *direction*
die Rückfahrkarte (-n)   *return ticket*
die S-Bahn (-en)   *metro/underground in Berlin*
der Schalter (-)   *ticket office*
das Schiff (-e)   *ship*
der Schnellzug (¨e)   *fast train*
der Speisewagen (-)   *buffet car*
die Station (-en)   *station*
die Straßenbahn (-en)   *tram*
das Taxi (-s)   *taxi*
der TEE-Zug (¨e)   *Trans-European-Express (train)*
die U-Bahn (-en)   *underground*
die Überfahrt (-en)   *crossing (sea journey)*
die Verspätung (-en)   *delay*
der Wagen (-)   *car, coach (of train)*
der Warteraum (¨e)   *waiting room*
der Wartesaal (-säle)   *waiting room*
der Zug (¨e)   *train*
der Zuschlag (¨e)   *supplement*

ab   *from*
an   *to, on*
direkt   *direct, non-stop*
einfach   *single, simple*
einmal/zweimal (*etc.*)   *one/two (etc.)*

hinten   *behind, in the back*
hin und zurück   *return*
langsam   *slow, slowly*
mitten   *in the middle*
schnell   *quick*
über (Frankfurt)   *via (Frankfurt)*
vorn(e)   *in the front*
werktags   *workdays*
wochentags   *weekdays*

abfahren (*sep.*)   *to depart, leave*
abfliegen (*sep.*)   *to depart (of plane), take off*
ankommen (*sep.*)   *to arrive*
aussteigen (*sep.*)   *to get off/out*
buchen   *to book*
einsteigen (*sep.*)   *to get in/on*
erreichen   *to reach, arrive at, catch*
festhalten (*sep.*)   *to hold tight*
kriegen   *to get*
landen   *to land*
nehmen   *to take*
reisen   *to travel*
reservieren   *to reserve*
rufen   *to call*
starten   *to start*
umsteigen (*sep.*)   *to change*
verlassen   *to leave*

Higher
der Abflug (¨e)   *departure, take-off (of flight)*
das Abteil (-e)   *compartment*
die Autofähre (-n)   *car ferry*
an Bord   *on board*
die Einzelkarte (-n)   *single ticket*
der Fahrausweis (-e)   *travel pass, ticket*
der Fahrpreis (-e)   *price (of journey)*
die Fähre (-n)   *ferry*
der Feiertag (-e)   *holiday (e.g. Sunday, public holiday)*
feiertags   *on Sundays and public holidays*
der Flug (¨e)   *flight*
die Gepäckannahme (-n)   *left luggage deposit*
die Gepäckaufbewahrung (-en)   *left luggage*
die Gepäckausgabe (-n)   *left luggage collection*
das Gepäcknetz (-e)   *luggage rack*
der Hubschrauber (-)   *helicopter*
der Liegewagen (-)   *couchette*
die Linie (-n)   *line, route*
die Mehrfahrtenkarte (-n)   *ticket valid for a number of journeys*
das Reisebüro (-s)   *travel agent's*
der Schaffner (-)   *ticket collector*
der Schlafwagen (-)   *sleeping car*
das Schließfach (¨er)   *left luggage locker*
der Sicherheitsgurt (-e)   *seat belt, safety strap*
die Stewardeß (-ssen)   *stewardess*
der Treffpunkt (-e)   *meeting point, rendezvous*
die Verspätung (-en)   *delay*

erhältlich   *available*
gültig   *valid*
verspätet   *delayed*
zuschlagspflichtig   *supplement payable*

(sich) anschnallen (*sep.*)   *to put on (one's) seat belt*
dauern   *to last*
hinauslehnen (*sep.*)   *to lean out*
kontrollieren   *to check (tickets, passports)*
lösen   *to buy (tickets)*
melden   *to report, announce*
verkehren   *to travel*
verpassen   *to miss (bus, train, etc.)*
verreisen   *to go on a long journey*

TRAVEL BY ROAD

Basic

Achtung! *beware! danger!*
die Ausfahrt (-en) *exit*
das Auto (-s) *car*
die Batterie (-n) *battery*
die Baustelle (-n) *building site, roadworks*
das Benzin (*no plural*) *petrol*
das Diesel (*no plural*) *diesel*
die Einbahnstraße (-n) *one-way road/street*
die Einfahrt (-en) *entry, entrance, drive*
das Fahrrad (-̈er) *bicycle*
der Führerschein (-e) *driving licence*
Gas geben *to accelerate*
die Gefahr (-en) *danger*
der Lastkraftwagen (-) *lorry*
der Lkw (-s) *abbreviation for 'Lastkraftwagen'*
der Luftdruck (-̈e) *air pressure*
das Mofa (-s) *moped*
das Motorrad (-̈er) *motorcycle*
Normal *2-star petrol*
der Notruf (-e) *emergency phone call*
das Öl (*no plural*) *oil*
das Parkhaus (-̈er) *multi-storey car park*
der Parkplatz (-̈e) *car park, parking space*
der Pkw (-s) *short for 'Personalkraftwagen': saloon car*
das Rad (-̈er) *cycle, wheel*
das Rad/Hinterrad/Vorderrad (-̈er) *wheel/back wheel/front wheel*
der Radfahrer (-) *cyclist*
der Rasthof (-̈e) *service station*
der Rastplatz (-̈e) *service area, parking area*
die Raststätte (-n) *service station*
der Reifen (-) *tyre*
der Reifendruck (-̈e) *tyre pressure*
die Reparatur (-en) *repair*
die Selbstbedienung/SB *self-service (SB = abbreviation)*
das Selbsttanken (-) *self-service*
die Straße (-n) *street, road*
Super *3/4-star petrol*
die Tankstelle (-n) *petrol station*
die Umleitung (-en) *diversion*
die (grüne) Versicherungskarte (-n) *(green) insurance card*
die Vorfahrt (-en) *right of way, priority*
Vorsicht *care, precaution*
der Wagen (-) *car*
die Warnung (-en) *warning*
die Werkstatt (-̈e) *garage (for repairs)*
die Zufahrt (-en) *access*

besetzt *taken, occupied, engaged (phone)*
frei *free*
gefährlich *dangerous*
gesperrt *closed (of road)*
gestattet *allowed*
kaputt *broken*
verboten *forbidden*

einordnen (*sep.*) *to order, get in lane*
erlauben *to allow*
freihalten (*sep.*) *to keep free*
nachsehen (*sep.*) *to look after/out for, to check (e.g. oil)*
parken *to park*
prüfen *to test, check*
radfahren (*sep.*) *to cycle*
reparieren *to repair*
tanken *to fill up (with petrol), to put petrol in*
volltanken *to fill the tank*

Higher

der Abschleppwagen (-) *breakdown vehicle*
Abstand halten *to keep a distance (from the car in front)*
per Anhalter fahren *to hitch-hike*
das Autobahndreieck (-e) *motorway junction*
das Autobahnkreuz (-e) *motorway junction/crossing*
die Autowäsche (-n) *car wash*
die Bremse (-n) *brake*
der Dienst (-e) *service*
der Durchgangsverkehr (*no plural*) *through traffic, all routes*
das Fahrzeug (-e) *vehicle*
der Fehler (-) *mistake*
die Gebühr (-en) *fee*
gebührenpflichtig *fee payable*
die Geldstrafe (-n) *spot fine*
die Geschwindigkeit (-en) *speed*
die Hochgarage (-n) *multi-storey car park*
die Höchstgeschwindigkeit (-en) *speed limit*
der Kofferraum (-̈e) *boot (of car)*
der Lieferwagen (-) *van*
der Motor (-en) *engine, motor*
die Panne (-n) *puncture, breakdown*
der Parkschein (-e) *parking ticket*
die Parkuhr (-en) *parking meter*
das Parkverbot (*no plural*) *no parking*
die Reifenpanne (-n) *puncture*
der Roller (-) *scooter*
der Scheinwerfer (-) *spotlight, headlamp*
Schritt fahren *to drive at walking pace*
der Stau (-s) *queue, jam (on roads)*
das Steuerrad (-̈er) *steering wheel*
die Strafe (-n) *punishment, fine*
die Tiefgarage (-n) *underground garage*
der Unfall (-̈e) *accident*
die Verkehrsstauung (-en) *traffic jam*
die Versicherung (-en) *insurance*
die Windschutzscheibe (-n) *windscreen*
der Zusammenstoß (-̈sse) *crash, collision*

abschleppen (*sep.*) *to tow away*
abstellen (*sep.*) *to turn off (engine)*
anlassen (*sep.*) *to start (engine)*
bremsen *to brake*
überfahren *to run over*

HOLIDAYS

Basic

der Austausch (-e) *exchange*
der Ausweis (-e) *identity card, documentation*
der Bodensee *Lake Constance*
die Broschüre (-n) *brochure*
das Camping *camping*
der Campingplatz (-̈e) *campsite*
die Donau *the Danube*
Europe *Europe*

die EWG *the EEC (European Economic Community)*
die Ferien (*plural*) *holidays*
das Gasthaus (-̈er) *hotel*
der Gasthof (-̈e) *hotel*
das Hotel (-s) *hotel*
die Jugendherberge (-n) *youth hostel*
Köln *Cologne*
die Kosten (*plural*) *costs*

München *Munich*
Nord- *north* . . .
in den Norden *to the north*
im Norden *in the north*
die Nordsee *North Sea*
Ost- *east* . . .
in den Osten *to the east*
im Osten *in the east*
die Ostsee *Baltic*
die Papiere (*plural*) *papers, documentation*
der Paß (Pässe) *passport*
die Paßkontrolle (-n) *passport control*
der Plan (¨e) *plan*
die Reise (-n) *journey*
der Reisepaß (¨sse) *passport*
der Rhein *Rhine*
die Sandburg (-en) *sandcastle*
eine Sandburg bauen *build a sandcastle*
der Stadtplan (¨e) *town plan*
Süd- *south* . . .
in den Süden *to the south*
im Süden *in the south*
der Urlaub (-e) *holiday*
das Verkehrsamt (¨er) *tourist office*
West- *west* . . .
in den Westen *to the west*
im Westen *in the west*
Wien *Vienna*
der Zeltplatz (¨e) *campsite for tents*

der Zoll (*no plural*) *customs*
das Zollamt (¨er) *customs house*
der Zollbeamte (-n) *customs official*
die Zollkontrolle (-n) *customs control*

auspacken (sep.) *to unpack*
bauen *to build*
bleiben *to stay*
einpacken (*sep.*) *to pack*
fahren *to travel, go*
organisieren *to organise*
planen *to plan*
reisen *to travel*
verbringen *to spend (time)*
braun werden *to get brown*
zelten *to camp (in a tent)*

Higher

der Aufenthalt (-e) *stay*
die Grenze (-n) *border, limit*
der Kanal *the English Channel*
das Mittelmeer *the Mediterranean*
das Reisebüro (-s) *travel agent*
die Sehenswürdigkeit (-en) *tourist sight*
die Unterkunft (¨e) *accommodation*

sehenswert *worth seeing*
verzollen *to declare (at customs)*
vorhaben (sep.) *to plan, intend*
vorzeigen (sep.) *to show (documentation)*

ACCOMMODATION

AT THE HOTEL (General)

Basic

das Abendessen (-) *evening meal (hot)*
die Anmeldung (-en) *booking (in)*
das Bad (¨er) *bath(room)*
die Bar (-s) *bar*
die Bedienung (-en) *service*
das Doppelzimmer (-) *double room*
die Dusche (-n) *shower*
das Einzelzimmer (-) *single room*
der Empfang (¨e) *reception*
die Empfangsdame (-n) *receptionist (female)*
das Essen (-) *food, meal*
der Fahrstuhl (¨e) *lift*
das Formular (-e) *form*
das Frühstück (-e) *breakfast*
das Gästehaus (¨er) *hotel*
das Gepäck *luggage*
das Hotel (-s) *hotel*
der Koffer (-) *suitcase*
der Lift (-e *or* -s) *lift*
die Mehrwertsteuer (-n) *VAT (Value Added Tax)*
MWS *VAT (short for 'Mehrwertsteuer')*
das Mittagessen (-) *lunch*
die Nacht (¨e) *night*
der Parkplatz (¨e) *car park, parking space*
die Pension (-en) *boarding house*
der Portier (-e) *porter*
der Preis (-e) *price*
der Reisescheck (-e *or* -s) *traveller's cheque*
die Reisetasche (-n) *suitcase*
der Scheck (-e *or* -s) *cheque*
das Schloßhotel (-s) *castle hotel*
der Schlüssel (-) *key*
der Speisesaal (-säle) *dining room*
der Stock (Stockwerke) *.floor, storey*
das Telefon (-e) *telephone*
die Übernachtung (-en) *(overnight) stay, accommodation*

das Zimmer (-) *room*
das Zimmermädchen (-) *chambermaid*

ab wann? *from when?*
allein *alone*
bequem *comfortable*
frei *free (not booked)*
pro *for, per*
wann? *when?*

ausfüllen (sep.) *to fill in, complete (form)*
bleiben *to stay*
essen *to eat*
frühstücken *to have breakfast*
kosten *to cost*
nehmen *to take*
parken *to park*
reservieren *to reserve*
telefonieren *to telephone*
übernachten *to stay (overnight), spend the night*
unterschreiben *to sign*

Higher

der Aufenthalt (-e) *stay*
die Aussicht (-en) *view*
der Blick (-e) *view*
das Erdgeschoß (-sse) *ground floor*
das Fremdenheim (-e) *boarding house*
das Fremdenzimmer (-) *room*
die Halbpension *half board*
die Vollpension *full board*
der Wasserhahn (¨e) *tap*
der Zimmernachweis (-e) *room indication*

inbegriffen/inbegr. *inclusive*
inklusiv *inclusive*
mit fließendem/heißem Wasser *with running/hot water*
warme Küche *hot meals*

sich anmelden (*sep.*) *to book in*
sich beklagen *to complain*
sich beschweren *to complain*

AT THE YOUTH HOSTEL

Basic

der Gast (⁻e) *guest*
die Herberge (-n) *hostel*
die Herbergseltern *wardens*
die Herbergsmutter (⁻) *warden (female)*
der Herbergsvater (⁻) *warden (male)*
die Jugendherberge (-n) *youth hostel*
die Person (-en) *person*
der Schlafraum (⁻e) *dormitory*
der Schlafsack (⁻e) *sleeping bag*

verboten *forbidden*

erlauben *to allow*
leihen *to borrow, lend*

Higher

das Mitglied (-er) *member*
das schwarze Brett *board with notices about duties*

AT THE CAMPSITE

Basic

die Abreise (-n) *departure*
die Ankunft (⁻e) *arrival*
die Batterie (-n) *battery*

das Büro (-s) *office*
das Camping *camping*
der Campingartikel (-) *camping equipment*
der Campinggas *camping gas*
der Campingkocher (-) *camping stove*
der Campingplatz (⁻e) *campsite*
der Dosenöffner (-) *tin opener*
das Feuer (-) *fire*
der Laden (⁻) *shop*
der Rucksack (⁻) *rucksack*
der Schatten (-) *shade*
der Waschraum (⁻e) *washroom*
der Wohnwagen (-) *caravan*
das Zelt (-e) *tent*
der Zeltplatz (⁻e) *tent site*

zelten *to camp (in a tent)*

Higher

der Abfall (⁻e) *rubbish*
der Abfalleimer (-) *rubbish bin*
die Gebühr (-en) *fee*
der Klappstuhl (⁻e) *folding chair*
der Klapptisch (-e) *folding table*
die Luftmatratze (-n) *lilo*
die Spülküche (-n) *kitchen (for washing up)*
der Strom *electricity*

klappbar *folding*
tragbar *portable*

abbauen (*sep.*) *to take down (tent)*
aufbauen (*sep.*) *to put up (tent)*
aufschlagen (*sep.*) *to put up (tent)*

SOCIAL RELATIONSHIPS

ON THE TELEPHONE

Basic

am Apparat *on the phone, speaking*
Hallo! *hallo!*
hier bei Neumann *this is the Neumanns*
hier Dieter *Dieter here*
wer spricht? *who's speaking?*
wer ist dort? *who's there?*
(auf) Wiederhören! *goodbye (on the phone only)*
besetzt *engaged (of phone), occupied*

anrufen (*sep.*) *to telephone (someone)*
sprechen (mit) *to speak (to)*
telefonieren *to telephone*
eine (falsche) Nummer wählen *to dial a (wrong) number*
falsch wählen *to dial the wrong number*
bitte warten! *please wait!*

POSTCARDS AND LETTERS

Basic

der Absender (-) *the sender*
Abs. *short for 'Absender'*
der Brief (-e) *letter*
der Brieffreund (-e) *pen friend (male)*
die Brieffreundin (-nen) *pen friend (female)*
(viele) Grüße (aus) *greetings (from + place)*
mit den besten Grüßen/Wünschen *(with) best wishes*
mit freundlichem Gruß *(with) kind regards, friendly greetings*
mit freundlichen Grüßen *(with) kind regards, friendly greetings*

herzliche Grüße *sincere greetings*
alles Gute *all the best*
hochachtungsvoll *yours sincerely*
sehr geehrter Herr, *dear Sir*
sehr geehrter/verehrter Herr . . . *dear Mr . . .*
sehr verehrte Dame, *dear Madam*
sehr geehrte/verehrte Frau *dear Mrs . . .*
sehr geehrte/verehrte Herr und Frau . . . *dear Mr and Mrs . . .*
liebe Ingrid *dear Ingrid*
lieber Dieter *dear Dieter*

beilegen (*sep.*) *to enclose*
bekommen *to receive*
erhalten *to receive*
sich freuen *to be pleased*
Grüße bestellen *to send greetings, greet*
grüßen *to greet*
es grüßt . . . herzlich *best wishes from . . .*
Schluß machen *to finish, close (e.g. letter)*
schicken *to send*

MEETING PEOPLE

Basic

die Ahnung (-en) *idea*
keine Ahnung *no idea*
die Einladung (-en) *invitation*
die Entschuldigung (-en)/Entschuldigung! *apology/excuse me!*
Feuer haben *to have a light*
der Freund (-e) *friend (male)*
die Freundin (-nen) *friend (female)*
die Idee (-n) *idea*

der Kollege (-n) *colleague (male)*
die Kollegin (-nen) *colleague (female)*
die Leute *people*
    Lust haben *to feel like*
die Mahlzeit (-en) *mealtime*
die Party (-s) *party*

aber *but*
ach (so)! *oh (really)!*
ach (du lieber) Gott! *good God!*
also *so, that's why*
auch *also, too*
ausgezeichnet *excellent*
bestimmt *definite, certain, definitely, certainly*
bis später/nachher *see you later/afterwards*
bis gleich/morgen/dann *till soon/tomorrow/then*
bitte (schön/sehr) *please, here you are, that's OK*
danke (schön/sehr) *thank you (very much)*
dann *then*
denn *because, for*
doch *but, however*
eben *just, quite*
es freut mich *I'm pleased/glad*
es/das geht (nicht) *that's (not) fine/OK*
es ist mir egal *I don't mind, it's the same to me*
es kann (nicht) sein *it can(not) be*
es macht nichts *it doesn't matter*
es tut mir leid *I'm sorry*
frohe Ostern! *happy Easter!*
frohe/fröhliche Weihnachten! *happy Christmas!*
frohes/glückliches Neujahr! *happy New Year!*
grüß Gott! *hallo (in South Germany)*
gute Besserung! *I hope you get well soon!*
gute Fahrt! *have a good journey! bon voyage!*
gute Heimfahrt! *have a good journey home!*
gute Nacht! *good night!*
guten Abend! *good evening!*
guten Appetit! *bon appétit, enjoy your food*
(guten) Morgen! *good morning!*
(guten) Tag! *good day! hello!*
komm' gut nach Hause! *safe journey home!*
(auf) Wiedersehen! *goodbye!*

furchtbar *terrible, terribly*
gleichfalls *the same to you (polite not rude!)*
gut *good*
herein! *come in!*
herzlichen Glückwunsch! *congratulations!*
Himmel! *goodness!*
hoffentlich *I hope so/that*
ja *yes, indeed, really*
klasse! *great! first class!*
leider *unfortunately*
mach's gut! *all the best!*
mal *just*
mein Gott! *my God! goodness!*
Mensch! *crikey! wow! man!*
na *well*
nee *no (colloquial for 'nein')*
nein *no*
nicht *not*
nicht wahr? *isn't it? aren't they? etc.*
prima! *great!*
Prosit!/Prost! *cheers!*
Quatsch! *rubbish! nonsense!*
schlaf gut! *sleep well!*

schon *already*
schrecklich *terrible, terribly*
Servus! *hallo!*
so? *is that so (true)? really?*
so was! *well really!*
Spaß haben *to have fun*
Spaß machen *to be fun*
toll *terrific, great*
träume süß *sweet dreams*
Tschüs(chen) *bye! cheers! see you!*
Tschüß *bye! cheers! see you!*
vielen Dank! *thanks a lot!*
viel Glück! *good luck!*
viel Spaß! *have fun!*
wie bitte? *pardon?*
willkommen *welcome*
wunderbar *wonderful*

abholen (*sep.*) *to fetch, collect (e.g. from station)*
bekannt machen *to introduce (people)*
danken *to thank*
denken *to think*
dürfen *to be allowed*
einladen (*sep.*) *to invite*
gern/lieber haben *to like/prefer*
hat's geschmeckt? *did it taste good?*
ich hätte gern *I'd like*
ich möchte gern *I'd like*
(sich) interessieren (für) *to be interested (in)*
meinen *to think*
mitmachen (*sep.*) *to take part*
probieren *to try*
schmecken *to taste (good)*
sollen *to be supposed/due to*
Spaß haben *to have fun*
Spaß machen *to be fun*
stimmen *to be right, agree*
das stimmt *that's right*
träumen *to dream*
(sich) vorstellen (*sep.*) *to introduce (oneself)*
warten *to wait*
wünschen *to wish*
Zeit haben *to have time*

Higher
abgemacht *agreed*
der Blödsinn *madness, nonsense*
ich habe nichts dagegen *I've nothing against it/that*
einverstanden *agreed*
der Namenstag(-e) *Saint's day, name day*
Pech haben *to be unlucky*
(wie) schade! *(what a) pity!*
die Überraschung (-en) *surprise*
die Verabredung (-en) *agreement, arrangement*
das Vergnügen (-) *pleasure, fun*
mit (großen/größtem/dem größten) Vergnügen *with (great) pleasure*
Verzeihung! *sorry! excuse me!*
zum Wohl! *cheers! your health!*
zufrieden *content, satisfied*

ablehnen (*sep.*) *to decline, refuse*
annehmen (*sep.*) *to accept*
ärgern *to annoy*
(sich) ärgern *to annoy/(get annoyed)*
begrüßen *to greet*
grüßen *to greet*
bitten *to ask, request*
duzen *to call 'du' (use familiar form when speaking)*

empfehlen *to recommend*
(sich) entschuldigen *to excuse (oneself)/ (apologise)*
genügen *to suffice, be sufficient*
gratulieren *to congratulate*
klappen *to work out, to fold (e.g. of chair)*
raten *to advise*
siezen *to call 'Sie' (use polite form when*
speaking)
(sich) treffen *to meet*
überraschen *to surprise*
sich verabschieden *to take one's leave, say goodbye*
vorschlagen (sep.) *to suggest*
vorziehen (sep.) *to prefer*

HEALTH AND WELFARE

PARTS OF THE BODY

Basic
der Arm (-e) *arm*
die Hand (¨e) *hand*
der Finger (-) *finger*
das Bein (-e) *leg*
der Fuß (¨e) *foot*
der Bauch *stomach*
der Magen *stomach*
der Rücken *back*
der Kopf (¨e) *head*
der Hals (¨e) *neck*
das Gesicht (-er) *face*
das Auge (-n) *eye*
der Mund (¨er) *mouth*
der Zahn (¨e) *tooth*
die Nase (-n) *nose*
das Ohr (-en) *ear*

das Bad (¨er) *bath*
sauber *clean*
schmutzig *dirty*

baden *to bath, have a bath*
sich duschen *to shower, have a shower*
sich waschen *to wash, have a wash*

das Handtuch (¨er) *hand towel*
die Seife *soap*
das Shampoo *shampoo*
das Haarwaschmittel *shampoo*
die Zahnbürste (-n) *toothbrush*
die Zahnpasta *toothpaste*

sich ausruhen (sep.) *to have a rest, relax*
schlafen *to sleep*
erkältet sein *to have a cold*
Fieber haben *to have a temperature*
die Grippe *flu, influenza*
Durst haben *to be thirsty*
durstig *thirsty*
Hunger haben *to be hungry, have an appetite*
hungrig *hungry*
satt *full (of food)*
gesund *healthy*
(un)fit *(un)fit*
krank *ill*
seekrank *seasick*
die Seekrankheit *seasickness*
müde *tired*
die Blutprobe *blood test*
die Spritze (-n) *injection*
der Durchfall *diarrhoea*
die Magenverstimmung *stomach upset*
mir ist heiß/kalt *I'm hot/cold*
mir ist übel/schlecht/schwindlig *I feel sick/ ill/giddy*
was fehlt? *what's wrong?*
was ist los? *what's the matter?*
weh tun *to hurt*
Heimweh haben *to be homesick*

Higher
der Körper (-) *body*
das Herz (-en) *heart*
die Brust (¨e) *breast, chest*
das Knie (-n) *knee*
die Schulter (-n) *shoulder*
der Daumen (-) *thumb*
die Zehe (-n) *toe*
die Zunge (-n) *tongue*

die Erkältung *cold*
der Schnupfen *cold*
verstopft *constipated*
die Verstopfung *constipation*
blind *blind*
stumm *dumb, mute*
taub *deaf*
dreckig *dirty*
sich bürsten *to brush oneself*
sich die Zähne bürsten/putzen *to brush/ clean one's teeth*
sich kämmen *to comb one's hair*
sich rasieren *to have a shave*
sich (wohl) fühlen *to feel (well)*
sich hinlegen (sep.) *to have a rest/lie down*
sich erholen *to recover*
genesen *to get well*
bluten *to bleed*

ACCIDENTS AND EMERGENCIES

Higher Level only
der Dienst (-e) *service*
der E111-Schein (-e) *E111 form*
die erste Hilfe *first aid*
der Feuerlöscher (-) *fire extinguisher*
der Feuerwehrwagen (-) *fire engine*
die Geldstrafe (-n) *fine*
der Gips (-e) *plaster (of Paris)*
das Heftpflaster (-) *plaster (elastoplast)*
der Husten (-) *cough*
die Krankenkasse (-n) *health insurance*
der Krankenschein (-e) *medical insurance record*
die Kur (-en) *treatment, cure; convalescence*
der Kurort (-e) *spa resort*
die Lebensgefahr *danger to life; danger!*
das Löschgerät (-e) *fire extinguisher*
die Medizin (-en) *medicine*
der Notausgang (¨e) *emergency exit*
der Notdienst (-e) *emergency service*
der Notruf (-e) *emergency phone call*
die Operation (-en) *operation*
der Patient (-en) *patient*
das Pflaster (-) *plaster (elastoplast)*
die Pille (-n) *pill*
das Rezept (-e) *prescription*
die Sprechstunde (-n) *surgery hours*
die Spritze (-n) *injection*
die Strafe (-n) *fine, punishment*
die Tablette (-n) *tablet*

der Termin (-e)   *time, appointment (time)*
das Thermometer (-)   *thermometer*
der Tod (-e)   *death*
der Tropfen (-)   *drop*
der Unfall (-e)   *accident*
der Verband (-e)   *bandage*
die Wunde (-n)   *wound*
der Zeuge (-n)   *witness*
der Zusammenstoß (-sse)   *crash*

atemlos   *breathless*
betrunken   *drunk*
blaß   *pale*
gebrochen   *broken*
körperbehindert   *physically handicapped*
tot   *dead*
verletzt   *injured*
verwundet   *wounded*

behandeln   *to treat (illness); to deal with*

sich das Bein/den Arm brechen   *to break one's leg/arm*

fallen   *to fall*
husten   *to cough*
ums Leben kommen   *to die*

löschen   *to extinguish, put out*
niesen   *to sneeze*
retten   *to save*
schwitzen   *to sweat*
sterben   *to die*
stürzen   *to rush; crash*
überfahren   *to run over*
überfallen   *to attack*
sich übergeben   *to be sick*
untersuchen   *to examine*
verunglücken   *to have an accident*
weinen   *to cry*

SHOPPING

SHOPS

Basic
die Apotheke (-n)   *chemist*
der Automat (-en)   *vending machine*
die Bäckerei (-en)   *baker's*
die Drogerie (-n)   *drugstore*
die Fleischerei (-en)   *butcher's*
der Friseur (-e)   *hairdresser's*
der Frisör (-e)   *hairdresser's*
der Gemüsehändler (-)   *greengrocer's*
das Geschäft (-e)   *shop, business*
die Geschäftszeiten (*plural*)   *opening hours, shop hours*
der Händler (-)   *trader, merchant*
die Handlung (-en)   *business, trade*
das Kaufhaus (-er)   *department store*
der Kiosk (-e)   *stand, kiosk*
die Konditorei (-en)   *cake shop, pâtisserie*
der Laden (-)   *shop*
das Lebensmittelgeschäft (-e)   *grocer's*
der Markt (-e)   *market*
die Metzgerei (-en)   *butcher's*
die Öffnungszeiten (*plural*)   *opening times*
der Supermarkt (-e)   *supermarket*
das Warenhaus (-er)   *department store*
der Zeitungsstand (-e)   *newspaper stand*

Einkäufe machen   *to shop, do the shopping*
einkaufen (*sep.*)   *to shop*
kaufen   *to buy*
verkaufen   *to sell*

Higher
die Abteilung (-en)   *department, section*
der Ausverkauf (-e)   *sale, special offer*
die Auswahl (-en)   *selection, choice*
der Einkaufskorb (-e)   *shopping basket*
der Einkaufswagen (-)   *shopping trolley (at supermarket)*
das Erdgeschoß (-sse)   *ground floor*
die Gebrauchsanweisung (-en)   *instructions (for use)*
die Hälfte (-n)   *half*
der Kassenzettel (-)   *till receipt*
das Pfand (-er)   *deposit*
die Quittung (-en)   *receipt*
der Rabatt (-e)   *discount*
die Rolltreppe (-n)   *escalator*
die Scheibe (-n)   *slice*
der Sommerschlußverkauf   *summer sale*

das Spülmittel (-)   *washing-up liquid*
der Topf (-e)   *pot*
der Umtausch (-e)   *exchange (of goods)*
das Untergeschoß (-sse)   *basement*
die Wahl (-en)   *choice*
das Waschpulver (-)   *washing powder*

günstig   *favourable*
umsonst   *in vain, free*

ausgeben (*sep.*)   *to spend (money)*
dienen   *to serve*
schälen   *to peel*
umtauschen (*sep.*)   *to exchange (goods)*
wiegen   *to weigh*

CLOTHES

Basic
der Anorak (-s)   *anorak*
der Anzug (-e)   *suit (male)*
die Armbanduhr (-en)   *wristwatch*
der Artikel (-)   *article*
der Badeanzug (-e)   *swimsuiit*
die Badehose (-n)   *swimming trunks*
die Bluse (-n)   *blouse*
die Brieftasche (-n)   *wallet*
die Brille (-n)   *glasses*
die Creme (-s)   *cream*
die Damenkonfektion   *ladies' wear*
die Farbe (-n)   *colour*
die Größe (-n)   *size*
der Gürtel (-)   *belt*
die Haarbürste (-n)   *hairbrush*
der Handschuh (-e)   *glove*
die Handtasche (-n)   *handbag*
das Hemd (-en)   *shirt*
die Herrenkonfektion   *menswear*
die Herrenmode (-n)   *men's fashion*
die Hose (-n)   *trousers*
die Jacke (-n)   *jacket*
die Jeans (*either feminine singular or plural*)   *jeans*
das Kleid (-er)   *dress*
die Kleider (*plural*)   *clothes*
die Kleidung (-en)   *clothing*
die Krawatte (-n)   *tie*
der Mantel (-)   *overcoat*
die Mode (-n)   *fashion*
das Paar (-e)   *pair*

das Papiertaschentuch (¨er) *paper handkerchief, tissue*
die Plastik *plastic*
das Portemonnaie *purse*
der Pulli (-s) *pullover*
der Pullover (-) *pullover*
die Qualität (-en) *quality*
der Regenmantel (¨) *raincoat*
der Rock (¨e) *skirt*
die Sandale (-n) *sandal*
der Schlafanzug (¨e) *pyjamas*
der Schlips (-e) *tie*
der Schuh (-e) *shoe*
die Socke (-n) *sock*
die Sonnenbrille (-n) *sunglasses*
die Sonnencreme (-s) *suncream*
die Sonnenmilch *suntan lotion*
das Sonnenöl *suntan oil*
der Strumpf (¨e) *sock, long sock*
die Strumpfhose (-n) *tights*
das Taschentuch (¨er) *handkerchief*
das T-Shirt (-s) *T-shirt*
die Uhr (-en) *clock, watch*
der Wecker (-) *alarm clock*
die Zahnbürste (-n) *toothbrush*
die Zahnpasta (-en) *toothpaste*

anhaben (*sep.*) *to have on, wear*
wählen *to choose, select*

Higher
die Baumwolle (-n) *cotton*
der Büstenhalter (-) (BH) *brassière (bra)*
das Gummi *rubber*
der Hut (¨e) *hat*
der Kamm (¨e) *comb*
das Kostüm (-e) *suit, costume (female)*
der Kunststoff (-e) *man-made material*
das Leder (-) *leather*
die Mütze (-n) *cap*
der Pantoffel (-n) *slipper*
der Regenschirm (-e) *umbrella*
der Schal (-e) *scarf*
die Seide (-n) *silk*
der Stiefel (-) *boot*
der Stoff (-e) *material*
die Unterwäsche *underwear*
die Wäsche *washing*
das Wildleder (-) *leather*
die Wolle (-n) *wool*

echt *real, genuine*

anprobieren (*sep.*) *to try on*
einreiben (*sep.*) *to rub in (cream etc.)*
reiben *to rub*
schützen *to protect*

FOOD AND DRINK

PLACES TO EAT AND DRINK

Basic
die Bar (-s) *bar*
die Bierhalle (-n) *beer hall*
das Café (-s) *café*
Erfrischungen (*plural*) *refreshments*
das Gasthaus (¨er) *hotel*
der Gasthof (¨e) *hotel*
die Gaststätte (-n) *hotel*
der Imbiß (-sse) *snack, snack bar*
der Imbißstand (¨e) *snack stand*
die Imbißstube (-n) *snack bar*
das Kaffeehaus (¨er) *coffee bar*
der Keller (-) *cellar*
der Kiosk (-e) *kiosk, stand*
die Konditorei (-en) *cake shop, pâtisserie*
die Milchbar (-s) *milk bar*
der Rasthof (¨e) *service station*
die Raststätte (-n) *service station*
der Ratskeller (-) *Town Hall Cellar Restaurant/Bar*
das Restaurant (-s) *restaurant*
der Schnellimbiß (-sse) *snack (bar)*
der Weinkeller (-) *wine cellar*
die Weinprobe (-n) *wine-tasting*
die Weinstube (-n) *wine bar*
der Würstchenstand (¨e) *hot sausage stand*

Herr Ober! *waiter!*
Fräulein! *waitress!*
Hallo (Bedienung)! *hallo (service please)!*
Bedienung bitte! *service please!*
die Rechnung bitte! *the bill please!*
Zahlen bitte! *I'd like to pay please!*

Higher
die Kneipe (-n) *pub*
die Schenke (-n) *bar*
der Stammtisch (-e) *regulars' table (public house)*

die Theke (-n) *counter*
die Wirtschaft (-en) *public house*
das Wirtshaus (¨er) *hotel*

EATING AND DRINKING OUT

Basic
das Abendbrot (-e) *evening meal (cold)*
das Abendessen (-) *evening meal (hot)*
die Bedienung (-en) *service*
das Essen (-) *meal, food*
das Frühstück (-e) *breakfast*
die Gabel (-n) *fork*
das Glas (¨er) *glass*
der Imbiß (-sse) *snack*
der Kellner (-) *waiter*
die Kellnerin (-nen) *waitress*
der Kinderteller (-) *children's meal/portion*
der Löffel (-) *spoon*
die Mahlzeit (-en) *meal, mealtime*
die Mehrwertsteuer (-n) *VAT (Value Added Tax)*
MWS *VAT (abbreviation for 'Mehrwertsteuer')*
das Menü (-s) *set menu*
das Messer (-) *knife*
zum Mitnehmen *to take away (food)*
das Mittagessen (-) *lunch*
das Öl (-e) *oil*
die Portion (-en) *portion, helping*
der Preis (-e) *price*
der Schnellimbiß (-sse) *snack (bar)*
die Speisekarte (-n) *menu*
die Tageskarte (-n) *menu of the day, specials*
die Tasse (-n) *cap*
der Teller (-) *plate*
die Untertasse (-n) *saucer*
die Weinkarte (-n) *wine list*
die Weinliste (-n) *wine list*
der Zucker (-) *sugar*

frisch   *fresh*
lecker   *delicious*
sauer   *bitter, sharp*
scharf   *spicy, sharp, strong*
süß   *sweet*

beißen   *to bite*
frühstücken   *to have breakfast*
geben   *to give*
grillen   *to grill*
kauen   *to chew*
reichen   *to pass (e.g. the salt)*
riechen   *to smell*
schlucken   *to swallow*
schneiden   *to cut*

Higher
das Gericht (-e)   *course*
die Getränkekarte (-n)   *drinks list*
der Getränkekellner (-)   *drinks waiter*
der Pfeffer   *pepper*
das Salz   *salt*
die Schale (-n)   *dish, bowl*
die Schüssel (-n)   *dish, bowl*
der Senf   *mustard*
der Strohhalm (-e)   *straw*
das Tablett (-e)   *tray*
der Weinkellner (-)   *wine waiter*

einschließlich/einschl.   *inclusive*
inbegriffen/inbegr.   *inclusive*
gebacken   *baked*
gebraten   *roast*
gemischt/gem.   *mixed*
paniert   *in breadcrumbs*

anbieten (sep.)   *to offer*
bieten   *to provide*
einschenken (sep.)   *to pour*
probieren   *to try*

THINGS TO EAT

Starters/Egg Dishes/Fish/Sausage and Cold Meat

Basic
die Gulaschsuppe (-n)   *goulash soup*
die Suppe (-n)   *soup*
die Tomatensuppe (-n)   *tomato soup*

das gekochte Ei (-er)   *(hard) boiled egg*
das Omelett (-e *or* -s)   *omelette*
das Rührei (-er)   *scrambled egg*
das Spiegelei (-er)   *fried egg*

der Fisch (-e)   *fish*

der Aufschnitt (-e)   *cold meat(s)*
die Bockwurst (-̈e)   *steamed sausage, like frankfurter but larger*
die Bratwurst (-̈e)   *fried sausage*
die Currywurst (-̈e)   *curried sausage*
die Leberwurst (-̈e)   *liver sausage/pâté*
der Schinken (-)   *ham*

Higher
die Hühnerbrühe (-n)   *chicken soup*
die Ochsenschwanzsuppe (-n)   *oxtail soup*
die Vorspeise (-n)   *starter*
die Forelle (-n)   *trout*
die kalte Platte (-n)   *cold buffet*

Meat and Poultry

Basic
das Brathähnchen (-)   *roast chicken*
das Curry (-s)   *curry*

das Fleisch   *meat*
die Fleischsorte (-n)   *kind/type of meat*
das Gulasch   *goulash*
das Hähnchen (-)   *chicken*
das Kotelett (-s)   *chop/cutlet*
die Leber (-n)   *liver*
das Rindfleisch   *beef*
das Schweinefleisch   *pork*
das Schnitzel (-)   *cutlet, escalope*
das Steak (-s)   *steak*
das Wiener Schnitzel (-)   *Wiener Schnitzel, Vienna cutlet*

Higher
der Braten (-)   *roast (dish)*
das deutsche Beefsteak   *German beefsteak*
der Eintopf (-̈e)   *vegetable soup, potage*
die Grillplatte (-n)   *(mixed) grill*
das Kalbfleisch   *veal*

Vegetables and Salads

Basic
die Bratkartoffel (-n)   *fried potato*
der Kartoffelsalat (-e)   *potato salad*
die Pommes frites (plural)   *chips*
der Reis   *rice*
der Salat (-e)   *salad/lettuce*
die Salzkartoffel (-n)   *boiled potato*
das Sauerkraut   *Sauerkraut, pickled cabbage*
die Tomate (-n)   *tomato*
der Wurstsalat   *sausage salad*

Higher
der Blumenkohl (Blumenköpfe)   *cauliflower*
die Bohne (-n)   *green bean*
der Champignon (-s)   *mushroom (small)*
die Erbse (-n)   *pea*
die Gurke (-n)   *gherkin, cucumber*
der Kartoffelbrei   *mashed potato*
das Kartoffelmus   *mashed potato*
der Knödel (-)   *dumpling*
der Pilz (-e)   *mushroom (large)*
die Zwiebel (-n)   *onion*

Desserts

Basic
die Creme   *cream*
der Eisbecher (-)   *ice-cream sundae*
die Erdbeere (-n)   *strawberry*
der Jogurt (- *or* -s)   *yoghurt*
die Himbeere (-n)   *raspberry*
der Käse (-)   *cheese*
die Kirsche (-n)   *cherry*
das Kompott   *apple sauce, stewed fruit*
der Obstsalat (-e)   *fruit salad*
der Pudding (-s)   *pudding, dessert (custard type)*
die Sahne (-n)   *cream*
die Schlagsahne (-n)   *whipped cream*
die Vanille   *vanilla*
die Zitrone (-n)   *lemon*
Zitronen-   *lemon-flavoured*

Higher
die Nachspeise (-)   *dessert, sweet*
der Nachtisch (-e)   *dessert, sweet*

Bread/Sandwiches/Cakes

Basic
der Apfelkuchen (-)   *apple cake*
das (belegte) Brot   *bread/(open sandwich)*
das Brötchen (-)   *roll*
das Butterbrot (-e)   *sandwich*

das Graubrot (-e)   *type of bread, very common*
der Käsebrot (-e)   *bread with cheese*
der Kirschkuchen (-)   *cherry cake*
der Kuchen (-)   *cake*
das Schinkenbrot (-e)   *bread with ham*
das Schwarzbrot (-e)   *black (rye) bread*
die Torte (-n)   *flan*
das Wurstbrot (-e)   *bread with cold meat*

Drinks

Basic

der Apfelsaft (⁼e)   *apple juice*
das Bier (-e)   *beer*
das Cola (-s)   *coke*
ein Dunkles   *a brown ale*
ein Helles   *a bitter/lager*
die Flasche (-n)   *bottle*
das Getränk (-e)   *drink*

der Kaffee (-s)   *coffee*
der Kakao   *cocoa*
das Kännchen (-)   *pot (of coffee/tea)*
die Limo   *lemonade*
die Limonade (-n)   *lemonade*
das Mineralwasser (-)   *mineral water*
der Orangensaft (⁼e)   *orange juice*
das Pils   *lager*
der Rotwein (-e)   *red wine*
der Sprudel (-)   *pop, fizzy drink, lemonade*
der Tee (-s)   *tea*
das Wasser   *water*
der Wein (-e)   *wine*
der Weißwein (-e)   *white wine*

Higher

der Schnaps (⁼e)   *spirits, schnaps*
der Sekt (-e)   *champagne*

SERVICES AT THE POST OFFICE

Basic

die Ansichtskarte (-n)   *(picture) postcard*
der Brief (-e)   *letter*
der Briefkasten (-)   *letter box*
die Briefmarke (-n)   *stamp*
der Briefträger (-)   *postman*
die Postkarte (-n)   *postcard*

Higher

das Ausland   *abroad*
      außer Betrieb   *out of action*
der Briefumschlag (⁼e)   *envelope*
der Einwurf (⁼e)   *slot (for posting)*
das Ferngespräch (-e)   *long-distance call*
der Fernsprecher (-)   *telephone*
das Gespräch (-e)   *conversation*
der Hörer (-)   *receiver*
das Inland   *inland*
die Leerung (-en)   *collection (from post box)*
die Luftpost   *air mail*
das Ortsgespräch (-e)   *local call*
die Post   *post office*
das Postamt (⁼er)   *post office*
die Postanweisung (-en)   *postal order*
die Postleitzahl (-en)   *postcode*
das Postwertzeichen (-)   *postage stamp*
die Rückgabe (-n)   *return (of money from coin box)*
das Rückgespräch (-e)   *reverse charges call*
der Schalter (-)   *counter*
die Taste (-n)   *button*
die Telefonzelle (-n)   *telephone kiosk*
das Telegramm (-e)   *telegramme*
der Umschlag (⁼e)   *envelope*
die Verbindung (-en)   *connection*

      postlagernd   *poste restante*

      abheben (*sep.*)   *to pick up*
      aufgeben (*sep.*)   *to hand in*
      drücken   *to press*
      durchwählen (*sep.*)   *to dial*
      verbinden   *to connect*

AT THE BANK OR EXCHANGE OFFICE

Basic

die Bank (-en)   *bank*

die Banknote (-n)   *banknote*
die Brieftasche (-n)   *wallet*
der Franken   *Swiss franc*
das Geld (-er)   *money*
der Geldwechsel   *change, exchange*
der Groschen (-)   *10 pfennig coin*
die Kasse (-n)   *cash desk, till*
das Kleingeld   *change (coins)*
die Mark   *mark*
      DM   *Deutschmark*
      D-Mark   *Deutschmark*
das Markstück (-e)   *one mark piece/coin*
der Paß (⁼e)   *passport*
der Pfennig (- or -e)   *pfennig*
      Pf.   *pfennig*
das Pfund (Sterling)   *pound*
das Portemonnaie (-s)   *purse*
der Reisescheck (-e or -s)   *traveller's cheque*
das Scheckbuch (⁼er)   *cheque book*
der Schein (-e)   *note*
der Schilling (- or -e)   *Austrian currency*
die Sparkasse (-n)   *savings bank*
das Taschengeld (-er)   *pocket money*
die Wechselstube (-n)   *exchange office*

      billig   *cheap*
      ein wenig   *a little*
      genug   *enough*
      kostenlos   *free*
      teuer   *expensive*
      viel   *much*

      arbeiten   *to work*
      kaufen   *to buy*
      kosten   *to cost*
      sparen   *to save*
      verdienen   *to earn*
      wechseln   *to exchange*

Higher

die Gebühr (-en)   *fee*
das Konto   *account*
die Kontonummer   *account number*
der Kurs   *exchange rate*
der Wechselkurs   *exchange rate*

      einlösen (*sep.*)   *to pay in*
      überweisen   *to transfer*

LOST PROPERTY

Basic

die Beschreibung (-en) *description*
die Enttäuschung (-en) *disappointment*
das Fundbüro (-s) *lost property office*
der Taschendieb (-e) *pickpocket*
die Überraschung (-en) *surprise*

dankbar *thankful, grateful*
sich bedanken *to thank*
beschreiben *to describe*
einreichen (*sep.*) *to hand in*
enttäuschen *to disappoint*
gehören *to belong*
liegenlassen (*sep.*) *to leave (behind), lose*
Pech haben *to be unlucky/have bad luck*
überraschen *to surprise*

verschließen *to lock*
verschwinden *to disappear*
versichern *to insure*

Higher

Angst haben (um) *to be afraid (about)*
Glück haben *to be lucky*
die Polizeiwache (-n) *police station*
der Polizist (-en) *policeman*

glücklich *happy, lucky*

aussehen (*sep.*) *to look, appear*
danken *to thank*
sich freuen *to be pleased*
vergessen *to forget*
verlieren *to lose*

WEATHER

Basic

der Blitz (-e) *lightning flash*
der Donner (-) *thunder*
das Eis *ice*
das Gewitter (-) *storm, thunderstorm*
der Himmel *sky*
der Regen *rain*
der Schatten (-) *shade*
der Schnee *snow*
die Sonne *sun*
der Sonnenschein *sunshine*
der Sturm (¨e) *storm*
das Wetter *weather*
der Wind (-e) *wind*
die Wolke (-n) *cloud*

heiß *hot*
herrlich *wonderful*
kühl *cool*
naß *wet*
sonnig *sunny*
stürmisch *stormy*
windig *windy*
wolkig *cloudy*

blitzen *to flash (of lighting)*
donnern *to thunder*
frieren *to freeze*
regnen *to rain*
scheinen *to shine*
schneien *to snow*

Higher

die Aufheiterung (-en) *brighter period*
die Bewölkung (-en) *cloud, clouding over*
der Grad (-) *degree*

Celsius *centigrade, celsius*
der Hagel *hail*
die Hitze *heat*
der Hochdruck (¨e) *high pressure*
die Höchsttemperatur (-en) *highest/maximum temperature*
die Kälte *cold*
das Klima (-s) *climate*
der Mond *moon*
der Nebel (-) *fog*
der Niederschlag (¨e) *precipitation (rain, snow, etc.)*
das Sauwetter *awful weather*
der Schauer (-) *shower*
der Stern (-e) *star*
die Tagestemperatur (-en) *daily temperature*
die Temperatur (-en) *temperature*
die Tiefsttemperatur (-en) *lowest/minimum temperature*
der Tiefdruck (¨e) *low pressure*
der Wetterbericht (-e) *weather report*
die Wetterlage (-n) *weather report/conditions*
die Wettervorhersage (-n) *weather forecast*

bewölkt *cloudy*
feucht *damp*
heiter *bright*
mild *mild*
neblig *foggy*
regnerisch *rainy*
schwül *sticky, oppressive*
trocken *dry*
trüb *dull*
veränderlich *changeable*
wolkenlos *cloudless, clear*

hageln *to hail*

CHAPTER

4

LISTENING: BASIC LEVEL

LISTENING SKILLS

NATIONAL CRITERIA

EXAM GROUP REQUIREMENTS

APPROACHING THE TESTS

PRACTICE WITH TAPE-RECORDINGS

EXAMINATION QUESTIONS

KEY TO THE QUESTIONS

TESTS WITH STUDENT ANSWERS

GETTING STARTED

'But they speak ever so fast! I can't understand a thing!' How often have you heard other people say that about people talking a different language? Perhaps you have even said or thought it yourself! In fact there is no evidence to suggest that people from other countries speak their language any more quickly than you might speak English. It may, however, be true that people find it difficult to understand other people talking a language which is foreign to them. Why is this, and what can we do about it?

E S S E N T I A L   P R I N C I P L E S

To begin with we need to focus on the skill of **listening** itself: what do we listen to and why, and what is the nature of that listening? So, what do **you** listen to? It is helpful to think about the different kinds of listening that you do in the ordinary course of events. You may well find that you listen to:

- the news, weather reports, travel announcements on the radio/TV
- announcements at a bus/train station, an airport or a port
- an interview on radio/TV
- a commentary about a particular event of interest
- the football results
- friends making plans or talking about recent events
- someone giving you a message on the telephone
- family and friends dealing with everyday matters, e.g. 'pass me the sauce!'

These are just a few of the common situations where you find yourself listening. In each case, though, you will not expect to remember **everything** you have heard. We all make a selection and remember what we need to or want to. (Sometimes we might even conveniently forget something we do not wish to hear: 'Don't sniff, child! How many times do I have to tell you?!')

You should try this out – listen to what someone is saying quite normally and then, say five minutes later, try to remember what he or she actually said. You will almost certainly not remember the exact words used, nor will you remember all that was said, but you will remember the **key points** or pieces of information which were important to you.

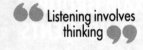

Listening involves thinking

By the same token, if you want to find out what the weather is going to be like, you listen to the forecast in a certain frame of mind. First you know the person is going to be talking about the weather (and not about the latest fashion), and second, you will be listening out for key pieces of information, e.g. hot, cold, wet.

So we can conclude that we do **not** need to understand every single word we hear, and that there are often certain expectations which can actually help us to understand. The same applies to foreign languages, including German.

So remember the following:

1   you do not have to understand every word
2   you should not be discouraged if you do not understand every word
3   you should try to build on your knowledge of key words and expressions
4   you should also get as much practice in listening to German as you can.

In this section we work through what you can expect to encounter in the Basic Listening examination. This is best done by looking first at the requirements as laid down in the National Criteria for Modern Languages and then seeing what that means in terms of the examination itself.

- 'Candidates should be expected, within a **limited range** of **clearly defined topic areas**, to demonstrate understanding of **specific details** in **announcements, instructions, requests, monologues** (e.g. weather forecasts, news items), **interviews** and dialogues. The material used should be based on language which was designed to be heard (and not involve texts which were intended to be read silently) and should be spoken by native speakers, i.e. recorded on tape. Candidates should be required to demonstrate only comprehension and no undue burden should be put on memory.' (The National Criteria for Modern Languages)

- 'Assessment of listening comprehension can best be carried out by means of questions in English to be answered by the candidate in his or her own words in English. Multiple-choice tests are also acceptable provided that they are not the only testing techniques being used within this skill area. Multiple-choice should preferably be in English, though experience shows that questions in German are also possible; if questions are in German they should be heard as well as read in order to preserve the emphasis on listening comprehension.' (The National Criteria for Modern Languages)

The two paragraphs above can be **summarised** as follows:

a)   the topic areas are limited and clearly set down
b)   you will have to show you can understand specific details (key points) in announce-ments, instructions, requests, 'monologues' (e.g. weather forecasts, news items), interviews and dialogues (conversations)
c)   the listening test will be recorded on tape by native German-speakers
d)   the questions will usually be in English
e)   you will usually answer the questions in English in your own words
f)   sometimes there may be other types of questions where you may be asked to select alternative answers or to match information.

We deal with all these points in detail later in the chapter.

EXAM GROUP REQUIREMENTS

As we saw in Chapter 3, each of the examining groups is required to set out in detail what candidates are expected to prepare for the examination. It must also set out the nature of the tests to be used. A useful source of information is the **syllabus**, which tells you about the length of the examination, the topic areas tested and the type of response expected. You will also find a detailed analysis of the vocabulary and grammar the examination may include. Much of this information is provided in Chapters 3, 13 and 15 of this book.

- For all of the examining groups the listening tests last between 20 and 30 minutes.
- In all of the tests there will be some brief announcements and instructions, some monologues and some dialogues. You will need practice in listening to as wide a variety of these as possible.

The **topic areas** covered in the listening tests will be:

- Personal Identification
- House and Home
- School
- Free Time and Entertainment
- Travel
- Holidays
- Accommodation

- Social Relationships
- Health and Welfare
- Shopping
- Food and Drink
- Services
- Language Problems
- Weather

APPROACHING THE TESTS

The questions in the examination, as we have already noted, will test your ability to understand the **key points**. In this section we will look at the kinds of things that can reasonably be asked.

In many cases the questions will be seeking an answer about

a)   Who?
b)   What?
c)   Where?
d)   When?

e)   How long?
f)   How many?
g)   How much?
h)   Why?

We need, then, to check what items could be included under these categories and you need to make sure that you are familiar with them and that you understand them when you hear them. Make certain you know your vocabulary.

a)   **Who?** people
   - family and friends
   - professions
   - descriptions: physical appearance, size, age etc.

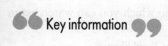
Key information

b)   **What?**
   - items relating to topic areas
   - what you have to do
   - instructions

c) **Where?** location
   - position: prepositions
   - places: buildings, landmarks, countries
   - directions
   - distances

d) **When?**
   - time of day
   - 24-hour clock
   - days, weeks, months, years
   - dates
   - moments of time: midnight, midday
   - length of time
   - frequency
   - expressions of time: today, yesterday etc.
   - seasons, important holiday periods: Christmas, New Year etc.
   - beginning, continuity, end

e) **How long?** duration
   - minutes, hours, days, weeks, months, years
   - until + time/point in time/day/week/month/year

f) **How many?**
   - numbers

g) **How much?** quantity
   - numbers
   - weights and measures
   - size: big, small

h) **Why?**
   - reason

The reason for concentrating on the above sub-headings will be more obvious when we consider some sample questions.

When practising listening, it is a good idea to make some **notes** as you hear the passage or extracts. This is especially true of numbers – e.g. times, dates, ages – but it is also true of other key points. Always **read the questions carefully**, with a view to planning the information you will be required to give. This will help you to pick out the vital points when you hear them spoken.

PRACTICE WITH TAPE-RECORDINGS

Listening, as we have already established, is a separate skill. To help improve your listening skills it goes without saying that you must above all have practice in listening. You will need to listen to as wide a range of voices as possible, and that of course means listening to recordings. Although that might at first seem easier said than done, let's just try and put things into perspective:

- most people these days have a cassette recorder or a walkman
- blank cassettes are cheap
- your teacher will probably have recorded cassettes you can borrow
- there is a cassette available with **this** book
- there are many good programmes on television and radio which you can watch/listen to and which in many cases you can record
- you can probably borrow records and cassettes from your local library
- if you are using your own cassette recorder you can stop and re-listen as often as you like

- you can also spend as long as you wish listening and then stop; it is generally a good idea to listen in short spells at first and gradually develop your ability to concentrate for longer periods. Intensive listening is hard work!

- if you have headphones you can listen without being disturbed (or disturbing others!)

So no more excuses! Make **listening** a regular part of your homework!

EXAMINATION QUESTIONS

The following extracts are on the *cassette*, which can be bought together with the book. All the extracts are written out in full in the text, so if you have bought the book separately get a friend on your course to *read out* the extract and then try to answer the questions.

EXTRACT ONE

The first extract on the cassette is about the topic area 'School'. It gives a selection of items similar to those you might hear in the exam. We shall use this extract to practise your **skill** in listening. Play the extract (or listen to your friend reading it) and imagine that your German friend is talking to you. Try to **note down** the key words and phrases in each item.

- PLAY EXTRACT ONE (or have your friend read out extracts (a) to (u) below)

❝❝ Anticipate key words ❞❞

We have printed each item below, and **ringed** some of the words and phrases that were likely to have been tested. Did you note these down? Written in English underneath each item are some of the **questions** these words and phrases might have helped you answer.

a) Hast du einen Wecker? Nein? OK, ich wecke dich dann. Gute Nacht.
   What does your friend want to know?   What will your friend do in the morning?

b) Du mußt um Viertel vor sieben aufstehen. Wir frühstücken um 7.
   When must you get up?.   What must you do at a quarter to seven?   When is breakfast?   Why must you get up at a quarter to seven?

c) Wir fahren um halb acht mit dem Schulbus. Also mußt du früher aufstehen als in England.
   At what time does the school bus go?   How will you get to school?   How are things different from life in England?

d) Die erste Stunde ist Mathematik. Bist du gut in Mathe?
   What is the first lesson?   When do you have Maths?   What does your friend want to know?

e) Die Englischlehrerin ist sehr nett. Sie spricht aber sehr schnell.
   Which teacher is nice?   What does your friend say about the English teacher?   What problem is there with the English teacher?

f) Der . . . lehrer ist streng/doof – ich mag ihn gar nicht.
   What does your friend say about this teacher?

g) Sie hat zwei Jahre in Birmingham gelebt.
   How long did the teacher spend in Birmingham?   What connection does the teacher have with Birmingham?

h) Sie hat in den Vereinigten Staaten studiert.
   What did the teacher do in the United States?   Where did the teacher study?

i) Um 9 Uhr 35 haben wir eine Pause. Dann essen wir unsere Butterbrote.
   When is the break?   What happens at 9.35?   What does your friend do then?

j) Wir können auch etwas zu trinken bekommen.
   What can you get during the break?

k) Was ißt du gern in deinen Butterbroten?
What does your friend want to know?

l) Willst du lieber Brot oder Brötchen?
What choice does your friend offer you?

m) Unser Klassenzimmer ist im zweiten Stock – Nummer R10b.
Where is your friend's classroom?   Why is the second floor important?

n) Also, das ist unser Klassenzimmer – ich sitze hinten, neben dem Fenster.
Where exactly does your friend sit?

o) In der vierten Stunde haben wir Vertretung – der Deutschlehrer fehlt heute.
What will happen in the fourth lesson?   Who is away?   When will you have a cover teacher?

p) In der fünften Stunde haben wir Sport. Ich treffe dich also vor der Sporthalle.
What is the fifth lesson?   When will you have sport?   Where should you meet your friend?

q) Nach der Pause schreiben wir eine Klassenarbeit für Geschichte. Du mußt dann in eine andere Klasse gehen. Du kannst vielleicht mit Rudi gehen.
What must your friend do after the break?   In which subject is there a test?   When must your friend do a History test?

r) Ach, die Klassenarbeit war aber schwer. Ich kriege bestimmt eine fünf.
What does your friend think of the test?   What mark does your friend expect?

s) Heute haben wir Schwimmen – vergiß' also dein Schwimmzeug nicht.
What should you remember to take with you to school?

t) Heute haben wir Schwimmen – du brauchst also dein Schwimmzeug – ich nehme ein Badetuch für dich mit.
What will your friend take for you?

u) Heute haben wir Sport – du brauchst also deine Turnschuhe und Sportzeug. Hoffentlich spielen wir draußen.
What should you take with you to school?   What lesson will you have?   What does your friend hope?

To repeat, it is important to understand how the **same stimulus** can be used to test **different items**. For example:

'We've got Sport today – you'll need your trainers and your sportsgear' might give rise to any one of the following questions:

- What lesson does your penfriend tell you about?
- What will you need to take to school today?
- When is the next Sport lesson?

EXTRACT TWO

The following type of listening test provides you with four possible answers to choose from. Even if you are unsure of the answer, be certain to put a tick in one box. Here are the instructions:

Questions 1–10

For each question listen to the German statement and then tick one of the boxes to indicate the most appropriate answer. There will be time for you to look at the suggested answers before you hear each recording. You will hear each German statement **twice**.

- PLAY EXTRACT TWO (or have a friend read out extracts 1 to 10 below)

1   The train you are travelling on arrives in Aachen, and you hear an announcement. How long does the train stop in Aachen?

☐ 5 minutes   ☐ 10 minutes   ☐ 15 minutes   ☐ 20 minutes

2   You plan to go out for the day, so you listen to the weather forecast on the radio. What should you take with you?

☐ an anorak   ☐ sunglasses   ☐ an umbrella   ☐ a woollen jumper

> Questions give clues as to what to expect

3   At a post office, the assistant tells you how much the stamps for your letters have cost. How much do you have to pay?

☐ DM 4,18   ☐ DM 4,80   ☐ DM 5,80   ☐ DM 8,40

4   You are shopping in a supermarket and you hear an advertisement. What is on special offer today?

☐ cheese   ☐ glasses   ☐ meat   ☐ wine

5   You are at the cinema, where you are given information about a film. When does it start?

☐ 7.15   ☐ 7.45   ☐ 8.00   ☐ 8.15

6   You are at a youth hostel. You need to buy some things, and you are told there is a shop nearby. What kind of shop is it?

☐ a baker's   ☐ a butcher's   ☐ a grocer's   ☐ a chemist's

7   You are at the tourist office, and the assistant answers your enquiry about a castle you want to visit. When is the castle open?

☐ Monday   ☐ Tuesday   ☐ Wednesday   ☐ Thursday

8   Your German penfriend invites you to a concert. Where is it being held?

☐ in the pub   ☐ in the theatre   ☐ in the concert hall   ☐ in the town hall

9   You are listening to the news on the radio. What was stolen?

☐ jewellery   ☐ some money   ☐ a television   ☐ antiques

10 You ask the way to the town centre. What are you told to do?

☐ go by train   ☐ go by bus   ☐ go by tram   ☐ get a taxi

(Total 10 marks)

To help you check your listening, a **written** version of the extract is provided below. Answers to each question are given at the end of this chapter.

1   Der Zug nach Köln fährt in fünf Minuten ab.
2   Die Wettervorhersage bis heute abend: warmes sonniges Wetter.
3   Also sechs Briefmarken zu achtzig . . . das macht vier Mark achtzig.
4   Sonderangebot: österreichischer Weißwein, drei Mark fünfzig die Flasche.
5   Die Vorstellung beginnt um Viertel vor acht.
6   Es gibt eine Bäckerei nur hundert Meter von hier.
7   Die Burg ist nur dienstags geöffnet.
8   Am Samstag ist ein Popkonzert im Rathaus.
9   Gestern abend haben zwei Einbrecher kostbare Ketten bei einer alten Dame gestohlen.
10 Am besten fahren Sie mit der Straßenbahnlinie drei.

EXTRACT THREE

In the following test you are asked to listen carefully to someone speaking, and then to write your answer in the space provided.

■ PLAY EXTRACT THREE

1   You are in a café in Germany and order something to eat. What does the waitress ask you?

_____ *(1)*

2   You are at a German station. The official tells you that the next train for Koblenz leaves in ten minutes. What else does he tell you?

_____   *(1)*

3   You are in a German shop. You buy a postcard. What does the shopkeeper ask you?

_____   *(1)*

4   You stop a passer-by and ask him the way to the nearest post office. What directions does he give you?

_____   *(1)*

5   You ask your penfriend if he wants to play tennis. Why can't he?

_____   *(1)*

6   You have arrived at a German Youth Hostel. What does the warden ask you?

_____   *(1)*

7   You are in a German baker's. What does the shopkeeper ask you?

_____   *(1)*

8   You have lost your umbrella. What does the man at the Lost Property Office ask you?

_____   *(1)*

9   You arrive at the beach with your friend. Why is he upset?

_____   *(1)*

10   You are staying with your German penfriend. You ask at what time you should get up in the morning. What does your penfriend's mother tell you?

_____   *(1)*

11   Whilst staying with your penfriend, you offer to help. What are you told you could do?

_____   *(1)*

12   You have bought some toothpaste for your friend and some soap and suntan oil for yourself. How much did the toothpaste cost?

_____   *(1)*

For checking purposes:

- The extract is printed below.
- Answers are provided at the end of the chapter.

1   *Kellnerin:* Sehr gut. Möchten Sie auch etwas dazu trinken?
2   *Beamter:* Der nächste Zug nach Koblenz? . . . in 10 Minuten, aber Sie müssen in Bonn umsteigen.
3   *Verkäufer:* Möchten Sie auch Briefmarken kaufen?
4   *Fußgänger:* Hier geradeaus. Die Hauptpost liegt am Marktplatz.
5   *Gerd:* Ja, aber leider muß ich für morgen meine Hausaufgaben machen.
6   *Herbergsvater:* Wieviele seid ihr denn?
7   *Verkäuferin:* Haben Sie sonst noch einen Wunsch?
8   *Beamter:* Ja . . . Wissen Sie so ungefähr, wo das war?
9   *Freund:* Ach! Wie doof! Ich habe die Badehose vergessen.
10 *Frau Müller:* Du bist ja müde. Das ist mir egal. Wann du willst.
11 *Frau Müller:* Das ist wirklich nett von dir. Könntest du vielleicht für mich den Tisch decken?

12 *Verkäuferin:* Also . . . Seife: DM 2,50
                eine Tube Zahnpasta: DM 2,75
                und eine Flasche Sonnenöl: DM 8,50
                Macht zusammen: DM 13,75

The German conversations you hear in Extracts 4 to 13 are rather longer. A **written** version of each of these extracts is provided on pages 56 to 58, with answers on pages 59 and 60.

EXTRACT FOUR

You are by the Rhine at Bonn. Listen to the conversation and then answer the questions.

■ PLAY EXTRACT FOUR

1   How often do the steamboats go?

_____ *(1)*

2   When is the next boat to Königswinter?

_____ *(1)*

3   What tickets does the tourist buy?

_____ *(2)*

EXTRACT FIVE

You are in a post office in Germany. Listen to the conversation and then answer the questions.

■ PLAY EXTRACT FIVE

1   What does the customer wish to do in addition to buying stamps?

_____ *(2)*

2   How much will it cost to do this?

_____ *(1)*

3   What information must be given on the form?

_____
_____ *(2)*

EXTRACT SIX

Answer as many questions as possible.
Write your answers, IN ENGLISH, in the spaces provided.

Travelling in Germany

You are travelling by train to stay in Germany.
You hear the following announcement at a railway station.

■ PLAY EXTRACT SIX

1   From which platform is the train leaving?

_____ *(1)*

2   At what time will it leave?

_____ *(1)*

You find the platform.
There is a further loudspeaker announcement.

3   What are you told to do?

_____ (1)

Your friend has told you to catch the airport bus.
When you arrive in her town you ask for the correct bus.

4   Where is the bus stop?

_____ (2)

5   How will you know which bus to get on?

_____ (1)

EXTRACT SEVEN   **At Home in Germany**
You have arrived at your destination and are being shown round the house.

   ■ PLAY EXTRACT SEVEN

1   What is your hostess asking you to admire from the bedroom window? (3 things)

_____

_____ (3)

2   Where is the bathroom?

_____ (2)

3   What time is breakfast?

_____ (1)

From the smell coming from the kitchen it is obvious that food is on the way!

You ask whether there is anything you can do to help.

Listen to the reply from your friend's mother, as you go into the dining room.

4   What does she ask you to do?

_____ (1)

5   How many people is she expecting?

_____ (1)

6   What does she ask you to get from the cupboard?

_____ (2)

EXTRACT EIGHT   **Buying a Present**
You go to a department store, looking for a tie to give to the father of the family you are staying with, who has a birthday.
First of all you hear the following announcement.

   ■ PLAY EXTRACT EIGHT

1   What is the special offer price of the jeans?

_____ (1)

2   By how much are they reduced?

_____   *(1)*

Jeans aren't a good idea for the present you need! – so you ask someone where you can buy a tie.

3   On which floor is the men's department?

_____   *(1)*

4   Where exactly on this floor is it?

_____   *(2)*

You have finally chosen the tie. It is a little more expensive than you expected, but you have some travellers' cheques. Listen though to this conversation at the cash desk – it may save you some time!

5   What can't the customer do?

_____   *(2)*

6   Where will he (and you!) have to go next?

_____   *(2)*

EXTRACT NINE   **A Treat! – But for whom?**
To celebrate the father's birthday, the whole family go to a café. The father orders without asking you what you want – he is obviously going to give **you** a special treat! See if you can make out, in advance, what you are going to get.

■ PLAY EXTRACT NINE

1   What are you **all** going to eat?

_____   *(1)*

2   What special trimmings are you going to get with it?

_____   *(2)*

3   What are you going to get to drink?

_____   *(1)*

During the conversation, the family start to talk about their holidays last year. Your friend fills in the details for you.

4   How long did the family spend there?

_____   *(1)*

5   Where did they stay?

_____   *(1)*

6   Which member of the family enjoyed it least?

_____   *(1)*

EXTRACT TEN

They all then start to plan an excursion for tomorrow – to show you some of the area. Complete the following card to a friend in England about your plans for tomorrow.

- PLAY EXTRACT TEN

Questions 1–5

Friday (1) _____

Dear Bill,

    Great time! Everyone really kind! Tomorrow we're going to (2) _____
During the day the weather is supposed to be (3) _____ *and (4)* _____
in the evening. So we are going on a trip to (5) _____
    Hope it all works out OK!
    See you.

(Total 5 marks)

The following extracts from Basic Listening tests are further examples of the kind of techniques you may have to practise.

EXTRACT ELEVEN

Questions 1–5
You have a holiday job as a receptionist at a German hotel, and have a conversation with a guest.
Look at the notepad below.
Now listen to the conversation and fill in, IN ENGLISH, the relevant information on the pad.
You will hear the conversation **twice**.

- PLAY EXTRACT ELEVEN

1 Datum _____
2 Wie viele Zimmer? _____
3 Wie viele Personen? _____ pro Nacht
4 Zimmerpreis _____
5 Name _____

(Total 5 marks)

EXTRACT TWELVE

Questions 1–5
You wish to visit a museum, and telephone to find out more about it. You hear a recorded message.
Look at the notes below about the museum.
Listen to the message and complete the notes IN ENGLISH.
You will hear the message **twice**.

- PLAY EXTRACT TWELVE

MUSEUM

1   Open from 10 a.m. until _____ p.m.

2   Open every day except _____

3   Admission price: Adults DM _____

4   Children over 3 years DM _____

5   Tickets can be bought at the museum and at _____

_____

(Total 5 marks)

EXTRACT THIRTEEN

Questions 1–2

You are on an exchange visit to Germany. As it is still term time, you go to school each day with your penfriend Inge.

Look at Questions 1 and 2.

Listen to the first part of the interview with Inge, and answer the following questions IN ENGLISH.

You will hear the interview **twice**.

■ PLAY EXTRACT THIRTEEN (Part one)

1   How does Inge usually travel to school?

_____

2   How far does she live from school?

_____

Questions 3–7

Now look at Inge's timetable below.

Listen to Inge as she describes her week at school, and complete, IN ENGLISH, Questions 3 to 7 **in the timetable**.

You will hear the description of her school week **twice**.

■ PLAY EXTRACT THIRTEEN (Part two)

LESSON	TIME	MONDAY	TUESDAY	WEDNESDAY
1	8.00	ART	ENGLISH	GEOGRAPHY
2	8.45	ART	MATHS	HISTORY
	9.30	——	B R E A K	——
3	9.50	**3**	**4**	MATHS
4	10.35	PHYSICS	FRENCH	MATHS
5	11.35	FRENCH	GEOGRAPHY	**7**
6	12.15	MATHS	**5**	BIOLOGY
7	13.00		**6**	

Questions 8–10
Now listen to the description of the rest of Inge's school week, and answer IN ENGLISH the questions that follow.
You will hear the description **twice**.

■ PLAY EXTRACT THIRTEEN (Part three)

8   When does she have Geography on Thursday?

_____

9   When does she have French on Friday?

_____

10   Give **one** reason why going to school on Saturday is not so bad.

_____

(Total 10 marks)

WRITTEN VERSION OF EXTRACTS 4–13

EXTRACT FOUR

— Tag! Wann fährt der nächste Dampfer nach Königswinter, bitte?
— Der Dampfer fährt alle 45 Minuten, also um 15.00 Uhr fährt der nächste ab. Die letzte Fahrt ist um 18.00 Uhr.
— Zweimal nach Königswinter, bitte – einfach.
— DM24 zusammen, bitte.

EXTRACT FIVE

— Geben Sie mir bitte zwei Briefmarken zu 90 Pfennig. Ich möchte auch dieses Päckchen nach Amerika schicken. Was kostet das, bitte?
— Moment mal! 500 Gramm nach Amerika kostet leider DM20,50. Füllen Sie bitte das Formular aus.
— Formular? Warum denn das?
— Sie müssen sagen, was in dem Päckchen ist, und wieviel es gekostet hat.
— Ach so!

EXTRACT SIX

Questions 1 and 2
Der Zug nach Heidelberg fährt um 14.50 von Gleis 13 ab.

Question 3
Achtung an Gleis 13. Bitte einsteigen. Die Türen schließen automatisch. Der Zug fährt sofort ab.

Questions 4 and 5
Zum Flughafen? Kein Problem. Gehen Sie zum Hauptausgang und dann gerade über die Straße. Da halten die Flughafenbusse. Die Linie Nummer 70, glaube ich, fährt zum Flughafen.

EXTRACT SEVEN

Question 1
Hier ist dein Zimmer. Es ist ziemlich klein, hat aber eine schöne Aussicht über den Fluß. Komm' . . . hier zum Fenster . . . Du hast hier einen ganz schönen Überblick . . . Komm' . . . ja, so . . . siehst du, da, die Bäume – schön, nicht wahr! Und die Kirche da drüben, direkt am Park, und da die Boote auf dem Fluß.

Question 2
Ja, gut . . . also . . . das Badezimmer findest du gerade um die Ecke, da.

Question 3
Normalerweise frühstücken wir um halb acht. OK?

Questions 4, 5 and 6

Das ist nett von dir. Kannst du bitte den Tisch decken? Hier . . . Moment . . . ja . . . hier ist die Tischdecke . . . wir nehmen die weiße. Teller und Tassen sind im Schrank, siehst du . . . da! OK? . . . Wir sind vier, und es kommt auch der Freund von Karl . . . also . . . fünf, ja?

EXTRACT EIGHT

Questions 1 and 2

Meine Damen und Herren! Im heutigen Sonderangebot haben wir preiswerte Jeans für DM 78,–. Normalerweise kosten sie DM 128,–. Also greifen Sie zu und sparen Sie DM 50,–.

Questions 3 and 4

Am besten versuchen Sie in der Herrenabteilung. Die ist auf der dritten Etage, links neben der Kasse.

Questions 5 and 6

— Ich möchte das Hemd hier. Kann ich mit Reiseschecks zahlen?

— Nein, leider nehmen wir keine Reiseschecks an. Sie müssen zur Sparkasse gehen, die ist hier gleich gegenüber.

— OK. Ich komme in ein paar Minuten wieder.

EXTRACT NINE

Questions 1, 2 and 3

— Herr Ober, wir möchten bestellen.

— Ja bitte.

— Also . . . viermal Himbeertorte ohne Sahne . . . und wir nehmen auch vier Kännchen Kaffee. Und dann, für unseren englischen Gast etwas Spezielles . . . natürlich auch Himbeertorte . . . die ist lecker . . . aber mit viel Sahne und etwas Eis dazu. Und zu trinken . . . ja zu trinken: Tee.

— Tee. Mit Milch oder Zitrone?

— Zitrone. Mit Milch kann man wohl jeden Tag in England Tee trinken.

Questions 4, 5 and 6

Wir haben zweieinhalb Wochen auf einem Campingplatz verbracht. Mitten im August sind natürlich immer viele Leute dort – meiner Mutter und meinen zwei Brüdern gefällt es dort in Jugoslawien sehr gut. Für meinen Vater ist es aber ein bißchen langweilig.

EXTRACT TEN

Questions 1 and 2

— Was machen wir am Wochenende?

— Wir können am Samstag etwas unternehmen.

— Wir können uns noch ein Rad leihen. Tscha . . . aber wollen wir uns zuerst in der Zeitung den Wetterbericht ansehen.

Questions 3 and 4

Also . . . das Wetter für morgen . . Samstag den 10. August . . . mmm . . . morgen . . . überwiegend Sonne, ab und zu wolkig; abends Regenschauer – ziemlich gut! erst abends ein bißchen regnerisch, sonst schönes Wetter.

Question 5

— Oh gut, dann können wir zur Burg fahren, oder möchtest du lieber an den Fluß?

— Nein, die Burg ist sehr interessant, da gibt es allerlei zu sehen.

EXTRACT ELEVEN

G.   Guten Tag.

R.   Guten Tag.

G.   Haben Sie ein Zimmer für eine Nacht?

R.   Für heute?

G.   Nein, für den sechsten Juli.

R.   Was für ein Zimmer soll es sein? Ein Einzelzimmer?

G.   Nein, ein Zimmer mit zwei Betten.
R.   Also für zwei Personen?
G.   Ja, das stimmt.
R.   Ich habe ein Zimmer mit Dusche.
G.   Was kostet das Zimmer?
R.   Fünfundvierzig Mark pro Nacht.
G.   Ja, das nehme ich.
R.   Wie ist Ihr Name?
G.   Klein.
R.   Also K...L...E...I...N.
G.   Ja, danke schön. Auf Wiedersehen.
R.   Bitte sehr. Auf Wiedersehen.

EXTRACT TWELVE

Das Museum ist jeden Tag von 10 bis 18 Uhr geöffnet, außer sonntags. Eintrittspreise: Erwachsene – sechs Mark, Kinder ab drei Jahren – drei Mark fünfzig. Eintrittskarten am Museum und vom Verkehrsamt.

EXTRACT THIRTEEN

Part one (Questions 1–2)
— Wie heißt du?
— Ich heiße Inge Bachmann.
— Und was für eine Schule besuchst du?
— Ich besuche eine Gesamtschule in Bremen.
— Wie kommst du zur Schule?
— Ich fahre meistens mit dem Rad, aber wenn das Wetter schlecht ist, fährt mich meine Mutter mit dem Wagen zur Schule.
— Wohnst du denn weit von der Schule?
— Anderthalb Kilometer.

Part two (Questions 3–7)
Die Schule beginnt um acht Uhr. Montags habe ich in der ersten und zweiten Stunde Kunst. Um halb zehn beginnt die Frühstückspause, und ich esse meine Butterbrote. In der dritten Stunde um neun Uhr fünfzig habe ich Englisch, dann Physik, Französisch und Mathe. Die Schule ist um dreizehn Uhr aus.

Dienstags beginne ich mit Englisch und Mathe. Nach der Frühstückspause habe ich Geschichte, dann Französisch und Erdkunde und schließlich in der sechsten und siebten Stunde Musik – eine Doppelstunde.

Mittwochs habe ich Erdkunde in der ersten und Geschichte in der zweiten Stunde. Nach der Frühstückspause habe ich Mathematik – eine Doppelstunde, in der fünften Stunde Deutsch und in der sechsten Biologie.

Part three (Questions 8–10)
Donnerstags habe ich Chemie in der ersten Stunde und Erdkunde in der zweiten. Um neun Uhr fünfzig habe ich Englisch, und um 10.35 Französisch. Der Schultag endet mit Deutsch – eine Doppelstunde.

Freitags habe ich zuerst Geschichte, dann Deutsch; nach der Pause kommt Französisch und dann in der vierten Stunde Biologie. Schließlich habe ich Sport.

Samstags ist es nur halb so schlimm. Erstens habe ich nur eine Doppelstunde Kunst und eine Doppelstunde Sport, und zweitens müssen wir nur jeden zweiten Samstag zur Schule gehen.

KEY TO THE QUESTIONS

EXTRACT ONE   –

EXTRACT TWO

1 5 minutes
2 sunglasses
3 DM 4,80
4 wine
5 7.45

6 a baker's
7 Tuesday
8 in the town hall
9 jewellery
10 go by tram

EXTRACT THREE

1 Do you want a drink?
2 You have to change in Bonn.
3 Do you want to buy stamps as well?
4 Straight on. It is in the market place.
5 He has to do homework for tomorrow.
6 How many are there of you?

7 Anything else?
8 Where, more or less, was it?
9 He's forgotten his trunks.
10 When you like.
11 Lay the table.
12 DM 2,75

EXTRACT FOUR

1 every 45 minutes
2 at 3.00 pm

3 two singles

EXTRACT FIVE

1 send a packet to America
2 DM 20,50

3 what is in the packet and how much it cost

EXTRACT SIX

1 13
2 2.50 pm
3 get in

4 straight ahead/across the road
5 No. 70

EXTRACT SEVEN

1 trees, church, park, boats on the river
2 round the corner
3 7.30

4 lay the table
5 5
6 plates and cups

EXTRACT EIGHT

1 DM 78
2 DM 50
3 third floor

4 on the left, near the pay desk
5 pay with travellers' cheques
6 to the bank opposite

EXTRACT NINE

1 raspberry gateau/flan
2 cream and ice cream
3 tea

4 2½ weeks
5 on a campsite in Yugoslavia
6 father

EXTRACT TEN

1 9th August
2 hire a bicycle
3 mainly sunny, occasionally cloudy

4 rainy
5 a castle

EXTRACT ELEVEN

1 6th July
2 one room
3 two people

4 DM 45
5 Klein

EXTRACT TWELVE

1 6 pm
2 Sunday
3 DM 6

4 DM 3,50
5 tourist office

EXTRACT THIRTEEN

1 bicycle
2 1½ kilometres
3 English
4 History
5 Music

6 Music
7 German
8 second lesson
9 after break
10 She has art and games (sports). They
     have school only every other Saturday.

TESTS WITH STUDENT ANSWERS

Here are some examples of Basic Listening tests with student answers. An experienced examiner has marked them and added comments. Notice that the total marks available are given in brackets after each question. This should indicate if and when two or more items are required in the answer. If your answer only has one item, and several marks are available for the answer, it is likely that your answer is incomplete.

TEST 1: PREPARING FOR VISITORS

This is the text the student heard:

Renate: Bist du fertig? Es ist fast acht Uhr.
Peter: Was haben wir vergessen?
Renate: Nichts. Ich habe den Weißwein auf den Balkon gestellt und das Bier in den Kühlschrank gelegt.
Peter: Und die Biergläser stehen schon auf dem Kaffeetisch im Wohnzimmer.

QUESTIONS AND STUDENT ANSWERS

1 What is the time?   (2)

Eight o'clock

    ❝ You have forgotten the word 'fast' (almost, nearly). 1 mark ❞

2 What had they forgotten?   (1)

nothing

    ❝ Fine! No problem here! 1 mark ❞

3 What is on the balcony?   (2)

the wine

    ❝ It should be *white* wine. 1 mark ❞

4 And where is the beer?   (1)

In the fridge

    ❝ Good! You know the difference between 'Schrank' and 'Kühlschrank'. 1 mark ❞

5 And where exactly are the beer glasses?   (3)

on the table

    ❝ Not enough! What sort of table and where is it? 1 mark ❞

 ❝ SIX marks out of a possible NINE. Could you have done better? ❞

TEST 2: AN INTERVIEW WITH GUNTHER SCHNEIDER

This the text the student heard:

Interviewer: Guten Tag, Günther. Was sind Sie von Beruf?
Günther: Ich studiere Chemie hier in Göttingen.
Interviewer: Und woher kommen Sie?
Günther: Ich komme aus Vlotho. Das ist eine Kleinstadt an der Weser, etwa hundertfünfzig Kilometer von Göttingen.
Interviewer: Und haben Sie Geschwister?
Günther: Ja, ich habe einen jüngeren Bruder.
Interviewer: Und was für Hobbys haben Sie?
Günther: Ich spiele Schach und ich gehe ziemlich oft ins Kino.

QUESTIONS AND STUDENT ANSWERS

1 What is Günther's job? (2)
    He's a student

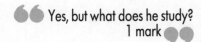 Yes, but what does he study? 1 mark

2 Where does the interview take place? (1)
    in Göttingen

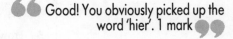 Good! You obviously picked up the word 'hier'. 1 mark

3 Where is Vlotho? (3)
    150 kms from Göttingen

You missed the phrase 'an der Weser' and you missed the word 'etwa' (about). 1 mark

4 Has he brothers and sisters? (2)
    yes, a brother

Yes, but you should have added 'younger'. 1 mark

5 What hobbies does he have? (2)
    chess and the cinema

Good! 'Schach' is a difficult word. Full marks for this one. 2 marks

SIX marks out of a possible TEN

TEST 3: AT THE STATION

This is the text the student heard:

Der Zug nach Frankfurt fährt um sieben Uhr vierzehn von Gleis vier ab.

QUESTIONS AND STUDENT ANSWER

Listen to the statement in German and tick the correct box.

The train leaves at:

a) 4.00 ☐
b) 7.14 ☒
c) 7.40 ☐
d) 17.14 ☐

The candidate has clearly understood the German but I am afraid I cannot give him/her the mark, because he/she has not read the instructions carefully

TEST 4: IN THE TRAVEL AGENCY

This is the text the student heard:

Frau Müller: Guten Tag. Ich möchte bitte eine Reise buchen.
Angestellte: Wo wollen Sie denn hinfahren?
Frau Müller: Wir wollen nach Österreich und zwar nach Kals in Osttirol.
Angestellte: Wollen Sie in einer Pension oder in einem Hotel übernachten?
Frau Müller: Lieber in einer Pension.
Angestellte: Und was für Zimmer brauchen Sie?

Frau Müller: Ja, zwei Doppelzimmer mit Bad und ein Einzelzimmer mit Dusche und WC.
Angestellte: Und wann möchten Sie hinfahren?
Frau Müller: Am dreizehnten vierten.
Angestellte: Und wie lange wollen Sie bleiben?
Frau Müller: Fünfzehn Tage.

QUESTIONS AND STUDENT ANSWERS

1 Where is Kals?   (3)

Austria, in Tirol

> Nearly! But it is *East* Tirol. 2 marks

2 What sort of hotel is she looking for?   (1)

a guest house

> Good! 1 mark

3 What accommodation does she require?   (5)
*2 double rooms with bath,
a single room with shower and toilet*

> Excellent! Five valuable marks picked up here. 5 marks

4 When does she wish to travel?   (2)

on the 13th

> You clearly don't know this German way of giving the month. 1 mark

5 How long does she want to stay?   (1)
15 days

> Yes. A fortnight would do as well. 1 mark

> Very good. TEN marks out of a possible TWELVE

TEST 5: AT THE SERVICE STATION

This is the text the student heard:

Frank: Guten Tag.
Tankwart: Guten Tag.
Frank: Ich möchte gern volltanken.
Tankwart: Dann müssen Sie den Motor ausschalten.
Frank: Oh. Entschuldigung!
Tankwart: Und rauchen dürfen Sie auch nicht.
Frank: Ach was!
Tankwart: So. Das wäre es. Fünfundvierzig Mark bitte.
Frank: Und können Sie bitte die Vorderreifen prüfen – und den Ölstand?
Tankwart: Ja, bitte schön. Alles ist in Ordnung. Gute Reise.

QUESTIONS AND STUDENT ANSWERS

1 What does Frank ask for?   (1)
Petrol

> Not good enough! He asks to have the tank filled. 0 marks

2 What does he fail to do?   (2)
*a) switch off engine
b) put out cigarette*

> Very good! Two useful marks

3 How much must he pay?   (1)

54 marks

> No! You have got the numbers the wrong way round! 0 marks

4 What else does he ask to have done?   (3)

tyres and oil checked

> Nearly. But it is the *front* tyres. 2 marks

> FOUR marks out of a possible SEVEN

Suggestions for *developing* your listening skills can be found in 'A Step Further' at the end of the next chapter.

LISTENING: HIGHER LEVEL

REQUIREMENTS

THEMES

EXAMINATION QUESTIONS

KEY TO THE QUESTIONS

TEST WITH STUDENT ANSWERS

A STEP FURTHER

G E T T I N G   S T A R T E D

Higher Level Listening is an optional paper. As with other optional papers, however, you have nothing to lose by attempting it. The Higher Listening tests for all of the examining groups are based on the same fundamental principles as for the Basic Listening tests (see Chapter 4). Many of the tests will overlap to some extent with the topic areas and vocabulary already covered at Basic Level. If you are confident and competent at Basic Listening, you should gain some credit at Higher Level.

ESSENTIAL PRINCIPLES

REQUIREMENTS

What do you have to do?

1   You will be expected to demonstrate the skills listed under Basic Listening over a **wider range of clearly defined topic areas** – check what is applicable in your case.

2   In addition you will be expected to show that you can:

   ■ identify the **important points** or **themes** of the material;
   ■ understand the **attitudes, emotions** and **ideas** of the speakers;
   ■ **draw conclusions** from what you hear;
   ■ identify the **relationship between ideas** expressed;
   ■ **infer meanings** from the extracts;
   ■ understand a variety of spoken German such as that heard on the radio and television, in the home, in formal and informal situations and by sixteen-year-olds in Germany, Austria and Switzerland.

As with Basic Listening, extracts may well contain natural hesitation, spontaneous repetition or rephrasing of sentences and a limited amount of background noise.

All extracts will be recorded by native German-speakers. Extracts will be heard twice. You will be able to make notes during the extracts. Longer extracts will be broken down into shorter sections so as not to place too much of a burden on your memory.

THEMES

What kind of themes or extracts can you expect?

As we saw in Chapter 4, the main sources for testing **listening comprehension** are likely to be:

   ■ **public announcements**, e.g. in public places, in shops, on the radio or television
   ■ **news, weather, traffic reports**
   ■ **telephone calls**
   ■ **guided tours**
   ■ **interviews**, on radio or television, **surveys**
   ■ **conversations, dialogues, discussions,** both **formal** and **informal**.

Some of the extracts, such as announcements, will be quite short, while others, such as discussions and interviews, are likely to be longer.

Obviously your understanding of a wide range of vocabulary is going to be put to the test, and you must make sure that you know most of the Higher Level vocabulary. But it is always helpful to know where to start and what to expect. It is, then, worth considering in more detail the topic areas mentioned above.

PUBLIC ANNOUNCEMENTS

You could expect to hear any of the following:

   ■ **announcements at a railway station, bus station, airport, ferry terminal** – these will inevitably deal with travel arrangements, such as times of departure and arrival, changes to timetables (e.g. delays), a reminder to change trains, requests to get off, to board, to go to Gate 3, to report to the reception
   ■ **announcements at a campsite, hostel, hotel** – these will tend to be about facilities offered (e.g. 'campers are reminded that fresh milk and groceries can be purchased in the camp shop'), special events such as evening barbecues, trips to places of local interest, excursions to nearby beauty spots, requests to come to reception, messages passed on by people telephoning or visiting, emergencies
   ■ **announcements in shops** – mostly in department stores, e.g. advertising goods, special offers, bargains, sales, cheese-tasting, wine-tasting, café/restaurant menus, holidays, etc.

- **Announcements on the radio or television** – these announcements could well include commercial advertising (e.g. by department stores planning a publicity drive (see above), travel agents advertising holidays, trips, special offers, local groups publicising activities and events) or local features (e.g. what's on in the region, diary of coming events such as films, plays, sports events, dances, exhibitions, special mini-reports).

NEWS, WEATHER, TRAFFIC REPORTS

You can expect these to include:

- **reports of current, topical news items**, such as visits, accidents, disasters, industrial unrest, strikes, protests, famous personalities, sports, special events, occasional 'funny stories'
- **weather forecasts** mentioning temperatures, general conditions, trends, features for holiday-makers or skiers, natural disasters such as floods
- **road conditions, motorway reports** (queues are very common on German motorways!) mentioning roadworks, diversions, accidents, advice/hints, features for holiday-makers.

TELEPHONE CALLS

These could include:

- messages of all kinds for someone who is not present
- a pen friend ringing you up to make arrangements, pass on information
- someone ringing to report reasons for a delay
- recorded messages, e.g. when you telephone a tourist information service and get a pre-recorded message.

GUIDED TOURS

These will obviously relate to places and features of interest. You are likely to be asked information about dates, ages, descriptions, special features, traditions, history, famous people, stories of interest.

INTERVIEWS ON THE RADIO OR TELEVISION, SURVEYS

These could well include:

- famous people talking about their lives, interests, careers
- experts talking about their specialist areas
- features of general interest, e.g. holidays, jobs, fashion, education, music, entertainment, sport
- ordinary people talking about any of the above, likes, dislikes, new schemes such as pedestrian zones
- open-call programmes.

CONVERSATIONS, DIALOGUES, DISCUSSIONS (FORMAL AND INFORMAL)

These could cover any of the areas mentioned above in interviews, but:

- **formal** discussions could include more serious matters and people, e.g. politicians
- **informal** conversations could well take place in the home environment, e.g. parents and children talking about holidays, free time, school, TV, etc. The tone is likely to be rather different.

Remember, at Higher Level you will be expected to understand details such as facts, in much the same way as at Basic Level, but you will also have to show that you can understand **what people think or feel about something, and why**. This is a very important development and the specimen questions will help to focus attention on this aspect.

EXAMINATION QUESTIONS

As with Basic Listening, you can expect a variety of question types. These are best summarised as follows:

- Questions in English requiring answers in English
- Multiple-choice questions in English
- Completing a table/form/note/grid
- Matching statements in English to the speakers in the extract.

Again you can play the extracts on the tape. Each extract is written out in full, so if you have bought the book separately, you can listen to your friend reading the extract to you. Sometimes the reader will need to play more than one rôle.

EXTRACT ONE

This is an example of what a 'matching statements' test might look like:

One evening during your stay in Germany you are listening to the local radio station and you hear a programme about the wine harvest. Four of the workers in the vineyards are interviewed about their jobs.

Look at the list of comments A–H below.

Listen to the interview and, next to each of the worker's names, write two letters to indicate which comments apply to him or her. (Each comment can only be used once.) You will hear the interview twice.

- PLAY EXTRACT ONE (or have your friend read out the extract)

A   enjoys working in the open

B   finds the work tiring sometimes   1   Christiane   ☐ ☐

C   worked once in the vineyards years ago

D   describes the work of a picker   2   Dirk   ☐ ☐

E   complains about the social life

F   is on holiday   3   Paul   ☐ ☐

G   is a student

H   says there are few grapes this year   4   Inge   ☐ ☐

The answer to this question is:

1. A, D   2. E, G   3. B, F   4. C, H

EXTRACT ONE
M1   An einem heißen Septembernachmittag bin ich nach Bernkastel an der Mosel gekommen. Ich stehe gerade in einem Weinberg, wo zahlreiche Leute dabei sind, die Trauben zu pflücken. Ich versuche jetzt, einigen von den Arbeitern ein paar Fragen zu stellen.

M3   CHRISTIANE

M1   Entschuldigen Sie bitte!
F1   Ja?
M1   Ja, würden Sie ein paar Fragen beantworten . . . über Ihre Arbeit hier im Weinberg?
F1   Ja gerne.
M1   Machen Sie das zum ersten Mal?
F1   Nein, nein, ich mache das jetzt seit drei Jahren.
M1   Und die Arbeit gefällt Ihnen?
F1   Ja, sie gefällt mir sehr.
M1   Und warum machen Sie das?

F1   Nun, zuerst mal um etwas Geld zu verdienen, aber auch weil wir im Freien arbeiten. Das macht schon Spaß.

M1   Und was machen Sie genau?

F1   Nun, wir stellen einen Korb unter die Trauben, unter den Weinstock . . . und wir schneiden die Trauben, also die Reben, ab.

M1   Nun, ich darf Sie nicht länger aufhalten, ich unterbreche ja Ihre Arbeit und Ihr Träger wartet auf Sie. Also, ich bedanke mich und wünsche Ihnen viel Spaß.

F1   Vielen Dank.

M3   DIRK

M1   Guten Tag! Ich habe gerade mit der Dame in der Reihe neben Ihnen geredet . . . darf ich fragen, wo Sie herkommen?

M2   Ich komme aus Hamburg.

M1   Extra zur Weinlese?

M2   Nein, ich bin Student in Trier und ich arbeite hier um etwas Geld zu verdienen.

M1   Sind Sie zum ersten Mal hier?

M2   Zum zweiten Mal.

M1   Gefällt es Ihnen?

M2   Hm, es geht.

M1   Sie scheinen ja nicht besonders begeistert zu sein.

M2   Nein – wir bekommen hier kein Essen und auch keine Unterkunft; als ich das erste Mal bei der Weinlese dabei war, da gab's Essen und Unterkunft . . . wir konnten uns dann abends nach der Arbeit treffen und zusammen bleiben, plaudern, uns unterhalten . .

M1   Und diese Trauben? Müssen Sie sie tragen? Sind Sie Träger oder Pflücker?

M2   Ich bin Träger.

M1   Das ist eine schwere Arbeit, oder?

M2   Ein bißchen schon, aber man gewöhnt sich doch daran.

M1   So, dann wünsche ich Ihnen viel Erfolg!

M2   Vielen Dank.

M3   PAUL

M1   Nach dem Hamburger kommt nun ein Engländer an die Reihe! Sie sind Engländer, nicht wahr?

M3   Ja, das stimmt.

M1   Sind Sie extra aus England zur Weinlese gekommen?

M3   Ja und nein . . . das heißt, ich bin auf drei Wochen Urlaub gekommen und die Weinlese ist ein Teil vom Urlaub.

M1   Und gefällt's Ihnen?

M3   Ja, sehr gut.

M1   Sind Sie zum ersten Mal hier bei der Weinlese?

M3   Nein, ich bin voriges Jahr zum ersten Mal hierhergekommen. Das ist also das zweite Mal.

M1   Aber die Arbeit ist schwer, nicht wahr?

M3   Manchmal ja. So am späten Nachmittag, da bin ich schon müde, aber sonst ist die Arbeit nicht zu schwer.

M1   Und was machen Sie? Pflücken Sie oder tragen Sie?

M3   Ich bin Träger.

M1   So, herzlichen Dank!

M3   Bitte sehr.

M3   INGE

M1   Entschuldigung, ich habe Ihrem Träger eben einige Fragen gestellt. Sie pflücken für ihn. Könnten Sie uns auch ein paar Fragen beantworten?

F1   Ja.

M1   Haben Sie heute viel gepflückt?

F1   Nein, nicht besonders viel. Dieses Jahr gibt es nicht so viele Trauben, aber mir gefällt die Arbeit. Meine Mitarbeiter sind ganz in Ordnung und die Stimmung bei der Arbeit ist sehr gut.

M1   Machen Sie das zum ersten Mal?

F1   Nein, ich war schon als Kind hier, mit meiner Mutter . . . nun das war wohl vor fünfzehn Jahren, als ich das letzte Mal hier war.
M1   Und Sie pflücken?
F1   Ja, ich pflücke.
M1   Und warum machen Sie das? Aus finanziellen Gründen? Um Geld zu verdienen?
F1   Ein bißchen schon, fürs Geld, aber vor allem wegen der netten Mitarbeiter. Es ist wirklich ein Vergnügen. Das macht schon Spaß, die Trauben zu pflücken.
M1   Besten Dank.

The majority of questions in the Higher Level Listening Tests will consist of **extracts in German** with **questions in English** to be **answered in your own words in English**.

As a rule, you will not be required to write your answers in complete sentences, and you will not be penalised for poor English, such as poor spelling. The clearer your English, however, the easier it will be for the examiner to understand your answer.

Some of the extracts will be quite short, while others will be longer. You must recognise that at **Higher** Level there will be a greater degree of unpredictability, and greater emphasis on picking up the meaning from the **gist** of what has been said.

Here are some examples of short items. The texts for these, and the other extracts, can be found in **written** form at the end of the chapter. You can also find **answers** to all the questions on pages 83–84.

EXTRACT TWO   **Questions 1–5**
When you are in Germany, you may not always receive the reply you expect or hope to receive. Listen carefully to these conversations. What replies were given?

■ PLAY EXTRACT TWO

1   In a shop.
_____ (1)

2   In town.
_____ (2)

3   At a hotel.
_____
_____ (2)

4   In town.
_____
_____ (2)

5   Asking a German schoolboy about his future.
_____
_____ (2)

EXTRACT THREE   A common theme at Higher Level is the theme of **health and illness**. Consider the following question:

You go to the chemist because you are suffering from a stomach upset. **Make notes on the advice he gives you.**

■ PLAY EXTRACT THREE

1   You should eat _____ *(1)*

2   You should drink _____ *(1)*

3   You should take the tablets _____ *(2)*

4   You should also _____ *(1)*

EXTRACT FOUR   Understanding a telephone call and making notes to show you have understood is also a likely test area. Consider the following example:

You are expecting a phone call from your German pen friend's mother to confirm arrangements for her visit to England. You will hear this in two parts.

■ PLAY EXTRACT FOUR (Part one)

1   In the first part you find out the following information:

She will arrive in _____

She will arrive at about _____ in the _____

She will be wearing _____ and _____

She will be carrying _____ and _____ *(7)*

■ PLAY EXTRACT FOUR (Part two)

2   From the second part of the message, what problems may arise and how could they be solved?

_____

_____

_____

_____ *(3)*

EXTRACT FIVE   This is a more difficult example based on the theme of accidents and emergencies:

You are staying with a German family. Your pen friend and her parents have gone to visit friends 100 km away, so you are alone in the house. The phone rings. You pick up the receiver. It is your pen friend's father.

Look at the questions 1–7 below.

Now listen to the phone call and answer the questions.

You will hear the phone call **twice**.

■ PLAY EXTRACT FIVE

1   Where exactly is the father ringing from?

_____

_____ *(3)*

2   What state is the car in?

_____ *(1)*

3   What state is the family in?

_____ *(1)*

4   What did the driver have to do after the accident?

_____ *(1)*

5   What did the driver do to try to avoid the accident?

_____ *(1)*

6   When will the family return home?

_____

_____ *(2)*

7   What does the father tell you to do?

_____ *(1)*

(Total 10 marks)

EXTRACT SIX

The topic area 'weather' is frequently examined. After all, weather forecasts are a common topic of conversation in everyday life. Here is an example:

You hear a weather forecast whilst camping in Southern Germany. Listen to the forecast and answer the questions.

■ PLAY EXTRACT SIX

1   What will the weather be like in your part of the country tomorrow?

_____

_____ *(3)*

2   What will the weather be like for you at the weekend?

_____ *(2)*

EXTRACT SEVEN

Conversations and discussions of one kind or another, across the full range of topics, are bound to occur within Higher Level tests. Here is an example concerning free time and entertainment:

Staying with a German family (questions 1–5)
You are staying with a German family and after supper your hosts discuss what to watch on TV.

Answer these questions in as much detail as possible. Write your answers, IN ENGLISH, in the spaces provided.

■ PLAY EXTRACT SEVEN

1   What programme is on TV?

_____ *(1)*

2   Why does Mr Müller think his wife found the previous night's programme boring too?

_____ *(1)*

3   Why do you think Mrs Müller wants to watch nevertheless?

_____ *(1)*

4   And what would Mr Müller have preferred to do?

_____ *(1)*

5   What sort of compromise do they reach?

_____

_____ *(2)*

EXTRACT EIGHT

This extract is concerned with daily routine in the house of the German family.

Staying with a German family (questions 6–11)
You are staying at your pen friend's house and wait for her to come back from school. Listen to her explanation why she is late, then answer these questions.

■ PLAY EXTRACT EIGHT

6 When exactly did this incident happen?

_____ *(1)*

7 Explain what happened and why it caused her to be late.

_____

_____ *(4)*

8 Approximately how late do you think she is?

_____ *(1)*

9 Why did she specially want to be home on time today?

_____

_____ *(2)*

10 What does she ask you to do?

_____

_____ *(2)*

11 What does she hope to avoid, by asking you?

_____

_____ *(1)*

EXTRACT NINE

This more difficult extract deals with a theme of current general interest. In this instance two young people are discussing a new motorway proposal.

You will hear two people talking about a new motorway proposal which will affect the Redachshausen area of Braunschweig.

Look at the questions below.

Now listen to the conversation and answer the questions IN ENGLISH.

You will hear the conversation **twice**.

■ PLAY EXTRACT NINE

1 How did Monika and Rolf react to the news of the new motorway proposals?

Monika: _____

Rolf: _____ *(2)*

2 Why can't Monika accept Rolf's opinion?

_____

_____ *(3)*

3 What effect does Rolf foresee?

_____ *(1)*

4 How will the new motorway affect people's leisure time?

_____
_____
_____ *(2)*

(Total 8 marks)

EXTRACT TEN Guided Tours or commentaries given during a sight-seeing tour are also likely sources at Higher Level Listening. Here is an example:

During your stay in Germany your penfriend takes you to Cologne and you join a sightseeing tour.

Listen to what is said and make notes, as you hope to return to Cologne with your class next year.

   ■ PLAY EXTRACT TEN

1 How long is the tour?

_____ *(1)*

2 Name the starting and the finishing points.

_____
_____ *(2)*

3 What effect, according to the guide, has the pedestrian zone had?

_____ *(1)*

The first stop is Cologne cathedral.

4 What is suggested as being of particular interest, and why?

_____
_____ *(3)*

5 What additional experience is available if you have the time, and what particular interest does it hold?

_____
_____ *(2)*

You continue with a walk down towards the river.

6 Explain the changes in this area which have occurred this century.

_____
_____ *(3)*

EXTRACT ELEVEN Another likely source is interviews. These could be TV or radio interviews, or interviews in the street. Themes could include holidays, jobs, and topics of general current interest. This interview deals with holidays.

You hear an interview on the radio in which a German talks about his family holidays in Norderney and Langeoog. Listen to the interview and answer the questions.

■ PLAY EXTRACT ELEVEN (Part (a))

1   Where in Germany are Norderney and Langeoog?

_____ *(2)*

2   Why is it more difficult to get to Langeoog?

_____ *(2)*

■ PLAY EXTRACT ELEVEN (Part (b))

3   Which part of the journey to Langeoog lasts ten minutes?

_____
_____ *(2)*

4   Why does the family now stay in a hotel in Langeoog?

_____
_____ *(2)*

(Total 8 marks)

EXTRACT TWELVE   The next interview is also about holidays, but the context is that of a survey.

The English Tourist Board is carrying out a survey of how the Germans like to spend their holidays. They are interviewing people outside a shop in Hamburg.

Look at the questions below.

Listen to the interview and answer the questions IN ENGLISH.

You will hear the interview **twice**.

■ PLAY EXTRACT TWELVE

1   What is the man's job?

_____ *(1)*

2   How long has he been married?

_____ *(1)*

3   What children does he have?

_____ *(1)*

4   How old is his son?

_____ *(1)*

5   Why does he choose to spend his holidays in Germany?

_____ *(1)*

6   Where exactly are they going for their holidays this year?

_____ *(1)*

7   What can the children do there?

_____
_____ *(2)*

8 What accommodation will they have there?

_____

_____ *(2)*
(Total 10 marks)

EXTRACT THIRTEEN This third example of an interview question includes two people being interviewed about their jobs.

You will now hear two separate interviews with people working on a building site in Düsseldorf.

The first interview is with Hans, the second with Mitra.

Look at the questions below.

Now listen to the interviews. You will hear both interviews once without interruption. Then you will hear each interview a second time.

After each interview answer the questions IN ENGLISH.

First listen to Hans being interviewed.
   ■ PLAY EXTRACT THIRTEEN (Part 1)

1 Where was Hans born?

_____ *(1)*

2 How long has he been working on the building site?

_____ *(1)*

3 What was his previous job?

_____ *(1)*

4 Why did he lose his job?

_____

_____ *(2)*

5 What does he think of his present job?

_____

_____ *(2)*

Now listen to Mitra being interviewed.
   ■ PLAY EXTRACT THIRTEEN (Part 2)

6 Where on the site does she work?

_____ *(1)*

7 Why does she like her job?

_____

_____ *(2)*

8 What happened to her when she left school?

_____ *(1)*
(Total 11 marks)

EXTRACT FOURTEEN

In this example you will hear someone being interviewed about her life in Germany.

An English student, Pauline Jackson, has just arrived in Munich to spend a year studying German at the University. She is being interviewed by her professor.

Look at the questions below.

Now listen to the interview, and answer the questions IN ENGLISH.

You will hear the interview **twice**.

■ PLAY EXTRACT FOURTEEN

1 Where would Pauline like to work?

_____ *(1)*

2 What does she like to do in her spare time?

_____ *(2)*

3 What does she think of German boys?

_____ *(1)*

4 What kind of place is she living in in Germany?

_____ *(1)*

5 What is the only disadvantage about this place?

_____ *(1)*

6 How did she manage to get the room?

_____ *(1)*

7 Where is the washing machine?

_____ *(1)*

8 What leisure facilities are there?

_____ *(2)*

(Total 10 marks)

EXTRACT FIFTEEN

This is an example of a **multiple choice** question with answers in English. Again, the subject area covered is employment, and the extract takes the form of an interview.

You will now hear an interview with Frau Schmidt, who is being asked about her career.

Look at the questions below.

For each question tick one of the boxes to indicate the most appropriate answer.

You will hear the interview **twice**.

■ PLAY EXTRACT FIFTEEN

1 She decided to become a teacher because of

☐ her uncle.   ☐ her parents.   ☐ good teachers.   ☐ her friend.

2 She prefers teaching

☐ the youngest pupils   ☐ adults.   ☐ pre-school children.   ☐ teenagers.
in the school.

3   When she stood in front of her first class she felt

☐ rather   ☐ extremely anxious.   ☐ quite calm.   ☐ very powerful.
nervous.

4   She was irritated most by pupils

☐ who never   ☐ who copied from   ☐ who looked out of   ☐ who
listened   each other.   the window.   constantly
chattered.

5   Which language did she herself find most difficult?

☐ Russian   ☐ French   ☐ Italian   ☐ English

6   Why is she learning Italian now?

☐ to be able to   ☐ to be able to   ☐ to keep her   ☐ to be able to
teach it   get by in Italy   mind active   work in Italy

(Total 6 marks)

EXTRACT SIXTEEN   This example concerns **completing a table**. It deals with the topic area 'weather'.

You are staying with friends in Germany. At breakfast time you hear the weather forecast on the radio.

Listen to the forecast for the Northern Region and see how the boxes in the table below for the Northern Region have been filled in.

You will hear the forecast **twice**.

■ PLAY EXTRACT SIXTEEN (Part 1)

Now listen to the forecasts for the other three regions and complete the boxes for those regions.

You will hear the forecasts **twice**.

■ PLAY EXTRACT SIXTEEN (Part 2)

REGION	WEATHER	MAXIMUM TEMPERATURE	WIND
NORTHERN	*sunny*	*4*	*Northwesterly*
WESTERN	1	2	3
SOUTHERN	4	5	6
CENTRAL	7	8	9

(Total 9 marks)

EXTRACT SEVENTEEN

In this second, more difficult example of completing a table, the setting of a slide-show in a German home is used.

Your German pen friend's father is interested in architecture, and shows you some slides of German buildings.

Listen to the father's comments on the buildings, and make brief notes IN ENGLISH, for your school project, about what he says. The answer for Slide 1 is given as an example. You could write about the kind of building, when it was built, any people connected with it, and about other features such as its surroundings.

In each case try to mention at least **three** points.

You will hear the commentaries **twice**.

Slide No. 1

> This is the picture of a monastery. It was built in 1922. Nurses are trained there. Many of them later work in Brazil. In front of the monastery is a lawn.

Slide No. 2

Slide No. 3

Slide No. 4

(Total 10 marks)

**WRITTEN VERSION
OF EXTRACTS 2–17**

EXTRACT TWO

1 *Du:* Ich hätte gern 6 Brötchen, bitte.
Verkäufer: Tut mir leid. Brötchen sind heute schon ausverkauft.

2 *Du:* Wann fährt der nächste Bus nach Darmstadt, bitte?
Beamter: Leider ist der letzte Bus schon gefahren.

3 *Du:* Ich hätte gern ein Einzelzimmer mit Bad, bitte.
Empfangsdame: Moment, mal . . . mm . . . ein Einzelzimmer mit Bad? – nein, wir haben nur noch ein Einzelzimmer frei, und das Zimmer ist mit Dusche.

4 *Du:* Entschuldigen Sie, bitte. Wo ist hier das Fundbüro?
Fußgänger: Das Fundbüro? Mm . . . es liegt am Markt neben dem Rathaus, aber es macht um fünf Uhr zu. Es muß jetzt schon seit einer halben Stunde zu sein.

5 *Du:* Du, Thomas, was machst du nächstes Jahr, wenn du die Schule verläßt?
Thomas: Wenn ich die Schule verlasse? Aber ich bleibe doch in der Schule, bis ich das Abitur habe; das heißt drei Jahre auf der Oberstufe.

EXTRACT THREE

Du: Guten Morgen. Ich habe Magenschmerzen und Durchfall. Haben Sie Tabletten? Mir ist auch übel, ich glaube, ich habe etwas Unbekömmliches gegessen.
Drogist: Ich kann diese Tabletten empfehlen. Ich würde auch raten, daß Sie 24 Stunden nichts mehr essen und nur Wasser trinken, dann sollte es Ihnen schon besser gehen.
Du: Danke schön. Die Tabletten kaufe ich. Wie oft muß ich sie nehmen?
Drogist: Dreimal am Tag mit Wasser und Sie müssen sich auch ausruhen.
Du: Danke. Was kosten die Tabletten?
Drogist: Eine Packung zu 20 kostet DM 9.

EXTRACT FOUR

Part one
Frau Braun: Hallo. Hier Frau Braun, die Mutter von Karin. Kannst du deiner Mutter bitte folgendes sagen? Also, Karin kommt, wie abgemacht, nächsten Dienstag in Hull an. Das Schiff soll gegen acht Uhr morgens in Hull ankommen. Falls du sie nicht sofort vom Foto erkennst, trägt sie folgendes: einen gelben Regenmantel, Sportschuhe und Jeans. Sie hat einen blauen Koffer und eine rote Tasche mit.

Part two
Frau Braun: Seitdem das Foto gemacht worden ist, hat sie sich die Haare schneiden lassen, aber trotzdem wirst du sie erkennen. Ich habe ihr aber gesagt, wenn es Schwierigkeiten geben soll, so soll sie neben dem Ausgang warten, bis ihr kommt. Alles klar? Vielen Dank. Wiederhören! Viele Grüße an deine Mutter!

EXTRACT FIVE

Hallo? Bist du's? Also, hör gut zu. Wir haben einen Unfall gehabt, aber keine Panik. Wir sind bei der Polizei in einem Dorf etwa 40 km von zu Hause entfernt. Gott sei Dank, wir sind nicht verletzt, aber das Auto läßt sich nicht mehr reparieren. Totalschaden. Wir sind mit etwa 80 auf der Landstraße gefahren. Die Mama saß am Steuer – ein Glück, daß sie nur Apfelsaft trinkt; man hat bei ihr eine Blutprobe gemacht – da ist plötzlich ein großer Hirsch aus dem Wald gesprungen. Die Mama hat gebremst, aber wir hatten keine Chance, wir sind mit ihm zusammengestoßen. Das Auto liegt jetzt am Straßenrand. Der Hirsch ist tot. Wir dürfen ihn leider nicht mit nach Hause nehmen – wir hätten das ganze Jahr gut davon essen können – aber er gehört dem Bauern. Ein Wunder, daß wir noch leben, aber wie gesagt, wir sind nicht verletzt. Etwas geschockt, natürlich, Mama zittert noch, aber du brauchst dich nicht zu beunruhigen. Ich weiß nicht, wann wir wieder zu Hause sein werden; es wird wohl ziemlich spät sein, aber du kannst ruhig schlafen gehen. Die Polizei bringt uns nach Hause. Alles klar? Hast du das alles verstanden?

EXTRACT SIX

Guten Abend, meine Damen und Herren! Es ist zwanzig Uhr fünf. Das waren die Nachrichten. Es folgt die Wettervorhersage für Deutschland bis morgen abend.
Über dem Ostatlantik ist ein breites Wolkenband erkennbar. In der kommenden Nacht

Abkühlung auf 4 bis 9 Grad. Einzelne Schauer im Bergland. Tageshöchsttemperaturen für morgen vormittag 11 bis 15 Grad. Im Südosten um 10 Grad.

Über dem nördlichen Teil der Bundesrepublik liegt ein breites Nebelfeld. Es gehört zu der Kaltfront eines finnischen Tiefs.

Südlich des Mains einzelne Schauer. Am Nachmittag gelegentlich etwas Regen. Schwacher bis mäßiger Wind aus westlichen Richtungen.

Die Vorhersage für das kommende Wochenende: im Süden weiterhin wolkig, im Norden wolkenarm und trocken. Tageshöchsttemperaturen um 17 Grad.

Es folgen die Verkehrsnachrichten.

EXTRACT SEVEN

Questions 1 and 2
Frau Müller: Was kommt gerade im Fernsehen?
Herr Müller: Nicht viel eben. Nur die Fortsetzung des Krimis von gestern abend. Wie heißt er denn? Ich weiß es nicht mehr. Aber er war doch furchtbar langweilig. Du bist ja schon gestern dabei eingeschlafen.

Questions 3, 4 and 5
Frau Müller: Schalt doch mal den Fernseher an. Ich habe keine Lust, was anderes zu machen.
Herr Müller: Wenn du unbedingt willst. Aber ich hätte doch lieber einen Blick in die Zeitung getan, und bei dem Krach kann ich das nicht. Aber bitte, wie du willst.
Frau Müller: Nun ja. Lassen wir es aus bis zur Tagesschau. Die möchte ich aber gerne sehen.
Herr Müller: Einverstanden.

EXTRACT EIGHT

Questions 6, 7 and 8
Das ist ja furchtbar, ich bin schrecklich spät daran, aber ich kann wirklich nichts dafür.

Beim Umsteigen ist mir die Mappe plötzlich aufgegangen, und alle Hefte sind auf den Bahnsteig gefallen. Also, da habe ich sie aufgehoben, und gerade wie ich einsteigen wollte, da sind mir die Türen vor der Nase zugegangen und der Zug ist abgefahren. Ich habe ganze zwanzig Minuten auf den nächsten warten müssen.

Questions 9, 10 and 11
Mensch, so ein Pech! Das Schlimmste ist, daß wir uns doch um halb fünf zum Schlittschuhlaufen treffen wollten. Kannst du bitte gleich Hans für mich anrufen und sagen, daß wir nachkommen. Sonst denkt er, wir kommen gar nicht.

EXTRACT NINE

M1: Sag, Monika, hast du schon gehört, daß durch Redachshausen eine Autobahn gebaut werden soll?
F1: Ja, das ist doch prima. Ich habe mich sehr gefreut, das gestern in der Zeitung zu lesen.
M1: Was! Also **ich** hab' mich furchtbar darüber geärgert, als ich gestern davon gehört habe.
F1: Das verstehe ich gar nicht. Denk doch zum Beispiel an mich und all die Braunschweiger, die an **der** Seite der Stadt wohnen; die können dann problemlos auf die Autobahn fahren und kommen schnell dort an, wo sie hinwollen. Wir haben die ganzen letzten Jahre immer morgens im Stau gestanden. Das wird uns das Leben viel leichter machen.
M1: Ja, aber dafür verlierst du doch das ganze Waldgebiet, in dem du am Wochenende so gerne spazierengehst. Ist es das denn wert, dafür daß man zehn Minuten schneller in der Schule ist?
F1: Ich denke schon, daß es das wert ist. Die zehn Minuten, die ich jeden Tag an Fahrzeit zur Arbeit spare, kann ich am Sonntag dazu benutzen, um zehn Minuten ins Grüne zu fahren und dann von dort aus zu laufen.
M1: Aber, wenn der Wald wegen der Autobahn abgeschlagen wird, heißt das doch, daß es viel weniger Wald für uns gibt. Dann müssen die Leute noch weiter fahren, um das bißchen Wald, das uns übrigbleibt, zu erreichen.
F1: Stimmt, das ist ein Argument, aber ich denke doch nicht, daß es das andere aufwiegt.

EXTRACT TEN

Questions 1, 2 and 3

Guten Tag, meine Damen und Herren. Ich bin Gabriele, Ihre Reiseleiterin, und werde Sie auf dieser Kurztour durch Köln begleiten. Die ganze Tour dauert anderthalb Stunden. Wir fangen hier am Hauptbahnhof an und beenden die Tour in der Altstadt, wo man die Rheinpromenade genießen kann.

Der größte Teil ist jetzt eine Fußgängerzone, was natürlich das Leben viel einfacher macht.

Questions 4 and 5

Zuerst sehen Sie den Dom – wie kann man ihn übersehen? Er ist einer der schönsten gotischen Bautens Deutschlands und es wurde 700 Jahre daran gebaut. Die Glasfenster sind sehr wertvoll und stammen aus dem dreizehnten Jahrhundert.

. . . Wenn Sie später noch Zeit haben, können Sie den Turm besteigen, man hat dort eine großartige Aussicht.

Question 6

Gehen wir weiter zur Altstadt. Sie wurde 1945 fast total zerstört, ist aber sehr naturgetreu wieder aufgebaut worden. Sehen Sie die alten engen Gassen, die steinernen Tore, die alten schiefen Dächer. Die Häuser stehen sehr eng zusammen, genau wie im Mittelalter.

EXTRACT ELEVEN

Part (a)

— Wenn du in Deutschland Urlaub machst, wo fährst du am meisten hin, Martin?
— Wir sind meistens an die Nordsee gefahren und zwar auf eine Insel – Norderney oder Langeoog. Das sind Inseln, die zur Gruppe der Ostfriesischen Inseln gehören. Wir sind dorthin gefahren, weil wir die mit dem Auto von uns in drei Stunden erreichen können. Aber auf Langeoog kann man nicht mit dem Auto; man muß das Auto auf dem Festland lassen und dann mit einem Schiff – das dauert ungefähr dreißig Minuten – bis zur Insel fahren.

Part (b)

— Man kommt im Hafen an und fährt dann mit einer kleinen Inselbahn ungefähr zehn Minuten bis in den Ort hinein, und da Langeoog nicht sehr groß ist, hat man sein Hotel immer ganz schnell erreicht.
— Ist die Insel sehr klein?
— Ja, die Insel ist ungefähr 15 Kilometer lang und im Durchschnitt 1,5 bis 2 Kilometer breit. Also ziemlich schmal.
— Wo wohnst du denn eigentlich, wenn du auf Langeoog Urlaub machst?
— Früher hatten wir eine Ferienwohnung – das war sehr angenehm. Jetzt ist es so, daß meine Frau auch einmal nicht kochen möchte, so daß wir dann in einem Hotel wohnen. Wir haben dann zwei Zimmer: in einem schlafen die beiden Jungen, und in dem anderen Zimmer schlafen meine Frau, die Tochter und ich.

EXTRACT TWELVE

F: Entschuldigen Sie bitte. Ich arbeite für das englische Verkehrsamt. Hätten Sie Zeit, einige Fragen zu beantworten?
M: Ja, natürlich.
F: Was sind Sie von Beruf?
M: Ich bin Verkäufer in einem großen Kaufhaus.
F: Sind Sie verheiratet? Haben Sie Familie?
M: Ich bin seit acht Jahren verheiratet. Ich habe zwei Töchter und einen kleinen Sohn – er ist erst vier Monate alt.
F: Wann haben Sie Ferien?
M: Ich habe im Juli drei Wochen Ferien.
F: Wo wollen Sie dieses Jahr Ihre Ferien verbringen? Hier in Deutschland, oder im Ausland?
M: Wenn man drei junge Kinder hat, ist es einfacher, in Deutschland zu bleiben.
F: Verbringen Sie Ihre Ferien in den Bergen, an der See oder auf dem Lande?

M: Wir fahren an die Nordsee. Da ist es so schön für die Kinder. Sie können Sandburgen bauen und in der See schwimmen.

F: Wohnen Sie in einem Hotel, bei Freunden, oder auf dem Campingplatz?

M: Ein Hotel wäre zu teuer, und leider wohnen keine Freunde von uns an der See. Wir wohnen auf dem Campingplatz – wir haben ein großes Zelt.

EXTRACT THIRTEEN

Part one

I: Entschuldigen Sie bitte. Woher kommen Sie?

H: Aus Düsseldorf. Ich bin hier geboren.

I: Wie lange arbeiten Sie schon hier auf der Baustelle?

H: Seit drei Monaten.

I: Ist das Ihre erste Stelle?

H: Nein, ich war früher Mechaniker. Ich habe Autos repariert. Das war wirklich interessant.

I: Und warum sind Sie jetzt hier?

H: Ich habe in der Reparaturwerkstatt Zigaretten geraucht. Als der Chef mich gesehen hat, hat er mich 'rausgeworfen. Eine Zeitlang war ich arbeitslos. Dann habe ich diesen Job bekommen.

I: Was machen Sie hier auf der Baustelle?

H: Ich bin Bauarbeiter, aber es gefällt mir nicht. Es ist so langweilig, und kalt ist es auch. Ich möchte eine andere Stelle finden.

Part two

Now listen to Mitra being interviewed.

I: Was macht denn eine junge Dame hier auf der Baustelle?

M: Auf der Baustelle ist ein Büro. Ich arbeite dort.

I: Und wie finden Sie die Arbeit hier?

M: Ganz interessant. Es ist schön, Geld zu verdienen. Ja, die Arbeit gefällt mir.

I: Ist das Ihre erste Stelle?

M: Ja, ich habe mit 15 Jahren die Schule verlassen. Dann war ich 8 Monate arbeitslos.

I: Wo kommen Sie her?

M: Aus Dortmund. Meine Eltern kommen aus der Türkei, aber ich bin in der Bundes-republik geboren.

I: Danke, Mitra.

EXTRACT FOURTEEN

Prof: Guten Tag, Fräulein Jackson, Ich wollte mich nur mit Ihnen bekannt machen und hören, ob Sie irgendwelche Probleme haben, hier im Ausland.

Frl. J: Danke, Herr Professor. Mir geht's bestens.

Prof: Sie sind Germanistin, das weiß ich natürlich. Was möchten Sie werden?

Frl. J: Das weiß ich immer noch nicht. Vielleicht Lehrerin – im Gymnasium könnte es ganz interessant sein, aber strapaziös.

Prof: Und was für Hobbys haben Sie?

Frl. J: Ich gehe ab und zu mal ins Theater oder ins Konzert, aber das ist ziemlich teuer geworden. Meine Freunde gehen lieber in die Disko.

Prof: Haben Sie einen Freund, wenn ich fragen darf?

Frl. J: Eine ganze Menge in England, aber keinen festen. Hier geht's mir genauso, ich finde die deutschen Jungen sehr nett.

Prof: Und wo wohnen Sie? Haben Sie schon ein Zimmer gefunden? Es kann schwierig sein, Unterkunft zu finden.

Frl. J: Ja, das stimmt. Ich wohne im Studentenwohnheim in der Adenauer-Straße, im vierten Stock. Es gibt zwar keinen Aufzug, aber sonst ist es prima dort. Ich habe wirklich Glück gehabt: kurz nach meiner Ankunft hat eine andere Germanistin ihr Studium aufgegeben, sie wollte lieber im Kaufhof arbeiten, und ich habe ihr Zimmer bekommen. Im Keller gibt es eine Waschmaschine, und es gibt auch einen Tischtennisraum und eine Kegelbahn. Wie gesagt, ganz prima.

Prof: Gut. Also ich freue mich, Sie kennengelernt zu haben, und daß alles in Ordnung ist. Auf Wiedersehen, Fräulein Jackson.

Frl. J: Auf Wiedersehen, Herr Professor.

EXTRACT FIFTEEN

I: Frau Schmidt, warum sind Sie eigentlich Lehrerin geworden?

FS: Eigentlich wollte ich nie Lehrerin werden, obwohl mein Onkel Lehrer war, für Chemie und Physik. Die guten Lehrer, die haben wir immer gern gehabt, die schlechten haben mir immer ein bißchen leidgetan. Aber meine beste Freundin ist Lehrerin geworden, und da habe ich es eben auch werden wollen.

I: Kinder bis zu welchem Alter wollten Sie dann unterrichten?

FS: Ich mag die Kleinen nicht besonders, also habe ich mich für die älteren Kinder gemeldet, das heißt, ich arbeite an einer Realschule, wo fünfzehn- bis sechzehnjährige die Altersgruppe ist, die ich am liebsten unterrichte.

I: Wie fühlten Sie sich, als Sie Ihrer ersten Klasse gegenüberstanden?

FS: Alle Lehrer an der Schule, in der ich mein Praktikum ablegte, haben mir gesagt, daß die Kinder zunächst abwarten würden, ob ich streng sei. Erst später würden sie wohl schwieriger werden. Also hatte ich gar keine Angst und war ganz ruhig.

I: Ist es denn auch so glatt weitergegangen?

FS: Nein, es kamen schon ein paar Probleme auf. Es gibt eben immer ein paar Kinder in der Klasse, die miteinander reden, beim Nachbarn abschreiben oder aus dem Fenster schauen. Ich konnte diejenigen am wenigsten leiden, die überhaupt nicht zuhörten, wenn ich sprach. Die waren mein größtes Problem.

I: Sie unterrichten Fremdsprachen, ist Ihnen da eine Sprache lieber als die anderen?

FS: Ich habe als kleines Kind ein paar Jahre mit meinen Eltern in Amerika verbracht, also habe ich schon früh Englisch gesprochen und ich finde es leicht. Ich habe auch Russisch als Fach und das hat mir interessante Möglichkeiten geboten. Französisch hatte ich in der Schule, aber ich fand es sehr schwer. Ich kann eigentlich nicht sagen, daß ich ein Fach lieber als das andere hätte – Sprachen machen mir einfach Spaß, und ich habe sogar angefangen, Italienisch zu lernen.

I: Wollen Sie das auch unterrichten?

FS: Nein, im Moment ist das nur zu meinem Privatvergnügen. Wir haben letztes Jahr in Italien Urlaub gemacht und ich konnte die Leute überhaupt nicht verstehen. Also, das war der eigentliche Grund, nämlich daß ich gern mit den Leuten sprechen möchte, wenn wir nächstes Jahr wieder hinfahren.

EXTRACT SIXTEEN

Part 1

Hier ist der Wetterbericht.

Im Norden meist sonnig aber kalt. Tageshöchsttemperatur um 4 Grad.

Der Wind kommt von Nordwesten.

Part 2

Im Westen regnerisch. Tageshöchsttemperatur 6 Grad. Der Wind kommt aus südwestlicher Richtung.

Im Süden herrscht Nebel. Tageshöchsttemperatur 7 Grad. Wind von Südwesten.

Im mittleren Deutschland Schnee. Tageshöchsttemperatur um 2 Grad. Wind von Westen.

EXTRACT SEVENTEEN

Hier siehst du das Franziskaner Kloster Bardel, das 1922 errichtet wurde. Hier werden Krankenschwestern ausgebildet, die später meistens in Brasilien arbeiten. Vor dem Kloster ist eine Grünfläche.

Die Kaiser-Wilhelm-Gedächtniskirche wurde am Ende des neunzehnten Jahrhunderts von Kaiser Wilhelm gebaut. Sie steht am Ende des vier Kilometer langen Kurfürstendamms in Berlin. Nach dem zweiten Weltkrieg war sie eine Ruine. 1961 ist ein moderner Turm angebaut worden.

Hier siehst du ein Schloß in Würzburg. Das Schloß wurde zwischen 1720 und 1744 gebaut. Die Bilder an der Decke wurden von dem berühmten Künstler Tiepolo gemalt. Vor dem Schloß sind ein Rasen und eine Steintreppe.

Hier sehen wir das Rathaus in Bremen. Das Rathaus wurde am Anfang des fünfzehnten Jahrhunderts erbaut und liegt am Marktplatz direkt neben dem Dom. Später hat der Baumeister Lüder das Rathaus mit einer neuen Fassade ausgestattet.

KEY TO THE QUESTIONS

EXTRACT TWO

1 Rolls are sold out.
2 The last bus has gone.
3 They have only one single room with shower.

4 It closed half an hour ago.
5 He is staying at school till he has his Abitur. That's three years in the 6th form.

EXTRACT THREE

1 nothing
2 water

3 3 times a day with water
4 rest

EXTRACT FOUR

1 Hull
8.00/morning
a yellow raincoat, trainers, jeans
a blue case, a red bag

2 She has had her hair cut since the photo was taken, so may not be immediately recognisable. If there are problems she will wait by the exit.

EXTRACT FIVE

1 From the police station in a village about 40 kilometres from home.
2 it's a complete wreck (a write-off)
3 not injured
4 have a blood test

5 braked
6 They don't know. Probably late that night.
7 go to sleep

EXTRACT SIX

1 Temperature about 10 degrees. Isolated showers but rain in the afternoon. A weak to moderate wind from the west.

2 Cloudy. Highest temperature about 17 degrees.

EXTRACT SEVEN

1 a continuation of yesterday evening's crime story
2 She fell asleep.
3 She does not want to do anything else.

4 He would prefer to read the paper.
5 No TV until the news, which they will watch.

EXTRACT EIGHT

1 when changing trains
2 Her school bag fell open and all her exercise books fell out. She had to pick them up. The train doors shut in her face and the train left.
3 about 20 minutes

4 They wanted to go ice skating at 4.30.
5 Ring Hans and say you will be coming late.
6 that Hans might think they were not coming at all

EXTRACT NINE

1 Monika is pleased and Rolf is cross.
2 Because it would save her a lot of time. Up till now there has always been a traffic jam. It will make life easier.

3 They will lose the whole wooded area.
4 They will have to go further away to get into the country. There will be less woodland area.

EXTRACT TEN

1 1½ hours
2 Start – the main station. Finish – the old part of the city.
3 It makes life easier.
4 The stained glass windows. They are valuable and date from the 13th century.

5 To climb the tower. It provides a wonderful view.
6 It was almost totally destroyed in 1945, but has been faithfully rebuilt.

EXTRACT ELEVEN

1 On the North Sea, part of the East Friesian Islands.
2 You can't take your car on to the island.
3 The island railway from the harbour to the village.
4 Because his wife does not want to cook for once.

EXTRACT TWELVE

1 salesman
2 eight years
3 two daughters and a son
4 four months
5 with three young children it is simpler
6 the North Sea
7 build sand castles and swim in the sea
8 a large tent on a campsite

EXTRACT THIRTEEN

1 Düsseldorf
2 three months
3 car mechanic
4 He smoked cigarettes in the repair workshop.
5 He does not like it. It is boring and cold.
6 in the office
7 It's interesting and she earns money.
8 She was unemployed for eight months.

EXTRACT FOURTEEN

1 in a grammar school
2 going to the theatre or to concerts
3 She thinks they are very nice.
4 in a students' hostel.
5 It has no lift.
6 Another student of German gave up her studies and left the room.
7 in the cellar
8 table tennis and bowling

EXTRACT FIFTEEN

1 her friend
2 teenagers
3 quite calm
4 who never listened
5 French
6 to be able to get by in Italy

EXTRACT SIXTEEN

1 rain
2 6
3 south-westerly
4 fog
5 7
6 south-westerly
7 snow
8 2
9 westerly

EXTRACT SEVENTEEN

1 –
2 It's the Kaiser-Wilhelm-Gedächtnis-kirche at the end of the Kurfürsten-damm (4 kms long) in Berlin. It was built at the end of the 19th century by Kaiser Wilhelm. After the 2nd World War it was a ruin. A modern tower was built in 1961.
3 A castle in Würzburg, built between 1720 and 1744. The paintings on the ceiling are by Tipolo. There is a lawn and stone steps in front.
4 The town hall in Bremen, built at the beginning of the 15th century. It is on the market place next to the cathedral. A new facade was added later.

TEST WITH STUDENT ANSWERS

Here is an example of the Listening Test at Higher Level. A student has answered the questions and an examiner has marked them, adding comments.

HOLIDAYS ABROAD

This is the text the student heard:

Frau Brock: Ich war dieses Jahr Anfang Februar in Italien. Es war wirklich wunderschön. Das Wetter war sehr angenehm und da waren keine Touristen. Wir hatten siebzehn Grad und keine Wolke am Himmel.
Herr Meyer: Und wie lange waren Sie dort?
Frau Brock: Ich war anderthalb Wochen in Venedig und dann noch eine Woche an der Küste.
Herr Meyer: Und was haben Sie in Venedig gemacht?
Frau Brock: Ja, wir konnten draußen auf der Terrasse sitzen und Kaffee trinken. Und dann haben wir Verwandte in der Nähe, und da waren wir drei oder viermal zu Besuch.
Herr Meyer: Und wie war es an der Küste?
Frau Brock: Sehr schön. Es war natürlich zu kalt zum Baden, aber wir haben schöne Wanderungen auf dem Strand gemacht. Wir interessieren uns für Vögel, wissen Sie, und da war sehr viel zu sehen. Wir haben auch einen Wagen gemietet und waren sehr oft unterwegs, meistens in den kleinen, abgelegten Dörfern im Gebirge.
Herr Meyer: Und nächstes Jahr?
Frau Brock: Das wissen wir noch nicht. Vielleicht Ungarn oder sogar die Türkei.

QUESTIONS AND STUDENT ANSWERS

1 When exactly was Frau Brock in Italy? (2)

This year in Febmary

> You have forgotten the word 'Anfang' (beginning). 1 mark

2 Why was it so nice? (3)

No tourists and the weather was nice

> You should add all details. In this case you should have mentioned the temperature and the cloudless skies. 1 mark

3 How long was she in Italy? (1)

2 weeks

> 'Anderthalb' means one and a half. So the answer should be two and a half weeks. 0 marks

4 What did she do in Venice? (3)

Drank coffee on the terrace and visited friends

> 'Verwandte' are relations, not friends. 2 marks

5 What were their main activities at the sea? (2)

Walking on the beach and bird watching

> Good! Full marks for this one. 2 marks

6 What else did they do whilst on the coast? (4)

Drove to small villages in the hills

> They *hired* (mieten) a car. The villages are *remote* (abgelegt). 2 marks

7 What plans does Frau Brock have for next year? (2)

Perhaps Turkey

> You missed 'Ungarn' (Hungary). 1 mark

> NINE marks out of a possible SEVENTEEN. You have clearly understood most of the German, but your lack of vocabulary has let you down

L I S T E N I N G : B A S I C   A N D   H I G H E R A   S T E P   F U R T H E R

Listening ought to be easy, but we are not very good at it. Every day we hear a great deal to which we pay no attention: radio, TV, lessons in school, people talking, traffic, birds, the wind and so on.

But in learning a foreign language, listening is the most important of the four skills, because all the others depend on it. We cannot speak a language unless we first hear it and understand it. Reading is made easier if we can hear in our heads the sounds of the printed word. And the ultimate test of the accuracy of what we write is whether or not it sounds right if we say it out loud.

So don't treat listening as a soft option which you can just absorb as you go along. That may have worked when learning to speak your own language, but look how long it took you! We haven't got that amount of time. So we have to take short cuts.

Here then are a few suggestions for positive listening.

THE CLASSROOM

Everything starts here. All language courses now have cassettes to go with them and they are usually of excellent quality. No doubt your teacher uses them often. But if not, then ask him or her to let you hear more German. Similarly, if you are not satisfied with the sound quality of the equipment used, then say so. Your teacher may well be glad of your support in pressing for better resources. A small single-speaker cassette recorder is not usually adequate for a classroom unless it has extension speakers. Some schools now have extension speakers on a wall or on a shelf and they make a great difference.

You may of course have access at school to small cassette recorders with headsets, or even a language laboratory. If this is the case, then there should be facilities to allow you to use them individually, either in lesson time or in free time. Perhaps the school has cassettes belonging to a course it no longer uses. Ask if you can borrow them to listen to on your own.

If you have a German assistant at school, then he or she may be prepared to record some German for you. If so then there is no copyright problem, and the school could make multiple copies for pupils to use at home.

WALKMAN

Have you got a personal stereo? Well, why not use it for German as well? If you haven't got one, then someone may be persuaded to buy one for you as long as it is occasionally used for 'educational purposes'. If someone has helped you to buy this book, then clearly you have friends or relatives on your side!

COMMERCIAL LANGUAGE COURSES

There are some excellent German courses available in bookshops for people learning at home or in evening classes. Your teacher will probably know about them. Even if they are fairly basic – such as *Get by in German* – they provide a lot of very good language practice, recorded by German speakers, on themes which are relevant to your course. You are sure to pick up extra vocabulary, too.

RADIO AND TV

There are almost always German courses of various levels on radio and TV. Sometimes they are at inconvenient times of the day, but you may be able to record them and play them when you are in the right frame of mind. Remember that schools programmes nearly always continue in your half-term week, and if you are mildly ill and have to be off school, the long, boring day can be relieved with some of the excellent radio and TV programmes.

Several German radio stations can be received very clearly in Britain. It would be worth searching for them on the radio or, better still, writing to the BBC for advice. News bulletins are particularly good, because they deal with matters which are to some extent familiar to you.

FILMS

More and more German films are now being shown on TV or at certain cinemas. Look out for these, but check carefully that they are subtitled. A dubbed version may be entertaining, but it is not going to help your German.

PEN FRIENDS

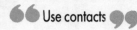 Use contacts

If you have a link with a German boy or girl, have you considered exchanging tapes as well as letters? This is excellent language practice for both sides and can keep you both up to date with sport and pop music and anything else you may have in common.

FAMILY AND FRIENDS

Revision is always more enjoyable if you can do it with someone else. An obvious area to practise with a member of the family or with a friend is **numbers**. They are a constant stumbling block in foreign languages and require a lot of practice. One person reads out numbers in German and the other writes down the figures. Make the numbers gradually bigger and bigger and read them out faster and faster. Include prices (Marks, Schillings, Swiss Francs), telephone numbers, weights, distances and times of day.

OTHER SOURCES

Does your teacher make use of Inter Nationes? This is a German firm which produces a large amount of high-class German language material for use in schools and colleges outside Germany. The material is free! Many of the cassettes would be suitable for class or individual use.

There may also be a German Language Centre near you (such as the Hatfield Polytechnic German Centre in Hertfordshire) which will lend material. The Goethe-Institut has branches in London, Manchester and Glasgow, and it too has a lot of material to lend.

But it is important to remember that these organisations can **only** be approached officially through your school.

So you see there are plenty of ways of improving your listening skills, and much of what we have suggested will help you in your other language skills as well. Do not worry if your progress seems to be slow. It is difficult to measure progress in listening skills. But every bit will help, and slowly you will find that you are understanding more and more, that you need to concentrate less and less on meaning, and that you are thinking less and less in English.

G E T T I N G   S T A R T E D

The Basic Level Reading Tests form part of the compulsory common core for all the examining groups, so Basic Reading will definitely be part of the work you have to do. However, most students seem to find reading the easiest skill to cope with. This is probably because it is the easiest skill to develop on an **individual** basis. To begin with, we all read at different speeds and we don't all understand the same words. So we usually read and learn at our **own** pace. Another important reason why reading may seem easier is that there is more material readily available.

E S S E N T I A L   P R I N C I P L E S

READING SKILLS

Before we consider reading German, it is worth spending some time looking at the skill of reading itself. What do you read in English, and why? We would like to suggest that you read quite a variety of things and that you also read them with a variety of different purposes or intentions.

You may well find that you read some or many of the following: newspapers, magazines, advertisements, brochures, public notices, messages, postcards, letters, novels, plays, poetry, reference books and much more. In each case, though, you will not expect to **understand** every single word and you will certainly not **remember** every single detail that you have read. You may be reading for **specific information**, e.g. to find out what time your favourite television programme is on, and you will 'skip over' or ignore information which is not relevant. On the other hand, you may be reading a novel where you are **interested** in the 'story', but again you will sift out the information you think is important to the story. You could try this out by doing some reading and then seeing how much you remember, and why. You will certainly not remember the exact words used! However, you will remember the key points or information relevant to you.

Equally, if you are reading a holiday brochure, you will approach the reading with a fair amount of **knowledge**. For instance, you have a reasonable idea of the likely content of the brochure: you expect to find information about accommodation, leisure activities and facilities, travel arrangements, prices, excursions, temperatures, etc. You won't expect to find the football results! You will be looking out to make a selection of what for you is the relevant information, e.g. double rooms with a shower, full board, deep-sea fishing, windsurfing, flight times.

We can conclude that we do not need to understand every single word we read, and that there are often certain expectations which can actually help us to understand. The same applies to German.

So remember:

1   you do not need to understand every word
2   you should not be discouraged if you do not understand every word
3   you should try to build on the knowledge of key words and expressions
4   you should get as much practice in reading German as you can.

NATIONAL CRITERIA

In this section we will work through what you can expect to encounter in the examination. This is best done by considering the requirements set out in the **National Criteria**.

■ 'Candidates should be expected, within a limited range of clearly defined topic areas, to demonstrate understanding of public notices and signs (e.g. menus, timetables, advertisements) and the ability to extract relevant specific information from such texts as simple brochures, guides, letters and forms of creative writing within the experience of, and reflecting the interests of, sixteen-year-olds . . .'

We can **summarise** the paragraph and other sections of the national requirements as follows:

a)   the topic areas are limited and clearly set down
b)   you will have to show you understand specific details (key points) in public notices and signs, simple brochures, guides, letters and imaginative writing
c)   the items or articles to be read will be relevant
d)   the material will be presented in as realistic a fashion as possible. This means that you can expect postcards and letters to be handwritten, so you must become as familiar as possible with **German handwriting**. There will be many examples in your course books, but if you know any native speakers of German, then use them to get additional practice.
e)   the questions will usually be in English, to be answered in your own words in English.

Now let's consider Basic Reading in more detail.

REQUIREMENTS

As with the other tests, each of the examining groups has set down the vocabulary and topic areas it will include in this part of the test. As we have already noted, there are some differences between the groups, so the first thing to do is make sure you know exactly what your examining group requires.

Detailed lists of the words you will be expected to understand are provided by the examining groups, and your teacher will have this information. There are some important differences between the groups on this matter, so in the **topic areas** in Chapter 3 and the **alphabetical list** in the last chapter of the book we have attempted to include those words which are most common. Although the list is not exhaustive, it certainly contains most words you will need to know. Make sure you check the requirements of your group.

Learning vocabulary is a chore, and always will be, but unfortunately it is an essential one for foreign languages. However, let's be positive: you know the **topics** to be covered, you know the **words** on which you can be tested, you know you don't need to show that you understand **every single word**. That's a lot better than starting to learn a dictionary! What you need to do is to develop **ways** of taking the pain out of learning vocabulary and to make vocabulary learning a regular part of your revision programme.

LEARNING VOCABULARY

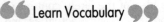

You may find the following suggestions helpful.

- It's better to have regular, short bursts of learning than longer periods. Ten minutes a day is much better than one spell of 50 minutes.
- Every time you learn vocabulary, you must test yourself.
- You may like to give yourself a small reward for reaching your targets.
- Learning with someone else can be a change, but you need to test each other.
- Be systematic about what sections of vocabulary you learn, and when.
- Develop some ways to put some interest into your vocabulary learning, e.g. by timing yourself and improving your speed and accuracy. Use the lists to help you.
- You can make your own lists. If you have access to a computer with a word processor, you can use it to help you with your German. It's a great revision asset, if it's used wisely.

APPROACHING THE QUESTIONS

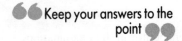
Keep your answers to the point

Most of the items are short, so the length will not be off-putting.

- Read the instructions carefully: very often there will be a sentence or two to set the scene, and these can be very helpful.
- You don't need to write long answers – often a few words will be sufficient – but make sure you provide all the information required.
- For each question there will usually be an indication of the number of marks available. This will provide you with a clear idea of the points you need to mention in your answer.
- You will usually answer the questions in English using your own words.
- You may be required only to tick a box for some questions.

THEMES

You can expect any of the following reading materials to be included in the examination:

PUBLIC NOTICES AND SIGNS

- Advertising posters, e.g. announcing coming events
- Traffic signs, e.g. highway code, places in town, motorway signs
- Signs in public places, e.g. at the railway station or in the supermarket
- Directions, e.g. when to take medicine
- Warnings, e.g. Beware of the dog!
- Price lists, e.g. at a hotel, campsite, shop
- Menus, e.g. restaurant, café, snack bar
- Timetables, e.g. train, bus
- General, e.g. public handouts about promotional activities, events

SIMPLE BROCHURES

- Holidays, e.g. resorts, riding holidays
- Accommodation, e.g. hotels, guest houses
- Leisure activities, e.g. sports, excursions

- Special events, e.g. exhibitions, festivals
- Special offers, e.g. train, boat packages

GUIDES

- Places of interest, e.g. tourist sights/buildings
- Monuments, e.g. *Kölner Dom*
- Towns, e.g. sightseeing tour – *Stadtbesichtigung von Berlin*
- Regions, e.g. trip along the Rhine

LETTERS

- Informal, e.g. from a pen friend
- Formal, e.g. from a hotel
- Semi-formal, e.g. letters page of a magazine

A wide range of topics could be covered in letters. Postcards are also likely to be included.

IMAGINATIVE WRITING

- Descriptions, e.g. of an event of interest
- Interviews, e.g. with a famous person
- Stories of interest

Remember, though, that there are also other possibilities for each of these sections, so get as much practice as you can in reading all kinds of German!

EXAM HINTS

The questions in the examination, as we have already noted, will test your ability to understand the key points. In this section we will look at the kinds of things that can reasonably be asked.

In many cases the questions will be seeking an answer about:

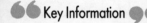 Key Information

a) Who?
b) What?
c) Where?
d) When?

e) How long?
f) How many?
g) How much?
h) Why?

So we need to check what items could be included under these categories, and you need to make sure that you are familiar with them and that you understand them when you meet them. Make sure you know your vocabulary.

WHO?

People:

- family and friends
- professions
- descriptions: physical appearance, size, age, etc.

WHAT?

Items relating to the full range of Basic Level topic areas:

- what you have to do: instructions, requests, payments, etc.
- what other people do/will do/have done, e.g. likes, dislikes, school, work, free-time activities

WHERE?

Location:

- position: prepositions
- places: buildings, landmarks
- places: countries
- directions
- distances

WHEN?

- time of day
- 24-hour clock
- days, weeks, months, years
- dates
- moments of time: midnight, midday
- length of time
- frequency, sequence, rapidity
- expressions of time: today, yesterday, etc.
- seasons, important holiday periods, e.g. Christmas, New Year
- beginning, continuity, end

HOW LONG?

Duration:

- minutes, hours, days, weeks, months, years
- until + time/point in time/day/week/month/year

HOW MANY?

- numbers

HOW MUCH?

Quantity:

- numbers
- weights and measures
- size: big, small

WHY?

- reason

The importance of these sub-headings will be more apparent when we consider some sample questions.

E X A M I N A T I O N   Q U E S T I O N S

SHORTER ITEMS

66 Questions give clues 99

The first questions in the examination will be very short. You may only have one word to read in some cases! Typically the early sections will deal with the signs and public notices you could expect to see around you in a town or village. Read and study the questions carefully before answering them.

During a walk round a German town you see the following signs and notices.

1   You see this notice on the door of a shop.

> **Mittwoch-
> Nachmittag
> geschlossen**

When is the shop shut? _____ *(1)*

2   In the shopping centre you see this notice.

> **Radfahren
> in der Passage
> verboten!**

What is forbidden there? _____ *(1)*

3   You are looking in the window of a dry-cleaner's.

Sofort - Dienst		
PREISE		
Hose ● Rock	je DM	3,30
Kleid ● Anorak		4,30
Jacke		3,80
Mantel		6,40
Pulli ● Pullover	ab	1,80
gut gereinigt, gebügelt		

How much would it cost to have a skirt cleaned? _____ *(1)*

4   What would you obtain here?

FAHRKARTEN

_____ *(1)*

5   What is Dr Schmidt's profession?

**Dr. med. dent
A. Schmidt**
Zahnarzt

_____ *(1)*

6   You are in swimming pool and see this sign.
What does it remind you to do?

BADEN NUR MIT
BADEMÜTZE GESTATTET

_____ *(1)*

7   You see this notice on a door:
What does it ask you to do?

BITTE DRÜCKEN

_____ *(1)*

8   What would you look for when you saw this sign?

WARNUNG VOR DEM HUND

Write your answer here _____ *(1)*

The theme of **motoring** is certain to be included at Basic Level Reading. Consider the following examples. Note the importance of common signs.

9   When driving along the Autobahn, you see
this sign. How does it affect your route?

UMLEITUNG

_____ *(1)*

10   You see the following notice:

P NUR FÜR SCHLOSS- UND PARKBESUCHER

Why can't you leave your car here if you wish to go shopping?

_____ *(2)*

The theme of **shopping** is an obvious choice for inclusion. In this exercise, again, you only need look out for key vocabulary. Check the topic area of food and drink!

Aktuelle Angebote *zu Vorteilspreisen*

EDEKA						
Brechbohnen	850-ml-Dose	-.99	Apfelmus	720-ml-Glas	-.69
Mandarin-Orangen	315-ml-Dose	-.88	Rotkohl	720-ml-Glas	-.69
Ananas, ganze Scheiben	850-ml-Dose	1.79	Weinkraut	850-ml-Dose	-.88
Pfirsiche halbe Frucht	850-ml-Dose	-.99	Gurken	720-ml-Glas	-.99

11 The following items are on your shopping list.
    Which can and which can't you buy at Edeka?

	YES	NO
peaches	☐	☐
cucumber	☐	☐
peas	☐	☐
red cabbage	☐	☐
wine	☐	☐
pineapple	☐	☐
apples	☐	☐
orange juice	☐	☐

12 You are in a department store and see the following sign:

TIEFPARTERRE	PARTERRE	1. ETAGE	2. ETAGE
Blusen	Pullis	Kleider	Mäntel
Röcke	Hosen	Cocktail	Pelze
Brautkleider		Jeans-Shop	Jacken
			Kostüme

On which floor would you buy a raincoat?

_____ *(1)*

Sometimes you will be presented with **multiple-choice** questions. They will usually test whether you know which sign to look out for in particular situations. Here are some examples.

13 Which of these signs would you expect to see when looking for a room for the night?

    A   Sommerschlußverkauf
    B   Zimmer frei
    C   Keine Zimmer
    D   Kein Eintritt

    Write your answer here _____ *(1)*

14 Which of these signs would you expect to see at a building site?

    A   Achtung Baustelle!
    B   Achtung bissiger Hund!
    C   Achtung Ausfahrt!
    D   Achtung Glatteis!

    Write your answer here _____ *(1)*

15 You are visiting your pen friend's uncle in hospital. Which of these notices would you look for?

    A   Eingang für Besucher
    B   Eintritt frei
    C   Kein Eingang
    D   Einfahrt für Krankenwagen

    Write your answer here _____ *(1)*

LONGER ITEMS

Typically these will include brochures, postcards, letters and descriptions. Remember that you do not need to understand every single word. If you find words you don't understand, look them up in a dictionary afterwards, make a written note of them and learn them! It's very likely that the same words will appear in many different pieces. Read and study the following questions carefully before answering them.

The next questions give examples of the treatments of **leaflets and brochures**. Here you are required to extract relevant key information.

16 In a leaflet giving advice to hitch-hikers you read the following:

> So wenig wie möglich Gepäck mitnehmen!
>
> In allen Ländern ist das Trampen auf Autobahnen und Schnellstraßen verboten. (Das heißt: Dort darf man keine Autos anhalten, weil es zu gefährlich ist.
>
> Tramper dürfen nur auf Parkplätzen oder an Tankstellen stehen.)
>
> Nach Möglichkeit nicht am Wochenende trampen!

State three pieces of advice given. _____

_____ *(3)*

17 Study the information on Cuxhaven given below and answer IN ENGLISH the questions that follow.

Your answers need not be in complete sentences.

a) Apart from tennis and golf, name **three** other activities popular in Cuxhaven.

_____

_____ *(3)*

b) How does the size of Cuxhaven compare with that of other resorts in North Germany?

_____ *(1)*

Imaginative writing is likely to include **letters and articles** found in magazines. Study the following examples.

18 The following letter on the problem pages of a teenage magazine catches your eye.

a) What is Monika's problem? _____
_____ *(1)*

b) Why is this particularly noticeable?
_____
_____ *(1)*

c) Who else in the family has this problem? _____
_____ *(3)*

> ## Hilfe! Mit 16 schon graue Haare
>
> Ich bin 16 Jahre alt und habe schon viele graue Haare. Meine Eltern, beide um die fünfzig, sind schon ganz grau, ebenso meine drei Schwestern (18 bis 28), und sogar mein 12jähriger Bruder bekommt schon graue Strähnen.
>
> Da ich dunkles Haar habe, sieht man die grauen Haare besonders gut. Soll ich sie färben?
>
> Monika H.,Brixon

19   Read the following descriptions of four young people who are not German but who live
in Germany, then answer the questions.

Anna-Maria aus Italien ist von ihren Klassenkameradinnen kaum zu unterscheiden, un doch fühlt sie sich ausgeschlossen, weil ihr die Familie nicht erlaubt, ohne Begleitung auszugehen oder eine Jugenddiskothek zu besuchen wie ihre Klassenkameradinnen. Sie muß hier nach italienischer Sitte leben.

Gülei hat es deswegen schwerer als andere, weil sie in ihrer Freizeit auch noch eine türkische Schule besucht. Sie will mit ihren Eltern zurück in die Türkei.

Maria aus Griechenland fürchtet sich davor, mit ihren Eltern zurückzumüssen. Hier lebt sie fünf Jahre, hat hier alle ihre Freundinnen und möchte hier bleiben. Dort kennt sie niemanden.

Cetin hat es geschafft, er ist nicht mehr ausgesondert. Er sitzt als Dolmetscher zwischen dem Schulsprecher und der Protokollführerin. Cetin weiß, was er will. Er wird weitergehen und Fernsehtechniker werden.

a)   Who wants to return to their own country? Name only one person. _____
_____ (1)

b)   Who has made a lot of friends in Germany? Name only one person. _____
_____ (1)

c)   Who has decided on their career? Name only one person. _____
_____ (1)

d)   Why is it difficult for an Italian girl to make friends in Germany? _____
_____ (2)

e)   Why does Gülei have less free time than the others? _____
_____ (1)

Other letters will be the kind that you might get from a friend. Equally, a friend might ask
you for help with a letter he or she has received. Study the following examples.

20   Nicola has just received this letter from her brother's girlfriend Sabine in Germany.

Lauterbach, den 5 Juni

Liebe Nicola,

vielen Dank für Deinen Brief. Ich will gleich wieder schreiben, denn ich habe Dir einige Neuigkeiten zu berichten. Ich habe endlich eine neue Stelle gefunden, in einem Reisebüro in der Stadtmitte. Zur Zeit bin ich 'Mädchen für alles', aber es ist interessant.
Jeden Dienstagabend und den ganzen Donnerstag gehe ich zur Berufsschule und lerne Französisch, Schreibmaschine und Stenographie. Ich muß mindestens zwei weitere Abende für die Schule arbeiten. So bleibt nicht viel Zeit für meine Hobbies.
Aber das macht nichts, so kann ich Geld für die Ferien sparen. Ich werde mit Freunden im Juli nach Bayern fahren. Das ist billig für uns, denn meine Eltern haben einen Wohnwagen am Chiemsee. Es ist noch ein Platz frei, hast Du Lust mitzukommen, es wäre vom 26. Juli bis zum 9. August.
Rufe bitte sofort an, wenn Du Interesse hast daran. Ich würde mich sehr freuen, Dich endlich mal wiederzusehen.
Bis auf bald
Herzliche Grüße
Deine Sabine

She wants to know:

a) where Sabine is now working _____ *(1)*

b) whether she likes the work _____ *(1)*

c) how often she goes to college _____ *(2)*

d) what subjects she is taking _____ *(3)*

e) how much homework she has to do _____ *(1)*

You must now explain the invitation.

f) When is Nicola being invited to Bavaria? _____ *(1)*

g) Who is Sabine going on holiday with? _____ *(1)*

h) What accommodation are they going to be using? _____ *(1)*

i) What must Nicola do if she wants to accept the offer? _____ *(1)*

21 Read the following letter carefully, then answer the questions as fully as you can.

Braunschweig, den 4. Oktober

Lieber Peter,

Es tut mir leid, daß ich nicht früher geschrieben habe! Als Dein Brief bei uns ankam, war ich schon bei meinem Onkel in Norddeutschland, nicht weit von der dänischen Grenze. Da habe ich fünf Wochen Ferien verbracht. Mein Onkel hat ein kleines Geschäft, wo er Herrenartikel verkauft, vor allem Anzüge und Mäntel, aber auch Schuhe. Ich habe ihm dabei geholfen. Es war sehr interessant, manchmal auch ganz lustig.

An einem Tag kam ein junger Mann in den Laden. Ich habe ihn gefragt: „Ja, bitte, Sie wünschen?"

„Ein Paar schwarze Schuhe, Größe 9."

Das fand ich komisch. – „Größe 9, das haben wir nicht."

„Ach schade", sagte er.

Da merkte ich, daß er einen leichten Akzent hatte. „Sind Sie Deutscher?" fragte ich.

„Nein, ich bin Engländer."

„Ach, jetzt verstehe ich. Das ist eine englische Größe. Sie meinen Größe 44."

Da haben wir beide gelacht.

Hast Du auch in den Ferien gearbeitet? Schreib mir bitte bald.

Mit herzlichen Grüßen,

Dein Ralf

a) Where in North Germany does Rolf's uncle live? _____ *(1)*

b) What does Rolf's uncle do for a living? _____ *(2)*

c) What did Rolf do while he was staying with his uncle? _____ *(1)*

d) What mistake did the English customer make? _____ *(1)*

KEY TO THE QUESTIONS

1   Wednesday afternoon
2   cycling
3   DM 3,30
4   tickets
5   dentist
6   put on a bathing hat
7   push
8   a dog
9   diversion
10 The car park is only for people visiting the castle or the park.
11 Yes for peaches, cucumber, red cabbage, pineapple.
    No for peas, wine, apples, orange juice.
12 second floor
13 B
14 A
15 A
16 Take as little luggage as possible.
    On motorways, only ask for a lift in car parks and service stations.
    If possible avoid the weekend.
17 a) swimming, sailing, windsurfing, riding
    b) It's the biggest.
18 a) She is sixteen and her hair is going grey.
    b) She has dark brown hair.
    c) Her parents, her three sisters and her brother.

19 a) Gülei
    b) Maria
    c) Cetin
    d) Her parents do not allow her to go out alone or to a disco.
    e) She goes to a Turkish school in her free time.
20 a) in a travel agency in the town centre
    b) yes, it's interesting
    c) Tuesday evening and all day Thursday/2 days a week
    d) French, typing, shorthand
    e) two evenings a week
    f) July 26th – August 9th
    g) friends
    h) a caravan
    i) ring straight away
21 a) near the Danish border
    b) He runs a men's clothes shop.
    c) He helped in the shop.
    d) He gave an English shoe size, not continental.

TESTS WITH STUDENT ANSWERS

The following two tests have been answered by a candidate. An examiner has marked them and has added his comments.

TEST ONE This is an article from a magazine, in which an unemployed German girl writes about her mother's work.

Meine Mutter paßt vormittags auf einen kleinen Jungen auf. Er heißt Hans und wohnt in der Nähe. Sie kommt meistens um zwei bis drei Uhr nachmittags wieder. Ich finde das sehr gut, weil ich mehr allein zu Hause bin und nicht immer zuhören muß, was meine Mutter sagt, zum Beispiel: „Mach den Rekorder leiser" oder „geh jetzt raus und sitz nicht immer im Zimmer rum". So kann ich mir meine Zeit selbst organisieren. Ich habe noch zwei Brüder 14 und 6 Jahre alt. Mit dem großen gehe ich oft ins Kino, und er hilft mir manchmal bei den Hausarbeiten.

QUESTIONS AND STUDENT ANSWERS

1 What does her mother do in the morning? (1)

She looks after a small boy called Hans.

Excellent! 1 mark

2 Why is the girl pleased that her mother is out of the house? (2)

She is alone and doesn't have to listen to her mother moaning.

Only half right. She can also organise her time herself. 1 mark

3 Give two examples of what her mother tells the girl to do. (2)

1. Turn your recorder down.
2. Don't sit around inside all day.

Well done! Full marks: 2 marks

4 Give two things the girl says about her brothers. (2)

They are 14 and 6 and she goes to the cinema with them.

She goes to the cinema with the older brother only (mit dem großen).
1½ marks

Good answers to these questions on the whole. FIVE AND A HALF out of a possible SEVEN. You see that you do not have to understand every word in order to get high marks. In this case it was small details that let you down.

TEST TWO Read the letter sent by Martina Schmidt to the warden of the youth hostel in Worms, and answer IN ENGLISH the questions that follow:

Martina Schmidt,
Kiesstr. 12,
6109 Mühltal

Sehr geehrte Herbergseltern!

Ich und zwei Freundinnen planen eine Fahrradtour den Rhein entlang. Zwei Tage wollen wir in Worms verbringen und würden daher gerne vom 18. Juni zum 19. Juni in Ihrer Jugendherberge übernachten. Für folgende Informationen wären wir dankbar: Wieviel kostet eine Übernachtung mit Abendbrot und Frühstück pro Person? Wieviel kostet das Leihen von Bettzeug, und wie erreicht man die Jugendherberge, wenn man auf der B6 vom Norden nach Worms kommt?

Auf jeden Fall möchten wir drei Betten für oben erwähnte Nacht buchen. Könnten Sie uns bitte mitteilen, ob das möglich ist?

Hochachtungsvoll,

Martina Schmidt

QUESTIONS AND STUDENT ANSWERS

1 What are Martina and her two friends planning? (2)

A cycle tour along the Rhine

Excellent! Full marks – 2 marks

2 How many nights would they like to spend in the Youth Hostel in Worms? (1)

Two

No! Only one. 0 marks

3 What **three** things does Martina ask about specifically in her letter? (5)

1. How much is bed + breakfast
2. How much is it to hire a sheet sleeping bag?
3. How do you get to the Youth Hostel from the B6?

Good, but you have forgotten *Abendbrot* (supper) and that they are coming from the *north* (vom Norden). 3 marks

Not bad! FIVE marks out of a possible EIGHT. Be sure to include all relevant details!

CHAPTER

READING: HIGHER LEVEL

REQUIREMENTS

THEMES

EXAMINATION QUESTIONS

KEY TO THE QUESTIONS

TESTS WITH STUDENT ANSWERS

A STEP FURTHER

GETTING STARTED

Higher Level Reading is an optional paper. As with other optional papers, however, you have nothing to lose by attempting it. As mentioned in Chapter 6, many students find reading German easier than the other skills. Perhaps the most important factor is that you can work at your own pace, so even if you don't think you can do all of the paper well, it would be a good idea to attempt Higher Level Reading if you want to get one of the higher grades.

ESSENTIAL PRINCIPLES

REQUIREMENTS

The Higher Level Reading tests for all of the examining groups are based on the same fundamental principles as for the Basic Reading tests (see Chapter 6). Many of the tests will overlap to some extent with the topic areas and vocabulary already covered at Basic Level, and if you are confident and competent at Basic Reading you should gain some credit at Higher Level.

If you have not yet worked your way through Chapter 6, then you should do so now before progressing to the detail of the Higher Level requirements.

What do you have to do?

1 You will be expected to demonstrate the skills listed under Basic Reading over a wider range of clearly defined topic areas – check what is applicable in your case.

2 In addition you will be expected to show that you can:

- identify the important points or themes of the material
- understand the attitudes, emotions and ideas of the characters
- draw conclusions from what you read
- identify the relationship between ideas expressed
- infer meanings from the extracts
- understand a variety of written German, in short and extended pieces, such as that found in public places, in magazines and in the press, in the home, in formal and informal situations and in writings by sixteen-year-olds in Germany, Austria and Switzerland.

THEMES

What kind of **themes** or extracts can you expect?

As we saw in Chapter 6, the main sources for testing reading comprehension are likely to be:

- Public notices and signs
- Simple brochures
- Guides
- News, weather, traffic reports
- Letters and messages
- Imaginative writing

At **Higher** Level the full range of topics and vocabulary will be covered, extracts will be longer, there will be more extended pieces from magazines and newspapers, and generally more extended pieces of formal and informal writing. Remember, though, that there are also other possibilities for each of these sections, so get as much practice as you can in reading all kinds of German!

Obviously your understanding of a wide range of vocabulary is going to be put to the test, and you must make sure that you know most of the Higher Level vocabulary, but it is always helpful to know where to start and what to expect. It is, then, worth considering in more detail the themes mentioned above.

PUBLIC NOTICES AND SIGNS

You can expect any of the following:

- **signs relating to everyday movements around towns or villages** – motoring, as a pedestrian or cyclist, as a tourist
- **notices and signs and other information at a railway station, bus station, airport, ferry terminal** – these will inevitably deal with travel arrangements such as times of departure and arrival, changes to timetables, special offers, tours
- **notices and signs and other information at a campsite, youth hostel, hotel** – these will tend to be about facilities offered (e.g. groceries which can be purchased in the camp-shop), special events such as evening barbecues, trips to places of local interest, excursions to nearby beauty spots, messages passed on by people telephoning or visiting, warnings, emergencies
- **notices and posters in shops** – mostly in department stores, e.g. advertising goods, special offers, bargains, sales, cheese-tasting, wine-tasting, café/restaurant menus, holidays, etc.

BROCHURES AND GUIDES

These could include:

- **commercial advertising**, e.g. by department stores planning a publicity drive (see above), tourist office brochures, travel agents advertising holidays, trips, special offers, local groups publicising activities and events
- **local features**, e.g. what's on in the region, diary of coming events such as films, plays, sports events, dances, exhibitions, special mini-reports, free handouts
- **guided tours** – these will obviously relate to places and features of interest. You are likely to be asked to select information about dates, ages, descriptions, special features, traditions, history, famous people, stories of interest.

NEWS, WEATHER, TRAFFIC REPORTS

You can expect these to include:

- **reports of current, topical news items**, such as visits, accidents, disasters, industrial unrest, strikes, protests, famous personalities, sports, special events, occasional 'funny stories'
- **weather forecasts** mentioning temperatures, general conditions, trends, features for holiday-makers or skiers, natural disasters such as floods
- **road conditions, motorway reports** (queues are very common on German motorways!) about roadworks, diversions, accidents, advice/hints, features for holiday-makers.

WRITTEN MESSAGES

These could be messages of all kinds for someone who is not present, such as:

- a pen friend giving details of arrangements, passing on information
- someone outlining reasons for a delay or change of plan
- a written message giving details of a phone call you were unable to take
- a note asking you to do something, e.g. carry out a particular job.

LETTERS

Letters could be of the formal kind or informal. **Formal** letters are most likely to be typewritten, but **informal** letters from a friend will usually be handwritten. Remember to get practice in reading **German** handwriting.

- **Formal letters** will tend to relate to accommodation, holidays and jobs, but other topic areas could be included. The most obvious themes would be reservations for hotels, campsites, youth hostels, details of holiday bookings, lost property (left while on holiday), job application correspondence.
- **Informal letters** will cover a wide range of material and topics, just as you would in a letter you might write in English! The most obvious themes will be current 'news', school, free time, recent activities (e.g. a party or trip), future plans, making arrangements.
- **Semi-formal** letters could also figure in this part of the examination. These are likely to be from someone you know or have a connection with but who is not actually a friend or close friend. A parent of your exchange partner writing to your parents is an example of such writing. The other kind of semi-formal letter to expect would be letters you might find in a magazine, where the writer relates something of special interest to him/her which would also be of general interest to other people.

INTERVIEWS IN MAGAZINES AND SURVEYS

These could well include:

- famous people talking about their lives, interests, careers
- experts talking about their specialist areas
- features of general interest, e.g. holidays, jobs, fashion, education, music, entertainment, sport
- ordinary people talking about any of the above, likes, dislikes, school, new schemes such as pedestrian zones.

Remember, at Higher Level you will be expected to understand details such as facts, in much the same way as at Basic Level, but you will **also** have to show that you can understand what people think or feel about something, and why. This is a very important development and the specimen questions will help to focus attention on this aspect.

E X A M I N A T I O N   Q U E S T I O N S

As with Basic Reading, you can expect a variety of question types. These are best summarised as follows:

■ questions in English requiring answers in English
■ multiple-choice questions in English
■ completing a table/form/note/grid
■ matching statements in English to material contained in the extract.

The majority of questions in the Higher Level Reading Test will consist of extracts in German with questions in English to be answered in your own words in English.

As a rule, you will not be required to write your answers in complete sentences, and you will not be penalised for poor English, such as poor spelling. The clearer your English, however, the easier it is for the examiner to understand your answer!

Some of the extracts will be quite short, while others will be longer. You must recognise that at Higher Level there will be a greater degree of unpredictability and greater emphasis on understanding the 'gist' or general meaning of what you are reading.

SHORT ITEMS

Although Higher Level Reading involves coping with much longer extracts than at Basic Level, you can still expect some quite short pieces. Usually they will be extracts of an informative nature, such as notices and advertisements. Holidays and travel are common themes. Consider the following examples.

1 You see this notice at a tram stop:

> 40. DM SIND DER PREIS, DEN UNSERE PRÜFER FORDERN, WENN SIE EINEN ZUG DER FRANKFURTER STRASSENBAHN OHNE GÜLTIGEN FAHRAUSWEIS BETRETEN. FAHRSCHEINE BEKOMMEN SIE AUS DEM AUTOMATEN.

What does this notice warn you about and what does it tell you to do?

_____

_____

_____ *(3)*

2 Here is an advertisement:

> FAHR AB AUF TRANSALPINO
> MIT TRANSALPINO SPART IHR BIS ZU 40% AUF FAHRPLAN-
> MÄSSIGEN ZÜGEN ZU ÜBER 300 STÄDTEN IN
> DEUTSCHLAND, EUROPA UND NORDAFRIKA
> TRANSALPINO – DAS BILLIGE BAHN-TICKET FÜR ALLE
> ZUGVÖGEL UNTER 26 GIBT'S ÜBERALL, WO DER GRÜN-WEISSE
> TRANSALPINO- STICKER KLEBT

a) Give two advantages of travelling on a Transalpino ticket.

_____ (2)

b) What restriction is there on the Transalpino ticket?

_____ (1)

3   The following information is given to passengers who wish to take their bicycles with them on suburban trains:

> An Sonntagen, Feiertagen und Samstag ab 14.00 Uhr können Sie ein Fahrrad (normale Bauart) in der U- und S-Bahn mitnehmen. Das geht aber nur auf den Linien U 1 bis U 4, S 1 bis S 6 und S 14/S 15.
>
> Für Ihr Fahrrad brauchen Sie einen gültigen Fahrschein. Der kostet 2,00 DM. Sie kaufen ihn vor Fahrtbeginn am Automaten: 'Zuschlag 1. Klasse' (Erwachsene).
>
> Die Fahrrad-Einstiegtüren sind durch ein Symbol markiert. Nur hier gibt es Stellplätze. Für maximal 2 Fahrräder.
>
> Aus Sicherheitsgründen und um andere Mitreisende nicht zu belästigen, müssen die Fahrräder während der Fahrt festgehalten werden. – (Nicht vergessen: Kinder unter 12 brauchen zum Fahrrad eine Begleitperson über 18!)
>
> Fahrgäste ohne Fahrrad haben Vorrang. Nehmen Sie bitte Rücksicht.

a) What are passengers under 12 with bicycles required to have?

_____

_____ (1)

b) What special regulation applies on trains on Saturday mornings?

_____ (1)

c) What must you do with your bicycle during the journey, and why?

_____

_____ (2)

d) How do you know which door of the train you must use?

_____ (1)

Newspaper reports of news items or interesting/unusual stories are likely to be common sources at this level. Usually, however, the articles will be reasonably short. Here is an example covering a report of a news item.

4   Here is a news item from the Süddeutsche Zeitung. Read it carefully and then answer, IN ENGLISH, the questions which follow.

> SÜDDEUTSCHE ZEITUNG – Montag, den 15. Oktober 1984
>
> *Casino in San Remo überfallen*
>
> Vorgestern haben zwei mit Pistolen bewaffnete Männer das Spielcasino in San Remo an der italienischen Riviera überfallen. Die mit roten Tüchern maskierten Räuber drangen in das Büro des Casinos ein, zwangen zwei Angestellte und einen Wächter, sich auf den Boden zu legen, öffneten den Geldschrank mit einem dem Wächter weggenommenen Schlüssel und entkamen in einem Auto. Ein dunkelgrüner Mercedes, der schon am Tag vorher gestohlen worden war, wird von der Polizei gesucht.

a) What incident is reported in this news item? _____ (1)

b) What were the employees made to do? _____ (1)

c) How were the criminals able to open the safe? _____ (2)

d) What are the police looking for and why? _____ (2)

Extracts and articles about famous people are likely to appear in this section of the examination. After all, most of us are interested in the stars!

5   Read this article about one of Austria's well-known singers and answer the questions in English.

> Nach einjährigem Hollywood-Aufenthalt ist Uschi Regers, Österreichs international erfolgreichste Rock-Sängerin, wieder in Deutschland.
>
> Vor drei Jahren geschieden lebt sie jetzt mit ihren Zwillingstöchtern, zwei Katzen und einem riesengroßen Schäferhund in einem Münchener Vorort.
>
> Mit rotgestreifer Punkfrisur und schwarzbemalten Lippen schockiert sie noch weiter die meisten Eltern. Trotzdem hat sie so viel Geld verdient, daß sie ihren größten Traum erfüllen und ihr eigenes Theater im Stadtzentrum kaufen kann. Von ihrem privaten Leben weiß man wenig. Sie spricht kaum davon und läßt die Reporter nie ins Haus. Wirklich hat sie zwei Gesichter – aggressiv auf der Bühne, aber zu Hause eine liebevolle Mutter.

a) How long did Uschi Regers spend in Hollywood? _____ (1)

b) When did she get divorced? _____ (1)

c) Where does she now live in Germany and who lives with her? _____
_____ (2)

d) Describe her appearance. _____ (2)

e) What is her greatest dream? _____ (2)

f) How does she manage to keep her private life to herself? _____
_____ (2)

g) What do you think is meant by saying that she has two faces? _____
_____ (2)

Letters, whether formal or informal, are likely to be used to test the kind of comprehension required at Higher Level. Study this example of an informal letter.

6   Read the letter below and answer IN ENGLISH the questions that follow.

German Style handwriting

> Kassel, den 11. November
>
> Liebe Carol!
>
> Vielen Dank für Deinen Brief, den ich vor drei Wochen bekommen habe. Entschuldige bitte, daß ich erst heute schreibe. Ich bin ja sehr schreibfaul! Du auch, nicht? Oder schreibst du gern Briefe?
>
> Bei mir war in letzter Zeit ziemlich viel los. Wir haben nämlich in unserer Stadt ein neues Sportzentrum, wo ich dreimal in der Woche hingehen darf. Da kann man allerlei Sport treiben. Man zahlt natürlich Eintritt, aber das ist eigentlich ganz günstig, und wenn man Sportartikel braucht, gibt es sie dort zu mieten. Das finde ich gut, denn ich könnte es mir sonst nicht leisten, Federball, Tischtennis und dergleichen zu spielen. Mein Lieblingssport aber – was wir leider bei uns nicht treiben können – ist Skilaufen. Dieses Jahr fahre ich zum dritten Mal mit der Klasse nach Österreich.
>
> Ich finde es klasse, daß Du Gitarre spielst. In meiner Freizeit spiele ich öfters Klavier. Später will ich in einer Jazzband spielen.
>
> Zum Schluß habe ich eine Bitte. Ich sammle eifrig Briefmarken und habe bis jetzt nur wenige aus England. Hast Du vielleicht welche, die Du mir zuschicken kannst?
>
> So, Schluß für heute. Viele Grüße,
> Deine Karin

a) When did Karin receive Carol's letter?

_____ (1)

b) What does Karin say about writing letters?

_____ (1)

c) What does Karin say about the cost of using the sports centre?

_____ (1)

d) What facility does the sports centre offer?

_____ (1)

e) What is Karin's regret about the sports centre?

_____ (1)

f) What does Karin say about her musical interests?

_____
_____ (2)

g) What request does Karin make at the end?

_____
_____ (1)

7   Below is a copy of a preview of a German TV programme. Your pen friend from Hamburg sent it to you as she knows that you are very interested in 'the alternative way of life' many Germans try to find.

Read through it and answer the following questions.

The Boysens made a dramatic change in their life.

a) Now describe the change of environment.

_____ (1)

b) What sort of jobs did Jens and Jutta originally train for?

_____ (2)

c) How have Jutta's attitudes to life changed?

_____
_____ (2)

d) Jens had bought 'Kate' – a cottage – in 1975. What were his initial reasons for buying this building?

_____ (2)

e) What happened on 9th July 1979?

_____ (1)

f) What evidence do you find in the text of his attitude to his new daughter?

_____
_____ (2)

g) What are the Boysens' feelings about their new way of life?

_____
_____ (2)

Umsteiger

Nie wieder in die Stadt!

Von der Großstadt auf eine Insel – Jens und Jutta Boysen begannen auf Pellworm ein neues Leben

Alles hinwerfen, abhauen, von vorn anfangen... Jutta (32) und Jens Boysen (35) haben das getan, woran andere manchmal denken. Vor zwei Jahren stiegen die Kellnerin und der Lehrer um in ein neues Leben: aus der Zwei-Millionen-Stadt Hamburg auf die nordfriesische Marschinsel Pellworm.

Die treibende Kraft war Jutta: „Damals stank mir alles, der Job, die Stadt, das ganze Leben." Sie saß fest, mit zwei Kindern aus erster Ehe, ohne Stellung und „ohne Vorstellung, wie es weitergehen sollte".

Aber da war ja noch die Kate auf Pellworm. Juttas Freund Jens, auf der Insel geboren, hatte sie 1975 gekauft „für die Ferien und für das Alter".

Am 9. Juli 1979 heiraten Jutta und Jens. Einen Monat später packten sie ihre Sachen und ließen mit den Kindern Arne und Meike, damals elf und acht Jahre, ihr altes Leben hinter sich.

Seit Jenny geboren ist, hat sie ohnehin genug Trubel. Die jüngste Boysen ist jetzt acht Monate alt. Sie ist der Grund dafür, daß Jens im letzten Jahr „relativ wenig gearbeitet hat".

Zurückkehren würden sie „nie wieder!". „Eher ziehen wir noch weiter hinaus."

1 „Ich bin ausgestiegen" **Donnerstag, 20.8., 16.15 Uhr**

Here are some questions based on TV programmes, but the tasks to be completed show a different format.

8 Below are some descriptions of Sunday programmes on German television.

Match the descriptions with the titles of the programmes alongside the following boxes.

Write in the box the letter of the description that most aptly describes the title.

a) **Der Internationale Frühschoppen**
Current Affairs discussion ☐ *(1)*

b) **Unsere kleine Farm**
Popular American serial
A little girl gets lost ☐ *(1)*

c) **Beatrix – Hollands neue Königin**
A new Queen for Holland ☐ *(1)*

d) **Solange es Menschen gibt**
American film (1959) ☐ *(1)*

TV AM SONNTAG

A 21.05	**B** 17.45	**C** 16.25	**D** 12.00
Mary und Laura wollen für den Biologie-unterricht Insekten sammeln. Sie nehmen ihre kleine Schwester Carry mit. In einem unbeaufsichtigten Moment stürzt das Kind in einen Ventilations-schlacht einer still-gelegten Kohlenmine	Dokumentarbericht zum bevorstehenden Thron-wechsel am 30. April in den Niederlanden.	Die Schauspielerin Lora Meredith arbeitet verbissen an ihrer Karriere. Ein Star zu werden bedeutet ihr mehr als ihre kleine Tochter Susie. Sie gibt das Kind in die Obhut ihrer farbigen Haus-hälterin.	Thema: Kuba und andere Unruheherde zwischen Karibik und Anden. Teilnehmer: Don J. Jordan (USA), Jürgen Koch (Kuba), Oswald Iten (Schweiz), Jorge Chirions Velarde (Peru), Anton-Andreas Guha (Deutschland) und Werner Höfer.

LONGER ITEMS

Longer extracts at Higher Level Reading will often involve people presenting their views and opinions about a particular topic. School is a theme on which many young people have something to say!

9 In the passage below five young Germans give conflicting views about the ideal length for a school day.

Read the passage and answer the questions that follow.

Ganztags- oder Halbtagsschule?

Schüler in der Bundesrepublik haben meistens von acht Uhr früh bis etwa ein oder zwei Uhr mittags Unterricht. Der Nachmittag ist frei. Aber oft braucht man die meiste Zeit für Hausaufgaben. In anderen Ländern gibt es die Ganztagsschule. Die Schüler haben auch nachmittags Unterricht und kommen erst um vier oder fünf Uhr nach Hause. Aber meistens haben sie dann keine Hausaufgeben mehr. Was ist besser: den ganzen Tag in der Schule sein, oder nachmittags noch zu Hause für die Schule arbeiten? Wir fragten die Schüler der 9. Klasse eines Gymnasiums in Wiesbaden.

Matthias (14): Den ganzen Tag Schule – das ist ja wie ein Arbeitstag bei den Erwachsenen. Ich finde das zuviel.

Oliver (15): Ich war in einer Ganztagsschule in der Schweiz. Da hatte man nicht soviel Freizeit wie hier. Wir hatten Unterricht von 7.45 Uhr bis 11.30 Uhr und nochmal von 13.45 Uhr bis 15.45 Uhr. Trotzdem hatte man den Rest des Nachmittags auch noch Hausaufgaben. Am Mittwochnachmittag war frei und am Samstagnachmittag auch. Also in der Woche konnte man nicht soviel unternehmen wie hier.

Renate (15): Ich glaube, es gibt auch andere Formen von Ganztagsschulen, wo man noch in der Schule seine Hausaufgaben machen kann. Wenn ich um vier nach Hause komme und bin dann aber fertig mit der Arbeit – das ist doch dasselbe wie jetzt bei der Halbtagsschule: Da komme ich um eins nach Hause und esse und mache dann Hausaufgaben bis um vier...

Karin (15): Aber dann finde ich es doch besser, wenn man die Hausaufgaben gleich in der Schule macht. Es ist doch ein ganz gutes Gefühl, wenn man nach Hause kommt, und man ist fertig mit der ganzen Arbeit.

Martin (14): Ja, aber ich habe zum Beispiel einen französischen Brieffreund – wenn der nach seiner Ganztagsschule nach Hause kommt, dann hat der zusätzlich noch Hausaufgaben. Die Ganztagsschule bringt, glaube ich, gar nicht so viele Vorteile. Man lernt nämlich gar nicht so viel, denn so nach vier oder fünf Stunden läßt die Konzentration doch unheimlich nach. Und außerdem: Man kann ja gar nichts anderes mehr machen an dem Tag. Ich meine, ich habe ja auch noch andere Interessen außer Schule und so. . .

a) Why does Matthias think a longer day at school would be too much?

_____

_____ (2)

b) What experience did Oliver have of the longer school day?

_____ (1)

c) In Oliver's experience what was the disadvantage of the longer school day and why?

_____

_____ (2)

d) Why did Renate conclude that she was already working as hard as if she stayed at school until 4 pm?

_____

_____ (2)

e) Which system does Karin seem to favour and why?

_____

_____ *(2)*

f) Why does Martin seem to be opposed to the idea of the longer school day?

_____

_____

_____ *(3)*

10 The following article appeared in a German youth magazine. Read it and answer the questions below.

Free time

Wie 312 Schüler und 658 Schülerinnen ihre Freizeit verbringen ist schon ganz erstaunlich. Für den Nachmittag in der Woche haben viele sogar einen richtigen Stundenplan entwickelt. Diesen Wochenplan schickte uns Barbara: **Montag:** Schularbeiten, 15 bis 17 Uhr Klavierstunde; **Dienstag:** Schularbeiten, 15 bis 17 Uhr Volleyball, abends Chor; **Mittwoch:** Schularbeiten, Freundinnen besuchen; **Donnerstag:** Schularbeiten, 15 bis 17 Uhr Konfirmandenunterricht; **Freitag:** Schularbeiten, 18.30 bis 20 Uhr Trompete spielen, anschließend Jazzdance."

Aber nicht nur die Mädchen sind so beschäftigt, auch die Jungen haben viele Aufgaben. Thomas geht zum Beispiel zweimal in der Woche in einen Turnverein, zweimal wöchentlich in die Tanzstunde und hat auch noch Gitarrenunterricht. Viele von euch hören nicht nur sehr gerne Musik, sondern spielen auch selbst ein Instrument: Klavier, Flöte, Gitarre und Akkordeon wurden am meisten angegeben.

Karin klagt, wie einige andere von euch auch, über das tägliche Üben: „Meine Mutter muß mich immer ans Üben erinnern, und manchmal möchte ich auch eine Klavierstunde ausfallen lassen, aber dann gehe ich doch immer wieder hin."

Auf Sabines Karte stand: „Ich verbringe meine Freizeit fast nur mit Sport." Sport spielt eine große Rolle in eurer Freizeit. Beliebt sind Leichtathletik (Turnverein) und Schwimmen. Fußball steht bei den Jungen natürlich an erster Stelle, die Mädchen gehen dagegen gerne reiten und spielen Tennis. Einfach so, nach Lust und Laune, ohne feste Termine, organisieren also die wenigsten ihre Nachmittage in der Woche. Auch wenn die Aufgaben fast alle freiwillig sind. Euer Wochenende ist nicht ganz so verplant: „Das verbringe ich zusammen mit meinen Eltern und Geschwistern. Meistens gehen wir meine Oma besuchen, sonst kann ich machen was ich will." Ähnlich wie für Thomas ist das Wochenende dazu da, auch mal zu tun, wozu man gerade Lust hat. Zum Beispiel mit „meinem Bruder zu streiten und zu spielen," schrieb Matthias. Was ihr alle gerne macht: spielen, basteln, Freunde besuchen und natürlich fernsehen! Und das fanden wir auch interessant: Jungen schrieben öfters als Mädchen, daß sie im Haushalt helfen müßten. Und Nachhilfestunden müssen sehr viele am Nachmittag auch noch machen. Fernsehen ist vor allem auch ein Mittel gegen Langeweile.

---

a) What activity occupies most of Barbara's free time?

_____ *(1)*

b) Name two activities that Thomas does twice a week.

_____

_____ *(2)*

c) What does Karin complain about?

_____ *(1)*

d) In what way are weekend activities different from weekday ones?

_____ *(1)*

e) Name two weekend activities which are stated to be common to most teenagers.

_____

_____ *(2)*

f) What do you find out about helping in the home?

_____ *(1)*

KEY TO THE QUESTIONS

1 a fine of DM 40 if you get on the tram without a ticket
to buy tickets from the machine

2 a) You save up to 40% of the normal fare. There are trains to over 300 towns in Germany, Europe and North Africa.
   b) You must be under 26.

3 a) Somebody over 18 must accompany them.
   b) No bicycles allowed.
   c) You must hold it for safety reasons and so as not to annoy other passengers.
   d) The door is marked with a symbol.

4 a) an attack on a casino in San Remo
   b) to lie down on the floor
   c) They had taken the keys from the guard.
   d) A dark green Mercedes used as the getaway vehicle.

5 a) one year
   b) 3 years ago
   c) in a Munich suburb with her twin daughters (and two cats and a huge Alsatian dog)
   d) red striped punk hairstyle and black lips
   e) to buy her own theatre in the town centre
   f) She does not talk about it and she does not let reporters into the house.
   g) She gives a different impression on stage from when she is at home with her daughters.

6 a) 3 weeks ago/within the last month
   b) She's lazy.
   c) It's quite reasonable.
   d) It hires out equipment.
   e) You cannot ski there.
   f) She plays the piano and wants to play in a jazz band.
   g) Could Carol send her English stamps?

7 a) from a city to an island
   b) teacher and waitress
   c) She hated the city, her job and her life. Now she is much happier.
   d) for holidays and for his old age
   e) Jutta and Jens got married.
   f) He did not work so much during the child's first year. He presumably looked after the baby.
   g) They would never return to the city. They would rather move even further away.

8 a) D
   b) A
   c) B
   d) C

9 a) It's like an adult workday.
   b) He attended a full-day school in Switzerland.
   c) They had less free time. They had lessons in the afternoon and then homework.
   d) Because her homework took her till 4 o'clock.
   e) A full-day school where you finish homework at school. It is nice to feel free when you get home.
   f) His French pen friend has a full-day school and then homework. Concentration weakens after 4–5 hours. He has other interests besides school.

10 a) schoolwork
   b) gymnastics club and dancing lessons
   c) daily piano practice
   d) They are not as planned as the weekdays.
   e) playing, making things, visiting friends, watching TV
   f) Boys said more often than girls that they helped at home.

TEST WITH STUDENT ANSWERS

Here is an example of a Higher Reading Test, answered by a candidate and marked by an examiner.

The following account appeared in a North German newspaper. Read it carefully and then answer, IN ENGLISH, the questions which follow.

Putzfrau im Fahrstuhl steckengeblieben

Die 48jährige Putzfrau Marthe Sirola hat vierzehn Tage in einem Fahrstuhl eines Hamburger Hochhauses verbracht. Der Fahrstuhl war zwischen Erdgeschoß und Keller steckengeblieben, ohne daß jemand merkte, daß sich Frau Sirola darin befand. In dieser Zeit hat sie 3500 DM „verdient".

Frau Sirola hat nur überleben können, weil sie eine Flasche Limonade bei sich hatte. So konnte sie ihren Durst löschen. Als die arme Frau nicht zur Arbeit erschien, nahm man an, sie sei krank und sei zu Hause geblieben. Deshalb suchte man sie nicht. Endlich entdeckte ein Mechaniker am 28. Mai die bewußtlose aber noch lebende Frau im Fahrstuhl.

Die Firma, bei der die Putzfrau arbeitet, hat ausgerechnet, was Frau Sirola an Über- und Sonntagsstunden „verdient" hat. Die Zeit im Fahrstuhl gilt als Arbeitszeit, denn sie hatte im steckengebliebenen Fahrstuhl einen Besen und einen Eimer Wasser bei sich, als das Unglück geschah. An den beiden Sonntagen, die sie in dem Fahrstuhl verbrachte, „verdiente" sie sogar 300 Prozent mehr als an den gewöhnlichen Werktagen.

QUESTIONS AND STUDENT ANSWERS

a) What had happened to Frau Sirola? (4)

She was stuck for 14 days in a lift in a Hamburg skyscraper.

> Very good. A pity you did not add 'between ground floor and cellar.' 3 marks

b) How did she manage to survive? (1)

She had a bottle of lemonade.

> Full marks! 1 mark

c) Why was she not missed? (2)

They thought she was ill and had stayed at home.

> Full marks again! 2 marks

d) What was the one good outcome of her experience? (1)

They gave her 3500 Marks

> Not quite. She earned (verdient) the money. ½ mark

e) How was the amount calculated? (2)

By working out overtime and Sunday time.

> Good! Full marks! 2 marks

f) What particular circumstances qualified her to receive this? (2)

She was ill.

> No! She had a broom and a bucket of water with her (einen Besen und einen Eimer Wasser) and so she was technically 'at work'. 0 marks

> Good. EIGHT AND A HALF out of a possible TWELVE

READING:
BASIC AND HIGHER
A STEP FURTHER

Much of the reading material at Basic Level is taken from notices, signs, menus and leaflets. Your course books will have some examples of these things, or you may have copies of Harrap's *German Sign Language* at school. But it should be possible to get hold of authentic material without too much trouble. After all, it is easy enough to pick up free leaflets in Britain – at the station, theatre, travel agency, information office and so on. This is where your contacts with Germany come in useful. If you have a pen friend, you could exchange packets of leaflets. Or if you know someone who is going to Germany, you could ask them to look out for suitable material.

Don't throw away any letters you may have which are written in German. It is important to get used to German handwriting (how is it different from English handwriting?) and the kind of expressions which are common in letters.

But understanding what you read is basically a matter of knowing the words. If you don't know the days of the week, then you cannot tell on which days the shop is closed. If you don't know the meaning of the word *Auskunft* then you cannot know what is on offer there. (Actually it means 'information'.)

So words simply have to be learnt, and it's no good just hoping they will sink in without your making any effort. Lack of vocabulary is a constant barrier to success at exam time, so we have got to devise ways of learning lists of words in as painless a fashion as possible. Here, then, are a few suggestions for ways of taking some of the drudgery out of learning vocabulary.

1   Take the number **ten** as your norm and **find ten words** on one subject. For example, think about **transport**:

das Auto, der Wagen	das Flugzeug
das Fahrrad, das Rad	das Motorrad
der Bus	das Schiff
das Taxi	die Fähre
der Zug	das Luftkissenfahrzeug

Now **make up a sentence** for each one, e.g. *Ich fahre mit dem Zug nach Bremen.*

Other subjects to tackle in this way could be:

- clothes
- weather
- school subjects
- countries
- towns in Germany
- furniture
- shops
- professions
- fruit and vegetables
- sports
- hobbies other than sports
- food you like
- buildings other than shops

No doubt you can think of plenty more by looking at your topic lists and vocabulary lists.

2   Use a **vocabulary book**. Make sure you write carefully and neatly. Nothing is worse than revising from a grubby note book which is full of mistakes. Give yourself plenty of space, putting the German on one side of the page and the English on the other. Then you can cover up one side and test yourself. Alternatively, put the meaning on the next page, so that you always have to make the effort of turning the page to find the answer.

3 Another simple way of learning vocabulary is to take a **rough piece of paper** and to **fold it** into four or six like this:

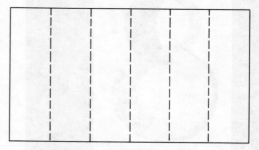

You then write out, say, twenty difficult German words in column one. Then write out the English in column two. Now fold back column one so that you cannot see it. Now you only have the English in front of you. Try to write out the German again in column three. Then check with column one and fill in the gaps. Now continue in the same way.

But beware! It is quite easy to learn words on a short-term basis like this. The real test is whether you still remember them in a few weeks' time.

4 Some people develop a habit of writing **lists** of words on pieces of paper or card about the size of a postcard. They use these cards as bookmarks or pin them on the wall, prop them up by a mirror or leave them anywhere where they are bound to notice them.

5 Here is another suggestion for those with an orderly mind. Find a small long, deep box, the sort of box which After Eights come in. Cut up lots of small cards (you can cut up old Christmas cards) to fit into the box like filing cards. Write the German word(s) at the top of the card, and write the English in the same way on the back.

You can then work your way through the cards either from the German side or from the English, gradually replacing the words you know with new ones. You can also write on the bottom of the cards and turn the whole set upside down. This scheme could clearly be developed to include phrases and sentences, or questions and answers, just as in Trivial Pursuit!

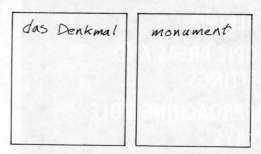

6 Do not forget that words have little meaning until they are put together into sentences. So **read** German whenever you can. If you have worked through the *Lesekiste* sets, the school probably has readers to follow that. There may well be discarded textbooks in school too, which could provide excellent reading practice. And what about the school library or the local library? One school I know had an excellent scheme for providing cheap reading material. Every English member of an exchange group took to Germany a paperback which he or she no longer needed. The German group brought books to England, so that each school was able to build up a small collection of books in the foreign language.

In all your revising, remember that learning does not have to be done sitting at a table. Try speaking German as you walk about the room. Work out German phrases in your mind as you watch TV or as you cycle to school. Identify each article as you tidy your room or as you lay the table. Prop your vocabulary book up in front of you as you do the washing up.

If you can't get to sleep at night, go over groups of words in your mind. The possibilities are endless! But above all make the language something alive, something to be used, something to be enjoyed.

SPEAKING: BASIC LEVEL – ROLE-PLAYS

TALKING

TOPIC AREAS AND SETTINGS

APPROACHING ROLE-PLAYS

EXAMINATION QUESTIONS

A STEP FURTHER

GETTING STARTED

All the examining groups require you to take part in rôle-plays at Basic Level and at Higher Level. This is hardly surprising, since one of the primary aims of the GCSE is to help you to cope with the German needed for everyday situations.

E S S E N T I A L   P R I N C I P L E S

TALKING

The rôle-plays will require you to take the initiative, so be prepared to talk! You will need to be able to:

- ask for goods, e.g. in a shop
- ask for information, e.g. in a tourist office
- give information, e.g. reporting lost property
- make arrangements, e.g. over the telephone
- understand and answer the questions of other people.

You will perform the rôle-plays with your teacher, who will be asked to take the part of a helpful native speaker of German. Usually the test will be recorded, so it is a good idea to practise speaking into a microphone and getting used to the sound of your own voice. Your teacher may mark the test or may send the recording to the examining group for marking.

In most cases you will have to do **two** rôle-plays. You will be required to arrive at the examination room approximately 15 minutes before your test actually begins to allow for your preparation time. Make sure that you do not have to make a rush at the last minute; it is important to be as calm as you possibly can be in the circumstances. You will be given the rôle-play cards on which you will be tested, and then you have some 10 minutes to prepare yourself to carry out the instructions on the cards. The instructions will be in English, and will indicate clearly what you have to do.

You are not required or expected to use perfect German. The main point is for you to make yourself understood. That means you need to speak as clearly as you can and pronounce the words as well as you can, so that the other person can understand. At all stages your teacher will attempt to be as helpful as possible, to allow you to show exactly what you can do. Remember, in the GCSE you always get credit for what you **can** do.

So be positive from the start.

TOPIC AREAS AND SETTINGS

The rôle-play situations will be drawn from the **topic areas** and **settings** listed for Basic Level. It is vital, then, that you know the material relevant to you. Check exactly what your examining group states and study carefully the **language tasks** and **vocabulary** sections in Chapter 3.

Remember that material listed in any topic area can be tested in a variety of settings. To remind you what they are, they are listed below.

Topics	Settings
Personal Identification	Town
House and Home	Home
Life at Home	School
School	Places of work
Free Time and Entertainment	Places of Entertainment
Travel	Public Transport
Holidays	Private Transport
Accommodation	Tourist Information Office
Meeting People	Shops, Markets
Shopping	Cafés, Restaurants
Food and Drink	Hotels, Campsites, etc
Services	Dentist, Doctor, Chemist
Work and Future	Garage, Petrol Station
Language Problems	Bank, Exchange Office
Weather	Lost Property, Police Station

Some topic areas and settings lend themselves more readily to rôle-plays than others, so listed below are the most common situations you are likely to meet in this section of the examination. You must prepare yourself to cope in situations which may involve:

Key Situations

- asking the way
- shopping
- cafés and restaurants
- booking accommodation

- petrol stations, garages
- places of entertainment
- visiting a German-speaking family
- school

- trains, buses, stations
- banks, post offices
- tourist offices
- customs

- minor illnesses and complaints
- reporting lost property
- making arrangements to go out
- meeting new people.

Please remember that this list only represents the most likely situations to be covered. It is not an exhaustive list and you should be prepared to deal with other possibilities.

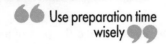

APPROACHING ROLE-PLAYS

Use preparation time wisely

Now that you are more confident about what to expect, it is time to look at the rôle-plays in detail, and how best to prepare for them.

As with all tests, a **systematic** approach is sensible.

The first thing you need to do is **read the instructions carefully** and work out exactly what the tasks are and what you have to say. Let's look at an example.

- You are at the railway station in Germany. You are talking to the ticket clerk. The rôle of the ticket clerk will be played by the examiner.

  1 Ask for a return ticket to Hamburg.

  2 Ask when the train leaves.

  3 Ask from which platform it goes.

  4 Ask if you have to change trains.

  5 Ask if you can get something to eat on the train.

- The first thing, then, is to work out exactly what you have to say. You will probably end up with something like this:

  1 'A return ticket to Hamburg, please.'

  2 'When does the train leave?'

  3 'Which platform does it go from?'

  4 'Must I change trains?'

  5 'Can I get something to eat on the train?'

- The next stage is to think of the German you know to convey and ask for the information required and to obtain what you need. You will have to do this in your head as you are not allowed to make notes during your preparation time. Remember that there are many different ways of saying the same thing and it does not matter which you use as long as you get your message across. Whatever else you do, do not try to translate word for word from English into German! Don't forget that your teacher will be as helpful as possible, too.

  You will probably end up saying something like this:

  1 *'Einmal hin und zurück nach Hamburg, bitte.'*

  2 *'Um wieviel Uhr fährt der Zug ab?'*

  3 *'Von welchem Gleis fährt der Zug?'*

  4 *'Muß ich umsteigen?'*

  5 *'Kann ich im Zug etwas zu essen kaufen?'*

Now **you** try the following situation. Use the same steps as we have looked at for the previous rôle-play.

- You are at the reception desk in a hotel. The examiner will play the part of the hotel receptionist.

  1 Say that your father/mother has reserved two rooms.

  2 Give your surname and nationality.

3   Ask what floor the rooms are on.

4   Check that breakfast is included in the price.

5   Ask where the car can be parked.

■ You should have ended up with something like this:

1   'My father/mother has reserved two rooms.'

2   'My name is Wilson and I'm English.'

3   'What floor are the rooms on?'

4   'Is breakfast included in the price?'

5   'Where is the car park?'

■ That would lead you to say something like:

1   *'Mein Vater/Meine Mutter hat zwei Zimmer reserviert.'*

2   *'Mein Familienname ist Wilson, ich bin Engländer.'*

3   *'In welchem Stock sind die Zimmer?'*

4   *'Ist das Frühstück eingeschlossen?'*

5   *'Wo ist der Parkplatz?'*

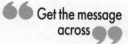
Get the message across

Remember that there are many ways of getting your message across – you do not always need to use complete sentences, you can take easier solutions. You should, however, make an effort to be polite. If you make a mistake, don't worry or panic, just correct yourself as you would in English.

In many rôle-plays you will also have to listen out carefully for what your teacher says. Again, don't panic if there is something you do not understand, but ask for it to be said again, e.g. *Wie bitte?*

The next section will provide a number of different rôle-plays for you to work through. Get as much practice as you can. Perhaps you can work with a friend or someone at home. Make up your own rôle-plays and test each other. The more fun ideas you come up with, the easier you will find it to make progress.

EXAMINATION QUESTIONS

For the following rôle-plays we have provided a sample dialogue with the part played by the **candidate** indicated by the letter *C*, and that of the **examiner** by the letter *E*. We have also given an English translation. Before you study the sample dialogue, however, you should try to work out how **you** would tackle the situation. Only when you have done that should you compare what you would say with the German we have provided. Remember that there are many different ways of saying the same thing, so it does not matter if you come up with a version which is not identical, as long as it conveys the message.

There are also some notes to highlight useful pointers.

AT THE RAILWAY STATION

You are staying with your pen friend in Bonn. One day he/she has a hospital appointment and you decide to visit Köln for the day. You go to the railway station to buy your ticket and check on the details of the journey. The rôle of the booking-clerk will be played by the examiner.

which preposition?

1 Ask for a return ticket to Köln.

very common tasks

2 Ask how much it is.

3 Ask what platform the train leaves from.

key words

4 Ask at what time the train arrives in Köln.

try to anticipate what this could be

5 Be prepared to respond to any other question or observation from the clerk about your journey.

MEG

SAMPLE DIALOGUE

C: Eine Rückfahrkarte nach Köln bitte.
A return to Cologne please.

E: Eine Rückfahrkarte nach Köln, bitte sehr.
A return to Cologne, here you are.

C: Was kostet das?
How much is it?

E: Achtundzwanzig Mark.
28 Marks.

C: Von welchem Gleis fährt der Zug?
What platform does the train go from?

E: Von Gleis 7B.
From Platform 7B.

C: Wann kommt der Zug in Köln an?
When does the train arrive in Cologne?

E: Um elf Uhr zwanzig. Was machen Sie denn in Köln?
At 11.20. What are you going to do in Cologne?

C: Ich will den Dom sehen.
I want to see the cathedral.

E: Schön. Viel Spaß.
Fine. Enjoy yourself.

AT THE POST OFFICE

You are at the post office in Germany. You are talking to the clerk at the counter. The examiner will play the part of the clerk.

which preposition?

1 Ask how much it costs to send a postcard to England.

2 Buy three stamps at that amount.

key idiom – comes up in many situations

3 Say you would like to send a parcel also.

4 Ask if you can make a phone call to England.

5 Ask if the clerk has any change.

MEG

SAMPLE DIALOGUE

C: Was kostet eine Postkarte nach England?
How much is a postcard to England?

E: Nach England? Achtzig Pfennig.
To England? 80 Pfennig.

C: Drei Briefmarken zu achtzig Pfennig bitte.
Three 80 Pfennig stamps please.

E: Bitte schön. Das macht also zwei Mark vierzig.
Here you are. That's 2 Marks 40 then.

C: Ich möchte auch ein Paket schicken.
I would also like to send a parcel.

E: Jawohl. Das kostet sechs Mark dreißig.
Certainly. That's 6 Marks 30.

C: Kann ich nach England telefonieren?
Can I telephone to England?

E: Aber natürlich. Gehen Sie bitte in Kabine drei.
But of course. Go into booth 3 please.

C: Haben Sie Kleingeld?
Do you have any change?

E: Ja. Hier haben Sie zehn Mark klein.
Yes. Here's 10 Marks in change.

AT THE TOURIST OFFICE

You are in the tourist office of a German town enquiring about a museum. The examiner will play the part of the tourist information officer.

1 Ask if there is a museum in the town.

2 Ask where it is.

key idiom

3 Ask if there is a bus or tram there.

key vocabulary

4 Ask what time the museum is open.

5 Ask for a town plan.

MEG

SAMPLE DIALOGUE

C: Gibt es ein Museum in der Stadt?
Is there a museum in the town?

E: Ja, natürlich. Das Stadtmuseum ist sehr interessant.
Yes of course. The Stadtmuseum is very interesting.

C: Wo ist das Museum?
Where is the museum?

E: Das ist ziemlich weit, im westlichen Teil der Stadt.
It's quite a way, in the western part of the town.

C: Fährt ein Bus oder eine Straßenbahn dorthin?
Does a bus or tram go there?

E: Ja. Es gibt eine Straßenbahn – die Linie sechs.
Yes. There's a tram – number 6.

C: Wann ist das Museum offen?
When is the museum open?

E: Von zehn bis achtzehn Uhr. Aber das Museum ist montags geschlossen.
From 10 o'clock until 6. But the museum is closed on Mondays.

C: Danke. Haben Sie einen Stadtplan?
Thank you. Do you have a town plan?

E: Aber sicher. Bitte schön.
But of course. Here you are.

C: Vielen Dank. Auf Wiedersehen!
Thank you very much. Goodbye!

E: Auf Wiedersehen!
Goodbye!

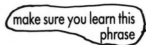

ASKING THE WAY   You are looking for the railway station and ask a passer-by for help. The examiner will play the part of the passer-by.

(make sure you learn this phrase)   1   Ask how to get to the main railway station.

   2   Ask how far away it is.

(another key idiom)   3   Thank the person and say goodbye.

ULEAC

SAMPLE DIALOGUE

E: Ja, mein Herr/mein Fräulein?
Yes Sir/Madam?

C: Entschuldigung, können Sie mir sagen, wie ich zum Hauptbahnhof komme, bitte?
Excuse me, can you tell me how to get to the main station please?

E: Zum Bahnhof? Kein Problem. Gehen Sie geradeaus bis zur Kreuzung, dann links bis zur Ende der Straße. Da ist der Bahnhof. Sie können es nicht verfehlen.
The station? No problem. Go straight on to the crossing, then left to the end of the street. The station is there. You can't miss it.

C: Ist das weit von hier?
Is it a long way from here?

E: Nein, gar nicht, nur ungefähr drei Minuten.
No, not at all, only about three minutes.

C: Vielen Dank. Auf Wiedersehen.
Thanks very much. Goodbye.

E: Auf Wiedersehen.
Goodbye.

ACCOMMODATION   You are at the reception desk of a hotel and you are talking to the receptionist. The rôle of the receptionist will be played by the examiner.

   1   Ask if the hotel has room for one person.

   2   Say you want to stay three nights.   *(key vocabulary)*

   3   Ask if the rooms have a shower.

   4   Ask how much the rooms cost.

(obvious kind of task)   5   Choose a room from those offered.

MEG

SAMPLE DIALOGUE

C: Guten Tag. Haben Sie ein Einzelzimmer frei?
Hello. Do you have a single room free?

E: Guten Tag. Ja, wir haben Zimmer. Wie lange wollen Sie bleiben?
Hello. Yes, we have rooms free. How long do you want to stay?

C: Drei Nächte.
Three nights.

E: Drei Nächte, sehr gut.
Three nights, very well.

C: Haben die Zimmer eine Dusche?
Do the rooms have a shower?

E: Ja, wir haben Zimmer mit Dusche oder mit Bad. Zimmer acht mit Dusche und Zimmer zehn mit Bad.
Yes, we have rooms with a shower or bath. Room 8 with a shower and Room 10 with a bath.

C: Was kosten die Zimmer?
    How much are the rooms?

E: Zimmer acht 60 Mark, Zimmer zehn 65 Mark.
    Room 8 60 Marks, Room 10 65 Marks.

C: In Ordnung, ich nehme das Zimmer acht.
    Fine, I'll take Room 8.

E: Sehr wohl. Hier ist der Schlüssel, das ist Zimmer acht.
    Very good. Here is the key, that's Room 8.

AT THE PETROL STATION

You are travelling through Austria by car with your family. You call at a petrol station and, as you speak German, your parents ask you to talk to the attendant. The rôle of the attendant will be played by the examiner.

1 You require a full tank of petrol.

2 You require two litres of oil. *obvious tasks to expect*

3 Enquire about cost.

key question!! 4 Ask where the toilets are.

try to anticipate the question 5 Be prepared to respond to any other question or comment about your journey.

MEG

SAMPLE DIALOGUE

C: Guten Tag. Volltanken bitte.
    Hello. Fill it up please.

E: Guten Tag. Bitte sehr.
    Hello. Here you are.

C: Ich brauche auch zwei Liter Öl.
    I also need two litres of oil.

E: Zwei Liter Öl, bitte schön.
    Two litres of oil, there you are.

C: Was macht das?
    What does that come to?

E: Sechsunddreißig, fünfzig.
    DM 36,50.

C: Wo sind die Toiletten?
    Where are the toilets?

E: Drüben, neben dem Büro. Wo fahren Sie jetzt hin?
    Over there, next to the office. Where are you travelling to now?

C: Nach Deutschland, nach München.
    To Germany, to Munich.

E: Gute Fahrt! Auf Wiedersehen.
    Have a good journey! Goodbye.

C: Danke. Auf Wiedersehen.
    Thanks. Goodbye.

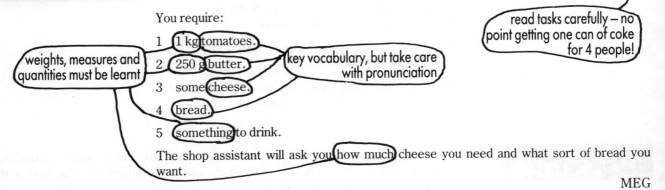

SHOPPING FOR FOOD

You decide to have a picnic so you stop at a *Lebensmittelgeschäft*. You need to cater for four people. The rôle of the shop assistant will be played by the examiner.

read tasks carefully – no point getting one can of coke for 4 people!

You require:

1 1 kg tomatoes.
2 250 g butter.
3 some cheese.
4 bread.
5 something to drink.

weights, measures and quantities must be learnt

key vocabulary, but take care with pronunciation

The shop assistant will ask you how much cheese you need and what sort of bread you want.

MEG

SAMPLE DIALOGUE

E: Guten Tag. Was darf es sein?
      Hello. Can I help you?

C: Guten Tag. Ich möchte ein Kilo Tomaten.
      Hello. I'd like a kilo of tomatoes.

E: Ein Kilo Tomaten, sehr wohl.
      A kilo of tomatoes, very good.

C: Und zweihundertfünfzig Gramm Butter.
      And 250 grammes of butter.

E: Ja. Ist das alles?
      Yes. Is that all?

C: Nein, ich möchte auch Käse.
      No, I'd also like some cheese.

E: Wieviel denn?
      How much then?

C: Ein halbes Kilo.
      Half a kilo.

E: Bitte schön. Sonst noch etwas?
      Here you are. Anything else?

C: Ja, ich brauche Brot.
      Yes, I need some bread.

E: Ja, was für ein Brot nehmen Sie?
      Yes, what kind of bread do you want?

C: Ein Weißbrot.
      A white loaf.

E: Ein Weißbrot.
      A white loaf.

C: Und eine große Flasche Limonade.
      And a large bottle of lemonade.

E: Bitte schön. Das macht DM 16,25.
      Here you are. That makes DM 16,25.

AT THE TOURIST OFFICE

You are at a tourist information office in Köln. The examiner will play the part of the assistant.

1 Ask for a map of the city.

2 Thank the assistant and say that you would also like some leaflets about Köln.

3   Ask if the cathedral is open today.

4   Ask how much it costs to go up to the tower.

5   Ask if you can buy theatre tickets at the tourist office.

ULEAC

SAMPLE DIALOGUE

C: Guten Tag. Haben Sie einen Stadtplan bitte?
Hello. Do you have a plan of the city please?

E: Guten Tag. Ja natürlich. Bitte schön.
Hello. Yes of course. Here you are.

C: Vielen Dank. Ich möchte auch einige Broschüren über Köln.
Thank you very much. I would also like some brochures about Cologne.

E: Nun, da sind sie. Nehmen Sie, was Sie brauchen.
There they are. Take what you need.

C: Ist der Dom heute offen?
Is the cathedral open today?

E: Aber natürlich.
But of course.

C: Was kostet es zum Turm zu steigen?
What does it cost to climb to the tower?

E: Zwei Mark.
Two Marks.

C: Kann ich hier Eintrittskarten für das Theater bekommen?
Can I get tickets for the theatre here?

E: Leider nicht. Wir verkaufen hier keine Eintrittskarten. Sir müssen zum Theater oder zu einem Reisebüro gehen.
Unfortunately not. We don't sell any tickets here. You have to go to the theatre or to a travel agent.

C: Vielen Dank. Auf Wiedersehen.
Thank you very much. Goodbye.

E: Auf Wiedersehen.
Goodbye.

| **AT THE LOST PROPERTY OFFICE** | You have lost your passport and are at the lost property office. The examiner will play the part of the official. |

1   Say that you have lost your passport.

2   Say that you are English and on holiday.   *key items*

obvious task   3   Say that you had it when you went to the bank yesterday.

ULEAC

SAMPLE DIALOGUE

E: Guten Tag. Kann ich Ihnen behilflich sein?
Hello. Can I help you?

C: Guten Tag. Ich habe meinen Paß verloren.
Hello. I've lost my passport.

E: Das tut mir leid. Was ist Ihre Staatsangehörigkeit?
I'm sorry. What's your nationality?

C: Ich bin Engländer(in). Ich bin auf Urlaub hier.
I'm English. I'm on holiday here.

E: So. Wann hatten Sie den Paß zum letzten Mal?
       I see. When did you last have your passport?

C: Gestern, als ich zur Bank ging.
       Yesterday, when I went to the bank.

E: So.
       Right.

AT A RESTAURANT

You go to a restaurant with two friends to celebrate your birthday. You are looking forward to a good meal. The rôle of the waiter/waitress will be played by the examiner.

1   Greet the waiter/waitress and ask for a table for three.
2   Ask for the menu.
3   Say you want chicken.   key vocabulary
4   Say you would like chips.
predictable task   5   Order something to drink.

MEG

SAMPLE DIALOGUE

C: Guten Abend. Ein Tisch für drei bitte.
       Good evening. A table for three please.

E: Guten Abend. Auf der Terrasse ist ein schöner Tisch noch frei.
       Good evening. There's a nice table free on the terrace.

C: Wir möchten die Speisekarte bitte.
       We'd like the menu please.

E: Bitte schön.
       Here you are.

C: Ich nehme das Hähnchen.
       I'll have the chicken.

E: Mit Reis?
       With rice?

C: Nein, mit Pommes frites.
       No, with chips.

E: Sehr gut. Und zu trinken?
       Very good. And to drink?

C: Einen Orangensaft.
       An orange juice.

E: Einen Orangensaft.
       One orange juice.

AT A CAFE

You are with two friends in a café in Austria; they would both like an ice-cream and a coffee; you only want a coffee. You call the waiter/waitress and order for yourself and your friends. The rôle of the waiter/waitress will be played by the examiner.

1   Greet the waiter/waitress and say that you would like three coffees.
2   Ask if they have ice-cream.
3   Say that you would like two strawberry ice-creams.   key vocabulary
4   Ask if the service is included.
5   Be prepared to respond to any other question or observation from the waiter/waitress about your order for ice-cream.

MEG

SAMPLE DIALOGUE

E: Guten Tag. Was darf es sein?
Hello. What would you like?

C: Guten Tag. Drei Kaffees bitte.
Hello. Three coffees please.

E: Sonst noch etwas?
Anything else?

C: Haben Sie Eis?
Have you got any ice-cream?

E: Aber natürlich. Wir haben Schokolade, Erdbeer, Zitrone und Vanille.
But of course. We have chocolate, strawberry, lemon and vanilla.

C: Gut, dann zweimal Erdbeereis.
Good, two strawberry ice-creams then.

E: So, dreimal Kaffee und zweimal Erdbeereis.
Right, three coffees and two strawberry ice-creams.

C: Ist die Bedienung eingeschlossen?
Is the service included?

E: Ja, die Bedienung ist eingeschlossen. Wer bekommt das Eis?
Yes, the service is included. Who is the ice-cream for?

C: Also ich nicht.
Not for me.

MEETING PEOPLE AT A PARTY

You are at a party in Germany and meet someone who is especially interested in talking to you because you come from Britain. The examiner will play the part of the German person.

1 Say hello and introduce yourself.

2 Say where you come from.

3 Say if it is a village or a town.

4 In answer to the question mention one thing you like doing in Germany.

5 Say yes and ask when.

MEG

SAMPLE DIALOGUE

C: Hallo. Ich heiße Michelle.
Hello. My name's Michelle.

E: Hallo Michelle. Woher kommst du?
Hello Michelle. Where are you from?

C: Aus Weymouth.
From Weymouth.

E: Ist das ein Dorf?
Is that a village?

C: Nein, das ist eine Stadt.
No, it's a town.

E: Und was machst du gern hier in Deutschland?
And what do you like doing here in Germany?

C: Ich gehe gern ins Freibad.
I like going to the open-air pool.

E: Ich auch. Vielleicht können wir morgen zusammen gehen?
Me too. Perhaps we can go together tomorrow?

C: Ja. Um wieviel Uhr?
     Yes. When?

E: Schön. Ich komme um drei zu dir.
     Good. I'll come round for you at three o'clock.

A STEP FURTHER

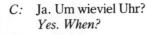

Here are some other examples, but this time without the sample dialogues. Use these for practice.

AT THE MARKET

You are shopping for fruit at a market in Germany. The examiner will play the part of the stallkeeper.

1   Ask how much the large apples are.

2   Ask for half a kilo.

3   Say that is all you want, thank the stallkeeper and say goodbye.

                                                                    ULEAC

AT A CAFÉ

You go to a café with a friend in Germany. Your friend asks you to order while he/she makes a quick telephone call. The part of the waiter/waitress will be played by the examiner.

1   Order an orange juice for yourself.

2   Order a lemonade for your friend.

3   Ask where the toilets are.

                                                                    ULEAC

There are student answers with examiner comments at the end of the next chapter, together with other suggestions for practising rôle-play situations.

CHAPTER

SPEAKING: HIGHER LEVEL – ROLE-PLAYS

REQUIREMENTS

APPROACHING ROLE-PLAYS

EXAMINATION QUESTIONS

PRACTICE SITUATIONS

TESTS WITH STUDENT ANSWERS

A STEP FURTHER

GETTING STARTED

The Higher Level Speaking Tests are optional, but you have nothing to lose by attempting them and, if you are aiming at one of the higher grades, you would be well advised to try them. As with the other Higher Level tests, all candidates will have to complete the Basic Level tests, and the material covered at Basic Level will also feature at the Higher Level.

ESSENTIAL PRINCIPLES

REQUIREMENTS

❝ Accuracy becomes more important ❞

If you enter for the Higher Level, you will have slightly longer to prepare the situations you will be tested on. You will usually begin with the Basic Level rôle-play situations and then go on to the Higher Level rôle-plays. The examining groups, apart from NEA, require you to perform one Higher Level rôle play; NEA requires you to do two.

As with Basic Level, **communication** is the key. You should be able to pronounce the sounds of German accurately enough for a native speaker to understand without difficulty, and to speak with a certain degree of correct intonation and stress. Note that at Higher Level the degree of accuracy expected is greater than at Basic Level, but the important thing is still 'getting the message across'. The more accurate your German is, though, the easier it is for the examiner to understand.

So what is different about the Higher Level rôle-play tests?

- You will be expected to cope with rôle-plays from the full range of situations, settings and topics defined in the syllabus.
- The rôle-plays will contain elements of unpredictability and problem-solving. This means you have to try to anticipate what the problems may be; be prepared to listen carefully to what the examiner says, and then to think and react quickly.

The extra topics for Higher Level include:

- lost property
- repairs and complaints
- more serious medical problems
- accidents and emergencies
- telephoning and more complex situations at the post office
- banking and currency exchange
- travel by air or sea.

You must remember, though, that Basic Level topics can also be included, but that they will be given a different and more demanding emphasis.

The length of the individual rôle-plays will vary somewhat from one examining group to another in terms of the number and complexity of the tasks required. You can also expect the stimuli or instructions to be more complicated, sometimes presented in a novel way. In the main the instructions will be in the form of an outline in English, but could include some kind of a visual stimulus such as a town plan. Again, you must check exactly what your examining group requires.

APPROACHING ROLE-PLAYS

So how do you go about preparing for and tackling these Higher Level rôle-play situations?

As always, a methodical approach will pay dividends. A thorough preparation of the material covered in the Basic Level rôle-plays is of course essential (see Chapter 8) before you concern yourself too much about the detail of the Higher Level situations. Assuming that you are ready, however, these steps should help you:

1 Make sure you know just what topics are in the syllabus for Basic and Higher Level.
2 Check the settings and language tasks and make sure that you can cope with the German you will need to use and understand. Cross check with the lists in Chapter 3 and the details provided by your examining group.
3 Study as many rôle-play situations as you can and get practice. You can practise with a friend, or you can test yourself. Use your checklists.
4 There are often useful courses or programmes on radio or television. Check what is available and listen or watch whenever possible. You may also be able to tape some programmes, but you will have to check on copyright procedures. There is also an increasing number of courses with tapes, some of which can be borrowed from local libraries.
5 Try making up your own rôle-play situations and then try them out with a friend. This can be fun as well as being good practice. You could try being a 'difficult' shop assistant, hotel receptionist, etc.

When studying the rôle-play instructions, the following points should be helpful:

■ Check what the crucial element(s) in each task is and work out what you are going to say. Remember that there are many different ways of saying the same thing.

Be ready for unexpected twists

■ Try and work out what you think the examiner might say, and the possible 'twists' to the dialogue. In most cases these will in fact be reasonably predictable. A simple example of this would be if you were instructed to buy a kilo of apples. The examiner might say that he/she has no apples but the pears are very good. How about a kilo of pears instead? You will have to make a quick decision. The more practice you get, the more 'predictable' these twists will become.

■ Don't panic! There may well be something that at first you don't understand, but that doesn't really matter. Equip yourself with a series of useful phrases to ask the examiner to repeat something, to ask the examiner to say something more slowly, to explain that you didn't quite catch what he/she said. As long as you can do this in German you will not lose credit.

SAMPLE RÔLE-PLAY

Let's look at an example.

Making Arrangements

Study the following situation and be prepared to perform the rôle indicated. In addition, you must respond to any other questions or observations which the examiner may make.

You are making a telephone call to your pen friend in Switzerland to invite him/her to come and visit you. The examiner will play the rôle of your pen friend.

key points

1 Ask if he/she would like to stay with you in the summer holiday or at another convenient time.

2 Tell him/her you will fetch him/her by car from the airport.

key points

3 Answer his/her question about what he/she could do during his/her stay in Britain.

MEG German (adapted)

This might seem at first to be a fairly straightforward situation, but let's look at the examiner's rôle:

first twist **You must respond to this suggestion.** **You must do the work!**

1 Say you are going to Italy, but you could go to England at Christmas. Wait until you are invited at Christmas or until another arrangement is suggested, then accept.

You have to listen hard and understand.

2 Thank him/her for the offer to fetch you and ask what you will do during your stay in England.

awkward customer!

3 Say you don't like the first activity mentioned and agree an alternative, allowing the candidate to take the initiative.

Be prepared to take the initiative.

Problem-solving

A close reading of the two sets of instructions reveals one of the key features of the Higher Level situations – the area of **problem-solving**. In fact it makes the test considerably more interesting and rewarding. You can see in this example that the examiner has been given the brief to be a rather 'awkward customer' in that he/she does not agree with your suggestions and forces you to think of other possibilities. This is very realistic; just think of how often it happens to you in everyday life! The important thing is to try and anticipate well in advance what the examiner might spring on you in the way of surprises, twists, difficulties and 'unexpected' questions.

The rôle-play might have gone something like this:

C: Hallo, Jochen, hier Peter.
    Hello, Jochen. It's Peter.

Try to include normal pleasantries.

E: Hallo, Peter, wie geht's?
    Hello, Peter. How are you?

good use of word order

C: Danke gut. Jochen, willst du in den Sommerferien nach England kommen?
    Fine thanks. Jochen, do you want to come to England in the summer holidays?

E: Na, das ist eine schöne Idee, aber ich fahre im Sommer nach Italien. Es geht also leider nicht.
    Well, that's a nice idea, but I'm going to Italy in the summer. So unfortunately I can't.

C: Ah, das ist schade. Kannst du vielleicht zu Weihnachten kommen?
    Oh, that's a pity. Can you maybe come at Christmas?

good response

very useful expression

E: Ja, das wäre toll. Ich war zu Weihnachten noch nie in England.
    Yes, that would be great. I've never been to England at Christmas.

C: Das freut mich. Wir werden dich vom Flughafen abholen.
    I'm pleased. We'll pick you up from the airport.

good; a common error is to use 'treffen' here

E: Vielen Dank! Sag' mal, was machen wir denn alles, wenn ich bei euch bin?
    Thanks a lot. Listen, what will we do altogether when I'm staying with you?

nice variation of word order

C: Ja, wir können nach London fahren. Das ist immer schön. Auch können wir zum Jugendklub gehen.
    Well, we can go to London. That's always nice. We can also go to the Youth Club.

E: Na ja. In London war ich schon oft. Das finde ich nicht so toll.
    Hm. I've already been to London a lot. I don't think that's so good.

convincing and interesting response

C: Dann fahren wir nicht nach London. Wir können vielleicht meine Schwester in Schottland besuchen. Da ist zu Weihnachten immer viel los!
    Well, we won't go to London then. Perhaps we can visit my sister in Scotland. There's always a lot going on there at Christmas.

E: Oh, das finde ich schon viel besser. Zu Neujahr muß das wirklich lustig sein. Also, ich muß die Sache mit meinen Eltern noch besprechen, dann schreibe ich dir einen Brief. Vielen Dank für den Anruf. Tschüs!
    Oh, I think that's much better. At New Year that must be really fun. Well, I must talk things over with my parents, then I'll write you a letter. Thanks for the call. Bye!

useful expression

C: Tschüs.
    Bye!

EXAMINATION QUESTIONS

In this section we provide a number of rôle-play situations which are typical of the kind to expect in the examination, and which cover a range of topic areas. Each rôle-play includes a possible sample dialogue. We have also provided an English translation and some comments.

ACCOMMODATION

You have just arrived in Germany by car for a two-week stay near Augsburg in South Germany. On the way you have some problems with the car and are delayed. It is getting late and you realise that it is not possible to reach your destination, so you decide to stay at a local campsite near Heidelberg. The examiner will play the part of the campsite manager/manageress.

1   Say that you are looking for a campsite for the night.

2 Ask what you can do.

3 Say that it is too far to go.

4 Ask if there are any hotels nearby.

5 Be prepared to respond to any other questions or observations the examiner might make.

MEG French (adapted)

Try and work out what the examiner may say here.

SAMPLE DIALOGUE

C: Guten Abend, wir suchen einen Campingplatz für heute abend.
Good evening, we're looking for a campsite for tonight.

Good. Not 'heute Nacht', which means 'last night'!

useful idiom

E: Guten Abend. Es tut mir leid, hier ist alles belegt.
Hello. I'm sorry, we're completely full up.

one obvious word that can be used in many situations

C: Schade, Können Sir mir einen anderen Campingplatz empfehlen?
That's a pity. Can you recommend another campsite?

E: Ja, es gibt einen großen Campingplatz etwa 40 Kilometer weiter. Dort finden Sie immer Platz.
Yes, there's a big campsite about 40 kilometres further on. You'll always find room there.

no need always to answer at great length

C: Das ist zu weit.
That's too far.

E: Ich kann dort anrufen, wenn Sie wollen.
I can ring up if you like.

C: Gibt es Hotels hier in der Nähe?
Are there any hotels nearby?

E: Ja, sicher. Was brauchen Sie denn eigentlich?
Yes, of course. What exactly do you need then?

C: Wir brauchen ein Einzelzimmer und ein Doppelzimmer.
We need a single room and a double room.

straightforward predictable tasks, but you still have to get them right!

E: So, dann gehen Sie am besten zum Hotel Schreber. Das ist gar nicht so weit und ganz preiswert. Fahren Sie hier links und Sie sehen das Hotel schon auf der rechten Seite. Das ist ungefähr einen Kilometer.
Well then, the best thing you can do is go to the Hotel Schreber. It's not far at all and quite reasonable. Go left here and you'll see the hotel on your right. It's about a kilometre.

C: Vielen Dank. Auf Wiedersehen.
Thanks a lot. Goodbye.

E: Bitte schön. Auf Wiedersehen.
That's all right. Goodbye.

SHOPPING While window-shopping in Germany you see a T-shirt you like in a shop window. You go into the shop to take a closer look. The examiner will play the part of the shop assistant.

1 Indicate the T-shirt and say you would like to try it on.

2 Say that you are not sure of your size – it might be 42.

What is your size? German sizes are different. Find out.

Try to anticipate what it could be.

3 Agree to the shop assistant's suggestion and choose a colour.

4 You are in a hurry, so react appropriately to the assistant's next question.

Think about it!

5 Say you will take the T-shirt, check the price, and if you are happy with it, pay.

ULEAC French (adapted)

SAMPLE DIALOGUE

E: Guten Tag. Kann ich behilflich sein?
        Hello. Can I help you?

C: Guten Tag. Das T-Shirt dort finde ich schön. Kann ich es anprobieren?
        Hello. I like the T-shirt there. Can I try it on?

E: Aber selbstverständlich. Welche Größe?
        But of course. What size?

C: Das weiß ich nicht genau . . . 42 vielleicht.
        I'm not exactly sure . . . 42 perhaps.
        (very useful phrase)

E: Es tut mir leid, ich habe es nur noch in 44. Möchten Sie es anprobieren?
        I'm sorry, I've only got it in 44. Would you like to try it on?

C: Ja, es ist gut, aber ich möchte das Blaue.
        Yes, it's OK but I'd like the blue one.
        (perfectly adequate response)

E: Bitte schön. Wollen Sie nicht in die Kabine gehen?
        Here you are. Don't you want to go into the changing room?

C: Nein, ich hab's eilig. Das geht so.
        No, I'm in a hurry. It's all right like this.
        (Make sure you learn this idiom.) (useful expression)

E: Wie Sie wünschen.
        As you like.

C: Ja, das geht in Ordnung. Was kostet es?
        Yes, that's fine. How much is it?

E: 28 Mark.
        28 Marks.

C: Gut. Das finde ich ganz preiswert. Ich nehme es.
        Good. That's good value. I'll take it.
        (good conclusion)

LOST PROPERTY

Here we look at two situations involving lost property.

1 A LOST CAMERA

You have just arrived back at your hotel in Frankfurt after a visit to the famous Senkenberg museum and you discover that you have lost your camera. You seek help from the hotel receptionist. The rôle of the receptionist will be played by the examiner.

1   Say that you have lost your camera.

2   Say that you have been to the Senkenberg museum.

3   Say that you travelled by bus.

4   Ask at what time the office at the bus station closes.

(Again, try to anticipate)

5   Be prepared to respond to any other question or observation from the receptionist about the camera.

                                                                    MEG (adapted)

SAMPLE DIALOGUE

C: Guten Tag.
        Hello.

E: Guten Tag.
        Hello.

C: Ich habe meinen Fotoapparat verloren. Können Sie mir helfen?
        I've lost my camera. Can you help me?
        (Short responses, but quite adequate. Better to be simple and accurate than make life too difficult!)

E: Ich hoffe. Wo waren Sie denn?
        I hope so. Where have you been, then?

C: Ich komme jetzt vom Senkenberg-Museum.
I've just come from the Senkenberg Museum.

E: Wie sind Sie gefahren?
How did you travel?

C: Ich bin mit dem Bus gefahren.
I went by bus.

E: Ja, da könnten Sie zum Busbahnhof gehen und da fragen.
Well, you could go to the bus station and ask there.

C: Wann schließt das Büro dort?
When does the office there close?

E: Ich glaube um 18 Uhr. Ich kann für Sie anrufen, wenn Sie mir den Apparat ein bißchen beschreiben.
At six o'clock, I think. I can ring up for you, if you can describe the camera for me.

C: Das ist nett. Der Apparat ist ein Kodak 133, schwarz, ganz neu.
That's kind. The camera is a Kodak 133, it's black and quite new.

E: In Ordnung, ich rufe dann jetzt an.
Fine. I'll ring now, then.

C: Vielen Dank.
Thank you very much.

E: Nichts zu danken.
You're welcome.

2 A LOST BAG

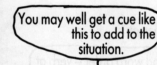
You may well get a cue like this to add to the situation.

During a visit to Germany you lose a bag containing:

- an expensive camera
- approximately 200 Marks
- a watch of no great value – but given to you by your grandmother.

You went to the cinema yesterday and then went on to the café next door:

- Cinema 2.15–4.00
- Café 4.00–5.30

Loss (first) noticed when paying (attempting to pay) bill.

You are now in the lost property office. The part of the official will be played by the examiner.

1 Say what you have lost.
2 Give contents of bag.
3 Give value of articles.
4 Say where and when you lost the bag.
5 Tell how the loss came to be noticed.   ULEAC (adapted)

SAMPLE DIALOGUE

E: Guten Tag. Kann ich irgendwie behilflich sein?
Hello. Can I help you at all?

C: Guten Tag. Ich habe eine Tasche verloren.
Hello. I've lost a bag.

E: Und was hatten Sie in der Tasche?
And what did you have in the bag?

C: Eine Uhr, 200 Mark und einen Fotoapparat.
     A watch, 200 Marks and a camera.

E: Und was für einen Wert hatten die Uhr und der Apparat?
     And how much were the watch and camera worth?

useful phrase for lots of situations

C: Ich weiß nicht genau . . . der Apparat war aber ziemlich teuer.
     I don't know exactly . . . but the camera was quite expensive.

E: Und die Uhr?
     And the watch?

C: Die Uhr ist nicht viel wert.
     The watch is not worth very much.

E: Das Wichtigste ist also der Apparat?
     The most important thing is the camera then?

Very good. Note how important it is not to translate directly. This is the best and easiest way of dealing with the task.

C: Ja, aber . . . die Uhr war ein Geschenk von meiner Großmutter.
     Yes, but . . . the watch was a present from my grandmother.

E: Wann haben Sie die Tasche verloren?
     When did you lose the bag?

C: Gestern nachmittag . . . (ich weiß nicht genau) . . . zwischen Viertel nach zwei und halb sechs.
     Yesterday afternoon . . . (I'm not sure exactly) . . . between a quarter past two and half past five.

E: Und wo?
     And where?

C: Ich war im Kino und dann im Café.
     I was in the cinema and then in a café.

E: Wann haben Sie gemerkt, daß Sie die Tasche verloren hatten?
     When did you notice that you had lost the bag?

good word order – verb at end of clause after 'als'

C: Als ich im Café zahlen wollte.
     When I wanted to pay in the café.

No need for complete sentences, sometimes they are quite unnatural.

E: So, bis jetzt ist nichts abgegeben worden. Am besten kommen Sie morgen nachmittag wieder.
     Well, so far nothing has been handed in. The best thing is to come again tomorrow afternoon.

TOURIST INFORMATION

You have just arrived in Saarlouis, where you want to spend a few days during a tour of Germany. You go to the tourist office to get help with accommodation. The examiner will play the part of the clerk in the tourist office.

fairly uncomplicated tasks but you still need to concentrate

1 Greet the clerk.

2 Explain that you have just arrived in Saarlouis, and ask for a list of accommodation for the town.

3 Find out the meaning of 'HG' and the location of the Hotel Ratskeller.

4 Ask the price of a single room with a shower and with breakfast.

5 Explain apologetically that it is too expensive for you, and enquire about alternative cheaper hotels in the area.

6 Say this suggestion seems fine. Find out how far it is and how best to get there.

ULEAC (adapted)

SAMPLE DIALOGUE

C: Guten Morgen / Guten Tag.
     Good morning / Hello.

AT THE POST OFFICE	You are in a post office in Germany. The examiner will play the part of the counter clerk.

Your tasks are:

1 to greet the clerk,   4 to enquire where the letter-box is,

2 to post a parcel,   5 to say thank you and goodbye.

3 to buy stamps,

ACCOMMODATION – CAMPSITE

Candidate's Instructions

SITUATION	You arrive at a German campsite late one evening, hoping to find accommodation. Your teacher will play the part of the site warden.
REMEMBER	You have not booked in advance, but you need to find some accommodation for the night either here or at another campsite.
YOU MUST	1 Open the conversation by asking if there is any room left. 2 Respond to any suggestions your teacher puts to you. 3 Find out where you can obtain suitable accommodation.

NEAB

MEETING PEOPLE/ MAKING ARRANGEMENTS

Candidate's Instructions

SITUATION	You are on holiday in Germany and have made a new acquaintance. Your teacher will play the part of the new acquaintance.
REMEMBER	You wish to meet him again tomorrow and you are free all day. Arrange a meeting.
YOU MUST	1 Open the conversation by suggesting a time to meet. 2 Respond to any suggestions your teacher puts to you. 3 Arrange something to do, and when and where to meet.

NEAB

AT THE YOUTH HOSTEL

You arrive with a friend at a German youth hostel, where you have booked accommodation in advance. Your teacher will play the part of the hostel warden.

He greets you.

a) Return the greeting, give your name, and say you have booked two beds.
The warden seems to be having difficulty in finding your reservation, and asks you whether you phoned or wrote.

b) Say you wrote three and a half weeks ago.
He finds the letter and asks if you need bed-linen.

c) Say you need four sheets and two pillows.

NEAB

FREE TIME AND ENTERTAINMENT

You want to go to the pictures in Germany. You phone the cinema to see if there are any seats left. Your teacher plays the part of the booking-office clerk.

He answers the telephone.

a) Ask if they have two tickets for tonight's showing.
He asks what kind of seats you want.

b) Say in the stalls – you want to sit at the front.
He tells you when the film starts.

c) Ask when you have to pick up the tickets.
He tells you.

NEAB

TESTS WITH STUDENT ANSWERS

Here are two examples of rôle-play tests with student responses. An examiner has marked them and has added comments. Remember, however, that the candidate writes nothing down in this test, so that the examiner is not at all interested in spelling – only in seeing that the messages are successfully communicated.

TEST 1: AT THE MARKET

You are shopping at the cheese stall of a market in Germany. The examiner will play the part of the stallholder.

1 Ask how much the Emmental cheese costs.

2 Ask for 300 grammes of it.

3 Ask where you can buy milk.

STUDENT RESPONSES

Examiner: Guten Tag. Bitte schön?
Candidate: Was kostet Emmental?
Examiner: Der Emmentaler? Zwölf Mark das Kilo.
Candidate: Dreihundert.
Examiner: Dreihundert Gramm? Bitte schön.
Candidate: Wo ist Milch?
Examiner: Im Supermarkt. Dort an der Ecke.

66 Under the circumstances the meaning is clear, but only just! 99

66 Again the meaning is conveyed 99

66 Not really clear. Do you want to drink milk or buy it? The stallholder is *very* sympathetic 99

66 This candidate would pass this test at basic level, but not with full marks. Better responses would be: 1 GutenTag. Was kostet der Emmentaler Käse, bitte? 2 Dann nehme ich dreihundert Gramm, bitte. 3 Wo kann man hier in der Nähe Milch kaufen, bitte? 4 Danke schön. Auf Wiedersehen. 99

TEST 2: IN A CAFÉ

You are in a café in Germany and you are ordering for yourself and for a friend. The examiner will play the part of the waiter.

1 Order a cup of tea with lemon for yourself and a drink of orange juice for your friend.

2 Ask if they have ices.

3 Choose two different ices.

STUDENT RESPONSES

Examiner: Guten Tag. Was wünschen Sie?
Candidate: Tee bitte und Orange.
Examiner: Bitte schön.
Candidate: Haben Sie Eis?
Examiner: Ja natürlich. Schokolade, Mokka und Pralinen.
Candidate: Schokolade und Kaffee, bitte.
Examiner: Bitte schön.

66 You didn't ask for the lemon; and did you want orange juice or an orange? 99

66 Excellent! 99

66 But you chose an ice which we do not have! 99

66 Three major errors of communication here, so no more than half marks. Better responses would be: 1 Guten Tag. Eine Tasse Tee mit Zitrone für mich, bitte, und einen Orangensaft für meinen Freund/meine Freundin. 2 Haben Sie Eis, bitte? 3 Dann nehmen wir einmal Schokolade und einmal Mokka, bitte. 99

A STEP FURTHER

There is really only one way to practise rôle-play and that is to act it out with a partner. No doubt you have plenty of opportunity to do this in the classroom, but with a bit of initiative you could easily organise it for yourselves. There are lots of rôle-play situations in most course books and there are many in this book too.

If you are working with a friend on the same course, I suggest you go about it in a businesslike way.

1 Decide who is going to play which part.
2 Read the parts through as a dialogue.
3 Repeat, but this time, instead of actually reading word by word, glance at the phrase you have to say, and then look up and say it.
4 This time try to say it by heart.
5 Now finally leave your book on the table, stand up and act it out, putting in *Guten Tag, danke, auf Wiedersehen* and so on as appropriate.

You may need several attempts at some of the stages, but you will improve in this kind of learning very quickly. When you are satisfied, change parts.

This is a much better way of learning than simply reading the parts through. With this method you will really make the words and phrases part of your own language repertoire and you will be able to use them in a variety of situations both in the examination and in Germany.

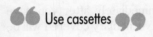

❝ Use cassettes ❞

There is an alternative method if you have not got a partner. That is to record on tape the part played by the examiner, leaving a suitable gap for your own part. Then play it over again and again, putting in your own part, gradually making yourself less and less dependent on the book. Finally, do it while walking round the room, with appropriate gestures and facial expressions. (Don't worry. No one is looking!)

SPEAKING: BASIC AND HIGHER – CONVERSATION

GETTING STARTED

At GCSE you will be required to take Basic Level Speaking, and in addition to the rôle-play tasks you will have a short conversation with your teacher. This will usually take place immediately after you have completed the rôle-plays. The topic areas and vocabulary covered will be those listed for Basic Level only. Again, just check the exact requirements for your individual case.

At Higher Level general conversation is a compulsory part of the test for all the examining groups, in addition to the rôle-play tasks. At this level the conversation can cover the full range of vocabulary and topic areas. There are, however, a few additional topics at Higher Level which would be covered in the conversation. The most important is the area of work and the future, i.e. your future plans.

ESSENTIAL PRINCIPLES

**THE TEST – BASIC
LEVEL**

This part of the test will be very brief and will not go into much detail. In essence, you will be asked some 10 to 20 straightforward questions (depending on your examining group) and you will be expected to provide fairly simple answers.

The marks awarded will again depend on your ability to make yourself understood, to **communicate** some meaning. Your teacher will be trying to help you by taking the rôle of a sympathetic native speaker, and if there is something he or she does not understand then he or she will react just as if it were a real-life situation. For instance, in real life, if you met a German teenager at a party and asked how old he or she was and you got the reply 'forty', you wouldn't just leave it there and go on to another question! You would probably express surprise (!) and say something like 'Forty? I'm sure you don't mean that!' The German teenager would then have a chance to correct the previous answer: 'No, I mean fourteen'. This is what happens in natural conversation, and although your teacher has to ask you a particular number of questions, he or she will be trying to make this part of the test as natural as possible. Try to be as natural as you can, too!

The conversation is not a cross-examination! The idea is not to probe into your secrets, but simply to assess your ability to speak German. The conversation in German will be based on the material you have covered throughout your course. The oral examination is the equivalent of the coursework element in other subjects, so the questions and topic areas covered will sample what you have been doing all along in your oral work in class and at home. Your teacher will not be trying to 'trick' you or catch you out.

Given that you now know that every effort is made to help you, make sure you help yourself by being prepared to **say** something!

The **topics** you are likely to be asked about will include:

- yourself, your home and family
- your home town, village or area
- your school
- your interests and hobbies
- your leisure activities
- your daily routines
- your holidays
- your visits abroad
- your friends.

❝ Be prepared to talk ❞

A conversation is a **two-way** affair, and you need to play your part. You will not be expected to give long, elaborate answers at this level, but you will be expected to say more than *ja* and *nein*! If, for instance, you are asked *Siehst du gern fern?*, then don't just say *ja* or *nein*, but volunteer some other information, e.g. *Mein Lieblingsprogramm ist East-Enders*. Most of the questions asked will in fact give you an opportunity to say a few words or a couple of sentences. Remember, this part of the examination assesses your ability to speak German, so **you must speak!**

The questions you will be asked are questions with which you should be familiar, but if there is a question you do not understand, don't panic. Ask the teacher to repeat the question:– *Wie bitte?* or *Noch einmal bitte*. Make sure you have a few phrases 'up your sleeve' to help you out of such difficulties.

**THE TEST – HIGHER
LEVEL**

The main difference between the Basic Level and Higher Level conversation is that you are expected to **say more**! The initiative lies with you much more than it does with the examiner. The questions asked will require more than a brief response. Your teacher, as the examiner, will ask questions of a more open nature, giving you a cue to talk on a particular topic. An example could be something like 'You say you are very interested in sport. Can you tell me more?' This question form is a clear invitation to you to say what you can, so at this level you must be prepared to string a number of sentences together on a variety of themes.

Another important feature will be the actual language you use. Communication will still be very important, but this is the chance for you to really 'show off' what you know. You should be looking to make your answers **interesting** in terms of content, vocabulary, idiom, structure. Remember, if you don't use it, you cannot be awarded credit for knowing it!

As stated earlier, the topic areas covered will be much the same as for Basic Level (see above), with the addition of **work and future plans**. This topic area is likely to cover:

- your immediate plans for school, e.g. leaving, staying on into sixth form
- future studies, subjects, interests – give reasons for your choice
- part-time job, summer job – what you will do with the money you earn
- employment and career interests – give reasons
- where you would like to work or live – give reasons.

The conversation will cover a range of these topics and will usually follow a fairly logical sequence. You are likely to be asked two or three questions on one topic area before going on to a different one.

APPROACHING THE TEST

❝ Choose what interests you ❞

Students have often claimed that it is not possible to revise or prepare for an oral examination, but that simply is not true.

Once you have checked the **topic areas**, you can work out small groups of questions for each topic area and make sure that you can answer them. The **vocabulary** and **language tasks** in Chapter 3 will help you to do so. See also the examples given in the next section.

The first thing to do is pick out areas of **special interest** to you. After all, if you are interested in something, you are likely to have something to say! You should then prepare these topics thoroughly. The conversation will not be very long, but it's a good idea to string together some notes and sentences so that you can talk confidently on the individual subjects for about a minute. In the examination you will not be allowed to give a pre-learnt talk, but you will be expected to volunteer ideas and information.

Next you should concentrate on the **other possible themes** which are perhaps of less interest to you. Remember, though, that you should aim to be interesting yourself in the examination, so pretend! Think of ways to convey enthusiasm, e.g. by using particular items of vocabulary or idioms. I remember planning my own Advanced Level French oral as a student: I had recently spent a very enjoyable term at a school in Germany and it seemed a good idea to talk about it. I began by mentioning the channel crossing, but instead of just saying the French equivalent of 'the journey was good', I said enthusiastically, 'the crossing was superb!' The effect on the examiner was very positive. You are advised to think of similar 'tricks', so instead of *die Fahrt war gut*, say something like *die Überfahrt war wirklich toll, obwohl es ein bißchen stürmisch war.*

EXAMINATION QUESTIONS – BASIC LEVEL

Here are some examples of the kind of questions you can expect in this part of the examination. As most of these questions will be familiar to you we have not added the English equivalent. However, if you have difficulty understanding you could:

- ask a friend or relative
- look up words in the vocabulary list (Chapter 15)
- ask your teacher.

YOURSELF, YOUR HOME AND FAMILY

Wie heißt du?
Wie alt bist du?
Wann hast du Geburtstag?
Hast du Geschwister?
Wie ist dein Bruder?
Wie ist deine Schwester?

Hast du Haustiere?
Was ist dein Vater von Beruf?
Was ist deine Mutter von Beruf?
Wie ist dein Haus?
Beschreibe bitte dein Haus.

YOUR HOME TOWN, VILLAGE OR AREA

Wo wohnst du?
Wo ist Great Staughton?
Ist das eine Stadt?
Ist das ein Dorf?

Wohnst du gern in Great Staughton?
Was gibt es in Great Staughton zu sehen?
Was gibt es in Great Staughton zu tun?
Wie lange wohnst du schon in Great Staughton?

YOUR SCHOOL

Wie kommst du in die Schule?
Um wieviel Uhr kommst du in die Schule?
Wie ist deine Schule?
Was lernst du in der Schule?
Was ist dein Lieblingsfach?

Seit wann lernst du Deutsch?
Was machst du in der Pause?
Wo ißt du zu Mittag?
Was für Sport treibst du in der Schule?

YOUR INTERESTS AND HOBBIES

Was sind deine Hobbys?
Was machst du nach der Schule?
Wo machst du das?
Wie oft machst du das?

Wo spielst du Tischtennis?
Mit wem spielst du Tennis?
Ist das teuer?
Spielst du ein Instrument?

YOUR LEISURE ACTIVITIES

Was machst du in deiner Freizeit?
Siehst du gern fern?
Was siehst du gern im Fernsehen? Warum?
Was ist deine Lieblingssendung? Warum?
Was für Musik hörst du gern?
Wer ist dein Lieblingssänger?

Wo kannst du tanzen?
Was machst du am Wochenende?
Liest du auch gern?
Was liest du gern?
Bekommst du viel Taschengeld?
Was machst du mit deinem Taschengeld?

YOUR DAILY ROUTINE

Um wieviel Uhr stehst du gewöhnlich auf?
Was machst du dann?
Was ißt du zum Frühstück?
Wer vorbereitet das Frühstück bei euch?
Um wieviel Uhr verläßt du morgens das Haus?

Um wieviel Uhr ißt du abends?
Wann gehst du gewöhnlich ins Bett?
Wie hilfst du zu Hause?
Hilfst du gern zu Hause?
Um wieviel Uhr stehst du sonntags auf?

YOUR HOLIDAYS

Wohin gehst du auf Urlaub?
Mit wem gehst du auf Urlaub?
Wie lange bleibst du dort?
Wie fährst du dorthin?
Fliegst du gern?
Gefällt dir Blackpool? Warum (nicht)?

Was machst du gern auf Urlaub?
Was machst du abends?
Was hast du im letzten Urlaub gemacht?
Wie war dein letzter Urlaub?
Was machst du diesen Sommer?

YOUR VISITS ABROAD

Bist du nach Deutschland gefahren?
Kennst du Deutschland?
Wo warst du?
Wann war das?
Bist du in einem Hotel geblieben?
Was hat dir (nicht so) gut gefallen?
Bist du ins Ausland gefahren?
War das mit einem Austausch?
Möchtest du in Deutschland wohnen? Warum (nicht)?
Warum gefällt dir Frankreich?

YOUR FRIENDS

Wie heißt dein bester Freund/deine beste Freundin?
Wie ist er/sie?
Wo wohnt er/sie?
Warum hast du ihn/sie gern?
Was macht ihr gern zusammen?

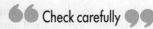 Check carefully   As you can see, there is a good deal of overlap in terms of the kinds of question to expect, but your teacher will use a mixture. There are many other possible questions which could be asked. Make sure you check what you cover during your lessons and listen carefully to what your teacher says about preparation for this section of the examination. In some cases there will be special information about a final selection of topics to be covered shortly before the examination itself.

In some cases a visual stimulus may be used as a basis for conversation. You will be asked a few simple questions and then more general conversation will follow. At the moment this applies only to SEG at this level, but it is a possible future development. The SEG specimen question for this exercise is included here.

Pre-set questions on a written or visual stimulus
Sample material and questions:

GRUGA essen PARK

Gruga · Vogelpark
Botanischer Garten

Külshammerweg 32 · 4300 Essen 1 · Telefon (0201) 88–7807

EINTRITTSPREISE

Tageskarten:		März – Oktober	November – Februar
● Erwachsene		DM 3,00	DM 1,00
● Erwachsene ab 19.00 Uhr (April – September)		DM 1,50	
● Kinder/Jugendliche (6–17 Jahre)		DM 1,00	DM 0,50
● Kinder unter 6 Jahren in Begleitung eines Erwachsenen		frei	frei

ÖFFNUNGSZEITEN

Sommersaison
April bis Sept.: 8.00 bis 24.00 Uhr – Kassenschluß: 20.30 Uhr

Wintersaison:
Oktober bis März: 9.00 Uhr bis zum Eintritt der Dunkelheit
Kassenschluß: 16.30 Uhr

Gaststätten im Grugapark

| Grugabad | Tel. 79 39 31 | Cafeteria | Tel. 77 84 36 |
| Landhaus | Tel. 77 96 12 | Schänke am Tierhof | Tel. 78 84 04 |

Diverse Verkaufsstände im Park.

**Rollstuhl-Ausleihe an den Erste-Hilfe-Stationen:
Haupteingang Telefon 88-7888 · Rollschuhbahn Telefon 88-7889.**

1 Was kostet der Eintritt im Winter?
2 Ist der Park am Abend offen? (Bis wann?)
3 Ab wieviel Uhr (ab wann) ist der Eintritt billiger?
4 Wo kann man ein Glas Bier (oder eine Tasse Kaffee) trinken?
5 Wann (in welchem Monat) beginnt der Wintersaison?

EXAMINATION QUESTIONS –
HIGHER LEVEL

As mentioned earlier, the questions asked at Higher Level will be of a much more open nature – an invitation to talk, to express your ideas and opinions. The questions will fall into two main categories:

■ The questions may simply follow up something you have already mentioned, e.g. *Du hast gesagt, du hast London (nicht) gern. Warum eigentlich (nicht)?*
■ The questions may pick up something quite new, e.g. *Welche Pläne hast du für die Zukunft?*

In both examples, you have been given the 'green light', so take the opportunity!

The following are further examples of the kind of question to expect:

Du hast viele Geschwister. Wie findest du das?
Beschreibe mir ein bißchen dein Haus.
Wohnst du gern in deinem Haus?
Welche Vorteile/Nachteile hat das Leben in der Stadt?
Warum möchtest du auf dem Lande wohnen?
Warum gefällt dir die Schule (nicht)?
Warum gefällt dir die Schuluniform (nicht)?
Was trägst du gern am Wochenende, und warum?
Was machst du gewöhnlich am Samstagabend?
Was machst du mit deinem Taschengeld?
Bist du nach Deutschland gefahren?
Wie war der Austausch?
Bist du ins Ausland gefahren?
Würdest du gern im Ausland wohnen?
Welche Länder möchtest du besuchen?
Warum bleibst du an der Schule?
Was für eine Stelle suchst du (nachher)?
Welche Ferienpläne hast du für den Sommer?

OTHER EXAMINATION QUESTIONS

In some cases, as at Basic Level, a visual stimulus may be used as a basis for conversation. Currently this applies to MEG and SEG, so if you are following their syllabus you will need special practice and training for this part of the examination. The principles will, however, be the same in that the stimuli are intended as a basis for you to show what you are able to say. The specimen tests for MEG and SEG are included below.

MEG Specimen Test

The plan printed below gives an outline of a holiday in Germany last summer.

Tell the examiner about the journey and what happened on it. You need not mention every detail of the outline on the page. You can decide whether it was you who made the trip or someone you know.

Be prepared to respond to any questions or observations the examiner might make.

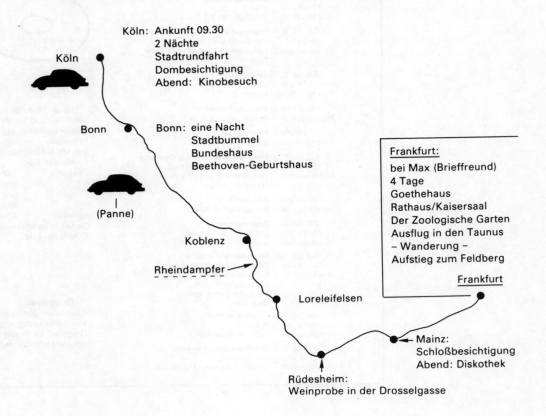

Köln: Ankunft 09.30
2 Nächte
Stadtrundfahrt
Dombesichtigung
Abend: Kinobesuch

Köln

Bonn

Bonn: eine Nacht
Stadtbummel
Bundeshaus
Beethoven-Geburtshaus

(Panne)

Koblenz

Rheindampfer

Loreleifelsen

Frankfurt:
bei Max (Brieffreund)
4 Tage
Goethehaus
Rathaus/Kaisersaal
Der Zoologische Garten
Ausflug in den Taunus
– Wanderung –
Aufstieg zum Feldberg

Frankfurt

Mainz:
Schloßbesichtigung
Abend: Diskothek

Rüdesheim:
Weinprobe in der Drosselgasse

SEG Specimen Test

Questions 1–5, which are set for General Level candidates, **must** be asked. The remainder are given as a guide to the type of question to be put to Extended Level candidates. If these actual questions are not used the examiner will substitute questions of a similar standard and type. Questions should require some manipulation of the text by the candidate, not merely the answers 'yes' or 'no'. Not all the questions will necessarily be used for each candidate.

1. Was kostet der Eintritt im Winter?
2. Ist der Park am Abend offen? (Bis wann?)
3. Ab wieviel Uhr (ab wann) ist der Eintritt billiger?
4. Wo kann man ein Glas Bier (oder eine Tasse Kaffee) trinken?
5. Wann (in welchem Monat) beginnt der Wintersaison?
6. Warum ist im Winter der Eintritt nach 16.30 Uhr nicht möglich?
7. Wo kann man Vögel sehen?
8. Wann ist der Eintritt im Sommer billiger?
9. Was kann man am 6. Juli machen?
10. Wohin würdest du gehen, wenn du Frisbee-Golf sehen möchtest?
11. Für wen kostet es nichts, in den Park zu kommen?
12. Können Kinder den Park immer besuchen?
13. Was für andere Möglichkeiten gibt es im Grugapark?
14. Was verstehst du unter 'Grugabahn'?
15. Kannst du mir etwas Information über das Grugabad geben?
16. Wie fährst du am besten zum Grugapark (, wenn du kein Auto hast)?
17. Wo und wann kann man die Peter Weisheit Band hören?
18. Was kostet der Eintritt für einen Vierzehnjährigen?
19. Im Grugapark gibt es eine Gaststätte, die Grugabad heißt. Warum, meinst du, heißt ein Gasthaus eigentlich Gruga*bad*?

VERANSTALTUNGS
PROGRAMM
86

JULI

SA. 5. 7. 15–18 Uhr Musikpavillon	**Mit Pauken und Trompeten** Es spielt das Bundesbahn-Orchester und die Blizza-Harmonica-Gang
SO. 6.7. 15–18 Uhr Musikpavillon	**Tanznachmittag** mit der Fred Sellman Big Band
FR. 11. 7. 9–18 Uhr Tummelwiese	**Frisbee-Golf** Europameisterschaft Veranstalter: Deutscher Frisbee Sport-Flugscheiben Verband
SA. 12. 7. 15–18 Uhr Musikpavillon	**Ein guter Sound** gespielt von der Gruppe Musik-Transfer
18.30 Uhr Musikpavillon	**Abendgottesdienst** Weigle-Haus · Essen
9–18 Uhr Tummelwiese	**Frisbee-Golf** Europameisterschaft
SO. 13. 7. 15–18 Uhr Musikpavillon	**Melodien aus Oper und Operette** Aufführung mit dem Theater und dem Philharmonischen Orchester Essen
9–18 Uhr Tummelwiese	**Frisbee-Golf** Europameisterschaft
SA. 19. 7. 15–18 Uhr Musikpavillon	**Zigeunerklänge** mit dem „Trio Farfarello" und den „Les Gitanes Swing"
SO. 20. 7. 15–18 Uhr Musikpavillon	**Musizierende Jugend** Bunter Nachmittag mit dem Schönebecker Jugendblas-Orchester und dem 1. Essener Akkordeon-Orchester
Sa. 26. 7. 15–18 Uhr Musikpavillon	**... noch einmal** mit der Peter Weisheit Band
SO. 27. 7. 15–18 Uhr Musikpavillon	**Mit Musik geht's besser** Unterhaltung mit den Siegtaler Musikanten

Park und Verwaltung sind mit Straßenbahn, Bus und U-Bahn zu erreichen.
Straßenbahnlinie: 111
Haltestelle: Gruga
Von Mai bis Oktober, täglich im 10-Minuten-Takt.
Buslinien: 142 und 152 aus Richtung Kettwig
149 aus Richtung Wuppertal
Haltestelle: Alfred-Brücke
Diese Busse fahren ebenfalls im 10-Minuten-Takt.

Grugabad

Räumlich in den Park einbezogen, aber für Besucher abgetrennt, liegt das Grugabad. Es ist eines der größten und schönsten Freibäder Deutschlands.

A STEP FURTHER

The German word for language is *Sprache*, which also means 'speaking'. This reminds us of the obvious fact that in a normal day we use language more for speaking than for reading or writing. Speaking is also the criterion by which people will normally judge your ability in a language. They will say 'Oh, you are learning German, are you? Go on, say something in German!' And later on, when working, a colleague may say, 'Oh, you did German at school, didn't you? Can you deal with this visitor or customer?'

So in real life it is our speaking of the language which is likely to be put to the test most often. Anyway, most of us like talking, so let us think of ways of improving our conversation skills.

First ask yourself this question. If you had a conversation with a non-English-speaking visitor, would you prefer that his English should be lively, interesting, with plenty of mistakes and a funny accent, or that he should speak slowly and laboriously but correctly? The answer is obvious. A slow conversation with long pauses is boring in the extreme, so make up your mind that this is not for you!

A German conversation should ideally take place in Germany, Austria or Switzerland with a German-speaking person. A satisfactory alternative would be a conversation with a German in this country, or with your teacher. But in the real world this is not often possible in the limited time available, so we shall have to think of other ways of practising.

If you have a good friend with whom you can work, then this will be fine, but let us think of the many times when you are having to revise on your own.

READING

A language is for speaking out loud, and your accent and fluency will not improve until you get into the habit of reading or speaking German out loud as a regular thing. If you are learning a part for a play, you know that it really only works if you say it out loud. So start by **reading** German out loud to yourself. If this embarrasses you at first, then put your elbows on the table and your hands over your ears and read it quietly.

SPEAKING

Take a topic from the list – say, 'yourself, your home and family' – and think for a few minutes of how you might talk about it to someone who doesn't know you. When you feel ready, try talking for a minute fairly fluently. Use an alarm clock or a watch if you wish, and if possible record what you say on cassette. Make it sound chatty and interesting. **Don't** make it sound as though you are reading it or as if you have learnt it off by heart. If you are not satisfied, do it again. To make it more interesting, tell a pack of lies, exaggerating your own skills, explaining how your mother is a lead singer in a pop group and your father plays in goal for West Ham.

But be careful to tell the truth in the exam. An examiner may not check up on all your family details, but if you say *die Sonne scheint* when the rain is lashing against the window, then you can't expect to score on that question!

Of course this exercise would be much better if you could turn it into a conversation. One way of getting round the problem would be to record a series of questions on cassette, leaving a gap after each question long enough for a full answer. Your teacher or German assistant might do it for you, but you could always do it yourself.

TOPICS

Use your topic lists in the following way to help you with your conversation work. Take a piece of paper for each topic and make a list of 10–15 words or phrases to remind you of what you are able to say. For example, for the topic 'yourself, your home and your family' you could write these key words:

- Name
- Wie alt?
- Wohnen?
- Mutter, Vater
- Geschwister
- Haustiere

- Haus
- Schlafzimmer
- Hobbys
- Freunde, Freundinnen
- Ferien
- Schule

PARTNERS

Do you have a dog or a cat or a baby in the house? If so, you probably talk to them quite frequently without expecting much of a response. Try talking to your dog or cat in German: *Hallo Mitzi. Wie geht es dir? Hast du Hunger? Was willst du trinken? Milch? Tee? Whisky? Oh, das geht besser, nicht wahr?* and so on. The dog or cat won't mind and at least it will give you the feeling that you are talking to someone, even if the response is limited!

EXERCISE INTO CONVERSATION

Making an exercise sound like a conversation is really a very tricky thing to do. You should, particularly if you are doing the Higher Level, be aware of the many little words and phrases that the Germans put into their speech, which make it sound like authentic German. Here is an example of how a native German might respond to the questions on the topic of 'your leisure activities', with an explanation of the idiomatic phrases used.

YOUR LEISURE ACTIVITIES

E: Was machst du in deiner Freizeit?

C: Ja *das ist schwer zu sagen. Momentan* habe ich nicht viel Freizeit. Aber ich spiele gern Fußball und ich gehe manchmal ins Kino.

E: Siehst du gern fern?

C: Ja sehr gern, wenn ich Zeit habe.

E: Was siehst du gern im Fernsehen? Warum?

C: Erstens Sport. Ich finde das sehr interessant, und dann oft Filme, weil sie oft sehr gut sind. Es ist auch billiger als im Kino!

E: Was für Musik hörst du gern?

C: Ja, meistens Popmusik, aber auch *ab und zu* Jazz oder klassische Musik.

E: Was machst du am Wochenende?

C: *Das kommt darauf an.* Wenn das Wetter schön ist, gehe ich aus. Oder ich fahre in die Stadt und treffe meine Freunde.

E: Liest du auch gern?

C: Ja, *besonders* spät am Abend, wenn ich im Bett bin.

E: Was liest du gern?

C: Na ja, *das ist verschieden.* Krimis, Science Fiction und auch die Zeitung. Und Sie? Was lesen Sie gern?

E: Ich? Oh ja, ich lese auch gern, meistens Romane. Und bekommst du viel Taschengeld?

C: Nein! Viel zu wenig. Aber ich habe auch einen Job in einem Schuhgeschäft.

E: Was machst du mit deinem Taschengeld?

C: Ich kaufe Schallplatten oder ich gehe ins Kino. Ich glaube, das ist alles.

das ist schwer zu sagen	that is hard to say
momentan	at the moment
ab und zu	now and then
das kommt darauf an	that depends
besonders	especially
das ist verschieden	that varies

All these phrases could be used in almost any conversation and they add a lot of colour and interest. Note how the candidate often went further than just an answer to the question given. He even at one point turned the tables and asked the examiner a question! This gives an excellent impression.

This conversation is of course of a very high standard, but it gives you something to aim for.

WRITING: BASIC LEVEL

GETTING STARTED

Although writing is a very important part of learning a language, it is **not a compulsory paper** at GCSE examination level. You can take just the common core (Basic Listening, Basic Reading and Basic Speaking) but the maximum grade you can then obtain is a Grade E. **If you want to get a Grade C, you must take Basic Writing.** It does not matter how well you may do in the other tests; if you do not at least **attempt** the Basic Writing test, you will not be eligible for the award of a Grade C. But don't panic, read on! You will not be penalised if you do attempt Basic Writing and don't do well, so there is nothing to lose by 'having a go'.

ESSENTIAL PRINCIPLES

REQUIREMENTS

In many cases the tasks you have to do are the kinds of things you will have done to help you with the other skills. The tasks are designed to be fairly straightforward and predictable, and Basic Writing is not intended to be any more difficult than any of the other Basic Level Tests.

As with Basic and Higher Level Speaking, **you do not have to produce perfect German in order to score full marks.** The more accurate you are, however, the more marks you will gain. **If you are aiming at Grades A and B, you must sit Basic Writing AND Higher Writing.**

The writing tasks vary somewhat between the different examining groups, and you will need to check carefully which topic areas you are expected to cover and which exercises you are required to do. There is, however, major agreement in that you may be required:

- to write **simple lists,** e.g. a shopping list
- to write **simple messages,** e.g. a note left for a friend (20–40 words)
- to write **a postcard,** e.g. to a German pen friend, possibly in reply to a postcard received by you (20–40 words).
- to **complete a given form,** e.g. an application form
- to write a **simple letter, formal** or **informal**, in response to instructions in English or to a letter in simple German (60–100 words)
- to **fill in gaps,** e.g. in a letter in German (LEAG only).

In all exercises there will be clear instructions as to what you should include, and how much you are required to write.

We will look at the different kinds of question later in the chapter, in the section 'Examination Questions'.

The answer you have to provide will generally be outlined in English. However, you may be required to write a reply to a message, postcard or letter written in German and addressed to you. It is important for you to **get practice in reading and understanding German handwriting.** Your course book will no doubt contain examples. If you have a German pen friend or contact then note how he/she forms the individual letters. Some examples are provided in the sections on Reading Comprehension in Chapters 6 and 7 (a more likely area for German handwriting to appear in) as well as in the chapters on Writing.

APPROACHING THE QUESTIONS

1 You will need to communicate the information required in such a way that the person for whom the list/message/postcard/letter is intended can understand clearly what you mean.

    Clear handwriting is also an obvious advantage! If you do notice a mistake and wish to correct it, then do so clearly and neatly. You will not get credit for anything an examiner cannot decipher!

2 You do not have to write perfect German in order to get your meaning across, but do try to be as accurate as possible.

3 You must make sure that you include all the relevant information necessary to the exercise.

4 Make sure you keep within the word limits set for the question.

5 Think carefully about what you are going to write before you write your answer. This is especially important if you have to write your answer in a limited space, e.g. on a blank postcard or notepad. There should be 'rough paper' for you to use in the examination.

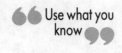

- Make notes in German, using vocabulary and expressions with which you are familiar.
- Always build on German that you know. It is a good idea to learn and remember vocabulary and grammar in a set phrase and then to use the phrase as a kind of building block. If you know that *ich möchte* means 'I would like', and that *ich möchte ein Kilo Äpfel* means 'I would like a kilo of apples', then you can go on to use *ich möchte . . .* to say what else you would like.

- Try to use interesting material wherever you can, but make sure it is relevant. Which of the following do you think is likely to create a better impression?
  — *es war gut*
  — *es war sehr gut*
  — *es war wirklich gut*
  — *es war einfach klasse/toll* (perhaps this is even the title of your course book!)
  We hope you see what we mean!

- Beware the so-called 'false friends'; that is, German words which are spelt or sound similar to English words and vice-versa, but which actually have a different meaning. Have you heard the German teacher's standard joke? 'A German tourist goes into a butcher's in England, and, getting rather fed up with waiting his turn, calls out: "When do I become a sausage?"' Ugh, but perhaps it will help you to remember the problem of become/*bekommen*.

- Although it is sometimes tempting, don't think of what you want to say in English and then try to translate it into German. Just look at what can happen. The task is to explain that you hope your friend is coming.
  — *Ich hoffe, du bist kommen(d).*   This is the sort of writing that has driven many a teacher or examiner prematurely bald!
  — *Ich hoffe, (daß) du kommst.*   This is fine.
  — *Hoffentlich kommst du.*   A fine alternative correct formulation.

Many possibilities

- There are many different ways of saying the same thing in English, and it is just the same with German (consider again the example above). You might, for instance, want to find out if there is a swimming pool nearby. It would be equally possible and equally acceptable to write:
  — *Gibt es dort in der Nähe ein Schwimmbad?*
  — *Ist dort in der Nähe ein Schwimmbad?*
  — *Habt ihr dort in der Nähe ein Schwimmbad?*
  — *Ist dort ein Schwimmbad? Ist es weit?*
  It's important, then, for you to think: 'How can I say that in German and make myself understood? What useful words and expressions do I know?'
  IF YOU DON'T KNOW IT, DON'T USE IT.

6 Make sure you check your work thoroughly. In particular, check spellings, genders, cases, verbs, and – above all else – that you have done all that is required of you. If, for example, there are five tasks, make sure that you have included them all.
  There is a comprehensive checklist in the next chapter which can be used and adapted to suit your needs.

The information provided by the examining groups will tell you which topics will be examined and what vocabulary and grammar you need to know. You will find helpful details elsewhere in the book on these subjects. It is up to you to prepare fully, so that you are not caught out by something unexpected.

You must also ensure that you get enough practice in the different exercises that may appear in the examination. Here are some suggestions which you may find practical and of benefit.

VOCABULARY

Little but often

- You cannot suddenly expect to sit down and learn 1500–2000 words. Be systematic and learn vocabulary regularly and in short bursts. 'Little but often' is a sensible approach.

- Get the vocabulary habit! 10 minutes twice a day soon builds up, but make sure you test yourself or get someone else to test you. Check spellings and try not to make the same mistakes next time.

- Try and think of some novel ways to help you to make learning items less boring.

- Set yourself realistic targets and allow yourself small rewards for the successful completion of a target.

- I have a friend who wrote out short lists which she left in prominent places, where she couldn't help seeing them: next to the mirror, by the radio, by the record-player, by the kettle, etc.
- Think of a topic area, give yourself a time limit and then see how many words you can write down in the time allowed.
- Think of a word and then see what new word comes into your head next, e.g. *Tisch, Tennis, Sommer, Sonne, Ferien, keine Schule* and so on (good fun with a friend).

You must have plenty of other ideas.

PRACTICE IN WRITING

- If you have contacts in or from Germany, Austria or Switzerland, then use them. Exchange letters and postcards, swap language, ask for help, make notes of vocabulary and expressions you think may help you.
- Go over as many specimen questions as you can. There will be many exercises in your course books similar to those which occur in the GCSE examination.
- Go over and revise exercises you have written in the past and try to do them again, only this time see if you can improve on your previous performance.
- Try to make note of any particular weaknesses which occur/have occurred regularly in your writing and try to do something about it. Ask your teacher for help if you don't understand or can't see why you often make the same mistake.

We shall now look at each type of writing task you are likely to meet.

WRITING LISTS

Writing a list is really not much more than showing that you have learnt certain items of vocabulary. Check the topic areas to be tested and learn the vocabulary! You can help yourself learn the vocabulary by actually testing yourself regularly. You can also devise your own test lists to fit in with the kind of exercise you may have to complete in this section of the examination.

The sort of list you will be required to write is likely to centre on the topic areas of **shopping** and **holidays, clothing** and **personal belongings,** though these may not be the only topics tested. Possible lists could be:

- shopping for food and drink, e.g. for a party or picnic
- shopping for presents, e.g. to take home from Germany, Austria, Switzerland
- describing the contents of a lost bag or case.

Apart from knowing the individual words, you may be required to give further information, e.g. stating an **appropriate quantity** or **amount** (for food and drink), or using **adjectives of size, colour and age,** e.g. to describe clothing.

Remember to make sure that what you include in your list makes sense for the task. For instance, if you are writing a shopping list for a picnic, it is unlikely that you would wish to take *Bratkartoffeln*! Nor is it likely that you would wish to take ten different things to drink and nothing to eat!

WRITING MESSAGES

The messages you have to write may not involve you needing to write in complete sentences – simple notes may be sufficient. Be careful, as always, to check all the instructions very carefully and cover all the tasks.

Again, refer to the topic areas tested in this section by your examining group. Some obvious possible messages/notes could include:

- leaving **instructions for a German-speaking visitor** explaining to him/her how to get to a particular place
- leaving a **telephone message**, e.g. 'Klaus rang up, he wants to go to the cinema tonight, the film is great, can you ring him at 6.30?'
- explaining **why you have gone out** and where, when you will be back, etc.
- **making arrangements** for some kind of activity, e.g. planning a trip to town or to a concert, football match, etc.

In order to be able to leave the right kind of message or note, you will need to be able to give details about:

- **directions and places:** first left, straight on, at the café etc.
  die erste Straße links, geradeaus, im Café, usw.

- **methods of transport:** on foot, by bus/train/taxi, etc.
  zu Fuß, mit dem Bus/Zug/Taxi, usw.

- **times and dates:** half past four, in the evening, on Friday, etc.
  halb fünf, am Abend, am Freitag, usw.

- **duration of time:** five minutes, half an hour, etc.
  fünf Minuten, eine halbe Stunde, usw.

- **activities of interest:** cinema, concert, theatre, swimming, etc.
  Kino, Konzert, Theater, Schwimmen, usw.

- **simple instructions/ suggestions:** Can you come to the party?
  Kannst du zur Party kommen?

The above is not intended to be a complete list, but rather to show some examples of the kind of message to expect.

WRITING POSTCARDS

As before, check all the instructions fully. You may have to write your answer on a blank postcard provided. This means you have to plan what you are going to write very carefully, and stick closely to the word limits.

As with writing a letter, there are some standard things you will be expected to know how to do:

1 state where you are writing from, and the date
2 start a postcard
3 end a postcard
4 write a German-style address.

You may not be required to show you can do all of these in any one postcard, but you should be prepared.

1 You should not write the full postal address. The standard way to state where you are writing from and the date is as follows:
— *Cambridge, den 4. Mai*
— *Marbella, den 11. August,* etc.
2 You can begin either with a greeting from wherever you are, or by greeting the person to whom you are writing, e.g.
—*Viele Grüße aus Blackpool, Frankreich,* etc.   OR
— *Lieber Bernd, Jochen, Dieter,* etc.
— *Liebe Sonja, Marianne, Inge,* etc.
You can also write *Lieber Bernd!* using the exclamation mark, but then the first word of your postcard must be written with a capital letter. Otherwise the first word of your postcard should be written with a small letter unless it is a name.
3 There are a number of different ways of ending a card. You could choose from the following:
— *viele Grüße* (but best avoided if you have begun with *Viele Grüße aus* . . .)
— *dein* (if you are male) or *deine* (if female) and your first name.
For example:
> *viele Grüße*
> *dein Brian / deine Sarah*
4 There are some important points to remember when addressing cards or letters to Germany/Austria/Switzerland:
— *Herr* becomes *Herrn* for Mr . . .
— the street is followed by the house number
— the post code *(Postleitzahl)* comes before the name of the town/village.
For example:
Herrn Rainer Hohenner
Am Glaskopf 36
3550 Marburg 1
It is a sensible idea to try to learn some addresses for possible inclusion. It could be the

address of a pen friend if you have one, or it could be an imaginary address using German-style layout. Some useful postcodes are:

6000 Frankfurt
7800 Freiburg
2000 Hamburg
5000 Köln
8000 München

EXAMINATION QUESTIONS

On the following pages you will find a variety of examples of tests for the Basic Writing section. A star against the number of the test indicates that a possible answer has been provided at the end of the tests. But do it yourself first!

1* Your exchange partner is staying with you and wants to go alone to the swimming pool on the bus and asks for directions in writing.

Write notes in German on the notepad below giving details of the number of the bus and where to catch it; how long it will take; how to get from the bus stop to the pool and any further useful information you can think of.

You need not write in complete sentences.

2 Your German visitor is arriving by train but unfortunately you cannot meet him at the station. With the help of the map, write approximately 30 words in German on how to get to your house, which is **2 Church Road**, on foot.

2 Church Road

3* You have returned to your pen friend's home after shopping to find no one in. There is a message for you which you read and which you must answer before going out again. The message, from your pen friend's mother, reads:

> John!
> bin bei meiner
> Schwester zum Kaffee einge-
> laden. Hatte vergessen, es Dir zu
> sagen. Wenn Du Hunger hast,
> nimm' Dir ein Stück Kuchen im
> Kühlschrank.
> Wenn Du ausgehst, schreib
> bitte auf, wann Du zurück-
> kommst.
> Bis später
> K. Hörner

Leave a message in German explaining to Frau Hörner that:

a) It is 4.00 pm.

b) You are going out.

c) You are going to play tennis with your English friend.

d) You will be back at 6.30 pm.

e) You have eaten a piece of the cake – thank you!

4* Imagine that you are staying with a German pen friend. You have just answered the phone and promised to give a message to your friend, who is out at present. You want to go out too, so you leave a message on the message pad.

Write a note in German saying:

who telephoned.

where he/she would like to go this evening.

when he/she will phone again.

5   You are going to stay with your German pen friend during the summer holidays.

Your pen friend has written asking for details of the time and date of your arrival in Munich and an idea of what you would like to do while you are there.

Reply on the blank postcard below by writing about 30 words in German. You need not use complete sentences. In addition to your 30 words, add, in the spaces provided, a German-style address, which may be real or invented.

6* The following postcard has been re-addressed to you in Cornwall where you are on holiday. It is from your German pen friend, who is on holiday in Germany.

Liebe Julie herzliche Grüße vom Rhein. Wir sind mit der Schule hier und waren heute in Bonn, der Hauptstadt. Interessant war eine Dampferfahrt auf dem Rhein mit Essen und Disko. Einfach Klasse! Was machst Du in den Ferien? Grüße an Deine Eltern und John. Alles Liebe Heidi

Miss
Julie Bastow
Main Street
Clacton-on-Sea
England

Write a similar postcard IN GERMAN to your pen friend.

Say you are staying at a campsite with your family. You went swimming today in an indoor pool, which was great because it is raining. Your new friend John is now at home and back at work. Send greetings to Heidi's parents and sister.

7   You are on holiday and wish to send a postcard to your pen friend's family, telling them about the place where you are staying, the weather, what you have done so far and what you are going to do in the last few days of the holiday. Write the message IN GERMAN, as they speak no English. Write about 30 words.

8* Write a letter in German, of 70–80 words, to the hotel in this advertisement, including the points below.

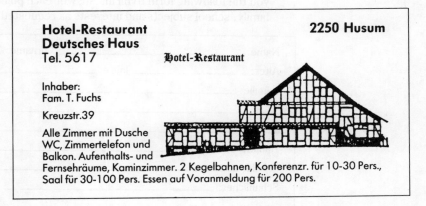

a) Give the dates when you want to stay at the hotel.

b) Say you want one double and one single room.

c) Say whether you want a bathroom or a shower.

d) Ask if the hotel is near the beach.

e) Ask if there is a disco at the hotel.

f) Ask if there is a car park.

Remember to start, date and end the letter correctly.

9 Write a letter in German of 60–70 words to your pen friend, inviting him/her to spend a fortnight with you. Make sure you include at least four of the points listed below, including one out of the last two.

Suggested dates – the best way to get to your town or village – information about your family – information about your home – what you might expect to do (e.g. swimming, walking, visits you might make).

10 Write a letter in German in reply to the letter below. You must write 60–70 words and refer to four points made in the letter. One of these must come from the second paragraph.

Lieber Fritz,
es ist schon so lange, daß ich von Dir höre. Wieso denn? Gehst Du immer noch jeden Freitag ins Kino, oder hast Du jetzt etwas anderes zu machen?
Wie geht es Deiner Freundin – Du weißt, – das Mädchen, das in Deiner Straße wohnt? Wie heißt sie? Ich hätte gern Ihre Adresse. Kannst Du sie fragen, ob sie mir schreiben möchte? Schreib mir auch über Dich selbst – und jene Reise nach Spanien, die Du planst.
Erwartungsvoll!
Dein Lumpi

11 You have sent your name and address to an agency in Germany which was advertising
for English teenagers to write to German children of the same age, and they have sent
you the following form to fill in. Answer each point IN GERMAN giving details of your
family, school subjects and interests as requested.

Name: _____ Vorname: _____

Alter: _____ Jahre: _____ Monate: _____

Familie: _____

_____

_____

Haustiere: _____

Schule: _____

Schulfächer: _____

Fremdsprachen: _____

_____

Freizeitbeschäftigung: _____

Sport: _____

Andere Interessen: _____

_____

Datum: _____ Unterschrift: _____

---

12 The following letter contains several numbered spaces. Using the list below the
letter, write out IN GERMAN the words which would apply to your own circumstances.

Norwich, _____(1)_____

Sehr geehrte Herren!

Ich möchte ____(2)____ mit ____(3)____ in Ihrem Hotel
übernachten. Können Sie uns ein _____ Zimmer mit Dusche
und   (4)

ein Doppelzimmer mit ____(5)____ für den ____(6)____
bis zum ____(7)____ reservieren.

Haben Sie ____(8)____ in Ihren Zimmern? Wir möchten am
liebsten ____(9)____ übernachten. Ich möchte auch
wissen, ob wir bei Ihnen ____(10)____ und ob ____(11)____
ein Schwimmbad ist.

Ich danke Ihnen im voraus für Ihre Bemühungen.

Hochachtungsvoll,

_____ Unterschrift

Answers

1 (today's date) _____

2 (how long?) _____

3 (who is accompanying you?) _____

4 (what kind of room?) _____

5 (washing facilities?) _____

6 (arrival date) _____

7   (departure date) _____

8   (TV) _____

9   (which floor?) _____

10 (have meals) _____

11 (near by) _____

OUTLINE ANSWERS

Below are corrected versions of student answers to the questions marked with a star.

1   Bus zum Schwimmbad – Nummer 17 vor der Kirche um 2.00, 2.30, 3.00 usw.
    Zwanzig Minuten – Haltestelle <u>Marktplatz.</u>
    Schwimmbad neben Atlantis Kino.
    Nicht vergessen – 50p und Bademütze!

3   Frau Hörner.
    Es ist 4 Uhr.
    Ich gehe aus. Ich spiele Tennis mit Martin.
    Ich komme um 18.30 zurück.
    Danke für den Kuchen! <u>Sehr</u> gut!

4   Manfred ruft an (3.00 Uhr).
    Er will heute abend zu uns kommen.
    Er ruft wieder an – gegen 6.00 Uhr.

6   Liebe Heidi, herzliche Grüße aus Devon. Ich bin auf einem Campingplatz mit der
    Familie. Heute regnet es! Wir sind also zum Hallenbad gegangen. Das war prima! John
    ist jetzt zu Hause und arbeitet wieder. Schade! Grüße an Deine Eltern und Sabine.

    Alles Liebe,
Julie

Examiner's comment

Notice how Julie has made maximum use of Heidi's card to **her**. She has quite rightly
copied some of Heidi's phrases and adapted others. She has also changed round some of
the English instructions a little so that they go into German more easily.

8   Hotel Deutsches Haus   Dundee, den 3. April
    2250 HUSUM

    Sehr geehrter Herr Fuchs!
         Wir fahren Ende Juli nach Schleswig-Holstein und möchten in Ihrem Hotel
    übernachten.
         Wir wollen am Montag dem 20. Juli ankommen und am Dienstag dem 28. Juli
    abfahren.
         Wir brauchen ein Doppelzimmer und ein Einzelzimmer, beide mit Dusche.
         Ist das Hotel weit vom Strand und gibt es eine Disko im Hotel? Und kann man am
    Hotel parken?
         Hoffentlich haben Sie noch Platz für uns!
              Hochachtungsvoll,
                   Ihre Anita Browning

Examiner's comment

Anita has worked her way through this letter very carefully. She has covered all the
required points and probably ticked them off on the question paper when she had dealt with
them. The beginning and ending are good, the letter is nicely divided into paragraphs and
she has sensibly kept her sentences short. The meaning is therefore totally clear.

TESTS WITH STUDENT ANSWERS

Here you will find three further examples of tests for the Basic Writing sections, which have been done by a candidate. An examiner has marked them and has added comments.

Your German friend is on holiday and has sent you this postcard.

TEST ONE

Grüße aus den Alpen! Viel Schnee
Wetter schön. Jeden Tag
Skilaufen. Abends sitzen wir
vorm großen Kamin und
spielen Karten.

Alles Gute zum Neuen Jahr!
Dein Karl.

You have also been away for Christmas, but where you are staying, the weather is cold and wet, you go into town every day and you go to the cinema or watch TV in the evenings. You should write about 30 words.

STUDENT ANSWER

Grüße aus Bridlington!
Es ist kalt (heir) und
es regnet. Ich gehe
in die Stadt
(jede Tag) und (im Abend)
(ich gehe) (in den Kino)
oder (ich sehe das)
(Fernsehen).
     Dein Michael

66 Excellent start! 99

66 'hier', otherwise a very good sentence. Keep it short! 99

66 'jeden Tag' (most 'time phrases' are in the Accusative) and this phrase should come before 'in die Stadt'. Remember: TIME MANNER, PLACE 99

66 Should be '*am* Abend' 99

66 'gehe ich': the verb must be the second idea 99

66 'Kino' is neuter, so it should be '*ins* Kino' 99

66 'ich sehe fern' is the best phrase 99

66 Excellent! 99

66 As you see, quite a few small mistakes, but you have answered all the points required, have made yourself totally clear, and have a very good start and end to the card. This would be given a high mark. Well done! 99

TEST TWO   You and your German friend are arranging a picnic for some friends.

Make a list in German of ten things for your German friend to buy. You could include items for making sandwiches, drinks, cakes, fruit and anything else you think suitable.

STUDENT ANSWER

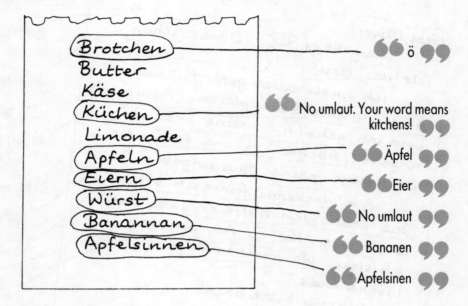

Brotchen ———————————————— 66 ö 99

Butter

Käse

Küchen ———————————— 66 No umlaut. Your word means kitchens! 99

Limonade

Apfeln ——————————— 66 Äpfel 99

Eiern ———————————— 66 Eier 99

Würst ———————————— 66 No umlaut 99

Banannan ——————————— 66 Bananen 99

Apfelsinnen ——————————— 66 Apfelsinen 99

66 An excellent list of which a dietician would approve! It would provide a well-balanced meal! 99

66 As you can see, some spelling mistakes in common words (often umlauts) but the meaning is totally clear. 99

TEST THREE   Write a letter to your German pen friend including the following points. Write about 60 words.

i)   Start the letter with the date and a suitable greeting.

ii) Thank him/her for his/her letter.

iii) Tell him/her what your hobbies are.

iv) Tell him/her what you normally do in the evenings.

v)   Say what you are going to do at the weekend.

vi) Ask what he/she does at weekends.

vii) Ask him/her to write to you soon.

viii) Sign off your letter with a suitable ending.

STUDENT ANSWER

Birmingham der 8. Mai — den (accusative)

Liebe Oliver! — Lieber (he's a boy)

Wie geht es dir? Danke schon — Dir and Dein etc. must have a capital in a letter

für das Brief. — schön (schon means already)

Ich spiele auch gern Fußball. — den (Brief is masculine)

Auch ich höre Schallplatten (Popmusik) — { Ich höre *auch* (verb second) / Auch höre ich

und ich gehe mit meine Freunde — meinen Freunden (dat. plural)

angeln. Abends ich sehe fern oder — word order (verb second)

ich mache meine Hausaufgaben. — Wochenende

Am Wochende fahre ich oft in — *die* Stadt

das Stadt. Ich treffe Freunde und — Kaffee

wir trinken Kaffe. Am Sonntag — Dreadful! (schlafe ich)

ich sleep. Was machen Du am — machst

Wochenende?

Schreib bitte bald.

Dein

Malcolm

Although at first sight there appear to be a lot of mistakes in this letter, there is also much to commend.

a) The ticks down the side indicate that every point has been adequately dealt with.

b) Communication is fine. Everything is easily understood.

c) The letter is well set out. The beginning and the end are good although there are errors.

d) There are some good phrases, e.g. *Wie geht es Dir?, Ich spiele auch gern Fußball, Ich höre Schallplatten, Ich mache meine Hausaufgaben, Ich treffe Freunde, abends, am Sonntag.*

However, there are errors which could have been avoided:

a) three spelling mistakes:– *schon, Wochende* (spelt correctly later on!) and *Kaffe*.

b) *ich sleep* is unforgivable and creates a very poor impression. If you cannot remember the correct word, think of something else to say. You did not *have* to say anything about sleeping. This is an *unforced error*!

c) There are errors of word order, case endings, gender and verb endings. Clearly these areas need revision.

In general terms this is a good piece of work at basic level, but would be inadequate for a high mark at higher level.

You will find further practical suggestions for improving your written German at the end of the next chapter.

WRITING: HIGHER LEVEL

REQUIREMENTS

APPROACHING THE EXAMINATION

IN THE EXAMINATION

EXAMINATION QUESTIONS

TEST WITH STUDENT ANSWER

A STEP FURTHER

GETTING STARTED

At Higher Level the examining groups will require you to write two pieces, usually a letter for one piece and a report, a narrative or an account for the other. In some cases you have a choice, e.g. to write an informal **or** a formal letter, but in others you will find that the questions are compulsory, with no choice. You will be required to write between 200 and 250 words in all.

ESSENTIAL PRINCIPLES

REQUIREMENTS

Find out exactly what your examining group requires:

- How much time is allowed?
- How many words are you expected to write?
- What kind of writing do you have to produce?
- How many pieces will you have to write?
- Is there a choice?
- What questions are you best at, if there is a choice?

MARK SCHEMES/CRITERIA FOR ASSESSMENT

At Higher Level the examining groups seek to reward answers by marking positively across three main areas. In some cases the emphasis is slightly different, and the three areas listed below are sometimes merged to form just two areas. Find out exactly what your examining group is doing! The three main areas are:

1 Communication
2 Accuracy
3 Quality of expression

It is worth considering these aspects in more detail.

1 Communication

This refers to the extent to which the relevant information is conveyed to the reader. Do you cover all the tasks and make yourself understood?

2 Accuracy

This refers to the extent to which grammatical accuracy helps to convey the relevant information. Do you just manage to get the message across, or are you able to get the message across clearly in largely correct German?

3 Quality of expression

This refers to the extent to which the language you use helps to make your writing interesting and appropriate to the task. Do you use a variety of vocabulary, idioms, tenses, grammatical structures? Does your writing show coherence as a whole?

APPROACHING THE EXAMINATION

- Check the topic areas to be tested in Higher Writing.
- Learn the vocabulary and structures required.
- Study as many specimen papers and past examination papers as possible.
- Devise a checklist which suits you, to help you to check your work for accuracy/ mistakes before and during the examination.
- Write as many practice essays/letters as you can before the examination. Work to the times allowed in the examination and use your checklist.

DEVISING A CHECKLIST

It is important that the **checklist** you adopt is simple but thorough, and also suits you. Outlined below is an example checklist for you to consider.

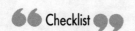 Checklist

1 Have you answered the question including all the relevant information?
2 Have you kept within the word limits?
3 Have you checked your work for accuracy?

Verbs

- Do subjects and verbs agree in number?
  der Mann kam ✓ *der Mann kamen* ✗

- Have you chosen the right form of the verb?
  die Frau sagte ✓ *die Frau sagtest* ✗

- Have you chosen the right auxiliary verb (*haben* or *sein*) with the perfect and pluperfect tense?
  ich bin nach Bonn gefahren   ich habe nach Bonn gefahren
- Have you chosen the right tense?
  als ich in die Schule ging ✓ *als ich in die Schule gehe* ✗

Genders

- Do articles agree with the nouns in number and gender? (It is surprising how often very common words are used with the wrong gender.)
  die Bücher ✓ *das Bücher* ✗
  das Mädchen ✓ *die Mädchen* ✗
- Do pronouns agree with the nouns they replace in number and gender?
  der Mann – er
  die Frau – sie
  das Buch – es

Adjectives

- Do adjectives have the right endings?

Cases

- Are all subjects in the nominative case?
- Are all direct objects in the accusative case?
- Are all indirect objects in the dative case?
- Have you chosen the right case after prepositions?
  Remember there are four main groups of prepositions:
  — those always followed by the accusative
  — those always followed by the dative
  — those followed by the accusative OR dative:
    'motion towards' + accusative
    'no motion towards' + dative
  — those always followed by the genitive.

Word Order

Have you chosen the correct word order?

- Adverbs: Time/Manner/Place (TMP)
- Nouns: Subject/Verb/Indirect Object/Direct Object
- Pronouns: Direct Object/Indirect Object
  Pronouns always come before nouns
- Inversion of verb + subject, e.g. after *dann, plötzlich*
- Verbs at end of subordinate and relative clauses, e.g. *das Wohnzimmer, wo wir jeden Abend sitzen*, . . .
- Past participles at end of clause, e.g. *Ich habe die Zeitung noch nicht gelesen.*
- Position of infinitives, e.g. *Er muß morgen früh in die Arbeit gehen.*

Spellings

- Do your nouns begin with a capital letter?
- Have you used correct plural forms?
  (It is surprising how many students do not know that the correct plural of *Mann* is *Männer*!)
- have you used umlauts where necessary?
- have you used ß where necessary?

For more information see Chapter 13, which deals with grammar.

IN THE EXAMINATION

It is helpful to have a plan of action for the things to do once you have been told that you may start the examination. Your teacher will certainly have discussed the importance of this, but here again are some useful reminders and suggestions that are worth considering.

1   Make a quick note of any memory aids or checklists you may wish to refer to. These may be in the form of mnemonics, e.g. VZ BANS GAME (initial letters of prepositions always followed by the dative case), or tables, e.g.
    Nom. *der/die/das*
    Acc. *den/die/das*
    Dat. *dem/der/dem*
    Gen. *des/der/des*

2   Read the instructions on the question paper carefully, and make a sensible choice (where appropriate) from the questions available.

3   Plan what you are going to write before you launch into the essay proper. Make a note of key vocabulary and expressions to be included.

4   Allow enough time for each question.

5   Allow enough time to re-read and check your work.

6   Write clearly and legibly. A well-presented script creates a favourable impression on examiners and is easier for them to mark.

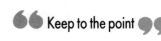 **Keep to the point**

7   Make sure that what you write is relevant to the question. Reproducing material learnt by heart, however correct, will lose you marks if it is not relevant to the question.

8   Only use German that you know. Don't plan an essay in English and then try to translate it into German. That's a recipe for disaster! Draw on the vocabulary, idioms, phrases and constructions that you are familiar with. On the other hand, it is important to 'show off' what you do know. The examiner can only award marks for what you have written, so make sure you reveal as full a range of your knowledge as you possibly can, i.e. a range of vocabulary, idiom, construction, etc.

9   Check that you have answered all aspects of the question.

10 Check that you have kept within the word limits.

11 Last but by no means least:
    CHECK YOUR WORK CAREFULLY FOR ACCURACY – use your checklist (see Chapter 14)!

EXAMINATION QUESTIONS

Here we provide a variety of examples of tests for the Higher Writing Examinations. A star against the number of the item indicates that a corrected version of a pupil's answer has been provided at the end of the tests. But attempt the questions yourself first!

WRITING LETTERS   All the examining groups include letter-writing at Higher Level. In some cases it is an optional element (e.g. for ULEAC) and in other cases you will have a choice between writing an informal letter, probably to a pen friend, or a formal letter, perhaps to a hotel manager.

Whatever letter you have to write, it is important to make sure that you include all the information required, so the first step is to establish just what tasks or areas you have to cover. Consider the following examples, and try to work out what you need to include in your letter before reading our suggestions.

EXAMPLE 1

Write a letter telling your pen friend about a holiday you have just spent with your uncle and aunt.

Say how you spent the fortnight there. Ask him/her questions about his/her holidays. Finish by inviting him/her to stay with you next summer.

Hints for Example 1

Here you would need to include:

- where you went
- who you went with
- what you did
- ask your pen friend about his/her holidays
- invite him/her to stay with you next summer.

Remember to try and make your letter interesting; perhaps mention something strange that happened, an interesting visit, a friend you made.

EXAMPLE 2

Write a formal letter to an Austrian hotel where you and your friend want to stay in August.

You may wish to say why you have chosen the hotel, what you require in terms of rooms or ask about activities which interest you and excursions which are available.

Hints for Example 2

Here you would need to mention:

- how many people you are
- when exactly you would like to stay at the hotel
- your reasons for choosing the hotel
- details of the rooms you require
- and enquire about activities and excursions.

Other questions involving letter-writing will allow you greater scope to be creative. Always look for ways of making your letter a little special by being imaginative.

This letter provides a loose framework with plenty of possibilities for a lively response.

EXAMPLE 3*

During your exchange visit in Germany you spent a day with your pen friend's mother at her place of work. She is a nurse at a local hospital. Write a letter to your pen friend's sister, who lives in Bonn. Describe your day there, how you were allowed to help, what sort of people you met and what sort of illnesses they had.

You must write about 100 words IN GERMAN. Credit will be given for variety of vocabulary and expressions, but irrelevant material will earn no marks.

Other letter-writing tasks will be in response to a letter you have received. Here are two examples – one informal, one formal. Again you will need to make sure that you include all the relevant information in your reply.

EXAMPLE 4

You have received this letter from your pen friend in Germany. Write a suitable reply IN GERMAN answering the questions and adding any information you may feel is necessary, using about 100 words.

Fulda, den 10. Juni

Lieber Michael,

vielen Dank für den letzten Brief und für die Einladung. Ich glaube, alles klappt. Du kommst am 28. Juli zu uns hier in Fulda und dann fahren wir im August nach Manchester zusammen.

Schreib uns bitte die Flugnummer und wohin Du fliegst – die ganze Familie möchte da sein, wenn Du ankommst!

Fliegst Du gern? Ich fahre lieber mit dem Zug. Weißt Du schon jetzt, was Du während Deines Aufenthaltes machen möchtest? Wir haben ja genug Zeit, alles im voraus zu planen, wenn Du uns die Pläne in Deinem nächsten Brief schreiben könntest.

Wir freuen uns sehr auf Deinen Besuch.

Bis bald,
Tschüß
Gerd

P.S. Wie war das Wochenende in Yorkshire?

Hints for Example 4

Here you could:

- thank Gerd for his letter
- say you are pleased that everything is going to work out
- give details of your flight number and where you are flying to
- say whether you like flying, travelling by train
- say what you would like to do in Germany
- mention anything else of interest or importance.

This formal letter is asking you for more information in order to establish whether the bag you have lost has been found in the Youth Hostel. Read the letter carefully to see exactly what you need to include in your reply.

EXAMPLE 5

You receive this letter from the Youth Hostel in reply to your earlier letter. Write a suitable reply IN GERMAN in about 100 words, making sure you include the relevant information, to get a more helpful reply from the hostel.

Stuttgart, den 8. Juni 1985.

Sehr geehrter Herr Wilson,

Ich habe Ihren Brief gestern erhalten und bin jetzt in der Lage, folgendes zu schreiben.

"Blaue Adidas" Sporttaschen haben wir zur Zeit zehn in unserem Fundbüro. Sieben darunter enthalten Sportsachen bzw. Trainingsanzüge, Hemden, kurze Hosen, Socken, Sportschuhe u.a.

Können Sie uns bitte Ihre eignen Sachen genauer beschreiben: nur dann können wir feststellen, ob wir Ihre Tasche hier haben oder nicht. Wir brauchen bitte eine Liste von allem, was in der Tasche steckte und auch einen kurzen Bericht, in dem Sie uns schreiben, wo Sie Ihrer Meinung nach die Tasche haben liegen lassen.

   Mit freundlichen Grüßen,

                                        M. Deutz
                                        Herbergsvater
                                        Jugendherberge
                                        Arltgasse 7
                                        Stuttgart.

Hints for Example 5

The key to what you need to write is indicated in the final paragraph of the letter. The Youth Hostel warden needs more detailed information about the contents of the bag and where you think you left it. If you want your bag back, then make sure you supply the necessary information!

REPORTS, NARRATIVES, ACCOUNTS

All the examining groups include at least one of these activities. The stimulus may be in the form of an outline presented in English or a visual stimulus, such as a series of pictures. In either case you should have ample opportunity to write an interesting piece. As with letter-writing, however, you must make sure that you include the necessary details and that your answer is a genuine response to the question.

These two examples offer considerable freedom, but use your words wisely – don't waste space and words unnecessarily, stick to the point!

Choose **one** of the two topics below and write about 150 words in German on the writing paper provided.

EXAMPLE 6*

You are spending a fortnight abroad as a guest of a German-speaking family.

You are interested in journalism as a career and you decide to write a piece for the local newspaper editor giving your impressions of the area and the way of life there.

EXAMPLE 7

You have recently returned to England after spending a holiday in Germany. Whilst abroad you were a witness to an accident.

The German police have written to you asking for your report on what happened. Write your account.

....

This example is much more specific, but you should have plenty to say about your home town!

EXAMPLE 8

You are staying with your German pen friend, who asks you to write an article for the school newspaper which is produced by him and his friends. He wants you to describe your home town or region, and he wants you to make it sound lively and interesting enough to attract a large group of applicants for next year's exchange visit. Write about 100 words IN GERMAN, including your own suggestion for a title.

Hint for Example 8

Remember to make your account appealing to people of your own age.

Visual stimuli always give you ideas, but plan what you are going to write carefully. Think about the most important aspects of each picture and try to cover each one equally. If you write 60 words about the first picture your narrative will lack balance. Do not waste words with over-elaborate descriptions such as *an einem schönen aber kühlen Sommertag . . .*, but do set the scene.

EXAMPLE 9

Imagine that you are any one of the characters portrayed in the story below. Tell the story, in the past, using about 100 words IN GERMAN.

EXAMPLE 10

Your pen friend asks you to describe the best event of your holidays. Instead you write about the event you would rather forget. Write your account IN GERMAN and base it on the pictures provided below. You should write about 100 words, and we have on this occasion made no suggestion as to how you should tackle it. However, try to remember the advice given in previous examples.

OUTLINE ANSWERS   Here are corrected versions of students' answers to the starred questions.

3

Krefeld, den 8. April

Liebe Anke!

Gestern war ein sehr interessanter Tag für mich. Ich ging mit Deiner Mutter zum Krankenhaus und war den ganzen Tag da.

Deine Mutter arbeitet jetzt im Kinderkrankenzimmer. Die Jungen und Mädchen sind von drei bis zehn Jahre alt. Die meisten haben Operationen gehabt, aber sie sind nicht mehr im Bett.

Ich habe mit ihnen gespielt. Wir haben Karten gespielt und wir haben gebastelt. Ein Junge plauderte die ganze Zeit, aber ich habe nicht viel verstanden. Er kommt aus der Türkei.

Nach dem Mittagessen haben die Kinder geschlafen und ich habe mein Buch gelesen. Dann habe ich einen kleinen Spaziergang mit zwei Mädchen gemacht. Sie waren sehr nett.

Am Abend war ich sehr müde. Ich möchte auch Krankenschwester werden, aber die Arbeit ist schwer.

Herzliche Grüße,

Deine Ruth

Examiner's comments

At first this question might seem a bit daunting. You might well say when faced with the instruction 'describe what sort of illnesses they had' that you don't know anything about serious illnesses in German. You may also feel that your vocabulary for the hospital is woefully inadequate.

But Ruth has successfully managed to avoid all these difficulties by sticking to the German that she knows, and using it in simple and accurate sentences.

6   Hallo! Ich bin David Bennett und ich komme aus Exeter in Südwestengland. Ich verbringe zwei Wochen hier in Detmold bei Jürgen meinem Brieffreund.

Es gefällt mir sehr gut hier. Das Wetter ist etwas wärmer hier als in England und wir sind fast die ganze Zeit im Freien.

Wir sind einmal zum Hermannsdenkmal gewandert und das war sehr interessant. Es ist so groß! Und der Wald ist wirklich schön – so ruhig und kühl. Man kann so lange wandern, ohne andere Leute zu sehen. Am Trimm-dich-Pfad haben wir viel Spaß gehabt. Das haben wir nicht so oft bei uns. Ich bin nicht so fit wie ich dachte!

Das Freibad in der Stadt finde ich auch toll. Das Wasser ist schön warm und die Wellen sind sehr gut!

Es gefällt mir auch, durch die Stadt zu bummeln. Die Geschäfte in der Fußgänger-zone sind erstklassig. Aber wo sind die neuesten Schlager? Ich finde sie nicht.

Schon zweimal haben wir Kaffee und Kuchen gehabt. Das ist aber fantastisch! Und so viel Schlagsahne! Ich darf aber nicht so viel essen! Sonst schimpft meine Mutter, wenn ich nächste Woche wieder zu Hause bin!

Examiner's comments

The candidate has made a really good job of this. The subject clearly suited him and gave him the opportunity to write about a part of Germany that he has visited. Notice that several of his sentences end with an exclamation mark and some even contain no verb. This gives a lively tone to the writing and is not at all difficult to do. He has also put in a question. This too is an excellent idea.

As with other candidates he too has kept his German simple and sentences short. If you ever get in a tangle with a sentence, split it into two or more. If it is difficult for you to write then it will be difficult for others to read! And that defeats the object of the exercise.

TEST WITH
STUDENT ANSWER

Here is a model question for the Higher Level Writing Test which has been answered by a student. It has been marked by an examiner who has added comments.

On a trip to Germany you made brief notes about your activities on a map of the town you visited. Using the map and the notes, write a full account of your visit for your school magazine. You must write about 100 words IN GERMAN. Credit will be given for variety of vocabulary and expressions, but irrelevant material will earn no marks.

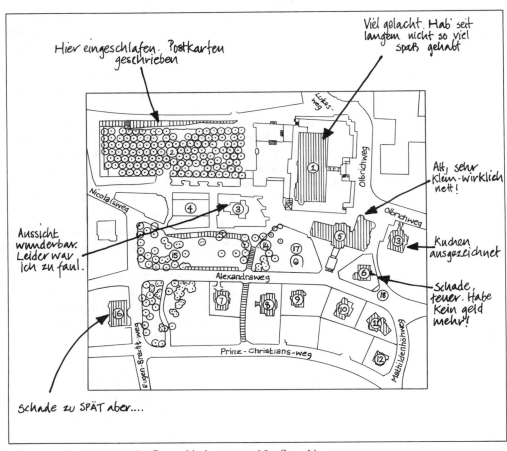

Hier eingeschlafen. Postkarten geschrieben

Viel gelacht. Hab' seit langem nicht so viel spaß gehabt

Alt, sehr Klein - wirklich nett!

Kuchen ausgezeichnet

Schade, teuer. Habe Kein geld mehr!

Aussicht wunderbar. Leider war ich zu faul.

Schade zu SPÄT aber....

1	Stadttheater	5	Peterskirche	16	Sternkino
2	Jugendherberge	6	Disko		
3	Fernsehturm	13	Café-Konditorei		

STUDENT'S ANSWER

Dieses (neuter)

bin gefahren

meinen (accusative)

nach for place names

Dieses Jahr habe ich zu Detmold gefahren um mein Freund Stefan zu besuchen. In der Stadt gibt es viel zu sehen.

very good sentence

excellent sentence

word order

Am Dienstag wir haben die Peterskirche gesehen. Sie ist alt und sehr klein aber wirklich nett. Dann haben wir ausgezeichnete Kuchen im Café-Konditorei gegessen und Kaffee getrunken. Am Abend wir waren im Stadttheater. Das Spiel war modern und sehr lustig. Ich habe nicht viel verstanden aber wir haben viel gelacht. Ich habe seit lange nicht so viel Spaß gehabt.

word order

Stück

can't copy!

wollte (past tense

good

Am Donnerstag war es sehr warm. Stefan will den Fernsehturm besteigen, aber leider war ich zu faul. Die Aussicht vonoben ist wunderbar, (sagt Stefan). Ich habe Postkarten geschrieben und habe eingeschlafen.

Detmold ist sehr schön! Kommt nächstes Jahr mit!

bin

excellent ending

two words

EXAMINER'S COMMENTS

In spite of a number of mistakes this is a reasonable piece of work at Higher Level. You have clearly studied the question very carefully before writing, and you have made full use of the German written on the town plan (in spite of the fact that you copied one word wrongly!). You have also included a variety of vocabulary and expressions (as requested) and all your material was relevant (also as requested).

Your main errors were in the fields of word order, verbs with *sein* and case endings. Otherwise your work is fairly accurate and would achieve a creditable mark at Higher Level.

WRITING: BASIC AND HIGHER A STEP FURTHER

Much of the writing work which you will need to do in preparation for the exam will be done in class and homework time and much of it will be marked and corrected by your teacher. But his or her time is limited, so it is worthwhile considering a number of ways in which you can help yourself to improve your writing skills.

ACCURACY

First of all take care that everything you write in German is spelt correctly, no matter how rough the work may be. And accuracy includes all the umlauts and capital letters. (Remember, too, that punctuation is more important in German than in English, and that there are strict rules which you should keep to.) Mistakes in **spoken** German are not so serious, but mistakes in the written part of the paper can count against you, particularly if you are hoping for a high grade.

LETTER-WRITING

In your vocabulary book or in your note book collect together all the phrases you can find which can be used in a variety of different letters. Beginnings and endings are particularly important. Look carefully at any letters which you may receive from a pen friend or which you come across in books, and learn their beginnings and endings and use them in your own work.

NOTES

If you have a like-minded friend, then try exchanging notes with him or her in German. For example:

Lieber Peter!
   Was machst Du heute abend? Ich gehe ins Kino. Kommst Du mit?
   Richard

Lieber Richard!
   Danke für Deinen Brief. Leider kann ich nicht kommen. Ich habe zu viele Hausauf-gaben. Bist Du schon fertig?
   Peter

. . . and so on. The notes need not be real. It is simply a way of enjoying using the language.

WRITING A DIARY

An excellent bit of writing practice is to write a diary in German for a few days. You don't have to write full sentences, you can say what you like, you don't have to show it to anyone. You don't even have to tell the truth. The golden rule is to keep it simple and to avoid making mistakes. Here is an example of the kind of thing you could write:

Montag, den 3. Oktober

Die Sonne scheint, aber es ist kalt. Der Winter kommt!
Ich stehe um acht Uhr auf. Zu spät! Ich trinke Tee – sehr schnell. Ich esse Weetabix – sehr schnell. Der Bus kommt.
Ich komme um neun Uhr in der Schule an.
1   *Englisch – viel Arbeit – Shakespeare gefällt mir nicht!*
2   *Mathe – Herr Morrison krank – wir arbeiten nicht viel.*
     Pause – gut, aber es regnet.
3   *Deutsch – der Rekorder is kaputt! Wir lachen.*
     Mittagessen – Wurst und Kartoffeln.
     Joghurt. Wasser. Nicht sehr gut.
4   *Erdkunde – langweilig.*
5   *Sport – es regnet nicht mehr. Fußball – sehr gut, aber ich bin schmutzig!*
Ich gehe um halb fünf nach Hause. Eine Tasse Tee. Wie sagt man 'biscuits' auf Deutsch?!
Hausaufgaben (Englisch und Deutsch)
Fernsehen – Fußball – England gegen Holland. England gewinnt 2–0!!
Ich lese und gehe ins Bett. Gute Nacht!

There! That is all very easy German, isn't it, and just the sort of thing you could do yourself.

DOUBLE TRANSLATION

This is a somewhat intellectual exercise which may appeal to those of you who are tackling Higher Level in writing.

Take a paragraph of four or five lines of fairly straightforward German from your course book or from a similar source. Translate it into English, close the book and then translate it back into German again. Check with the original. How did you get on? If you are not satisfied, do it again, at least in part.

CHAPTER 13

GRAMMAR

NOUNS AND ARTICLES

ADJECTIVES

VERBS

CASES AND PREPOSITIONS

PRONOUNS

ADVERBS

CONJUNCTIONS

INTERROGATIVES

NEGATIVES

WORD ORDER

NUMBER, QUANTITY AND TIME

GETTING STARTED

It is generally accepted that real competence in a foreign language depends on an understanding of grammar. This does not apply to our own language, where we depend more on our long experience of the language to determine the correctness of what we say and write. Some students of German at GCSE level may have lived in Germany or may have had extensive experience of the language to give them a real feeling for the sound of German. But for most of us there is no easy short cut.

Do not forget that a language grows by itself and is constantly changing. The 'rules' have been thought up to make some sort of sense out of an already established language. Much of the grammar in this chapter will be familiar to you. It is intended as a reference section, but there are areas where you are recommended to learn phrases by heart, and to use them wherever possible in a practical situation.

NOUNS AND ARTICLES

RECOGNITION

One of the most encouraging aspects of learning German is that many German nouns are instantly **recognisable** to English speaking people. If you knew no German at all you would have no difficulty in understanding *Mann, Haus, Garten, Hand, Finger, Hammer, Familie.* And even *Buch, Schule, Stuhl, Büro, Mantel* would pose few problems.

CASES

But each German noun has to be learnt with its gender and its plural form, and also in the four separate **case** forms. This sounds a daunting task, but with a little patience and application it should not prove to be too difficult.

Let us look at the familiar tables:

	Masculine	**Feminine**	**Neuter**	**Plural**
Nominative	der Mann	die Frau	das Kind	die Leute
Accusative	den Mann	die Frau	das Kind	die Leute
Genitive	des Mannes	der Frau	des Kindes	der Leute
Dative	dem Mann	der Frau	dem Kind	den Leuten

	Masculine	**Feminine**	**Neuter**	**Plural**
Nominative	ein Mann	eine Frau	ein Kind	keine Leute
Accusative	einen Mann	eine Frau	ein Kind	keine Leute
Genitive	eines Mannes	einer Frau	eines Kindes	keiner Leute
Dative	einem Mann	einer Frau	einem Kind	keinen Leuten

You will see that there are six words for 'the' and five words for 'a'. But the differences between the two tables are confined to *der – ein* and *das – ein*. Otherwise the case endings of the articles are identical in the two tables. This makes it much more manageable.

PATTERNS

The next point to remember is that the following words follow the **pattern** of *der*:

dieser	*this*	solcher	*such*
jener	*that*	welcher	*which*
jeder	*each*	mancher	*many a*

and these words follow the pattern of *ein*:

kein	*no, not a*		
mein	*my*	unser	*our*
dein	*your*	euer	*your*
sein	*his*	Ihr	*your*
ihr	*her*	ihr	*their*

GENDER

There are **some** rules of **gender** but they are only a rough guide and provide no substitute for the grim fact that all genders must be learnt with each noun. Nevertheless these guidelines should help:

Masculine nouns include:

- all seasons, months and days, e.g. *der Frühling, der Mai, der Sonntag*
- all words denoting a male being, e.g. *der Mann, der Bäcker, der Bruder*

Feminine nouns include:

- all words ending with *-ung, -heit, -ei, -schaft,* e.g. *die Zeitung, die Krankheit, die Bäckerei, die Freundschaft*
- almost all words denoting a female being, e.g. *die Frau, die Lehrerin, die Schwester*
- many words ending with *-e*, e.g. *die Straße, die Vase, die Tasse.*

Neuter nouns include:

- all nouns formed from the infinitive of verbs, e.g. *das Fischen, das Essen*
- most names of countries (but not *die Schweiz* or *die Türkei*)

- all nouns ending with *-chen* and *-lein*, e.g. *das Mädchen, das Fräulein*
- most words of foreign origin, e.g. *das Auto, das Hotel, das Taxi.*

PLURALS

Plurals are equally tricky. There are at least nine ways of forming plurals in German and the plural should be learnt with each noun as well as the gender. Experience will show you, however, that some plurals are much more common than others. For instance, *Eier* and *Kartoffeln* are more often found in the plural than in the singular, whereas the plural of *die Welt* is comparatively rare.

Here are a few hints to help you learn the plurals:

- Most nouns ending in *-er* and *-el* do not change in the plural, or they take an umlaut, e.g. *Brüder, Löffel, Messer, Onkel.*
- Most feminine nouns take *-n* or *-en*, e.g. *Vasen, Frauen, Zeitungen.*
- Most foreign words take *-s*, e.g. *Autos, Taxis, Sofas.*

WEAK MASCULINE NOUNS

These are oddities because they take an *-n* or *-en* in every case except the nominative singular, e.g.

	Singular	**Plural**
Nominative	der Mensch	die Menschen
Accusative	den Menschen	die Menschen
Genitive	des Menschen	der Menschen
Dative	dem Menschen	den Menschen

Some common weak masculine nouns are:

Junge	*boy*	Prinz	*prince*
Löwe	*lion*	Franzose	*Frenchman*
Neffe	*nephew*	Matrose	*sailor*
Schotte	*Scotsman*	Soldat	*soldier*
Bauer	*farmer*	Student	*student*
Russe	*Russian*	Polizist	*policeman*
Kunde	*customer*		

Don't forget *Herr* (sir, Mr, gentleman) which takes *-n* in the singular and *-en* in the plural.

POINTS TO REMEMBER

- Leave out the article when giving someone's profession, e.g. *Mein Vater ist Polizist –* My father is a policeman.
- Leave out the articles when using *weder . . . noch . . .*, e.g. *Ich habe weder Brot noch Käse –* I have neither bread nor cheese.
- Use the definite article in German for expressions using parts of the body or clothes, e.g.
  Er wäscht sich die Hände (*not* seine Hände).
  Er hob den Kopf (*not* seinen Kopf).
  Sie hatte den Koffer in der Hand (*not* ihren Koffer in ihrer Hand).
- Certain idomatic phrases have no article and they should be learnt by heart, e.g.

  er hat Fieber *he has a temperature*
  ich habe Kopfschmerzen *I have a headache*
  es ist schade *it is a pity*
  wir haben Besuch *we have visitors*

NOW TEST YOURSELF (1)

a) Give the genders of these words: *Onkel, Wohnung, Restaurant, Büchlein, Schneider, Engländerin, Laufen, Vater, Bluse, Mutter*
and these trickier ones: *Park, Name, Person, Balkon, Tür, Käse, Butter, Mädchen, Fräulein, Klub.*

b) Give the plural of these words: *Wagen, Bluse, Ausstellung, Café, Zimmer, Hotel, Traube, Tür, Radio, Kellner*
and these trickier ones: *Kartoffel, Nacht, Nummer, Freundin, Autobus, Schwester.*

c)   Translate into German:
- i) We have neither a cat nor a dog.
- ii) Herr Rabowski is a dentist.
- iii) The cars are not here.
- iv) I am brushing my teeth.
- v) She is my sister.
- vi) Our grandpa is at home.
- vii) These people are hungry.
- viii) Which boy can you see?
- ix) He's got toothache.
- x) Switzerland is beautiful.

Now look up the answers at the back of this chapter.

ADJECTIVES

SEPARATION

The easiest way to use an adjective in German is to separate it from the noun it describes, e.g. *Unser Haus ist groß.* In this way the adjective does not have to agree with the noun, and thus all problems are avoided. So if you are not sure of the correct endings in a sentence like *Wir haben ein großes Haus*, you could say *Wir haben ein Haus. Es ist sehr groß*, which avoids the necessity for an agreement.

AGREEMENT

However, there are times when you will have to put the adjective in front of the noun and it is then that you will have to know this table:

	Masculine	**Feminine**	**Neuter**
Nominative	{der große Baum {ein großer Baum	{die große Stadt {eine große Stadt	{das große Haus {ein großes Haus
Accusative	den großen Baum	die große Stadt	{das große Haus {ein großes Haus
Genitive	des großen Baumes	der großen Stadt	des großen Hauses
Dative	dem großen Baum	der großen Stadt	dem großen Haus

	Plural
Nominative	{die großen Häuser {meine großen Häuser
Accusative	die großen Häuser
Genitive	der großen Häuser
Dative	den großen Häusern

Assuming that you have already learnt the correct articles and genders, the adjectives should not present a great problem. Let us look at the facts from a different point of view.

- After *der, die* and *das*, and *eine* the adjective ends in *-e*. (Be careful with the exceptions in the feminine genitive and dative cases, and in the plural.)
- After *ein* the adjective ends in *-er* or *-es*.
- Otherwise the adjective ends in *-en*.

That surely reduces the problem a little.

USE AS NOUN

You can use an adjective as a noun, e.g.

der Arme   *the poor boy or poor man*
die Alte   *the old woman*
das Beste   *the best thing*
ein Deutscher   *a German*

GENDER

Notice that each gender has a characteristic letter:

Masculine = R
Feminine = E
Neuter = S

and this letter should wherever possible be apparent, eg:

der kleine Stuhl	ein kleiner Stuhl
die weiße Bluse	eine weiße Bluse
das kleine Kind	ein kleines Kind

OMISSION OF ARTICLE

In the same way, if the **article** is omitted, then the **adjective** should show the gender or number of the noun, e.g.

guter Wein
klassische Musik
frisches Obst
schöne Trauben

POINTS TO REMEMBER

- The characteristic letter (R, E and S) for the genders must only appear once in the masculine and neuter forms. So *der langer Garten* is definitely wrong and so is *das kleines Kind*!
- The adjective only agrees if it precedes the noun.
- The key letter for each gender can help you decide the gender of a word you do not know. For instance, *ein neues Geschäft* is clearly neuter.

NOW TEST YOURSELF (2)

Translate into German:

a) the red bus
b) a red bus
c) the narrow street
d) a narrow street
e) the small village
f) a small village
g) the white mountains
h) white mountains
i) cold weather
j) We have a large garden.
k) the old man
l) Our cat is stupid.
m) My poor head!

COMPARATIVES AND SUPERLATIVES

FORMATION

The comparatives and superlatives of adjectives are formed in much the same way as in shorter English adjectives. Just as 'small' becomes 'smaller' and 'smallest', so *klein* becomes *kleiner* and *kleinst*. Some adjectives take an umlaut.

Here are some common examples:

Adjective	Comparative	Superlative
klein	kleiner	kleinst
jung	jünger	jüngst
alt	älter	ältest
neu	neuer	neuest
modern	moderner	modernst
schön	schöner	schönst
groß	größer	größt

and a few irregulars:

gut	besser	best
nah	näher	nächst
hoch	höher	höchst
viel	mehr	meist

AGREEMENT

Do not forget that a comparative or a superlative must agree with the noun in the familiar way, e.g.

der kleinste Junge   *the smallest boy*
mein jüngerer Bruder   *my younger brother*
die längste Straße   *the longest street*

EXAMPLES

Look at the following examples and learn them by heart:

Ich bin größer als du.   *I am bigger than you.*
Herr Schneider ist (eben)so alt wie Herr Rabowski.   *Herr Schneider is as old as Herr Rabowski.*
Sabine ist nicht so alt wie Richard.   *Sabine is not as old as Richard.*
Das Wetter wird immer kälter.   *The weather gets colder and colder.*
Je mehr es regnet, desto lieber bleibe ich zu Hause.   *The more it rains, the more I prefer staying at home.*

POINTS TO REMEMBER

- Do not use *mehr* to translate 'more boring'. The German is *langweiliger*.
- Do not use *meist* to translate 'most interesting'. The German is *interessantest*.

NOW TEST YOURSELF (3)

Translate into German:
a) my older sister
b) the longest month
c) the most boring lesson
d) She is older than me.
e) It is not as cold as yesterday.
f) The nights are becoming shorter and shorter.
g) the best films
h) next year
i) a more modern school
j) most people

V E R B S

ENDINGS

Most people shudder at the thought of verbs and in some languages they do present serious problems. But in German, although there is much to learn, verbs are not a major stumbling block.

Every sentence contains a verb, so we must be prepared to use verbs as accurately as possible.

First of all, let us look at a straightforward present tense of a verb:

wohnen   *to live*

ich wohne *I live*	wir wohnen *we live*
du wohnst *you live*	ihr wohnt *you live*
er, sie, es wohnt *he, she, it lives*	Sie wohnen *you live*
	sie wohnen *they live*

These verb endings are the endings for the great majority of German verbs in every tense. Once you have learnt them you should never make mistakes such as *ich wohnen* or *er wohne*.

TYPES OF VERBS

German verbs can be divided into four groups:

- **Weak verbs** like *wohnen* which are regular and which form the majority of German verbs
- **Strong verbs** which are irregular and which must be learnt
- **Mixed verbs** which are also irregular and must be learnt
- **Modal verbs** which consist of six very common irregular verbs.

There is a list of strong and mixed verbs at the end of the section on verbs.

WEAK VERBS

The present tense of *wohnen* has already been given. The **imperfect** (or **simple past**) tense follows much the same pattern:

ich wohnte *I lived, I used to live*	wir wohnten
du wohntest	ihr wohntet
er, sie, es wohnte	Sie wohnten
	sie wohnten

The **perfect tense** uses the present tense of *haben* and the part participle of *wohnen*:

ich habe gewohnt *I lived, I have lived*	wir haben gewohnt
du hast gewohnt	ihr habt gewohnt
er, sie, es hat gewohnt	Sie haben gewohnt
	sie haben gewohnt

All other tenses can now be formed without further difficulty. This will be explained below.

STRONG VERBS

These verbs are irregular but often follow a common pattern, so they usually pose little problem to learners. Here is an example:

sehen   *to see*

PRESENT TENSE

ich sehe *I see, etc.*	wir sehen
du siehst	ihr seht
er, sie, es sieht	Sie sehen
	sie sehen

IMPERFECT TENSE

ich sah *I saw, etc.*	wir sahen
du sahst	ihr saht
er, sie, es sah	Sie sahen
	sie sahen

PERFECT TENSE

ich habe gesehen *I saw, have seen, etc.*	wir haben gesehen
du hast gesehen	ihr habt gesehen
er, sie, es hat gesehen	Sie haben gesehen
	sie haben gesehen

MIXED VERBS

These few verbs have characteristics of both weak and strong verbs and are listed in the verb table at the end of this section.

MODAL VERBS

There are six modal verbs and they are normally used with other verbs. They are:

| dürfen | *to be allowed to* | mögen | *to like to* | sollen | *to be supposed to* |
| könnten | *to be able to* | müssen | *to have to* | wollen | *to wish/want to* |

The **present tense** of these verbs is irregular as follows:

ich	darf	kann	mag	muß	soll	will
du	darfst	kannst	magst	mußt	sollst	willst
er, sie, es	darf	kann	mag	muß	soll	will
wir	dürfen	können	mögen	müssen	sollen	wollen
ihr	dürft	könnt	mögt	müßt	sollt	wollt
Sie	dürfen	können	mögen	müssen	sollen	wollen
sie	dürfen	können	mögen	müssen	sollen	wollen

The **imperfect tense** of these verbs is:

| ich | durfte | konnte | mochte | mußte | sollte | wollte |

In the **perfect tense** the past participle is rarely used, the infinitive is used instead, e.g.

Ich habe nicht arbeiten können.   *I have not been able to work.*

Now let us look at each tense in more detail.

THE TENSES

THE PRESENT TENSE

This tense, e.g. *ich wohne* translates 'I live', 'I do live' and 'I am living'. Be careful therefore not to think in English when writing German. If you think in terms of 'I am going to town' as *Ich bin . . .* then you are doomed to disaster. Think of 'I am going' as one idea for which the German is *Ich gehe . . .*

THE IMPERFECT TENSE (SIMPLE PAST)

This tense, e.g. *ich wohnte* means 'I lived', 'I was living' or 'I used to live'. Here again the German is simpler than the English form. This tense is used extensively in narrative German and sometimes in spoken German. However, in speech the perfect tense is more commonly used for describing events in the past.

THE PERFECT TENSE

This tense, e.g. *ich habe gewohnt* means 'I lived' or 'I have lived'. For most German verbs the perfect tense is formed with the present tense of *haben*. But some require *sein* instead (e.g. *ich bin gefahren* – I travelled) and these verbs must be learnt from the verb table. Remember that the past participle must go to the end of the sentence or clause, e.g. *Ich habe ein neues Motorrad im Park gesehen.*

THE PLUPERFECT TENSE

This translates 'I had . . .' and uses the **imperfect** tense of *haben* or *sein* with the past participle, e.g.

Ich hatte den Film schon gesehen.   *I had already seen the film.*
Er war zu Hause geblieben.   *He had stayed at home.*

THE FUTURE TENSE

This is formed by the present tense of *werden* with the infinitive of the main verb at the end of the sentence, e.g.

Ich werde nächstes Jahr ein Auto kaufen.   *Next year I will buy a car.*

But remember that for events in the immediate future the present tense may be used, just as in English, e.g.

Ich fahre heute nachmittag in die Stadt.   *I am going to town this afternoon.*

THE CONDITIONAL TENSE

This translates 'would' in a sentence such as 'If it wasn't raining I would play tennis'.
'Would' is translated by *würde* (the imperfect subjunctive of *werden*) with the infinitive at the end of the sentence, e.g.

Ich würde Tennis spielen, wenn . . .   *I would play tennis if . . .*
Was würdest du mit so viel Geld tun?   *What would you do with so much money?*

THE PASSIVE

You are unlikely to use the passive at this stage but you should be able to recognise it. It is formed with *werden* and the past participle of the main verb. Here are some examples:

Die Tür wird gestrichen.   *The door is being painted.*
Er wurde durch einen Tunnel geführt.   *He was led through a tunnel.*
Es wird oft gesagt . . .   *It is often said . . .*
Das Auto wurde verkauft.   *The car was sold.*

THE SUBJUNCTIVE

This also needs to be recognised but does not need to be used at this stage. It is used mainly in reported speech, e.g.

Er sagte, er habe wenig Geld.   *He said he had little money.*
Sie sagt, sie sei krank.   *She says she is ill* (sei *comes from* sein).

It is also used after *als ob* (as if), e.g.

Er lief so schnell, als ob er Angst hätte.   *He ran so fast as if he were afraid.*

The modal verbs and *haben* and *sein* are often found in the subjunctive. Look at these examples:

Ich könnte nicht schlafen.   *I wouldn't be able to sleep.*
Er müßte nach Hause gehen.   *He would have to go home.*
Ich möchte bitte . . .   *I would like . . .*
Ich dürfte nicht bleiben.   *I would not be allowed to stay.*
Ich hätte gern . . .   *I would like . . .*
Das wäre nett.   *That would be nice.*

POINTS TO REMEMBER

- Some phrases use a different tense in German from English, e.g.

  Ich wohne seit zwei Jahren in Hamm.   *I have been living in Hamm for two years.*
  Er lernte Deutsch seit sechs Wochen.   *He had been learning German for six weeks.*

- Some verbs do not take *ge-* in their past participle:
  a) those verbs beginning with *be-, ge-, er-, ver-, zer-, emp-, ent- (besuchen, gewinnen, erkennen, verlieren, zerbrechen, empfehlen, entscheiden).*
  b) those verbs ending in *-ieren (reparieren).*

- Modal verbs rarely use their past participles but use the infinitive instead, e.g.

  Ich habe schwer arbeiten müssen.   *I have had to work hard.*

NOW TEST YOURSELF (4)

a) Translate into English:
  i) Er stand vor dem Kino.
  ii) Der Zug war schon angekommen.
  iii) Es wird bald regnen.
  iv) Das Buch wurde sehr schnell geschrieben.
  v) Er sagte, er könne nicht arbeiten.
  vi) Ich wäre sehr dankbar.
  vii) Das würde DM 200 kosten.
  viii) Wohin bist du gelaufen?
  ix) Er bekam zwei Briefe.
  x) Er tat, als ob er nichts kaufen wolle.

b) Translate into German:
  i) He is learning Italian.
  ii) We used to live in Austria.
  iii) I would like some tomatoes, please.
  iv) Have you bought the house?
  v) I had already left.
  vi) Are you reading the paper?
  vii) I would stay at home, if . . .
  viii) They are tired.
  ix) We had already eaten.
  x) What did you find?

IMPERATIVES

Imperatives are used for giving commands. Here are the normal forms for the verb *arbeiten* – to work:

Arbeite! *work!* (du *form*)
Arbeitet! *work!* (ihr *form*)
Arbeiten Sie! *work!* (Sie *form*)
Arbeiten wir! *let us work!* (wir *form*)

You will notice that only the *du* form is different from the present tense. The *-st* is dropped and so frequently is the *-e* in more common verbs. Study these examples of the *du* form:

Gib mir dein Buch! *Give me your book!*
Steh auf! *Stand up! (or: Get up!)*
Komm mal her! *Come here!*
Geh weg! *Go away!*
Putz dir die Zähne! *Brush your teeth!*

REFLEXIVE VERBS

PRONOUN

These are normal verbs which add a reflexive pronoun, e.g. *sich waschen* – to wash oneself.

Present Tense

ich wasche mich *I get washed (literally: I wash myself)*	wir waschen uns *we get washed*
du wäschst dich *you get washed*	ihr wascht euch *you get washed*
er, sie wäscht sich *he, she gets washed*	Sie waschen sich *you get washed*
	sie waschen sich *they get washed*

POINTS TO REMEMBER

- In the perfect tense reflexive verbs use *haben*.
- In certain phrases, e.g. *ich wasche mir die Hände*, the reflexive pronoun becomes **dative**, because it is now the **hands** you are washing. In such cases the only changes are *mich* to *mir* and *dich* to *dir*. The other pronouns remain the same.

COMMON REFLEXIVE VERBS

Some common reflexive verbs are:

sich ängstigen *to become anxious*	sich setzen *to sit down*
sich beeilen *to hurry*	sich vorstellen *to introduce oneself, imagine*
sich erholen *to recover*	
sich erinnern an *to remember*	sich bemühen *to take the trouble*
sich erkälten *to catch cold*	sich anziehen *to get dressed*
sich interessieren für *to be interested in*	sich ausziehen *to get undressed*
sich kleiden *to get dressed*	sich entscheiden *to decide*
sich rasieren *to shave*	sich unterhalten *to converse*

SEPARABLE VERBS

PREFIX

These verbs have a **prefix** which can be separated from the main part of the verb. Study these examples of the verb *ausgehen* – to go out:

Present tense: Ich gehe jeden Abend aus. *I go out every evening.*
Perfect tense: Ich bin gestern ausgegangen. *I went out yesterday.*
Future tense: Morgen abend werden wir ausgehen. *We will go out tomorrow evening.*
Infinitive with *zu*: Meine Schwester hatte vor, auszugehen. *My sister planned to go out.*

COMMON SEPARABLE VERBS

These are some of the commonest separable verbs which you should be able to recognise and use:

ausgehen   *to go out*
ankommen   *to arrive*
abfahren   *to depart*
weggehen   *to go away*
aufstehen   *to get up*
aufwachen   *to wake up*
aufhören   *to stop*
teilnehmen   *to take part*
einsteigen   *to get in*
aussteigen   *to get out*
anfangen   *to begin*

umsteigen   *to change (trains)*
umziehen   *to move house*
sich anziehen   *to dress*
sich ausziehen   *to undress*
sich umziehen   *to change (clothes)*
fernsehen   *to watch TV*
zurückkommen   *to come back*
stattfinden   *to take place*
mitteilen   *to inform*
vorhaben   *to have in mind*

POINTS TO REMEMBER

- Do not confuse *umziehen* with *sich umziehen*.
- When hearing German or reading German watch out for the separable prefix at the end of the sentence. It can totally change the meaning of a sentence.

IMPERSONAL VERBS

These verbs or idiomatic phrases can only be used in the *es* form. Here are some examples:

es regnet   *it's raining*
es schneit   *it's snowing*
es friert   *it's freezing*
es blitzt   *there's lightning*
es donnert   *it's thundering*
es tut mir leid   *I'm sorry*

es tut mir weh   *it hurts (me)*
es gefällt mir   *I like it (it pleases me)*
es fällt mir ein   *it occurs to me*
es gelingt mir   *I succeed, I manage*
es ist mir kalt   *I'm cold*
es geht mir gut   *I'm well*

NOW TEST YOURSELF (5)

This covers the last few sections. Translate into German:
a) Go home! (all three forms)
b) Don't drive so fast! (all three forms)
c) Wash your hands! (all three forms)
d) Let's stay at home!
e) She's getting changed.
f) He's shaving.
g) We are chatting.
h) I get up at seven o'clock.
i) We watched TV last night.
j) What have you got in mind today?
k) How are you?
l) I don't feel so good.

TABLE OF STRONG AND MIXED VERBS

This list gives the third person singular (*er, sie, es* form) of all the common strong and mixed verbs. Candidates aiming for Higher Levels should be able to recognise and use all these verbs. Basic Level candidates should concentrate on those marked with an asterisk.

Infinitive	Meaning	Present	Imperfect	Perfect
backen	*to bake*	bäckt	backte	hat gebacken
befehlen	*to command*	befiehlt	befahl	hat befohlen
*beginnen	*to begin*	beginnt	begann	hat begonnen
beißen	*to bite*	beißt	biß	hat gebissen
*bekommen	*to get, obtain*	bekommt	bekam	hat bekommen
biegen	*to bend*	biegt	bog	hat gebogen
*bieten	*to offer*	bietet	bot	hat geboten
binden	*to bind, tie*	bindet	band	hat gebunden
*bitten	*to ask, beg*	bittet	bat	hat gebeten
blasen	*to blow*	bläst	blies	hat geblasen

Infinitive	Meaning	Present	Imperfect	Perfect
*bleiben	to remain	bleibt	blieb	ist geblieben
*brechen	to break	bricht	brach	hat gebrochen
*brennen	to burn	brennt	brannte	hat gebrannt
*bringen	to bring	bringt	brachte	hat gebracht
*denken	to think	denkt	dachte	hat gedacht
dringen	to pierce, penetrate	dringt	drang	ist gedrungen
*einladen	to invite	lädt ein	lud ein	hat eingeladen
*empfehlen	to recommend	empfiehlt	empfahl	hat empfohlen
*erlöschen	to die down, go out (of fire, light)	erlischt	erlosch	ist erloschen
erschrecken	to be frightened	erschrickt	erschrak	ist erschrocken
*essen	to eat	ißt	aß	hat gegessen
*fahren	to drive, ride	fährt	fuhr	ist gefahren
*fallen	to fall	fällt	fiel	ist gefallen
*fangen	to catch	fängt	fing	hat gefangen
*finden	to find	findet	fand	hat gefunden
*fliegen	to fly	fliegt	flog	ist geflogen
fliehen	to flee	flieht	floh	ist geflohen
*fließen	to flow	fließt	floß	ist geflossen
*fressen	to eat (of animals)	frißt	fraß	hat gefressen
*frieren	to freeze	friert	fror	hat gefroren
*geben	to give	gibt	gab	hat gegeben
*gehen	to go	geht	ging	ist gegangen
*gelingen	to succeed	gelingt	gelang	ist gelungen
genießen	to enjoy	genießt	genoß	hat genossen
*geschehen	to happen	geschieht	geschah	ist geschehen
*gewinnen	to gain, win	gewinnt	gewann	hat gewonnen
gießen	to pour	gießt	goß	hat gegossen
gleichen	to resemble	gleicht	glich	hat geglichen
gleiten	to glide	gleitet	glitt	ist geglitten
*graben	to dig	gräbt	grub	hat gegraben
*greifen	to seize	greift	griff	hat gegriffen
*haben	to have	hat	hatte	hat gehabt
*halten	to hold, stop	hält	hielt	hat gehalten
*hängen	to hang, be suspended	hängt	hing	hat gehangen
heben	to lift	hebt	hob	hat gehoben
*heißen	to be called	heißt	hieß	hat geheißen
*helfen	to help	hilft	half	hat geholfen
*kennen	to know	kennt	kannte	hat gekannt
klingen	to sound	klingt	klang	hat geklungen
*kommen	to come	kommt	kam	ist gekommen
kriechen	to creep	kriecht	kroch	ist gekrochen
*lassen	to let	läßt	ließ	hat gelassen
*laufen	to run	läuft	lief	ist gelaufen
*leiden	to suffer	leidet	litt	hat gelitten
leihen	to lend	leiht	lieh	hat geliehen
*lesen	to read	liest	las	hat gelesen
*liegen	to lie	liegt	lag	hat gelegen
lügen	to tell lies	lügt	log	hat gelogen
meiden	to avoid	meidet	mied	hat gemieden
messen	to measure	mißt	maß	hat gemessen
*nehmen	to take	nimmt	nahm	hat genommen
*nennen	to name, call	nennt	nannte	hat genannt
*raten	to advise, guess	rät	riet	hat geraten
reiben	to rub	reibt	rieb	hat gerieben
*reißen	to tear	reißt	riß	hat gerissen
*reiten	to ride	reitet	ritt	hat geritten
*rennen	to run	rennt	rannte	hat gerannt
*riechen	to smell	riecht	roch	hat gerochen
*rufen	to call	ruft	rief	hat gerufen
*scheinen	to appear, shine	scheint	schien	hat geschienen
*schieben	to shove, push	schiebt	schob	hat geschoben
*schießen	to shoot	schießt	schoß	hat geschossen
*schlafen	to sleep	schläft	schlief	hat geschlafen
*schlagen	to strike, hit	schlägt	schlug	hat geschlagen
schleichen	to creep	schleicht	schlich	ist geschlichen
*schließen	to shut	schließt	schloß	hat geschlossen
schmelzen	to melt	schmilzt	schmolz	ist geschmolzen
*schneiden	to cut	schneidet	schnitt	hat geschnitten

Infinitive	Meaning	Present	Imperfect	Perfect
*schreiben	*to write*	schreibt	schrieb	hat geschrieben
*schreien	*to cry out, shout*	schreit	schrie	hat geschrie(e)n
schreiten	*to stride*	schreitet	schritt	ist geschritten
*schweigen	*to be silent*	schweigt	schwieg	hat geschwiegen
*schwimmen	*to swim*	schwimmt	schwamm	ist geschwommen
schwingen	*to swing*	schwingt	schwang	hat geschwungen
schwören	*to swear*	schwört	schwor	hat geschworen
*sehen	*to see*	sieht	sah	hat gesehen
*sein	*to be*	ist	war	ist gewesen
*singen	*to sing*	singt	sang	hat gesungen
*sinken	*to sink*	sinkt	sank	ist gesunken
*sitzen	*to sit*	sitzt	saß	hat gesessen
*sprechen	*to speak*	spricht	sprach	hat gesprochen
*springen	*to spring, jump*	springt	sprang	ist gesprungen
*stehen	*to stand*	steht	stand	hat gestanden
*stehlen	*to steal*	stiehlt	stahl	hat gestohlen
*steigen	*to climb*	steigt	stieg	ist gestiegen
*sterben	*to die*	stirbt	starb	ist gestorben
*stoßen	*to push, knock, bump*	stößt	stieß	hat gestoßen
*streichen	*to paint, spread*	streicht	strich	hat gestrichen
*streiten	*to argue, fight*	streitet	stritt	hat gestritten
*tragen	*to carry, wear*	trägt	trug	hat getragen
*treffen	*to hit, meet*	trifft	traf	hat getroffen
*treiben	*to drive*	treibt	trieb	hat getrieben
*treten	*to step, kick (football)*	tritt	trat	hat getreten
*trinken	*to drink*	trinkt	trank	hat getrunken
*tun	*to do*	tut	tat	hat getan
*verbieten	*to forbid*	verbietet	verbot	hat verboten
verderben	*to spoil*	verdirbt	verdarb	hat verdorben
*vergessen	*to forget*	vergißt	vergaß	hat vergessen
*verlieren	*to lose*	verliert	verlor	hat verloren
*verschwinden	*to disappear*	verschwindet	verschwand	ist verschwunden
*verzeihen	*to pardon*	verzeiht	verzieh	hat verziehen
*wachsen	*to grow*	wächst	wuchs	ist gewachsen
*waschen	*to wash*	wäscht	wusch	hat gewaschen
weisen	*to show*	weist	wies	hat gewiesen
*werden	*to become*	wird	wurde	ist geworden
*werfen	*to throw*	wirft	warf	hat geworfen
wiegen	*to weigh*	wiegt	wog	hat gewogen
*wissen	*to know*	weiß	wußte	hat gewußt
*ziehen	*to draw, pull*	zieht	zog	hat gezogen
zwingen	*to force*	zwingt	zwang	hat gezwungen

CASES AND PREPOSITIONS

The four cases – nominative, accusative, genitive and dative – cause difficulties for English students of German. Your course book will no doubt deal with them thoroughly, and you will have had frequent practice in using the cases. This section summarises the main rules, and gives examples of the use of the different cases, often with prepositions, with a recommendation that some of the phrases should be learnt by heart and used wherever possible both in spoken and in written German.

THE CASES

NOMINATIVE

The **Nominative** case is the starting point. It is the case given in vocabularies and dictionaries. It is used for the **subject** of the verb.

ACCUSATIVE

The **Accusative** is used:

- for the *direct object* of the verb, e.g. *Ich habe einen Bruder; Kannst du die Berge sehen? Er hat seine Jacke verloren.*
- after the following prepositions: *für, um, durch, gegen, entlang, bis, ohne.*
- after the following prepositions when **motion towards** is indicated: *in, an, auf, über, vor, hinter, unter, neben, zwischen.*
- in many time phrases, e.g. *letztes Jahr, guten Morgen, nächste Woche, diesen Dienstag, den ganzen Tag.*

GENITIVE

The **Genitive** case is used:

- for possession, e.g. *das Zimmer meiner Eltern* – my parents' room, *ein Freund meines Bruders* – a friend of my brother.
- after the following prepositions: *wegen, während, trotz, anstatt, statt, außerhalb, innerhalb.*

DATIVE

The **Dative** case is used:

- for the **indirect object** of the verb, e.g. *Ich gebe meinem Vater* (i.e. **to** my father) *den Brief; Du sagst mir* (i.e. **to** me) *nichts.*
- after the following prepositions: *aus, bei, mit, nach, seit, von, zu, gegenüber.*
- after the following prepositions when **no motion towards** is indicated: *in, an, auf, über, vor, hinter, unter, neben, zwischen.*

POINTS TO REMEMBER

- The only difference in form between the nominative case and the accusative case is in the masculine *(der – den, ein – einen).*
- The preposition *entlang* **follows** the noun.
- *Gegenüber* often appears after the noun, and **always** after a pronoun, e.g. *dem Rathaus gegenüber, mir gegenüber.*
- The genitive case is slowly (very slowly) becoming less used, so that one sometimes hears *während den Ferien* (dative). Some people also avoid using the genitive by using a dative with *von* instead, e.g. *das Zimmer von meinen Eltern* rather than *das Zimmer meiner Eltern.*
- The accusative prepositions are best learned in the order given, which provides the word FUDGEBO!
- The dative prepositions are best learned as written, in alphabetical order, in the following jingle:

Aus, bei, mit, nach, seit, von, zu,
All take the dative and *gegenüber* too!

THE PREPOSITIONS   These words frequently indicate the position of objects. Their use is often idiomatic and you should therefore learn by heart the phases given here as examples. Many of them you will know already!

ACCUSATIVE

Accusative only:

für	*for*	Das ist für mich; Das ist für meinen Bruder.
um	*round, at*	um die Ecke, um den Tisch, um 8 Uhr
durch	*through*	durch den Garten, durch die Stadt, durch das Haus
entlang	*along*	die Straße entlang
bis	*until*	Bis nächsten Monat! Bis morgen!
ohne	*without*	ohne meine Bücher

GENITIVE

Genitive only:

wegen	*because of*	Wegen des Regens kann er nicht kommen.
während	*during*	Während der Mittagspause hat es geregnet.
trotz	*in spite of*	Trotz des schlechten Wetters ist es warm.
anstatt/statt	*instead of*	statt meines Freundes
außerhalb	*outside*	außerhalb des Dorfes
innerhalb	*inside*	innerhalb der Stadt

DATIVE

Dative only:

aus	*out of, from, made of*	Er ging aus der Küche. Ich komme aus Schottland. Ein Bett aus Holz
bei	*at the home of, near, at*	bei meiner Freundin, bei Köln beim Frühstück, bei schönem Wetter
mit	*with, by*	mit meinen Freunden, mit dem Rad
nach	*to, after*	nach Spanien, nach Ulm, nach dem Mittagessen, meiner Meinung nach
seit	*since*	seit den Olympischen Spielen, seit drei Jahren
von	*of, from*	das Haus von meiner Oma Der Zug fährt von Bonn nach Bingen.
zu	*to, at*	ich gehe zum Bahnhof, zu Weihnachten, zum Geburtstag, eine Briefmarke zu 90 Pfennig
gegenüber	*opposite*	gegenüber der Kirche, ihm gegenüber

ACCUSATIVE OR DATIVE

Prepositions taking accusative or dative:

in	*into, in*	Acc.	Er ging in die Stadt. *(into)*
		Dat.	Er arbeitet in der Stadt. *(in)*
an	*to, at*	Acc.	Wir fahren ans Meer. *(to)*
		Dat.	Kiel liegt am Meer. *(at, on)*
auf	*onto, on*	Acc.	Die Katze sprang auf den Tisch. *(onto)*
		Dat.	Meine Sachen liegen auf dem Tisch. *(on)*
über	*over, above*	Acc.	Lauf schnell über die Straße! *(over)*
		Dat.	Die Lampe hängt über der Straße. *(above)*

The remaining prepositions in this group are nearly always followed by the **dative** case:

vor	*in front of, before*	vor dem Kino, vor dem Frühstück
hinter	*behind*	hinter der Garage
unter	*under, below*	unter dem Sofa
neben	*near*	neben der Schule
zwischen	*between*	zwischen der Post und dem Rathaus

USEFUL PREPOSITIONAL PHRASES

Other useful prepositional phrases to learn:

bis zum Ende	*right to the end*
Tag für Tag	*day after day*
er geht nach Hause	*he's going home*
sie bleibt zu Hause	*she's staying at home*
Geh zu Bett!	*go to bed!*
zu Fuß	*on foot*
zum Glück	*fortunately*
am zweiten April	*on the second of April*

Frankfurt am Main   *Frankfurt on the Main*
Der Spiegel ist an der Wand.   *The mirror is on the wall.*
am Himmel   *in the sky*
Wir fahren aufs Land.   *We're going into the country.*
Der Bauernhof ist auf dem Land.   *The farm is in the country.*
auf deutsch   *in German*
auf diese Weise   *in this way*
auf jeden Fall   *in any case*
auf dem Markt   *in the market*
Ich gehe auf die Bank.   *I'm going to the bank.*
Fahren Sie in die Schweiz?   *Are you going to Switzerland?*
Ich gehe ins Kino / Theater / Konzert / in die Disko.   *I'm going to the cinema / the theatre / a concert / the disco.*
in der Nähe von Dortmund   *near Dortmund*
im Freien   *in the open air*
im ersten Stock   *on the first floor*
im Fernsehen   *on TV*
über Rotterdam   *via Rotterdam*
vor drei Wochen   *three weeks ago*
vor allem   *above all*
er hat Angst vor Spinnen   *he's afraid of spiders*
unter meinen Freunden   *among my friends*

POINTS TO REMEMBER

The word 'to' can be translated by *nach, zu, in, an* or *auf!*
Check carefully before making a wild guess.

- *nach* is used for place names of towns or countries
- *zu* is the most general word otherwise
- *in* means going **into** (*in die Schule, ins Büro*)
- *an* means going up to, but not into (*an den Fluß, ans Meer*)
- *auf* means going on to (*auf den Markt, auf das Land*).

NOW TEST YOURSELF (6)

Translate into German:
a) by train
b) in the country
c) to Belgium
d) to the Black Forest
e) opposite you
f) at half past six
g) on Friday
h) see you soon!
i) on the wall
j) made of plastic
k) at our house
l) at Easter
m) through the window
n) after lunch
o) at home
p) 10 years ago
q) on the radio
r) in English
s) in Switzerland
t) to Turkey

PRONOUNS

COMMON PRONOUNS

The table which follows reminds you of the pronouns with which you are already familiar:

	I	you	he	she	it	we	you	you	they
Nominative	ich	du	er	sie	es	wir	ihr	Sie	sie
Accusative	mich	dich	ihn	sie	es	uns	euch	Sie	sie
Dative	mir	dir	ihm	ihr	ihm	uns	euch	Ihnen	ihnen

PATTERNS	A quick count will show you that there are seven different words for 'you'! But having digested this unpleasant fact, there are two reassuring features of the table:

- The words for 'he', 'she', 'it' and 'they' follow exactly the pattern of the definite articles *der, die, das* and *die*.
- The word for 'we' is always *wir* and the word for 'us' is always *uns*.

POINTS TO REMEMBER	

- When writing a letter *Du, Dich* and *Dir* must be written with a capital letter. Similarly *Ihr* and *Euch*.
- 'In it' is not translated by *in ihm*, but by *darin*. Similarly *darauf, daran, damit, darüber* and so on.
- Do not forget the pronoun *man*, which is common in German, e.g. *Hier spricht man Englisch* – English spoken here.
- 'It's me' is translated by *Ich bin's*.

NOW TEST YOURSELF (7)	Translate into German:

a) for me

b) with you

c) without us

d) against it

e) without him

f) for her

g) at your house

h) with her

i) with me

j) on it

k) in front of it

RELATIVE PRONOUNS	## NOMINATIVE

Der Mann, <u>der</u> dort allein sitzt, ist mein Lehrer.   *The man who is sitting there alone, is my teacher.*

The word *der* which is underlined is a relative pronoun meaning 'who'. It is *der* because it relates back to a masculine noun (*der Mann*) and because it is the **subject** of its own verb (*sitzt*).

ACCUSATIVE

Der Mann, <u>den</u> du dort siehst, ist mein Lehrer.   *The man whom you see there is my teacher.*

This time the relative pronoun is den because it is the **object** of the verb in the clause (*siehst*).

DATIVE

Der Mann, mit <u>dem</u> du sprichst, ist mein Lehrer.   *The man with whom you are speaking is my teacher.*

Here *dem* is dative following the word *mit*.

SUMMARY

Here is the table for relative pronouns:

	Masculine	Feminine	Neuter	Plural
Nominative	der	die	das	die
Accusative	den	die	das	die
Genitive	dessen	deren	dessen	deren
Dative	dem	der	dem	denen

You will see that there are a few new words, but that most relative pronouns are the same as the definite articles.

EXAMPLES

Die Kinder, die hier wohnen, kommen aus Schottland.   *The children who live here come from Scotland.*

Die Freunde, mit denen ich Tennis spiele, kommen später nach Hause.   *The friends with whom I play tennis are coming home later.*

Der Mann, dessen Sohn im Krankenhaus liegt, heißt Müller.   *The man whose son is in hospital is called Müller.*

Here is an example of a different kind of relative pronoun:

Hier ist die Küche, wo wir gewöhnlich essen.   *Here is the kitchen where we usually eat.*

POINTS TO REMEMBER

- Remember that the relative pronoun sends the verb to the end of the clause.
- Be prepared to recognise these words both in reading and in listening.
- Only use them if you feel confident to do so correctly. Two short sentences would often do just as well.

A D V E R B S

COMPARISON WITH ADJECTIVES

Many adverbs in German are the same as the adjective. For instance, in the sentence *Er ist ein guter Arbeiter* the word *gut* is an adjective. But it can also be used as an adverb in the sentence *Er arbeitet sehr gut* (He works very **well**).

SUPERLATIVE

The superlative of adverbs, however, needs some attention. 'He runs the fastest' is translated as *Er läuft am schnellsten.* At this stage this form is largely for receptive use only, apart from the phrase *am liebsten* (best of all), e.g.

Ich esse gern Erbsen, aber am liebsten esse ich Bohnen.   *I like eating peas but I like eating beans best of all.*

COMMON ADVERBS

Many adverbs are easy to use but are often forgotten by candidates in German. Here are a few which you will know, but which you may not often put to active use. Make a serious effort to introduce them sensibly into your written and spoken work.

auch	*also*	kaum	*hardly*
bald	*soon*	lange	*for a long time*
dann	*then*	leider	*unfortunately*
damals	*at that time*	nur	*only*
eben	*just*	oft	*often*
erst	*not until*	manchmal	*sometimes*
(e.g. erst morgen	*not until tomorrow*)	schon	*already*
fast	*almost*	sogar	*even*
ganz	*quite, completely*	sonst	*otherwise*
genug	*enough*	vielleicht	*perhaps*
gerade	*just*	wohl	*I suppose*
immer	*always*	ziemlich	*fairly, rather*
jetzt	*now*		

CONJUNCTIONS

USES OF CONJUNCTIONS

Conjunctions are words which join clauses together to make them longer and more complex. A few do not alter the word order:

und	*and*	denn	*for, because*
oder	*or*	sondern	*but (on the contrary)*
aber	*but*		

Others send the verb to the end of the clause. The most common examples of these are:

als	*when, as*	ob	*whether, if*
bis	*until*	obwohl	*although*
bevor	*before*	seitdem	*since*
da	*as, since*	sobald	*as soon as*
daß	*that*	so daß	*so that*
falls	*in case, if*	während	*while*
indem	*while*	wenn	*when, if*
nachdem	*after*	weil	*because*
damit	*in order that*		

Als ich jung war, . . . *When I was young* . . .
Bevor wir das Haus verließen, . . . *Before we left the house* . . .
Nachdem wir gefrühstückt hatten, . . . *After we had had breakfast* . . .
Obwohl es sehr kalt war, . . . *Although it was very cold* . . .
Wenn ich Zeit habe, . . . *When (if) I have time* . . .
Weil ich momentan kein Geld habe, . . . *Because I haven't any money at the moment* . . .

POINTS TO REMEMBER

- Using these conjunctions makes the sentence more complex. If you are unsure of what you are doing, divide your sentence into two simpler sentences. For example:

  Ich werde Tennis spielen, weil das Wetter schön ist.
  Das Wetter ist schön. Ich werde Tennis spielen.

- *Bis* and *während* are also prepositions, but as such have a different meaning. Do not confuse their use as a conjunction and as a preposition.

- Do not confuse *nachdem* with *nach dem*.

- *Da* (as, since) also has other meanings.

NOW TEST YOURSELF (8)

Translate into German:
a) Because it's raining today . . .
b) Before I go to bed . . .
c) Although my mother is ill . . .
d) Whilst you are doing your home- work . . .
e) If the sun is shining . . .
f) I don't know if he is coming today.
g) As it is already nine o'clock . . .
h) I know that the film is good.
i) As soon as the train arrives . . .
j) Since we have been living here . . .

INTERROGATIVES

QUESTION WORDS

Questions in German are easy. All question words begin with 'w'.

was?	*what?*	wer?	*who?*
wo?	*where?*	wen?	*whom?*
woher?	*where from?*	wessen?	*whose?*
wohin?	*where to?*	wem?	*whom?*
wie?	*how?*	wieviel?	*how much?*

wieviele? *how many?*
warum? *why?*
welcher . . .? *which . . .?*

was für . . .? *what sort of . . .?*
womit? wovon? *with what? of what?*

Examples:

Woher kommst du? *Where do you come from?*
Wohin fährt dieser Zug? *Where is this train going?*
Wie ist Ihr Hund? *What is your dog like?*
Was für einen Lehrer habt ihr? *What sort of a teacher do you have?*
Mit wem hast du gesprochen? *Who(m) did you speak with?*
Womit schreiben Sie? *What are you writing with?*
Welches Buch hast du da? *What (which) book have you got there?*
Warum muß man immer arbeiten? *Why does one always have to work?*
Wessen Schuhe sind diese? *Whose shoes are these?*

POINTS TO REMEMBER

- *mit wem?* means 'with whom?' (i.e. a person)
  womit? means 'with what?' (i.e. a thing)
- *woher* and *wohin* can separate, e.g. *Wo gehst du hin? Wo kommst du her?*

NOW TEST YOURSELF (9)

Translate into German:
a) How much does that cost?
b) Why are you so tired?
c) What sort of a book is it?
d) How many people are here?
e) Where does this bus go?
f) What's the weather like?
g) Which lessons have we got?
h) What are you standing on?
i) Who is that?
j) Who(m) do you play tennis with?

NEGATIVES

BEGINNINGS

Negatives should cause little problem in German. Almost all negative words begin with the letter 'n'.

nicht *not*
nie *never*
nein *no*
nichts *nothing*
niemand *no one*
nirgendwo *nowhere*
nicht mehr *no longer*

noch nie *never yet*
noch nicht *not yet*
nicht wahr? *isn't it? don't you? etc.*
gar nichts *not at all*
weder . . . noch *neither . . . nor*
kein *no, not a*

Examples:

Meine Arbeit ist noch nicht fertig. *My work is not yet finished.*
Ich war noch nie in der Schweiz. *I have never been to Switzerland (yet).*
Da war nichts zu sehen. *There was nothing to see.*
Es regnet nicht mehr. *It's stopped raining.*
Ich lerne weder Physik noch Biologie. *I don't learn either physics or biology.*
Heute abend haben wir keine Hausaufgaben. *We haven't any homework tonight.*

POINTS TO REMEMBER

- 'not a' or 'no' is *kein, keine,* etc.
- 'not anything' is the same as 'nothing' (*nichts*)
- 'not ever' is the same as 'never' (*nie*)

NOW TEST YOURSELF (10)

Translate into German:
a) She doesn't love me any more.
b) It's not yet 9 o'clock.
c) I haven't got a brother.
d) He hasn't eaten anything.
e) I'm right, aren't I?
f) I have nothing at all to say.
g) Nobody knows.
h) It is nowhere to be found.
i) Never again.
j) Haven't you got a dog?

W O R D   O R D E R

BASIC RULES

1 The basic rule for word order is that the verb should stand as the second idea in the sentence. Look at the following sentences:

Mein Vater fährt am Donnerstag nach Berlin.
Am Donnerstag fährt mein Vater nach Berlin.

Although the order of the phrases has changed, the verb remains in the second place.

2 This rule holds for the perfect tense when the auxiliary verb is in second place with the past participle at the end:

Wir haben den Kuchen schon gegessen.

3 This also applies when a subordinate clause begins the sentence, as in:

Da er kein Geld hatte, blieb er zu Hause.

If we count *Da er kein Geld hatte* as the first idea, then *blieb* as the main verb is still in second place.

4 Past participles and infinitives go to the end, e.g.

Ich kann dieses Lied nicht leiden.
Warum hast du die Platte gekauft?

5 In questions or commands the verb is often first, e.g.

Kommst du heute abend oder nicht?
Geh schnell nach Hauses zurück!

6 If you have a number of phrases in a sentence, remember the order of TIME, MANNER, PLACE, e.g.

Wir fahren morgen früh   mit dem Wagen   nach Basel.
        TIME   MANNER   PLACE

POINTS TO REMEMBER

■ If you have too many phrases in your sentence, it is often easier to start with a time phrase, e.g. *Am Donnerstag fahre ich mit dem Zug nach Lübeck.* This does not in any way alter the meaning of the sentence.

■ Try reading out loud the sentences you write. If a sentence sounds wrong, think again. This is the test which we subconciously apply to our own language.

NOW TEST YOURSELF (11)

Rewrite these sentences with the words in the correct order:
a) muß mit Dover morgen fahren dem ich nach Schiff
b) einen es kalt wenn trage ich Pullover ist
c) schon Uhr acht es ist?
d) sieben Film um an fängt der

e) einen heute gekauft Rock Sabine Bluse hat und eine
f) Straße nicht Lärm macht so viel der in!
g) am in Stadt wirst Samstag du die fahren?
h) fährt entlang die die schnell Straßenbahn Straße
i) kommt uns Briefträger heute zu der nicht
j) wissen der ist kaputt daß wir Plattenspieler

NUMBERS, QUANTITY AND TIME

CARDINAL AND ORDINAL NUMBERS

Cardinal numbers

1	eins	21	einundzwanzig
2	zwei	22	zweiundzwanzig
3	drei	30	dreißig
4	vier	40	vierzig
5	fünf	50	fünfzig
6	sechs	60	sechzig
7	sieben	70	siebzig
8	acht	80	achtzig
9	neun	90	neunzig
10	zehn	100	hundert
11	elf	120	hundertzwanzig
12	zwölf	1,000	tausend
13	dreizehn	1,000,000	eine Million
14	vierzehn		
15	fünfzehn		
16	sechzehn		
17	siebzehn		
18	achtzehn		
19	neunzehn		
20	zwanzig		

Ordinal numbers

1st	der erste
2nd	der zweite
3rd	der dritte
4th	der vierte
5th	der fünfte
20th	der zwanzigste

TIME

Wieviel Uhr ist es? } *What time is it?*
Wie spät ist es?
Es ist ein Uhr.   *It's one o'clock.*
Es ist zwei Uhr *etc.*
um sechs Uhr   *at six o'clock*
gegen sieben Uhr   *about seven o'clock*
Es ist Viertel nach zwei.   *It's a quarter past two.*
Es ist halb drei.   *It's half past two.*
Es ist Viertel vor drei.   *It's a quarter to three.*
Es ist fünf (Minuten) nach acht.   *It's five past eight.*
Es ist fünfundzwanzig (Minuten) vor zehn.   *It's twenty-five to ten.*

DAYS AND MONTHS

Days of the week
Sonntag, Montag, Dienstag, Mittwoch, Donnerstag, Freitag, Samstag (*or* Sonnabend)
Months of the year
Januar, Februar, März, April, Mai, Juni,
Juli, August, September, Oktober, November, Dezember

A N S W E R S   T O   T H E   E X E R C I S E S

1 a) der Onkel, die Wohnung, das Restaurant, das Büchlein, der Schneider, die Engländerin, das Laufen, der Vater, die Bluse, die Mutter
      der Park, der Name, die Person, der Balkon, die Tür, der Käse, die Butter, das Mädchen, das Fräulein, der Klub

   b) die Wagen, Blusen, Ausstellungen, Cafés, Zimmer, Hotels, Trauben, Türen, Radios, Kellner
      die Kartoffeln, Nächte, Nummern, Freundinnen, Autobusse, Schwestern.

   c) i)   Wir haben weder Katze noch Hund.
      ii) Herr Rabowski ist Zahnarzt.
      iii) Die Autos (Wagen) sind nicht hier.
      iv) Ich putze mir die Zähne.
      v)   Sie ist meine Schwester.
      vi) Unser Opa ist zu Hause.
      vii) Diese Leute sind hungrig.
      viii) Welchen Jungen kannst du sehen?
      ix) Er hat Zahnschmerzen.
      x)   Die Schweiz ist schön.

2 a) der rote Bus
   b) ein roter Bus
   c) die enge Straße
   d) eine enge Straße
   e) das kleine Dorf
   f) ein kleines Dorf
   g) die weißen Berge
   h) weiße Berge
   i) kaltes Wetter
   j) Wir haben einen großen Garten
   k) der Alte
   l) Unsere Katze ist dumm.
   m) Mein armer Kopf!

3 a) meine ältere Schwester
   b) der längste Monat
   c) die langweiligste Stunde
   d) Sie ist älter als ich.
   e) Es ist nicht so kalt wie gestern.
   f) Die Nächte werden immer kürzer.
   g) die besten Filme
   h) nächstes Jahr
   i) eine modernere Schule
   j) die meisten Leute

4 a) i)   He stood outside the cinema.
      ii) The train had already arrived.
      iii) It will rain soon.
      iv) The book was written very quickly.
      v)   He said he couldn't work.
      vi) I would be very grateful.
      vii) That would cost DM 200.
      viii) Where did you run to?
      ix) He received two letters.
      x)   He acted as if he did not want to buy anything.

   b) i)   Er lernt Italienisch.
      ii) Wir wohnten in Österreich.
      iii) Ich möchte bitte Tomaten.
      iv) Haben Sie das Haus gekauft?
      v)   Ich war schon abgefahren.
      vi) Lesen Sie die Zeitung?
      vii) Ich würde zu Hause bleiben, wenn . . .
      viii) Sie sind müde.
      ix) Wir hatten schon gegessen.
      x)   Was haben Sie gefunden?

5 a) Geh nach Hause! Geht nach Hause! Gehen Sie nach Hause!
   b) Fahr (Fahrt, Fahren Sie) nicht so schnell!
   c) Wasch dir (Wascht euch, Waschen Sie sich) die Hände!
   d) Bleiben wir zu Hause!
   e) Sie zieht sich um.
   f) Er rasiert sich.
   g) Wir unterhalten uns.
   h) Ich stehe um sieben Uhr auf.
   i) Wir haben gestern abend ferngesehen.
   j) Was haben Sie heute vor?
   k) Wie geht es dir?
   l) Es geht mir nicht so gut.

6 a) mit dem Zug
   b) auf dem Lande
   c) nach Belgien
   d) in den Schwarzwald
   e) dir gegenüber
   f) um halb sieben
   g) am Freitag
   h) bis bald!
   i) an der Wand
   j) aus Plastik
   k) bei uns
   l) zu Ostern
   m) durch das Fenster
   n) nach dem Mittagessen

o)	zu Hause	r)	auf Englisch
p)	vor zehn Jahren	s)	in der Schweiz
q)	im Radio	t)	in die Türkei

7
a)	für mich	g)	bei dir
b)	mit dir	h)	mit ihr
c)	ohne uns	i)	mit mir
d)	dagegen	j)	darauf
e)	ohne ihn	k)	davor
f)	für sie		

8
a)	Weil es heute regnet, . . .	f)	Ich weiß nicht, ob er heute kommt.
b)	Bevor ich ins Bett gehe, . . .	g)	Da es schon neun Uhr ist, . . .
c)	Obwohl meine Mutter krank ist, . . .	h)	Ich weiß, daß der Film gut ist.
d)	Während du deine Hausaufgaben machst, . . .	i)	Sobald der Zug ankommt, . . .
e)	Falls die Sonne scheint, . . .	j)	Seitdem wir hier wohnen, . . .

9
a)	Wieviel kostet das?	f)	Wie ist das Wetter?
b)	Warum bist du so müde?	g)	Welche Stunden haben wir?
c)	Was für ein Buch ist es?	h)	Worauf stehen Sie?
d)	Wieviele Leute sind hier?	i)	Wer ist das?
e)	Wohin fährt dieser Bus?	j)	Mit wem spielen Sie Tennis?

10
a)	Sie liebt mich nicht mehr.	f)	Ich habe gar nichts zu sagen.
b)	Es ist noch nicht neun Uhr.	g)	Niemand weiß.
c)	Ich habe keinen Bruder.	h)	Es ist nirgendwo zu finden.
d)	Er hat nichts gegessen.	i)	Nie wieder.
e)	Ich habe recht, nicht wahr?	j)	Hast du keinen Hund?

11
a) Morgen muß ich mit dem Schiff nach Dover fahren.
b) Wenn es kalt ist, trage ich einen Pullover.
c) Ist es schon acht Uhr?
d) Der Film fängt um sieben an.
e) Sabine hat heute eine Bluse und einen Rock gekauft.
f) Macht nicht so viel Lärm in der Straße!
g) Wirst du am Samstag in die Stadt fahren?
h) Die Straßenbahn fährt schnell die Straße entlang.
i) Der Briefträger kommt heute nicht zu uns.
j) Wir wissen, daß der Plattenspieler kaputt ist.

A CHECKLIST OF LANGUAGE TASKS

GETTING STARTED

It is very important that you should keep a record of the work that you do, and this chapter is designed to help you do so. Each section is divided up into topics and on the right-hand side of each page are two blank columns. These are for you to use. In each square you should indicate that you have covered this area (first square) and that you have revised it satisfactorily (second square). You may even feel it wise to add a third square for a final revision check. You could write the date in the square or you could colour it in. You will see that the responsibility for this work is entirely yours, but it should allow you (if tackled properly) to approach the exam with maximum confidence.

PERSONAL IDENTIFICATION

HOUSE AND HOME

LIFE AT HOME

SCHOOL, EDUCATION AND FUTURE CAREER

FREE TIME AND ENTERTAINMENT

TRAVEL

HOLIDAYS

ACCOMMODATION

SOCIAL RELATIONSHIPS

HEALTH AND WELFARE

SHOPPING

FOOD AND DRINK

SERVICES

LANGUAGE PROBLEMS

WEATHER

PERSONAL IDENTIFICATION

You should be able to give information about yourself and others (e.g. members of your family or host family) and seek information from others on the following points:		
Names (including spelling out your own name)		
Home Address (including spelling out the name of your home town)		
Telephone Numbers		
Ages and Birthdays		
Nationality		
General Descriptions including sex, marital status, physical appearance, character or disposition of yourself and others		
Religion		
Likes and Dislikes (with regard to people and other topics in the syllabus)		

HOUSE AND HOME ## GENERAL

You should be able to discuss where and under what conditions you and others live, and should be able to do the following:		
Say whether you live in a house, flat, etc. and ask others the same.		
Describe your house, flat, etc. and its location.		
Find out about and give details of rooms, garage, garden, etc. as appropriate.		
Mention or enquire about availability of the most essential pieces of furniture, amenities, services.		
Say whether you have a room of your own and describe your room or the room where you sleep.		
Say what jobs you do around the home.		
Offer to help.		
Ask where places and things are in a house.		
Say you need soap, toothpaste or a towel.		
Invite someone to come in, sit down.		
Thank someone for hospitality.		
Offer and ask for help to do something about the house.		
Ask permission to use or do things when a guest of a German-speaking family.		

GEOGRAPHICAL SURROUNDINGS

You should be able to give information about your home town or village and surrounding areas, and seek information from others, with respect to:		
Location		
Character		
Amenities, attractions, features of interest, entertainment.		
You should also be able to express a simple opinion about your own town or someone else's town.		
You should also be able to give full descriptions of your home town/village or that of others, and of the surrounding area and region:		
Outline possibilities for sight-seeing.		
Give your opinion of your home town/village:		
what is good about it		
what is not so good about it		
how long you have been living there		
how you would improve it.		
Say which parts of Germany/Austria/Switzerland or the UK you know, and talk about them.		

LIFE AT HOME

You should be able to give and seek information about:		
Members of the Family		
Description of Members of the Family and their Occupations		
Description of Family Pets		
Daily Routine		
State at what time you usually get up and go to bed, have meals, how you spend your evenings and weekends. Ask others about the same.		
Say what you do to help at home.		
Say whether you have a spare-time job. If so, what job, what working hours, how much you earn.		
Say how much pocket money you get and what you do with it.		

SCHOOL

Exchange information and opinions about your school/college and its facilities:		
State the type, size and location of your school and describe the buildings.		
Talk about daily routines:		
when school begins, ends		
how many lessons there are and how long they last		
break times and lunch times		
homework		
how you travel to and from school		
your school year and holidays		
subjects studied and preferences		
clubs, sports, trips and other activities.		

EDUCATION AND FUTURE CAREER

You should be able to discuss:		
what sort of education you have had		
what you propose to continue with		
at what types of educational institution.		
Talk about examinations.		
Talk about special events in the school year, e.g. plays, sports day, visits.		
Discuss your plans and hopes for the future, giving reasons as appropriate, including:		
immediate plans for the coming months		
plans for the time after completion of compulsory education		
where you would like to work.		

FREE TIME AND ENTERTAINMENT

GENERAL

State your hobbies and interests.		
Ask about the hobbies and interests of other people.		
Discuss your evening, weekend and holiday activities, and those of other people.		
Discuss your interest and involvement in:		
sport and sporting events		
intellectual and artistic pursuits		
youth clubs, societies.		
Give and seek information about leisure facilities.		
Express simple opinions about:		
radio and TV, films, performances.		
Agree or disagree.		
Ask if someone agrees.		
Describe and comment on the leisure and entertainment facilities of the area you live in.		
Discuss in more detail your interests/activities.		
Discuss films, plays, concerts, etc. in greater detail.		
Describe how you spent a period of free time, e.g. an evening, a weekend.		
Describe what you would like to do if opportunities and finance permitted.		

PLACES OF ENTERTAINMENT

Buy entry tickets for cinema or theatre, concert, swimming pool, football match, sports centre.		
Find out the cost of seats or entry.		
Find out or state the starting/finishing times.		
State or ask what sort of film or play it is.		
Ask if the film or event is/was good.		
Express an opinion (about the film or event).		
Agree or disagree.		
Ask if someone agrees.		

TRAVEL GENERAL

Say how you get to your school/place of work (means of transport, if any; duration of journey).		
Understand and give information about other journeys.		

FINDING THE WAY

Attract the attention of a passer-by.		
Ask where a place is.		
Ask the way (to a place).		
Ask if it is a long way (to a place).		
Ask if a place is nearby.		
Ask if there is a place or an amenity nearby.		
Understand directions.		
Ask if there is a bus, train, tram or coach.		
Ask some to repeat what he/she has said.		
Say you do not understand.		
Say thank you.		
Give directions to strangers.		
State and enquire about distances.		

TRAVEL BY PUBLIC TRANSPORT

Ask if there is a bus, train, tram, tube or coach to a particular place.		
Buy tickets, stating:		
destination		
single or return		
class of travel		
day of travel.		
Ask about the cost of tickets.		
Ask about times of departure and arrival.		
Tell someone about proposed times of departure and arrival.		
Ask and check whether it is:		
the right platform		
the right station		
the right line or bus, tram, coach or stop.		
Ask about the location of facilities, e.g. bus stop, waiting room, information office, toilets.		
Ask if and/or where it is necessary to change buses, trains, trams or coaches.		
Ask or state whether a seat is free.		
Understand information given in brochures and tables.		
Write a letter about requirements for travel arrangements.		
Give above information to others.		
Say what you have lost at the lost property office.		

Ask how to get to a place by bus, train, tram, tube or coach.		
Give above information to others.		
Reserve a seat.		
Ask for information, timetables or a plan.		
Ask about price reductions and supplements.		
Make arrangements for taking, leaving or sending luggage.		
Deal with an element of the unexpected in travel arrangements, e.g. delayed or cancelled departures, mislaid tickets or documents, lost luggage.		

PRIVATE TRANSPORT

Buy petrol by grade, volume or price.		
Ask for the tank to be filled up.		
Ask the cost.		
Ask someone to check oil, water and tyres.		
Ask where facilities are.		
Ask about the availability of facilities nearby.		
Check on your route.		
Obtain and give information about routes, types of roads, traffic rules, parking facilities.		
Report a breakdown, giving location and other relevant information.		
Ask for technical help.		
Pay and ask for a receipt.		

TRAVEL BY AIR OR SEA

Buy a ticket.		
Ask about the cost of a flight or crossing.		
Say where you would like to sit.		
Ask about times of departure and arrival.		
Inform someone about your proposed times of arrival and departure.		
Check which is the right flight, ferry or hovercraft.		
Ask about the location of facilities.		
State whether you wish to declare anything at the customs.		

HOLIDAYS   GENERAL

Talk about holidays in general, saying:		
where you normally spend your holidays		
how long they last		
with whom you go on holiday		
what you normally do.		
Understand others giving the same information.		
Describe a previous holiday:		
where you went		
how you went		
with whom you went		
for how long		
where you stayed		
what the weather was like		
what you saw and did		
what your general impressions were.		
Understand others giving the same information.		
Describe your holiday plans.		
Say whether you have been abroad, e.g. to Germany/Austria/Switzerland, and give details if applicable.		
Understand others giving above information.		
Supply information about travel documents.		

ACCIDENT

You should be able to do the following:		
Ask or advise someone to phone (doctor, police, fire brigade, ambulance, consulate, acquaintance).		
Ask for someone's name and address.		
Suggest filling in a road accident form.		
Describe an accident.		
Report that there has been an accident.		
Ask or say whether it is serious.		
Deny responsibility and say whose fault it was.		

SHOPPING

GENERAL

You should be able to:		
Ask for information about supermarkets, shopping centres, markets, shops.		
Ask where specific shops and departments are.		
Discuss shopping habits.		

SHOPS AND MARKETS

You should be able to:		
Ask whether particular goods are available.		
Ask for particular items (mentioning e.g. colour, size, who it is for, etc.).		
Find out how much things cost.		
Say an item is (not) satisfactory or too expensive, small, big, etc.		
Say you (do not) prefer or want to take something.		
Express quantity required (including weights, volumes, containers)		
Find out opening and closing times.		
Say that is all you require.		
Say thank you.		
Enquire about costs and prices.		
Pay for items.		
Say whether things are (too) expensive.		
State whether you have enough money.		
Understand currencies used in German-speaking countries, including written and printed prices.		
Ask for small change.		
Return unsatisfactory goods and ask for a refund or replacement.		

FOOD AND DRINK

GENERAL

You should be able to do the following:		
Discuss your likes, dislikes and preferences and those of others.		
Discuss your typical meals, meal times, and eating habits.		
Buy food and drink (see Shops and Markets).		
Explain to a visitor what a dish is, or what it contains.		

CAFÉ, RESTAURANT AND OTHER PUBLIC PLACES

Attract the attention of the waiter/waitress.		
Order a drink or snack.		
Order a meal.		
Ask for a particular fixed-price menu.		
Say how many there are in your group.		
Ask for a table (for a certain number).		

Ask about availability of certain dishes and drinks.		
Ask the cost of dishes and drinks.		
Ask for an explanation or description of something on the menu.		
Express opinions about a meal or dish.		
Accept or reject suggestions.		
Ask if the service charge is included.		
Ask about the location of facilities (e.g. toilets, telephone).		

AT HOME

Express hunger and thirst.		
Ask about time and place of meals.		
Ask for food and table articles (including asking for more, a little, a lot).		
React to offers of food (accept, decline, apologise, express pleasure).		
Express likes, dislikes and preferences.		
Express appreciation and pay compliments.		
Respond to a toast, e.g. *Prost*		

SERVICES POST OFFICE

Ask where a post office or letter box is.		
Ask how much it costs to send letters, postcards or parcels to a particular country or within Germany/Austria/Switzerland.		
Say whether you would like to send letters, postcards or parcels.		
Buy stamps of a particular value.		
Find out opening and closing times.		
Say that is all you require.		
Give and seek information about where phone calls can be made.		
Ask if you can make a phone call.		
Ask for a phone number and give your own phone number.		
Answer a phone call, stating who you are.		
Make a phone call and ask to speak to someone.		
Ask someone to ring you up.		
Find out if others can be contacted by phone.		
Tell others you will ring up.		
Ask for coins.		
Ask for a reversed charge call.		
Send a telegram.		

BANK OR EXCHANGE OFFICE

Say you would like to change travellers' cheques or money (including sterling).		
Ask for coins or notes of a particular denomination.		
Give proof of identity (e.g. show passport).		
Cope with any likely eventuality that may arise while using a bank or foreign exchange office to change currency or cheques.		

LOST PROPERTY

Report a loss or theft:		
stating what you have lost		
saying when and where it was lost or left		
describing the item (size, shape, colour, make, contents).		
Express surprise, pleasure, disappointment, anger.		

HAVING THINGS REPAIRED AND CLEANED

Report an accident, damage done or breakdown.		
Ask if shoes, clothes, camera, etc. can be repaired.		
Explain what is wrong and ask if shoes, etc. can be repaired.		
Ask for, and offer, advice about getting something cleaned or repaired.		
Ask for an item of clothing to be cleaned.		
Arrange for clothing to be washed.		
Find out how long it will take, what it will cost, when an item will be ready.		
Thank people, complain, express disappointment, pleasure. Suggest the need for repair or cleaning and report or comment on any action taken.		

LANGUAGE PROBLEMS

State whether or not you understand.		
Ask someone to repeat what he/she has said.		
Ask for and understand the spelling out of names, place names, etc.		
Ask if someone speaks English or German.		
State how well or how little you speak and understand German.		
Ask what things are called in German or English.		
Ask what words or phrases mean.		
Say you do not know (something).		
Say that you have forgotten (something).		
Apologise.		
Ask whether, or state that, something is correct.		
Say for how long you have been learning German and any other languages you know.		
Ask someone to explain something, to correct mistakes.		
Ask how something is pronounced.		

WEATHER

Describe or comment on current weather conditions.		
Ask about weather conditions in Germany/Austria/Switzerland.		
Describe the climate of your own country and ask about the climate in Germany/Austria/Switzerland.		
Understand simple predictions about weather conditions.		
Understand spoken and written weather forecasts.		

TOURIST INFORMATION

Ask for and understand information about a town or region (maps, brochures of hotels and camp sites).		
Ask for and understand details of excursions, shows, places of interest (location, costs, times).		
Give above information about your own area or one you have visited to others, e.g. prospective tourists.		
React to (i.e. welcome or reject) suggestions about activities and places of interest.		
Write a short letter asking for information and brochures about a town or region and its tourist facilities or attractions.		

ACCOMMODATION   GENERAL

Describe accommodation you use or have used.		
Write a short letter asking about the availability and price of accommodation at a hotel, campsite or youth hostel and about amenities available.		
Write a short letter booking such accommodation.		
Read and understand relevant information about accommodation, e.g. brochures.		
Make complaints.		

HOTEL

Ask if there are rooms available.		
State when you require a room/rooms and for how long.		
Say what sort of room is required.		
Ask the cost (per night, per person, per room).		
Say it is too expensive.		
Ask to see the room(s).		
Accept or reject a room.		
Check in.		
Say that you have (not) reserved accommodation.		
Identify yourself.		
Ask if there is a particular facility (e.g. restaurant) in or near the hotel.		
Ask where facilities are, e.g. telephone, car park, lift, lounge.		
Ask if meals are included.		
Ask if meals are available.		
Ask the times of meals.		
Ask for your key.		
Say you would like to pay.		
Say thank you.		

YOUTH HOSTEL

Ask if there is any room.		
State when and for how long.		
State how many males and females require accommodation.		
Say whether you have reserved or not.		
Identify yourself.		
Ask the cost (per night, per person or facility).		
Ask if there is a particular facility in or near the hostel.		
Ask where facilities are.		
Say you would like to pay.		
Ask about meal times.		
Ask about opening and closing times.		
Ask about rules and regulations.		
Say you have a sleeping bag.		
Say you wish to hire a sleeping bag.		

CAMPSITE

Ask if there is any room.		
State when and for how long.		
Say whether you have reserved or not.		
Identify yourself.		
Say how many tents, caravans, people or vehicles there are.		
Say how many children and adults are in the group.		
Ask the cost (per night, per person, per tent, caravan, vehicle or facility).		
Say it is too expensive.		
Ask if there is a particular facility on or near the site.		
Ask where the facilities are.		
Buy essential supplies.		
Ask about rules and regulations.		

SOCIAL RELATIONSHIPS

RELATIONS WITH OTHERS (GENERAL)

Say whether you are a member of any clubs/groups; if so, which clubs and what activities are involved.		
Give information about your friends.		
Say if you have any friends in Austria/Germany/Switzerland.		

MAKING ACQUAINTANCES

Greet someone and respond to greetings.		
Ask how someone is and reply to similar enquiries.		
Say that you are pleased to meet someone.		
Introduce yourself (see also Personal Identification).		
Introduce an acquaintance to someone else.		
Give, receive and exchange gifts.		
Make a telephone call.		

ARRANGING A MEETING OR AN ACTIVITY

Find out what a friend wants to do.		
Ask what is on TV or at the cinema.		
Express preferences for an activity (e.g. watching TV, going out, visiting a friend).		
Invite someone to go out (stating when and where).		
Invite someone or suggest going to a particular place or event or on a visit.		
Accept or decline invitations.		
State that something is possible, impossible, probable or certain.		
Thank and apologise.		
Express pleasure.		
Ask about, suggest or confirm a time and place to meet.		
Ask about and state the cost (of entry, etc.).		
Express surprise, pleasure, regret, doubt, certainty.		
Apologise for late arrival.		
State likes and dislikes.		

CURRENT AFFAIRS

You should be able to follow the recounting or discussion of current issues and events of general news value, and of interest to 16-year-old students, and to express your reaction to such items.		

HEALTH AND WELFARE

GENERAL

State how you feel (well, ill, better, hot, cold, hungry, thirsty, tired).		
Ask others how they feel.		
Ask about taking a bath or shower.		
Ask for soap, toothpaste, towel.		
Refer to parts of the body where you are in pain or discomfort.		
Call for help.		
Warn about danger.		
Say you would like to rest or go to bed.		

ILLNESS AND INJURY

Report minor ailments (e.g. temperature, cold, sunburn).		
Ask for items in a chemist's and ask if they have anything for particular ailments.		
Say you would like to lie down.		
Respond to an enquiry about how long an ailment or symptom has persisted.		
Say you would like to see a doctor or dentist.		
Report injuries.		
Deal with contact with the medical services.		
Say whether you take medicine regularly and, if so, what.		
Say whether or not you are insured.		
Tell others about medical facilities, surgery hours.		

VOCABULARY

KEY TO SYMBOLS AND ABBREVIATIONS

GERMAN–ENGLISH VOCABULARY (COMPREHENSIVE)

ENGLISH–GERMAN VOCABULARY (SELECTIVE)

GETTING STARTED

The German word for 'vocabulary' is *Wortschatz* – a treasury of words. And that is just what this chapter is. It is a treasury of all the valuable words which you need to know. Do you know, for instance, what a *Hubschrauber* is? Or a *Schiedsrichter*? And do you know how to say in German 'congratulations' or 'good luck'? Well, it is all here!

The German–English list is **comprehensive**, covering the words required by all the examining groups. The English–German list which follows is **selective**, covering commonly used terms. There is also, in Chapter 3, a detailed breakdown of German words by **topic area** that can guide you when you are seeking the translation of a particular English word.

Und wir wünschen dir viel spaß und alles Gute!

KEY TO SYMBOLS AND ABBREVIATIONS

All words listed without a preceding symbol are for active and receptive use at Basic Level.

R All words listed with a preceding R are for receptive use only at Basic Level.
* All words listed with a preceding * are for active and receptive use at Higher Level.
H All words listed with a preceding H are for receptive use only at Higher Level.

All words for active or receptive use at Basic Level are automatically for active use at Higher Level.

Plurals of nouns are indicated by (-), (-e), (⁻e), (⁻er), (-n), (-en), (-s), (-se) as appropriate.

(*sep.*) indicates a separable verb.

Further explanations in English are given in brackets where relevant to clarify meanings, e.g. ausgeben *to spend (money)*.

GERMAN–ENGLISH VOCABULARY (COMPREHENSIVE)

The list which follows is based on a detailed analysis of the vocabulary listed by the individual examining groups. There are many common items, but there are some interesting discrepancies, omissions and additions. The list I have drawn up is fully comprehensive at both levels and should serve you well. It is intended primarily as a reference list and a means of cross-checking against vocabulary contained in the individual topic areas.

* ab *from*

* abbauen (*sep.*) *to take down, dismantle; mine*

R abbiegen (*sep.*) *to turn off (directions)*

der Abend (-e) *evening*

das Abendbrot (-e) *evening meal (cold: bread + . . .)*

das Abendessen (-) *evening meal (hot)*

abends *in the evening*

aber *but*

abfahren (*sep.*) *to depart, leave*

die Abfahrt (-en) *departure*

* der Abfall (¨e) *rubbish*

* der Abfalleimer (-) *rubbish bin*

abfliegen (*sep.*) *to fly, take off*

* der Abflug (¨e) *departure (of flights)*

* abgeben (*sep.*) *to hand/give in (lost property)*

abgemacht *agreed*

H abhängen (*sep.*) von + *dat to depend on*

es hängt von ihm ab *it depends on him*

* abheben (*sep.*) *to take off (hat, lid, cover)*

abholen (*sep.*) *to collect, meet (e.g. at station)*

* das Abitur *Advanced Level examination*

* ablehnen (*sep.*) *to decline, reject*

abräumen (*sep.*) *to tidy up, clear away/up*

* abschleppen (*sep.*) *to tow away, drag away*

* der Abschleppdienst *breakdown service*

* der Abschleppwagen *breakdown vehicle*

abschließen (*sep.*) *to lock (up)*

* die Abschlußprüfung (-en) *school-leaving examination*

* abschreiben (*sep.*) *to copy (cheat), write down*

der Absender (-) *sender (of letter)*

Abs. *abbreviation for* Absender

* abspülen (*sep.*) *to wash up*

H Abstand halten *to keep one's distance (driving)*

H abstellen (*sep.*) *to turn off (motor, engine)*

das Abteil (-e) *compartment (of train)*

* die Abteilung (-en) *department (in shop, office)*

abtrocknen (*sep.*) *to dry up*

abwaschen (*sep.*) *to wash up*

H achten auf + *acc. to pay attention to, look after*

Achtung! *look out! watch out! take care!*

ADAC *German AA motoring equivalent*

die Adresse (-n) *address*

* der Affe (-n) *ape, monkey*

R ähnlich *similar*

die Ahnung (-en) *idea*

(ich habe) keine Ahnung *I've no idea, I haven't a clue*

* aktuell *current, currently, topical*

all- *every, all*

alle sein *to be all gone*

mein Geld ist alle *my money is all gone*

allein *alone*

* die Allergie (-n) *allergy*

alles *everything*

alles Gute! *all the best!*

als *when (conj.), than (comparison)*

also *so, therefore*

alt *old*

älter *older*

das Alter *age*

altmodisch *old-fashioned*

die Altstadt (¨e) *old town*

am (an dem) *at the, on the*

Amerika *America*

der Amerikaner (-) *American (person)*

amerikanisch *American*

die Ampel (-n) *traffic lights*

an *at, on*

an . . . vorbei *past (e.g. to go past)*

an der Kirche vorbei *past the church*

* an Bord *on board*

* an sein *to be on (e.g. TV)*

* anbieten (*sep.*) *to offer*

R das Andenken (-) *souvenir*

ander- *other*

anders (als) *different (from)*

anderthalb *one and a half*

anderthalb Stunden *one and a half hours*

der Anfang (¨e) *beginning*

anfangen (*sep.*) *to begin*

R das Angebot (-e) *offer*

angeln *to fish*

* die Angelrute (-n) *fishing rod*

angenehm *pleasant; pleased to meet you!*

* der Angestellte (-n) *employee*
* die }

die Angst (¨e) *fear*

anhaben (*sep.*) *to have on, wear*

per Anhalter fahren *to hitch-hike*

ankommen (*sep.*) *to arrive*

die Ankunft (¨e) *arrival*

die Anlage (-n) *system, installation; park*

anlassen (*sep.*) *to start (car, engine)*

R Anlieger frei *residents only (road sign)*

anmachen (*sep.*) *to turn on (e.g. light)*

H sich anmelden (*sep.*) *to book in, report, enrol*

'R die Anmeldung (-en) *booking, enrolment, registration*

* annehmen (*sep.*) *to accept*

der Anorak (-s) *anorak*

anprobieren (*sep.*) *to try on*

der Anruf (-e) *telephone call*

anrufen (*sep.*) *to telephone, make a phone call*

ans (an das) *to the*

R der Ansager (-) *announcer (e.g. TV/ radio)*

H (sich) anschnallen (*sep.*) *to fasten (one's) seat belt*

R die Anschrift (-en) *address (e.g. on letter)*

ansehen (*sep.*) *to watch, look at*

die Ansichtskarte (-n) *postcard*

anstreichen (*sep.*) *to paint*

anstrengend *exhausting, hard work*

die Antwort (-en) *answer, reply*

antworten (auf + *acc.*) *to answer, reply (to)*

(sich) anziehen (*sep.*) *to put on, to dress/(get dressed)*

der Anzug (¨e) *suit*

der Apfel (¨) *apple*

der Apfelsaft (¨e) *apple juice*

die Apfelsine (-n) *orange*

die Apotheke (-n) *chemist's*

der Apotheker (-) *chemist*

der Apparat (-e) *telephone, camera, set, machine*

am Apparat *on the telephone, speaking*

der Appetit *appetite*

guten Appetit *enjoy your meal! bon appétit!*

der April *April*

die Arbeit (-en) *work*

arbeiten *to work*

der Arbeiter (-) *worker*

H der Arbeitgeber (-) *employer*

H der Arbeitnehmer (-) *employee*

R arbeitslos *out of work, unemployed*

R (sich) ärgern *to annoy/(get annoyed)*

arm *poor*

der Arm (-e) *arm*

das Armband (-e) *bracelet*

die Armbanduhr (-en) *wrist watch*

der Artikel (-) *article, item*

der Arzt (¨e) *doctor (male)*

die Ärztin (-nen) *doctor (female)*

* der Aschenbecher (-) *ashtray*

R atemlos *breathless*

auch *also, too*

auf *on, onto, to*

auf dem Lande *in the country*

auf deutsch *in German*

auf die Toilette gehen *to go to the toilet*

auf Wiederhören! *goodbye! (on telephone)*

auf Wiedersehen! *goodbye!*

* aufbauen (*sep.*) *to build up*

der Aufenthalt (-e) *stay*

* die Aufführung (-en) *performance, production*

die Aufgabe (-n) *exercise (school)*

* aufgeben (*sep.*) *to give up*

* aufheben (*sep.*) *to pick up (e.g. from the ground)*

H die Aufheiterung (-en) *brighter period (weather)*

aufhören (*sep.*) *to stop, give up, cease*

* der Aufkleber (-) *sticker*

aufmachen (*sep.*) *to open*

* die Aufnahme (-n) *photo, recording*

aufpassen (*sep.*) *to pay attention*

aufräumen (*sep.*) *to tidy up, clear away/up*

* aufschlagen (*sep.*) *to open; to pitch (tent)*

der Aufschnitt *cold meat(s)*

aufstehen (*sep.*) *to get up, stand up*

aufwachen (*sep.*) *to awake, wake up*

der Aufzug (¨e) *lift, elevator*

das Auge (-n) *eye*
der Augenblick (-e) *moment*
der August *August*
* die Aula (die Aulen) *(assembly) hall, lecture theatre*
  aus *out, out of, from, made of*
der Ausdruck (¨e) *expression*
die Ausfahrt (-en) *exit, drive (motoring)*
* ausfallen *(sep.)* *to be cancelled*
der Ausflug (¨e) *excursion, trip*
R ausfüllen *(sep.)* *to fill out, complete (forms)*
der Ausgang (¨e) *way out, exit*
* ausgeben *(sep.)* *to spend (money)*
  ausgehen *(sep.)* *to go out*
  ausgezeichnet *excellent*
die Auskunft (¨e) *information*
das Ausland *abroad*
* der Ausländer (-) *foreigner*
  ausmachen *(sep.)* *to turn off/out (e.g. light)*
  auspacken *(sep.)* *to unpack*
* ausreichend *satisfactory (German school grade)*
R sich ausruhen *(sep.)* *to relax, rest*
  ausschalten *(sep.)* *to switch off (e.g. TV/radio)*
  aussehen *(sep.)* *to look, appear*
  Außen- *outside . . .*
  außer *apart from, besides, except*
  außer Betrieb *out of order, out of action*
  außerdem *besides*
  äußerst *extremely, exceptionally*
die Aussicht (-en) *view, outlook*
* aussprechen *(sep.)* *to express, pronounce*
  aussteigen *(sep.)* *to get off/out*
die Ausstellung (-en) *exhibition*
der Ausstieg (-e) *exit (e.g. on bus, train)*
* austragen *(sep.)* *to deal with, cancel*
der Austausch (-e) *exchange (school visit)*
der Austauschpartner (-) *exchange partner*
  austrinken *(sep.)* *to drink up*
R der Ausverkauf *sale (reduced price)*
* ausverkauft *sold out*
* die Auswahl *selection, choice*
der Ausweis (-e) *identity card, papers*
  sich ausziehen *(sep.)* *to get undressed*
das Auto (-s) *car*
die Autobahn (-en) *motorway*
H das Autobahndreieck (-e) *motorway merging point*
H das Autobahnkreuz (-e) *motorway intersection*
* die Autofähre (-n) *car ferry*
der Automat (-en) *vending machine*
R die Autowäsche (-n) *car wash*
das Baby (-s) *baby*
* der Bach (¨e) *stream, brook*
  backen *to bake*
der Bäcker (-) *baker*
die Bäckerei (-en) *baker's*
das Bad (¨er) *bath, bathroom*
der Badeanzug (¨e) *swimsuit*
die Badehose (-n) *swimming trunks*
die Bademütze (-n) *bathing hat*

  baden *to bath, bathe, have a bath*
das Badetuch (¨er) *bath(ing) towel*
die Badewanne (-n) *bath, bath tub*
das Badezimmer (-) *bathroom*
das Badminton *badminton*
die Bahn (-en) *railway, track*
der Bahnhof (¨e) *railway station*
der Bahnsteig (-e) *platform (at station)*
der Bahnübergang (¨e) *level crossing*
  bald *soon*
der Balkon (-s) *balcony*
der Ball (¨e) *ball*
die Banane (-n) *banana*
die Bank (-en) *bank (of money)*
die Banknote (-n) *bank note*
die Bar (-s) *bar, pub*
der Bart (¨e) *beard*
  basteln *to make models, do handicraft, etc.*
die Batterie (-n) *battery*
der Bauch (¨e) *stomach*
  Bauchschmerzen *stomach ache*
  bauen *to build*
der Bauer (-n) *farmer*
der Bauernhof (¨e) *farm*
der Baum (¨e) *tree*
* die Baumwolle *cotton*
die Baustelle (-n) *building site, roadworks*
der Beamte (-n) *official, civil servant*
  beantworten *to answer*
* sich bedanken *to say thank you, express gratitude*
  bedauern *to regret*
  bedeckt *cloudy (of sky)*
R bedienen *to serve, wait on*
  sich bedienen *to serve/help oneself*
die Bedienung (-en) *service*
  sich beeilen *to hurry*
  sich befinden *to be situated, to be*
der Beginn (-e) *beginning, start*
  beginnen *to begin, start*
  begleiten *to accompany*
  begrüßen *to greet*
  behandeln *to treat (e.g. a patient)*
R behilflich *helpful, of assistance*
  bei *at (the house of), near, on*
  beide *both*
R beilegen *(sep.)* *to enclose*
  beim (bei dem) *at the, near the*
das Bein (-e) *leg*
das Beispiel (-e) *example*
  beißen *to bite*
  bekannt *well known, famous*
der) Bekannte (-n) *acquaintance*
die)
* sich beklagen *to complain*
  bekommen *to get, receive*
ein belegtes Brot (-e) *open sandwich, bread and . . .*
  Belgien *Belgium*
* der Belgier *Belgian (person)*
  belgisch *Belgian (adjective)*
  beliebt *popular, liked*
* bellen *to bark*
  bemerken *to notice*
* benutzen *to use*
das Benzin *petrol*
  beobachten *to watch, observe*
  bequem *comfortable*
der Berg (-e) *mountain*
  bergsteigen *to climb, go*

  mountaineering
R der Bericht (-e) *report*
der Beruf (-e) *profession*
* die Berufsberatung *careers advice*
* die Berufsschule (-n) *technical college*
* berufstätig *in paid work, employed*
  berühmt *famous*
  beschäftigt *busy, occupied*
der Bescheid (-e) *information, notification*
  Bescheid sagen *to let someone know, tell someone*
* beschließen *to decide*
  beschreiben *to describe*
R die Beschreibung (-en) *description*
* sich beschweren *to complain*
  besetzt *occupied, taken; engaged (phone)*
  besichtigen *to visit, see (sights)*
* die Besichtigung (-en) *visit*
  besonder(s) *special/(especially)*
* besorgen *to obtain*
  besser *better*
die Besserung *improvement, recovery*
  gute Besserung! *get well soon!*
  best- *best*
* das Besteck (-e) *cutlery, place setting (at table)*
* bestehen (aus) *to exist; consist (of)*
  bestellen *to order (food, books, etc.)*
  bestimmt *definite(ly), certain(ly)*
  bestrafen *to punish*
der Besuch (-e) *visit*
  besuchen *to visit*
  betreten *to enter; step on (e.g. grass)*
* der Betrieb (-e) *firm, factory, works*
  außer Betrieb *out of order, not working*
* die Betriebsferien *works' holidays*
* betrunken *drunk*
das Bett (-en) *bed*
  ins Bett/zu Bett gehen *to go to bed*
* die Bettdecke (-n) *blanket*
* die Bettwäsche *bed linen*
  bevor *before (conjunction)*
* sich bewegen *to move*
  beweisen *to prove*
* bewölkt *cloudy*
H die Bewölkung *clouding over, becoming cloudy; cloud*
  bezahlen *to pay (for)*
die Bibliothek (-en) *library*
das Bier (-e) *beer*
  bieten *to offer, provide*
das Bild (-er) *picture*
  billig *cheap*
* binden *to tie, bind, unite*
  Biologie *Biology*
die Birne (-n) *pear; light-bulb*
  bis *until, as far as; by (of time)*
  bis bald *see you soon!*
  bis gleich *see you soon/shortly!*
  bis morgen *until/see you/by tomorrow*
  bis später *see you later!*
  bis zu *as far as*

ein bißchen *a little, a bit*

bitte *please; that's all right, here*

bitte nochmals *again please, same again please*

bitte schön *here you are, that's all right*

bitte sehr *here you are, that's all right*

bitten *to ask, request*

* die Blaskapelle (-n) *brass band*
* blaß *pale*

R das Blatt (-er) *leaf (of tree), page (of book), sheet (of paper)*

blau *blue; drunk (slang)*

bleiben *to stay, remain*

der Bleistift (-e) *pencil*

* der Blick (-e) *view, look*
* blind *blind*

der Blitz (-e) *flash (photo), flash of lightning*

blitzen *to flash (of photo or lightning)*

der Block (-s or -e) *block (of houses, flats)*

die Blockflöte (-n) *recorder (instrument)*

* blöd *mad, stupid*
* der Blödsinn *madness, nonsense, stupidity*

blond *blond, fair*

die Blume (-n) *flower*

* der Blumenkohl (Blumenköpfe) *cauliflower*

die Bluse (-n) *blouse*

* das Blut *blood*
* bluten *to bleed*

die Bockwurst *sausage (large Frankfurter)*

der Boden *floor, ground*

der Bodensee *Lake Constance*

* die Bohne (-n) *green bean*

das/der Bonbon (-s) *sweet*

das Boot (-e) *boat*

böse *angry, cross; naughty*

* braten *to fry, roast*
* der Braten *roast (a roast dish)*

das Brathähnchen (-) *roast chicken*

die Bratkartoffel (-n) *fried potato*

die Bratwurst (-e) *fried sausage*

brauchen *to need*

braun *brown*

brav *good, well behaved*

die BRD (Bundesrepublik Deutschland) *FRG (Federal Republic of Germany)*

* brechen *to break*

breit *broad, wide*

die Bremse (-n) *brake*

* bremsen *to brake*
* das Brett (-er) *board, shelf; stage (slang)*

der Brief (-e) *letter*

der Brieffreund (-e) *pen friend*

der Briefkasten (-) *letter box*

die Briefmarke (-n) *stamp*

die Brieftasche (-n) *wallet*

der Briefträger (-) *postman*

der Briefumschlag (-e) *envelope*

die Brille (-n) *(pair of) glasses*

bringen *to bring*

die Broschüre (-n) *brochure*

das Brot (-e) *bread, loaf of bread*

das Brötchen (-) *bread roll*

die Brücke (-n) *bridge*

der Bruder (-) *brother*

* die Brust (-e) *breast, chest*

das Buch (-er) *book*

buchen *to book*

die Bücherei (-en) *bookshop*

H buchstabieren *to spell*

die Buchhandlung (-en) *bookshop*

* bügeln *to iron*
* die Bühne (-n) *stage (of theatre, concert)*
* bummeln *to wander, stroll (in town)*
* die Bundesliga *German Football League*

die Bundesrepublik *The Federal Republic*

der Bungalow (-s) *bungalow*

bunt *bright, brightly coloured*

die Burg (-en) *castle*

* der Bürgermeister (-) *mayor*

der Bürgersteig (-e) *pavement*

das Büro (-s) *office*

die Bürste (-n) *brush*

* sich bürsten *to brush (oneself)*

der Bus (-se) *bus*

der Busbahnhof (-e) *bus station*

die Bushaltestelle (-n) *bus stop*

die Butter *butter*

das Butterbrot (-e) *sandwich*

bzw. *(short for beziehungsweise) r-espectively; that is (to say)*

das Café (-s) *café*

* Campinggaz *calor gas for camping*

der Campingkocher (-) *camping stove*

der Campingplatz (-e) *campsite*

Celsius *Centigrade, Celsius*

* der Champignon (-s) *mushroom*

der Chef (-s) *boss, head*

Chemie *Chemistry*

Chips *crisps*

der Chor (-e) *choir*

die /das Cola (-s) *coke*

der Computer (-s) *computer*

* der Cousin (-s) *cousin (male)*
* die Cousine (-n) *cousin (female)*

die Currywurst (-e) *curried sausage*

da *there*

* da *since (conjunction)*
* das Dach (-er) *roof*
* der Dachboden *attic*
* dagegen *against (it/something)*

damals *then, at that time*

die Dame (-n) *lady*

Damen *or* D *Ladies (on public toilets)*

damit *with it; so that*

der Dampfer *steamer*

danach *afterwards*

der Dank *thanks*

vielen Dank *thanks a lot*

* dankbar *grateful*

danke *thank you*

danke schön/sehr *thank you very much*

danken *to thank*

dann *then*

das geht *that's all right/OK*

daß *that (conjunction)*

das Datum (Daten) *date*

dauern *to last*

* der Daumen (-) *thumb*

die DB (Deutsche Bundesbahn) *German Federal Railway*

die DDR (Deutsche Demokratische Republik) *GDR (German Democratic Republic)*

R die Decke (-n) *ceiling; blanket, cover (on bed)*

decken *to cover; lay (table)*

dein *your*

denken *to think*

* das Denkmal (-er) *monument*

denn *for, because*

* deutlich *clear, clearly*

deutsch *German*

die Deutsche Bundesbahn *German Federal Railway*

der⎫ Deutsche (-n) *German (person)*
die⎭

* deutsches Beefsteak *German beefsteak*

Deutschland *Germany*

R die Deutschemark *German Mark, Deutschmark*

der Dezember *December*

* das Dia (-s) *slide (photo)*

dick *fat*

der Dieb (-e) *thief*

* dienen *to serve*
* der Dienst (-e) *service*

der Dienstag *Tuesday*

Diesel *diesel*

dieser *this*

diesmal *this time*

das Ding (-er) *thing*

direkt *direct, non-stop, without changing*

der Direktor *director, headmaster*

die Diskothek (-en) *discotheque*

DJH *German Youth Hostel Association*

DM or D-Mark (Deutschemark) *German Mark, Deutschmark*

doch *but, however*

der Dom (-e) *cathedral*

die Donau *The Danube*

der Donner (-) *thunder*

donnern *to thunder*

der Donnerstag *Thursday*

* doof *stupid, mad*

das Doppelhaus (-er) *semi-detached house*

das Doppelzimmer (-) *double room*

das Dorf (-er) *village*

dort *there*

dort drüben *over there*

die Dose (-n) *tin, can, jar*

R der Dosenöffner (-) *tin-opener*

dransein (*sep.*) *to have one's turn/go*

ich bin dran *it's my turn/go*

dreckig *dirty*

dringend *urgent*

dritte *third*

die Drogerie (-n) *drugstore*

der Drogist *chemist*

* drohen *to threaten*

drüben *over there*

drücken *to press, push*

dumm *stupid*

dunkel *dark*

dünn *thin*

durch *through*

der Durchfall *diarrhoea*
* durchfallen *(sep.) to fail (test, examination)*
* der Durchgang *thoroughfare*
H der Durchgangsverkehr *through traffic*
der dürfen *to be allowed*
der Durst *thirst*
durstig *thirsty*
die Dusche (-n) *shower*
duschen *to shower*
* duzen *to use du when talking to people*
der D-Zug (-̈e) *fast train*
* der E111-Schein *E111 form (health insurance)*
eben *just, flat*
ebenso *just as*
* echt *genuine, real*
die Ecke (-n) *corner*
egal *equal, same*
das ist mir egal *it's all the same to me*
H die Ehe (-n) *marriage*
H die Ehefrau (-en) *married woman, wife*
H der Ehemann (-̈er) *married man, husband*
H das Ehepaar (-e) *married couple*
* ehrlich *genuine, honest*
das Ei (-er) *egg*
eigen *own, of one's own*
die Eile *hurry*
eilen *to hurry*
der Eilzug (-̈e) *fast train*
ein paar *a few*
ein wenig *a little*
die Einbahnstraße (-n) *one-way street/road*
einbrechen *(sep.) to break in*
R der Einbrecher (-) *burglar*
* der Eindruck (-̈e) *impression*
einfach *simple, easy; single*
die Einfahrt (-en) *entry, entrance*
das Einfamilienhaus (-̈er) *detached house*
der Eingang (-̈e) *entry, entrance*
einige *a few, some*
die Einkäufe machen *to shop, do the shopping*
einkaufen *(sep.) to shop, do the shopping*
* der Einkaufskorb (-̈e) *shopping basket*
* der Einkaufswagen (-) *shopping trolley*
* das Einkaufszentrum (-tren) *shopping centre*
einladen *(sep.) to invite*
die Einladung (-en) *invitation*
* einlösen *(sep.) to cash (cheques)*
einmal *once, single, one portion of*
einordnen *(sep.) to put in order; get into lane*
einpacken *(sep.) to pack*
* einreiben *(sep.) to rub in*
* einreichen *(sep.) to hand in*
* einschalten *(sep.) to switch on*
* einschenken *(sep.) to pour (in)*
* einschl. (einschließlich) *inclusive, included*
* einschlafen *(sep.) to fall asleep*

* einschließlich *inclusive, included*
einsteigen *(sep.) to get on/in*
der Einstieg (-e) *entry, entrance (bus, tram, etc.)*
der Eintritt (-e) *entrance (ticket)*
die Eintrittskarte (-n) *entrance ticket (e.g. to concert)*
* einverstanden *agreed*
einwerfen *(sep.) to post, put in slot*
R der Einwohner (-) *inhabitant*
der Einwurf (-̈e) *slit for inserting coins/letters*
H die Einzelheiten *details*
* die Einzelkarte (-n) *single ticket*
das Einzelkind (-er) *only child*
das Einzelzimmer (-) *single room*
das Eis (-e) *ice-cream; ice*
der Eisbecher (-) *ice-cream sundae*
die Eisenbahn (-en) *railway*
der Elefant (-en) *elephant*
der Elektriker (-) *electrician*
R elektrisch *electric*
* Elektro- *electric . . .*
die Elektrizität *electricity*
die Eltern *parents*
der Empfang (-̈e) *reception*
die Empfangsdame (-n) *receptionist (female)*
R empfehlen *to recommend*
das Ende *end*
enden *to end*
endlich *at last, finally*
das Endspiel (-e) *final (of competition)*
eng *narrow; close (of friendship)*
England *England*
der Engländer *Englishman/British*
die Engländerin *Englishwoman/ British*
englisch *English (thing/ language)*
* der Enkel (-) *grandchild, grandson*
* die Ente (-n) *duck*
entfernt *distant, away, far (away)*
entlang *along*
* (sich) entscheiden *to decide*
entschuldigen *to forgive, excuse*
sich entschuldigen *to apologise*
die Entschuldigung (-en) *apology, excuse*
Entschuldigung! *excuse me!*
* enttäuscht *disappointed*
* entweder *either*
der Entwerter (-) *(ticket) cancelling machine*
R die Erbse (-n) *pea*
die Erdbeere (-n) *strawberry*
die Erde *earth, ground*
das Erdgeschoß *ground floor*
Erdkunde *Geography*
* erfahren *to learn, experience*
* die Erfahrung (-en) *experience*
* der Erfolg (-e) *success*
R Erfrischungen *refreshments*
* das Ergebnis (-se) *result*
* erhalten *to receive, get*
* erhältlich *obtainable*
* sich erholen *to recover, get better*
* sich erinnern *to remember*
* sich erkälten *to catch a cold*
* erkältet sein *to have a cold*
* die Erkältung (-en) *cold (illness)*

R erkennen *to recognise*
erklären *to explain*
* sich erkundigen *to enquire*
erlauben *to allow*
R die Erlaubnis (-se) *permission*
R die Ermäßigung (-en) *reduction (of cost)*
R ernst *serious*
erreichen *to reach, catch (train/bus)*
H das Ersatzteil (-e) *spare part*
erscheinen *to appear, come into view*
erschrecken *to frighten*
* erschrocken *frightened*
erst *first, firstly*
erst (um) *not until, only (of time)*
erste *first (adjective)*
die erste Hilfe *first aid*
R erstaunt *surprised*
der Erwachsene (-n) *adult, grown-up*
* erwarten *to expect*
erzählen *to tell, relate*
* es freut mich *I'm pleased*
es geht *(it's) all right*
es gibt + acc. *there is, there are*
es ist mir egal *I don't mind*
es macht nichts *it doesn't matter*
es tut mir leid *I'm sorry*
das Essen *food, meal*
essen *to eat*
das Eßzimmer (-) *dining room*
die Etage (-n) *floor, storey*
etwa *about, approximately, somewhat*
etwas *something*
euer *your*
Europa *Europe*
R evangelisch *Protestant*
EWG/EG *EEC/EC/Common Market*
* das Examen *examination*
die Fabrik (-en) *factory*
der Fabrikarbeiter (-) *factory worker*
das Fach (-̈er) *subject (school)*
die Fachhochschule (-n) *college*
die Fachschule (-n) *technical college*
* der Fahrausweis (-e) *ticket*
die Fähre (-n) *ferry*
fahren *to go, travel, drive*
der Fahrer (-) *driver*
der Fahrgast (-̈e) *passenger*
die Fahrkarte (-n) *ticket*
der Fahrkartenschalter (-) *ticket office*
der Fahrplan (-̈e) *timetable (of transport)*
* der Fahrpreis (-e) *fare*
das Fahrrad (-̈er) *bicycle*
der Fahrschein (-e) *ticket*
der Fahrstuhl (-̈e) *lift, elevator*
die Fahrt (-en) *journey*
* das Fahrzeug (-e) *vehicle*
der Fall (-̈e) *case, event*
auf keinen Fall *in no way*
fallen *to fall*
fallen lassen *to drop*
* falls *in case*
falsch *false, incorrect, wrong*
die Familie (-n) *family*
der Familienname (-n) *surname*
der Fan (-s) *fan*

der Fanatiker (-) *fan(atic)*
    fangen *to catch*
die Farbe (-n) *colour*
der Fasching *Carnival*
    fast *almost, nearly*
    faul *lazy*
der Februar *February*
der Federball *badminton*
* das Federbett (-en) *quilt, duvet*
    fehlen *to be missing/absent*
der Fehler (-) *mistake*
* die Feier (-n) *celebration, party*
* der Feierabend *end of work, evening*
R   feiern *to celebrate*
R der Feiertag (-e) *public holiday*
    das Feld (-er) *field*
    das Fenster (-) *window*
    die Ferien *holidays*
* das Ferngespräch (-e) *long-distance call*
    der Fernsehapparat (-e) *television set*
        fernsehen (*sep.*) *to watch television*
    der Fernseher (-) *television set*
* der Fernsprecher (-) *(public) telephone*
        fertig *ready*
    das Fest (-e) *celebration, party*
        festhalten (*sep.*) *to hold onto/fast*
*   fett *fat*
R   feucht *damp*
    das Feuer (-) *fire*
        Feuer haben *to have a light (colloquial)*
R der Feuerlöscher (-) *fire extinguisher*
R die Feuerwehr *fire brigade*
* der Feuerwehrwagen (-) *fire engine*
    das Feuerzeug (-e) *cigarette lighter*
    das Fieber *temperature*
    der Film (-e) *film*
    der Filzstift (-e) *felt-tip pen*
        finden *to find*
    der Finger (-) *finger*
* die Firma (Firmen) *firm, company*
    der Fisch (-e) *fish*
        fit *fit*
*   flach *flat*
    die Flasche (-n) *bottle*
* der Flaschenöffner (-) *bottle-opener*
    das Fleisch *meat*
    der Fleischer (-) *butcher*
    die Fleischerei (-en) *butcher's shop*
        fleißig *hard-working, industrious*
    die Fliege (-n) *fly*
        fliegen *to fly*
        fließen *to flow*
*   fließend *flowing, running (water)*
    die Flöte (-n) *flute*
    der Flug (⁻e) *flight*
    der Fluggast (⁻e) *passenger (on flight)*
    der Flughafen (⁻) *airport*
    der Flugplatz (⁻e) *airport*
    das Flugzeug (-e) *aeroplane*
    der Flur (-e) *corridor, hall*
    der Fluß (Flüsse) *river*
        folgen *to follow*
R   folgend *following*
* die Forelle (-n) *trout*
R das Formular (-e) *form (to be completed)*

* der Forst (-en) *forest*
R der Fortschritt (-e) *progress*
    das Foto (-s) *photo*
    der Fotoapparat (-e) *camera*
        fotografieren *to take a photo*
    die Frage (-n) *question*
        eine Frage stellen *to ask a question*
        fragen *to ask*
    der Franken *Swiss franc*
        Frankreich *France*
R der Franzose (-n) *Frenchman*
    die Französin (-nen) *Frenchwoman*
        französisch *French (adjective)*
    die Frau (-en) *woman*
        Frau . . . *Mrs . . .*
    das Fräulein (-) *girl, waitress*
        Fräulein! *waitress!*
        Fräulein . . . *Miss . . .*
*   frech *cheeky*
        frei *free, open, not taken*
    das Freibad (⁻er) *open-air swimming pool*
R   freihalten (*sep.*) *to keep clear/free (e.g. drive)*
    der Freitag *Friday*
    die Freizeit *free time*
H die Freizeitbeschäftigung (-en) *leisure activity*
R das Freizeitzentrum *leisure centre*
        fremd *strange, foreign*
    der Fremde (-n) *stranger, foreigner*
* das Fremdenzimmer (-) *room (in guest house)*
    die Fremdsprache (-n) *foreign language*
*   fressen *to eat (of animals)*
        sich freuen *to be pleased*
    der Freund (-e) *friend*
        freundlich *friendly*
* der Frieden *peace*
H der Friedhof (⁻e) *cemetery, graveyard*
        frieren *to be cold, freeze*
H die Frikadelle (-n) *rissole*
        frisch *fresh*
R der Friseur/Frisör *hairdresser (male)*
R die Friseuse/Frisörin *hairdresser (female)*
* die Frisur (-en) *haircut, style*
        froh *happy, glad*
        frohe Ostern *Happy Easter*
        frohe Weihnachten *Happy/Merry Christmas*
        frohes Neujahr *Happy New Year*
        fröhlich *happy, cheerful*
        früh *early*
*   früher *earlier, previously*
    der Frühling *Spring*
    das Frühstück (-e) *breakfast*
        frühstücken *to have breakfast*
*   sich fühlen *to feel*
        führen *to lead, take*
    der Führerschein (-e) *driving licence*
* die Führung (-en) *guided tour; lead*
*   füllen *to fill*
* der Füller (-) *fountain pen*
    das Fundbüro (-s) *lost property office*
R   funktionieren *to function*
        für *for (preposition)*
        furchtbar *terrible*
    der Fuß (Füsse) *foot*
        zu Fuß *on foot, walking*

    der Fußball (⁻e) *football*
    der Fußballplatz (⁻e) *football ground/pitch*
    der Fußballspieler (-) *footballer*
    der Fußboden *floor (opposite of ceiling)*
    der Fußgänger (-) *pedestrian*
    die Fußgängerzone (-n) *pedestrian zone*
* das Futter *food (for animals)*
*   füttern *to feed (animals)*

    die Gabel (-n) *fork (cutlery)*
R der Gang (⁻e) *corridor; gear (of car)*
* die Gans (⁻e) *goose*
        ganz *quite, very (adverb); all (adjective)*
* die Ganztagsschule (-n) *day school*
        gar kein *no, none at all*
        gar nicht *not at all*
        gar nichts *nothing at all*
    die Garage (-n) *garage*
* die Garderobe (-n) *wardrobe; cloakroom*
* die Gardine (-n) *curtain*
    der Garten (⁻) *garden*
    das Gas *gas*
R   Gas geben *to accelerate*
    der Gast (⁻e) *guest*
    das Gasthaus (⁻er) *hotel*
    der Gasthof (⁻e) *hotel*
    die Gaststätte (-n) *hotel*
*   gebacken *baked*
* das Gebäck *biscuits*
    das Gebäude (-) *building*
        geben *to give*
* das Gebiet (-e) *area, region*
* das Gebirge *mountains, mountain range*
        geboren *born*
*   gebraten *roast, baked, fried*
H   gebrauchen *to use*
H die Gebrauchsanweisung (-en) *instructions for use*
H   gebraucht *used, second-hand*
H die Gebühr (-en) *fee, charge*
H   gebührenpflichtig *fee payable, chargeable*
R die Geburt (-en) *birth*
R das Geburtsdatum (-en) *date of birth*
R der Geburtsort (-e) *place of birth*
    der Geburtstag (-e) *birthday*
*   geduldig *patient*
R die Gefahr (-en) *danger*
        gefährlich *dangerous*
        gefallen *to please*
        es gefällt mir *I like it*
R das Gefängnis (-se) *prison*
        gegen *against, towards; about (time)*
R die Gegend (-en) *area, neighbourhood*
* das Gegenteil (-e) *opposite*
        gegenüber *opposite (preposition)*
* der Gehalt (-e) *content*
* das Gehalt (⁻er) *salary*
        gehen *to go*
R   gehören (+ *dat.*) *to belong (to)*
    die Geige (-n) *violin*
        gelaunt *tempered*
        gut/schlecht gelaunt *good/bad-tempered, in a good/bad mood*
        gelb *yellow*

das Geld (-er) *money*
der Geldbeutel (-) *purse*
die Geldbörse (-n) *purse*
* die Geldstrafe (-n) *(spot) fine (e.g. motoring offence)*
R der Geldwechsel (-) *exchange (of currency)*
H die Gelegenheit (-en) *opportunity, occasion*
H gelegentlich *occasional(ly)*
H gelingen (*impersonal*) *to succeed*
es gelingt mir *I succeed*
* gemischt/gem. *mixed*
das Gemüse *vegetables*
der Gemüsehändler (-) *greengrocer*
* gemütlich *cosy*
genau *exact(ly), precise(ly)*
genug *enough*
* genügen *to be enough, suffice*
geöffnet *open*
Geographie *Geography*
das Gepäck *luggage*
* die Gepäckannahme *left-luggage deposit*
* die Gepäckaufbewahrung *left-luggage office/section*
* die Gepäckaufgabe *left-luggage deposit*
* die Gepäckausgabe *left-luggage collection area*
* das Gepäcknetz (-e) *luggage rack/net*
* die Gepäckrückgabe *left-luggage return area*
der Gepäckträger (-) *porter*
gerade *straight, just*
geradeaus *straight on, straight ahead*
* das Gerät (-e) *piece of equipment, appliance*
* das Gericht (-e) *court (of law); course (meal)*
gern(e) *willingly, gladly*
* gern geschehen *my pleasure*
gernhaben (*sep.*) *to like*
ich hätte gern *I would like*
die Gesamtschule (-n) *comprehensive school*
das Geschäft (-e) *shop, business*
der Geschäftsmann (-er) *businessman*
R die Geschäftszeiten *opening/business hours*
* geschehen *to happen*
das Geschenk (-e) *present*
Geschichte *History*
die Geschichte (-n) *story, tale*
geschieden *divorced, separated*
* das Geschirr (-e) *crockery*
R das Geschlecht (-er) *sex*
geschlossen *closed, shut*
* der Geschmack (-e) *taste*
H die Geschwindigkeit (-en) *speed*
die Geschwister *brothers and sisters*
das Gesicht (-er) *face*
gesperrt *closed, blocked (of road)*
* das Gespräch (-e) *conversation*
R gestatten *to allow, permit*
R gestattet *allowed, permitted*
gestern *yesterday*
* gestrichen *painted*
* frisch gestrichen *wet paint*
gesund *healthy*

* die Gesundheit *health*
Gesundheit! *bless you! (after sneeze)*
das Getränk (-e) *drink*
R die Getränkekarte (-n) *drinks menu/list*
getrennt *separate(ly) (of paying a bill)*
H das Gewicht *weight*
gewinnen *to win*
* gewiß *certain(ly), definite(ly)*
das Gewitter (-) *thunderstorm*
* sich gewöhnen an + *acc.* *to get used to*
gewöhnlich *usually, usual*
* der Gipfel (-) *summit, top*
* der Gips (-e) *plaster cast*
die Gitarre (-n) *guitar*
das Glas (-er) *glass*
glauben *to think, believe*
gleich *immediately, straightaway; same*
es ist mir gleich *it's all the same to me*
gleichfalls *the same to you (polite)*
das Gleis (-e) *platform, track (railway)*
das Glück *luck, good fortune*
glücklich *happy, fortunate, lucky*
R glücklicherweise *fortunately*
der Glückwunsch (-e) *congratulation*
* das Gold *gold*
der Goldfisch (-e) *goldfish*
der Gott (-er) *God*
R der Grad (-e) *degree (of temperature)*
das Gramm (-e) *gram(me)*
das Gras *grass*
* gratulieren *to congratulate*
grau *grey*
* die Grenze (-n) *border, boundary, limit*
grillen *to grill, have a barbecue*
die Grippe *influenza*
der Groschen (-) *10 Pfennig coin; Austrian currency*
groß *big, large, tall*
* großartig *wonderful, superb*
die Großeltern *grandparents*
die Großmutter (-) *grandmother*
die Großstadt (-e) *large city*
der Großvater (-) *grandfather*
R großzügig *generous*
R die Größe (-n) *size*
grün *green*
* grüne Karte *green card (motoring)*
die Grundschule (-n) *primary school*
die Gruppe (-n) *group*
der Gruß (-e) *greeting*
grüß dich! *greetings! hello!*
grüß Gott! *hello! (South Germany/Austria)*
grüßen *to greet*
gucken *to look*
der/das Gulasch (-e) *goulash*
die Gulaschsuppe (-n) *goulash soup*
* gültig *valid (e.g. of tickets)*
* der/das Gummi *rubber*
* günstig *favourable, good value*
* die Gurke (-n) *cucumber*
der Gürtel (-) *belt, seat-belt*
gut *good*
gut gelaunt *in a good mood,*

good-tempered
gute Besserung! *get well soon*
gute Fahrt! *safe/good journey!*
gute Heimfahrt! *safe/good journey home!*
gute Nacht! *goodnight!*
gute Reise! *have a good journey!*
guten Abend! *good evening!*
guten Appetit! *enjoy your meal! bon appétit!*
guten Morgen! *good morning!*
guten Tag! *hello! good day!*
das Gymnasium (-ien) *grammar school*
das Haar (-e) *hair*
die Haarbürste (-n) *hairbrush*
das Haarshampoo *hair shampoo*
* der Haartrockner (-) *hairdrier*
* das Haarwaschmittel (-) *hair shampoo*
haben *to have*
der Hafen (-) *port*
* der Hagel *hail (weather)*
* hageln *to hail (weather)*
das Hähnchen (-) *chicken*
halb *half*
die Halbpension *half-board*
* die Hälfte (-n) *half*
die Halle (-n) *hall*
das Hallenbad (-er) *indoor swimming pool*
Hallo! *hello! (also to attract attention)*
der Hals (-e) *neck, throat*
der Halsschmerzen *sore throat*
halten *to hold, keep, store, stop*
die Haltestelle (-n) *stop (of bus, tram)*
der Hamster (-) *hamster*
die Hand (-e) *hand*
die Handarbeit *needlework*
der Handball (-e) *handball*
H sich handeln um *to be about (e.g. film, book)*
der Händler (-) *tradesman, dealer*
die Handlung (-en) *action, deed; business, trade*
der Handschuh (-e) *glove*
die Handtasche (-n) *handbag*
das Handtuch (-er) *handtowel*
Hannover *Hanover*
hart *hard*
hassen *to hate*
häßlich *ugly*
der Hauptbahnhof (-e) *main station*
die Hauptschule (-n) *secondary modern school*
die Hauptstadt (-e) *capital city*
die Hauptstraße (-n) *main road*
das Haus (-er) *house*
die Hausaufgabe (-n) *homework*
die Hausfrau (-en) *housewife*
R der Haushalt (-e) *household*
der Hausmeister (-) *caretaker*
die Hausnummer (-n) *house number*
das Haustier (-e) *pet*
* heben *to lift, pick up*
das Heft (-e) *exercise book*
* das Heftpflaster (-) *sticky plaster*
der Heilige Abend *Christmas Eve*
die Heimat (-en) *home country*
R die Heimfahrt (-en) *home journey*
Heimweh haben *to be homesick*
heiraten *to marry*

heiß *hot*

heißen *to be called*

H heiter *bright (of weather)*

R heizen *to heat*

R die Heizung *heating*

helfen *to help*

hell *bright, light (of colours)*

das Hemd (-en) *shirt*

her- *(towards the speaker)*

herein (etc.) *come in (etc.)*

die Herbergseltern *wardens of hostel*

der Herbergsvater (-) *hostel warden (male)*

die Herbergsmutter (-) *hostel warden (female)*

der Herbst *autumn*

der Herd (-e) *cooker, stove*

herein! *come in!*

der Herr (-en) *gentleman, sir*

Herr . . . *Mr . . .*

Herren *or* H *Gentlemen (on public toilets)*

Herr Ober! *Waiter!*

die Herrenmode *menswear*

herrlich *wonderful*

* herstellen (sep.) *to produce*

* das Herz (-en) *heart*

herzlich *warm, sincere*

herzliche Grüße *kind regards, warm greetings*

herzlichen Glückwunsch! *congratulations!*

heute *today*

heute abend *this evening*

* heutzutage *nowadays, currently*

hier *here*

die Hilfe (no plural) *help, aid*

erste Hilfe *first aid*

Hilfe! *help!*

die Himbeere (-n) *raspberry*

der Himmel *sky; Heaven*

hin- *(away from the speaker)*

hinaus! (etc.) *get out! (etc.)*

hin und zurück *return*

H hinauslehnen (sep.) *to lean out*

* sich hinlegen (sep.) *to have a lie down, rest*

sich hinsetzen (sep.) *to sit down*

hinten *behind (adverb)*

hinter *behind (preposition)*

die Hit (-s) *hit (success)*

die Hitparade (-n) *hit parade*

* die Hitze (-n) *heat*

H hitzefrei *time off school because of heat*

* die Hitzewelle (-n) *heat-wave*

das Hobby (-s) *hobby*

hoch *high, tall*

hochachtungsvoll *yours faithfully*

H der Hochdruck *high pressure (weather)*

H die Hochgarage (-n) *multi-storey car park*

* das Hochhaus (-er) *high-rise/multi-storey building*

* die Hochschule (-n) *technical college, university*

H die Höchstgeschwindigkeit (-en) *maximum speed*

H die Höchsttemperatur (-en) *maximum temperature*

die Hochzeit (-en) *wedding*

der Hof (-e) *yard, courtyard, playground (school)*

hoffen *to hope*

hoffentlich *it is to be hoped, I hope, etc.*

die Hoffnung (-en) *hope*

* höflich *polite*

holen *to fetch, get, collect*

Holland *Holland*

* der Holländer (-) *Dutchman*

* die Holländerin (-nen) *Dutchwoman*

* holländisch *Dutch (adjective)*

das Holz (-er) *wood (material)*

der Honig *honey*

hören *to hear, listen to*

R der Hörer (-) *receiver (telephone)*

die Hose (-n) *(pair of) trousers*

das Hotel (-s) *hotel*

* der Hubschrauber (-) *helicopter*

hübsch *pretty*

der Hügel (-) *hill*

der Hund (-e) *dog*

der Hunger *hunger*

Hunger haben *to be hungry*

hungrig *hungry*

* husten *to cough*

* der Hut (-e) *hat*

* die Hütte (-n) *hut*

die Idee (-n) *idea*

ihr *her (possessive)*

ihr *you (plural of du)*

ihr *their (possessive)*

Ihr *your (polite form possessive)*

R die Illustrierte (-n) *magazine*

im (in dem) *in the*

R im Freien *in the open*

* der Imbiß (-sse) *snack*

die Imbißhalle (-n) *snackbar*

die Imbißstube (-n) *snackbar*

immer *always*

immer noch *still*

in *in*

* inbegriffen/inbegr. *inclusive, including*

die Industrie (-n) *industry*

R der Ingenieur (-) *engineer*

H inklusiv *inclusive*

das Inland *domestic, home, inland*

innen *inner*

die Innenstadt (-e) *town centre, city centre*

ins (in das) *into*

das Insekt (-en) *insect*

die Insel (-n) *island*

das Instrument (-e) *instrument*

intelligent *intelligent*

der Inter-City-Zug (-e) *Inter-City train*

interessant *interesting*

das Interesse (-n) *interest*

interessieren *to interest*

sich interessieren für *to be interested in*

* irgend *some or other*

* irgendwann *sometime or other*

* irgendwas *something or other*

* irgendwie *somehow or other*

* irgendwo *somewhere or other*

Italien *Italy*

R der Italiener (-) *Italian (man)*

R die Italienerin (-nen) *Italian (woman)*

R italienisch *Italian (adjective)*

ja *yes*

* jagen *to hunt*

* der Jäger (-) *hunter*

das Jahr (-e) *year*

die Jahreszeit (-en) *season (of year)*

R das Jahrhundert (-e) *century*

R jährlich *annual, annually*

der Januar *January*

die Jeans (singular & plural) *jeans*

jeder *every*

R jedesmal *every time*

jedoch *but, however*

jemand *someone, somebody*

* jener *that*

jetzt *now*

der Job (-s) *job*

* joggen *to jog*

* das Jogging *jogging*

der/das Joghurt (-s) *yoghurt*

die Jugend (no plural) *young people, youth (collective)*

der Jugendclub (-s) *youth club*

der Jugendklub (-s) *youth club*

die Jugendherberge (-n) *youth hostel*

* der Jugendliche (-n) *young person, youth (individual)*

* die (individual)

das Jugendzentrum (-tren) *youth centre*

der Juli *July*

jung *young*

der Junge (-n) *boy*

jünger *younger*

der Juni *June*

R die Kabine (-n) *cabin; booth (e.g. of telephone)*

der Kaffee (-s) *coffee*

die Kaffeekanne (-n) *coffee pot*

* der Käfig (-e) *cage*

R der Kai (-e or -s) *quay, waterfront*

der Kakao (-s) *cocoa*

R das Kalbfleisch *veal*

der Kalender (-) *calendar*

kalt *cold*

* die kalte Platte (-n) *cold meal*

* die Kälte *cold (weather)*

die Kamera (-s) *camera*

R der Kamin (-e) *fireplace, fireside, chimney*

* der Kamm (-e) *comb*

* sich kämmen *to comb one's hair*

* der Kampf (-e) *fight, struggle*

* kämpfen *to fight, struggle*

* der Kanal (-e) *channel, English Channel*

das Kaninchen (-) *rabbit*

das Kännchen (-) *little pot (for tea/coffee)*

die Kantine (-n) *canteen*

* die Kapelle (-n) *band; chapel*

kapieren *to understand (colloquial)*

kaputt *broken*

die Karotte (-n) *carrot*

* die Karriere (-n) *career*

die Karte (-n) *card, ticket, map*

die Kartoffel (-n) *potato*

* der Kartoffelbrei *mashed potato*

die Kartoffelchips *potato crisps*

* das Kartoffelmus *purée of potato*

der Kartoffelsalat *potato salad*

der Käse (-) *cheese*

der Käsekuchen *cheesecake*
die Kasse (-n) *box office, till, check-out*
* der Kassenzettel (-) *till receipt*
die Kassette (-n) *cassette*
der Kassettenrecorder (-) *cassette recorder*
R der Kater (-) *tom cat*
H einen Kater haben *to have a hangover*
die Kathedrale (-n) *cathedral*
H der Katholik (-en) *Roman Catholic' (person)*
R katholisch *Catholic (adjective)*
die Katze (-n) *cat*
* kauen *to chew*
H der Kauf (⸚e) *purchase*
kaufen *to buy*
das Kaufhaus (⸚er) *department store*
der Kaufmann (⸚er) *businessman, merchant*
der Kaugummi *chewing gum*
* kaum *hardly, scarcely*
* kegeln *to bowl (10-pin, skittles)*
kein *no, not any*
der Keks (-e) *biscuit*
der Keller (-) *cellar*
der Kellner (-) *waiter*
kennen *to know (people, places)*
R kennenlernen (sep.) *to get to know*
* der Kerl (-e) *chap, guy; character*
* die Kerze (-n) *candle*
die Kette (-n) *chain, necklace, bracelet*
das Kilo (*plural not much used* -s) *kilo*
der Kilometer (-) *kilometre*
das Kind (-er) *child*
der Kindergarten (⸚) *kindergarten, nursery*
R der Kinderteller (-) *child's portion/ dish*
das Kino (-s) *cinema*
der Kiosk (-e) *kiosk*
die Kirche (-n) *church*
* die Kirmes (-sen) *fair, funfair*
die Kirsche (-n) *cherry*
* das Kissen (-) *cushion*
* klappbar *folding, collapsible*
* klappen *to fold, collapse; work out well*
* der Klappstuhl (⸚e) *folding chair*
* der Klapptisch (-e) *folding table*
klar *clear, evident, obvious*
klasse *great, terrific, first class*
die Klasse (-) *class (first, school)*
die Klassenarbeit (-en) *class test (formal)*
* das Klassenbuch (⸚er) *form book*
* die Klassenfahrt (-en) *class trip*
der Klassenlehrer (-) *form/class teacher*
* der Klassensprecher (-) *class speaker/representative*
das Klassenzimmer (-) *classroom*
klassisch *classical*
H klauen *to steal, pinch, nick (slang)*
das Klavier (-e) *piano*
* kleben *to stick*
das Kleid (-er) *dress; plural also = clothes*
die Kleider *clothes*

der Kleiderschrank (⸚e) *wardrobe*
die Kleidung *clothing, clothes*
klein *small, little*
das Kleingeld *(small) change (of money)*
* klettern *to climb, clamber*
* das Klima (-s or -ate) *climate*
klingeln *to ring (of bell, phone)*
die Klinik (-en) *clinic; hospital*
die Klippe (-n) *cliff*
das Klo (-s) *toilet, loo (colloquial)*
klopfen *to knock, beat, hit*
der Klub (-s) *or der* Club (-s) *club*
klug *clever*
* die Kneipe (-n) *pub, tavern*
R das Knie (-n) *knee*
knipsen *to photograph*
* der Knödel (-) *dumpling*
der Knopf (⸚e) *button, knob*
der Koch (⸚e) *cook*
kochen *to cook, boil*
Kochen *Cookery, Domestic Science*
der Koffer (-) *case, suitcase*
der Kofferkuli (-s) *luggage trolley*
R der Kofferraum (⸚e) *boot (of car)*
R der Kohl (-e) *cabbage*
* die Kohle (-n) *coal*
Köln *Cologne*
komisch *amusing, funny, strange*
kommen *to come*
* die Komödie (-n) *comedy*
kompliziert *complicated*
das Kompott (-e) *stewed fruit*
die Konditorei (-en) *cake shop, pâtisserie*
R die Konfektion *clothing/wear*
Damenkonfektion *ladies' wear*
der König (-e) *king*
können *to be able*
das Konto (-s) *account*
die Kontonummer (-n) *account number*
R die Kontrolle (-n) *check, control (e.g. customs)*
* kontrollieren *to check, control*
das Konzert (-e) *concert*
der Kopf (⸚e) *head*
* das Kopfkissen (-) *pillow*
der Kopfsalat (-e) *lettuce*
Kopfschmerzen haben *to have a headache*
* die Kopie (-n) *copy, duplicate*
* kopieren *to copy, duplicate*
der Korb (⸚e) *basket*
* der Körper (-) *body*
* körperbehindert *disabled*
* korrigieren *to correct*
R kostbar *expensive, dear*
kosten *to cost*
die Kosten (*plural*) *cost(s)*
kostenlos *free*
das Kostüm (-e) *costume, suit*
das Kotelett (-e) *chop, cutlet*
R der Krach *big noise, din, racket*
* die Kraft (⸚e) *strength*
H kräftig *hearty, strong*
krank *ill*
das Krankenhaus (⸚er) *hospital*
* die Krankenkasse (-n) *health insurance (company)*
* der Krankenpfleger (-) *male nurse*
* der Krankenschein (-e) *medical*

insurance record card
die Krankenschwester (-n) *female nurse*
der Krankenwagen (-) *ambulance*
die Krankheit (-en) *illness*
die Krawatte (-n) *tie*
die Kreide (-n) *chalk*
* der Kreis (-e) *circle; district*
R das Kreuz (-e) *cross*
die Kreuzung (-en) *crossing*
* der Krieg (-e) *war*
kriegen *to get (colloquial)*
R der Krimi (-s) *mystery, thriller (book or film)*
der Kriminalfilm (-e) *thriller*
die Küche (-n) *kitchen; cooking*
der Kuchen (-) *cake*
* die Kuckucksuhr (-en) *cuckoo clock*
der Kugelschreiber (-) *biro, ball-point pen*
die Kuh (⸚e) *cow*
kühl *cool*
der Kühlschrank (⸚e) *refrigerator*
der Kuli (-s) (Kugelschreiber) *biro*
R der Kunde (-n) *client, customer*
Kunst *Art*
R der Künstler *artist*
H künstlich *artificial*
* der Kunststoff (-e) *man-made/ synthetic material*
* die Kur (-en) *health cure; diet*
* der Kurort (-e) *spa, health resort*
R der Kurs (⸚e) *course; rate of exchange*
R die Kurve (-n) *curve, bend*
kurz *short*
die Kusine (-n) *female cousin*
R der Kuß (⸚sse) *kiss*
R küssen *to kiss*
die Küste (-n) *coast*

das Labor (-s or -e) *laboratory*
lächeln *to smile*
lachen *to laugh*
der Laden (⸚) *shop*
* die Lage (-n) *position, situation*
* das Lamm (⸚er) *lamb*
die Lampe (-n) *lamp*
das Land (⸚er) *country; state (of Germany)*
landen *to land*
die Landkarte (-n) *map*
die Landschaft (-en) *countryside*
die Landstraße (-n) *country road*
lang *long*
lange *for a long time*
* die Langeweile *boredom*
langsam *slow, slowly*
die Langspielplatte (-n) *LP record*
sich langweilen *to be bored*
langweilig *boring*
* der Lappen (-) *cloth, rag*
der Lärm (*no plural*) *noise*
lassen *to let, allow*
der Lastwagen (-) *lorry*
Latein *Latin*
laufen *to run, go by foot*
* die Laune (-n) *mood*
laut *loud*
läuten *to sound, ring*
leben *to live*
das Leben *life*
H die Lebensgefahr *danger to life*
die Lebensmittel (*plural*) *food/*

groceries

das Lebensmittelgeschäft
(-e) *grocer's shop*

die Leber (-n) *liver*

die Leberwurst (¨e) *liver sausage*

* lebhaft *lively*

lecker *delicious*

das Leder *leather*

* ledig *single*

leer *empty*

leeren *to empty*

H die Leerung (-en) *collection (post)*

legen *to lay*

sich legen *to lie down*

der Lehnstuhl (¨e) *armchair*

* die Lehre (-n) *apprenticeship*

der Lehrer (-) *teacher*

lehren *to teach*

das Lehrerzimmer (-) *staffroom*

* der Lehrling *apprentice*

leicht *light, easy*

* die Leichtathletik *athletics*

leid tun *to make one feel sorry, to hurt*

es tut mir leid *I am sorry*

* leiden *to suffer*

* leiden können *to bear*

ich kann ihn nicht leiden *I can't bear him*

leider *unfortunately*

R leihen *to lend*

leise *softly, gently*

* die Leistung (-en) *achievement, performance*

leiten *to lead*

* der Leiter (-) *leader*

* die Leitung (-en) *guidance, direction*

* das Lenkrad (¨er) *steering wheel*

lernen *to learn*

lesen *to read*

letzt *last*

die Leute *people*

das Licht (-er) *light*

lieb *dear*

liebe Birgit *dear (in letter)*

lieber Franz *dear (in letter)*

die Liebe (-n) *love*

lieben *to love*

lieber *rather*

lieber haben *to prefer*

Lieblings- *favourite . . .*

das Lieblingsfach (¨er) *favourite subject*

am liebsten *best of all, most of all*

das Lied (-er) *song*

* liefern *to deliver*

* der Lieferwagen (-) *delivery van*

liegen *to lie*

liegenlassen (*sep.*) *to leave around/behind*

* der Liegestuhl (¨e) *deckchair*

* der Liegewagen (-) *sleeping car*

der Lift (-e *or* -s) *lift*

die Limonade (-n) *lemonade*

* das Lineal (-e) *ruler*

die Linie (-n) *line*

linke *left*

links *on the left*

die Liste (-n) *list*

der/das Liter (-) *litre*

der LKW (LKWs) *lorry*

* loben *to praise*

das Loch (¨er) *hole*

der Löffel (-) *spoon*

* der Lohn (¨e) *reward; wage*

los *loose, off*

* löschen *to extinguish*

* der Löscher (-) *blotter, extinguisher*

* lösen *to cash, buy (tickets)*

der Löwe (-n) *lion*

die Luft *air*

der Luftdruck *air pressure*

* die Luftmatratze (-n) *airbed*

* die Luftpost *airmail*

* lügen *to tell a lie*

die Lust *wish*

Lust haben (auf + *acc.*) *to feel like*

lustig *amusing*

machen *to do, make*

das Mädchen (-) *girl*

* der Mädchenname (-n) *girl's/maiden name*

das Magazin (-e) *magazine*

der Magen *stomach*

Magenschmerzen *stomach ache*

mager *thin*

* mähen *to mow*

die Mahlzeit (-en) *mealtime, meal*

der Mai *May*

der Main *Main (river)*

mal *just*

das Mal (-e) *time*

malen *to paint*

man *one*

manchmal *sometimes*

mangelhaft *defective, lacking, weak*

der Mann (¨er) *man, husband*

* männlich *masculine, male*

die Mannschaft (-en) *team*

der Mantel (¨) *coat*

die Mappe (-n) *briefcase, satchel*

die Margarine *margarine*

die Mark *Mark (currency)*

das Markstück (-e) *Mark coin*

der Markt (¨e) *market*

der Marktplatz (¨e) *marketplace*

die Marmelade (-n) *jam*

der März *March*

die Maschine (-n) *machine, aeroplane*

Mathe *Maths*

Mathematik *Mathematics*

* der Matrose (-n) *sailor*

R die Mauer (-n) *wall*

die Maus (¨e) *mouse*

der Mechaniker (-) *mechanic*

die Medikamente (*plural*) *medicine*

das Meerschweinchen (-) *guinea pig*

die Medizin (*no plural*) *medicine*

das Meer (-e) *sea*

mehr *more*

mehrere *several*

* die Mehrfahrtenkarte (-n) *ticket valid for a number of journeys*

* mehrmals *often*

R die Mehrwertsteuer *VAT*

die Meile (-n) *mile*

mein *my*

meinen *to mean, think*

die Meinung (-en) *meaning, opinion*

meiner Meinung nach *in my opinion*

meist *most*

meistens *mostly*

* die Meisterschaft (-en) *championship*

R sich melden *to report, answer (phone)*

R die Menge (-n) *crowd*

der Mensch (-en) *person, man*

das Menü (-s) *set menu*

* merken *to notice*

* merkwürdig *remarkable*

* die Messe (-n) *mass, trade fair*

* messen *to measure*

das Messer (-) *knife*

der/das Meter (-) *metre*

der Metzger (-) *butcher*

die Metzgerei (-en) *butcher's shop*

die Miete (-) *rent*

mieten *to rent, hire*

die Milch *milk*

die Milchbar (-) *milk bar*

* mild *mild*

* mindestens *at least*

das Mineralwasser (-) *mineral water*

die Minute (-n) *minute*

* das Mißverständnis (-se) *misunderstanding*

mit *with*

mitbringen (*sep.*) *to bring (with you)*

* das Mitglied (-er) *member*

mitkommen (*sep.*) *to come along with, to accompany*

* das Mitleid *sympathy*

mitmachen (*sep.*) *to join in*

mitnehmen (*sep.*) *to take with you*

zum Mitnehmen *to take away*

mitspielen (*sep.*) *to play with, to join in*

der Mittag (-e) *midday*

das Mittagessen (-) *midday meal, lunch*

die Mittagspause (-n) *midday break*

die Mitte (-n) *middle*

mitteilen (*sep.*) *to communicate, tell*

das Mittel (-) *means*

mittelgroß *middle-sized, average*

* das Mittelmeer *Mediterranean*

mitten *middle, in the middle*

Mitternacht *midnight*

der Mittwoch *Wednesday*

* die Möbel (*plural*) *furniture*

* möbliert *furnished*

die Mode (-n) *fashion*

modern *modern*

modisch *in fashion, fashionable*

das Mofa (-s) *moped*

* mogeln *to cheat*

mögen *to like*

möglich *possible*

* die Möglichkeit (-en) *possibility*

die Möhre (-n) *carrot*

die Molkerei (-en) *dairy*

der Moment (-e) *moment*

Moment! *just a mo!*

der Monat (-e) *month*

* monatlich *monthly*

* der Mond (-e) *moon*

der Montag *Monday*

morgen *tomorrow*

morgen früh *tomorrow morning*

der Morgen *morning*

die Morgenpause (-n) *morning break*

morgens *in the mornings*
die Mosel *Moselle (river)*
der Moselwein *Moselle wine*
der Motor (-en) *engine*
das Motorboot (-e) *motor boat*
das Motorrad (¨er) *motorbike*
* die Mücke (-n) *mosquito, gnat*
müde *tired*
München *Munich*
der Mund (¨er) *mouth*
* mündlich *oral*
R die Münze (-n) *coin*
das Museum (Museen) *museum*
die Musik *music*
der Musiker (-) *musician*
müssen *to have to*
* der Mut *courage*
* mutig *courageous, brave*
die Mutter (¨) *mother*
* die Muttersprache (-n) *mother tongue*
Mutti *mum, mummy*
R die Mütze (-n) *cap*
die MWS (Mehrwertsteuer) *VAT*

nach *after, to, according to*
der Nachbar (-n) *neighbour*
R nachdem *after*
* nachdenken (sep.) *to think, reflect*
nachgehen (sep.) *to follow*
nachher *afterwards*
der Nachmittag (-e) *afternoon*
nachmittags *in the afternoons*
die Nachmittagspause (-n) *afternoon break*
der Nachname (-n) *surname*
die Nachrichten (plural) *news*
* nachschlagen (sep.) *to look up (a word)*
* nachsehen (sep.) *to check*
* nachsitzen (sep.) *to be kept in*
* die Nachspeise (-n) *dessert*
nächst *next*
die Nacht (¨e) *night*
* der Nachteil (-e) *disadvantage*
* der Nachtisch (-e) *dessert*
nachts *at night*
nah(e) *near*
die Nähe *vicinity*
in der Nähe (von) *near (to)*
nähen *to sew*
Nähen *Needlework*
R der Nahverkehrszug (¨e) *local train*
der Name (-n) *name*
* der Namenstag (-e) *name day*
die Nase (-n) *nose*
naß *wet*
* die Näße *damp, wet*
die Natur *Nature*
natürlich *of course, naturally*
Naturwissenschaften *Natural Sciences*
der Nebel (-) *fog*
neben *near*
nebenan *nearby, next door*
das Nebenfach (¨er) *subsidiary subject*
* die Nebenstraße (-n) *side street*
neblig *foggy*
nee *no (colloquial)*
der Neffe (-n) *nephew*
nehmen *to take*
nein *no*

nennen *to name, call*
R nervös *nervous*
nett *nice*
das Netz (-e) *net*
neu *new*
* neugierig *curious, inquisitive*
das Neujahr *New Year*
neulich *recently*
die Neustadt (¨e) *new town*
nicht *not*
nicht mehr *no longer*
nicht wahr *isn't it?*
die Nichte (-n) *niece*
der Nichtraucher *non-smoker*
nichts *nothing*
nichts zu danken *that's all right*
nie *never*
die Niederlande *Netherlands*
* der Niederschlag (¨e) *knock-out, precipitation*
* niedrig *low*
niemals *never*
niemand *no one*
* nirgends *nowhere*
* niesen *to sneeze*
noch *still, yet*
noch einmal *once again*
noch etwas *a bit more*
noch mal *again*
noch nicht *not yet*
Nord- *north . . .*
der Nord *north*
in den Norden *to the north*
im Norden *in the north*
nördlich *northerly*
die Nordsee *North Sea*
normal *normal*
Normal *2-star (petrol)*
normalerweise *usually*
die Not *need, emergency*
der Notausgang (¨e) *emergency exit*
* der Notdienst (-e) *emergency service*
die Note (-n) *mark*
R der Notruf (-e) *emergency call*
nötig *necessary*
R notwendig *necessary*
der November *November*
* die Nudeln (plural) *noodles*
null *nil, zero*
die Nummer (-n) *number*
nun *now, well*
nur *only*
* der Nuß (¨sse) *nut*
* nützen *to be of use*
* nützlich *useful*

ob *if, whether*
oben *above, upstairs*
nach oben *upstairs, upwards*
der Ober (-) *head waiter*
Herr Ober! *waiter!*
* das Obergeschoß (-sse) *upper floor*
* die Oberstufe (-n) *sixth form*
* obgleich *although*
das Obst (no plural) *fruit*
der Obstbaum (¨e) *fruit tree*
die Obsttorte (-n) *fruit flan or gateau*
R obwohl *although*
* die Ochsenschwanzsuppe (-n) *oxtail soup*
oder *or*
* der Ofen (¨) *stove, oven, cooker*
offen *open*

öffentlich *public*
Öffnen *to open*
die Öffnungszeiten (plural) *opening times*
oft *often*
ohne *without*
das Ohr (-en) *ear*
der Oktober *October*
das Öl *oil*
die Oma (-s) *granny*
das Omelett (-e or -s) *omelette*
der Onkel (-) *uncle*
der Opa (-s) *grandpa*
R die Operation (-en) *operation*
H operieren *to operate*
die Orange (-n) *orange*
der Orangensaft (¨e) *orange juice*
das Orchester (-) *orchestra*
ordentlich *tidy*
die Ordnung (-en) *order, tidiness*
in Ordnung *in order, OK*
Ordnung machen *to tidy up*
organisieren *to organise*
der Ort (-e) *place*
* das Ortsgespräch (-e) *local call (telephone)*
Ost- *east . . .*
in den Osten *to the east*
im Osten *in the east*
Ostern *Easter*
Österreich *Austria*
der Österreicher *Austrian (man)*
österreichisch *Austrian (adjective)*
östlich *easterly*
die Ostsee *Baltic Sea*

ein paar *a few*
das Paar *pair*
das Päckchen (-) *packet*
packen *to pack, wrap*
das Paket (-e) *parcel*
die Packung (-en) *packet*
* paniert *in bread crumbs*
die Panne (-n) *breakdown*
das Papier (-e) *paper*
das Parfum (-s) *perfume*
das Parfüm (-e or -s) *perfume*
der Park (-s) *park*
die Parkanlage (-n) *parkland*
parken *to park*
* das Parkett *stalls (cinema)*
das Parkhaus (¨er) *multi-storey car park*
der Parkplatz (¨e) *car park*
* der Parkschein (-e) *parking ticket*
* die Parkuhr (-en) *parking meter*
R das Parkverbot *no parking*
das Parterre *ground floor*
der Partner *partner*
die Partnerstadt (¨e) *twin town*
die Party (-ys or -ies) *party*
der Paß (Pässe) *pass, passport*
der Passagier (-e) *passenger*
R passen *to suit*
passieren *to happen*
* die Paßkontrolle (-n) *passport control*
* der Patient (-en) *patient*
die Pause (-n) *pause, break*
* Pech haben *to have bad luck*
* peinlich *painful, embarrassing*
R die Pension *guest house*
* per Anhalter *by hitch-hiking*

die Person (-en) *person*
* der Personalausweis (-e) *personal identity card*
der Personenzug (-̈e) *passenger train*
* persönlich *personally, in person*
* der Pfad (-e) *path*
* der Pfadfinder (-) *scout*
* der Pfannkuchen (-) *pancake*
der Pfeffer *pepper*
die Pfeife (-n) *pipe*
der Pfenning (-e) *Pfennig*
das Pferd (-e) *horse*
Pfingsten *Whitsun*
der Pfirsich (-e) *peach*
die Pflanze (-n) *plant*
* pflanzen *to plant*
* das Pflaster (-) *pavement, plaster*
die Pflaume (-n) *plum*
* pflegen *to nurse, look after*
* die Pflicht (-en) *duty*
* das Pflichtfach (-̈er) *compulsory subject*
das Pfund *pound*
Physik *Physics*
das Picknick (-e or -s) *picnic*
die Pille (-n) *pill*
das Pils (-) *beer (Pils)*
* der Pilz (-e) *mushroom*
R PKW *private car*
das Plakat (-e) *poster*
der Plan (-̈e) *plan*
planen *to plan*
R planmäßig *according to plan/timetable*
das Plastik *plastic*
die Platte (-n) *record*
der Plattenspieler (-) *record player*
der Platz (-̈e) *place, square*
Platz nehmen *to sit down, take a seat*
die Platzkarte (-n) *seat ticket*
* plaudern *to chat*
plötzlich *suddenly*
der Pokal (-e) *cup*
* die Politik *politics*
* der Politiker (-) *politician*
die Polizei (*no plural*) *police*
die Polizeiwache (-n) *police station*
der Polizist (-en) *policeman*
Pommes frites *chips*
die Popmusik *pop music*
das Portemonnaie (-s) *purse*
der Portier (-s) *porter*
die Portion (-en) *portion*
die Post *post, post office*
das Postamt (-̈er) *post office*
die Postanweisung (-en) *postal order*
das Poster (- or -s) *poster*
R das Postleitzahl (-en) *post code*
R das Postwertzeichen (-) *stamp*
praktisch *practical, convenient*
die Praline (-n or -s) *praline, chocolate*
der Preis (-e) *price, prize*
R preiswert *cheap, good value*
* die Presse (-n) *press*
prima! *great!*
pro *per*
probieren *to try*
das Problem (-e) *problem*
* der Profi (-) *professional*
das Programm (-e) *programme*

der Prospekt (-e) *prospectus, brochure*
Prosit! *cheers!*
Prost! *cheers!*
* protestieren *to protest*
prüfen *to test, check*
die Prüfung (-en) *test, examination*
der Pudding (-s) *pudding, dessert*
der Pulli (-s) *pullover*
der Pullover (-) *pullover*
* das Pult (-e) *desk*
der Punkt (-e) *point, full stop*
pünktlich *punctual*
die Puppe (-n) *doll*
putzen *to clean*

R der Quadratmeter (-) qm *square metre*
die Qualität (-en) *quality*
Quatsch! *rubbish!*
* die Querstraße (-n) *cross street*
R die Quittung (-en) *receipt*

H der Rabatt (-e) *discount*
das Rad (-̈er) *wheel, bicycle*
radfahren (*sep.*) *to cycle*
der Radfahrer (-) *cyclist*
* der Radiergummi *(India) rubber, eraser*
das Radio (-s) *radio*
der Rand (-̈er) *edge*
* der Rang (-̈e) *row*
der Rasen (-) *lawn*
der Rasierapparat (-e) *razor, shaver*
sich rasieren *to shave*
R das Rasthaus (-̈er) *hotel*
R der Rasthof (-̈e) *service station*
R der Rastplatz (-̈e) *service area, parking area*
R die Raststätte (-n) *service station*
* der Rat (Ratschläge) *advice*
* raten *to advise*
das Rathaus (-̈er) *town hall*
der Ratskeller (-) *town hall cellar*
R der Räuber (-) *robber*
rauchen *to smoke*
R der Raucher (-) *smoker*
der Raum (-̈e) *room, space*
die Realschule (-n) *secondary school*
rechnen *to count, reckon, calculate*
die Rechnung (-en) *bill*
* recht haben *to be right*
rechte *right (adjective)*
rechts *on the right*
* die Rede (-n) *speech*
* das Regal (-e) *shelf*
die Regel (-n) *rule*
* regelmäßig *regular(ly)*
der Regen *rain*
der Regenmantel (-̈) *raincoat*
der Regenschirm (-e) *umbrella*
* die Regierung (-en) *government*
regnen *to rain*
regnerisch *rainy*
reiben *to rub, grate*
reich *rich*
reichen *to reach, be sufficient, pass*
der Reifen *tyre*
der Reifendruck *tyre pressure*
* die Reifenpanne (-n) *puncture*
* die Reihe (-n) *row*
das Reihenhaus (-̈er) *terraced house*

* rein *clean, pure*
* reinigen *to clean*
* reinigen lassen *to have cleaned*
* die Reinigung *cleaning*
der Reis *rice*
die Reise (-n) *journey*
das Reiseandenken (-) *souvenir*
die Reiseauskunft *travel information*
das Reisebüro (-s) *travel agent*
* der Reiseführer (-) *guide*
R der Reiseleiter (-) *guide*
reisen *to travel*
der Reisende (-n) *traveller*
der Reisepaß (-̈sse) *passport*
der Reisescheck (-e or -s) *travellers' cheque*
reiten *to ride*
R die Reklame (-n) *advertisement*
die Religion *religion*
rennen *to run*
* der Rentner (-) *pensioner*
die Reparatur (-en) *repair*
die Reparaturwerkstatt (-̈e) *repair workshop*
reparieren *to repair*
der Reporter (-) *reporter*
reservieren *to reserve*
reserviert *reserved*
die Reservierung (-en) *reservation*
das Restaurant (-s) *restaurant*
* retten *to save, rescue*
* sich retten *to save oneself*
* die Rettung (-en) *rescue*
* die Rettungsaktion (-en) *rescue action*
das Rettungsboot (-e) *rescue boat*
* der Rettungsdienst (-e) *rescue service*
* der Rettungsgürtel (-) *safety strap*
* das Rezept (-e) *recipe, prescription*
der Rhein *Rhine (river)*
richtig *correct*
die Richtung (-en) *direction*
riechen *to smell*
das Rindfleisch *beef*
der Ring (-e) *ring*
der Rock (-̈e) *skirt*
R die Rolle (-n) *rôle*
* der Roller (-) *scooter*
* das Rollo (-s) *roller blind*
* der Rollschuh (-e) *rollerskate*
* die Rolltreppe (-n) *moving staircase, escalator*
* der Roman (-e) *novel*
R romantisch *romantic*
rosa *pink*
* der Rotkohl *red cabbage*
der Rotwein *red wine*
der Rücken *back*
die Rückfahrkarte (-n) *return ticket*
die Rückfahrt (-en) *return journey*
* die Rückgabe *return (of luggage)*
* das Rückgespräch (-e) *money call (telephone) reverse charge*
der Rucksack *rucksack*
rückwärts *backwards*
* das Ruderboot (-e) *rowing boat*
rudern *to row*
der Ruf (-e) *call, shout, reputation*
rufen *to call, to shout*
die Ruhe *peace, quietness*
ruhen *to rest*
R der Ruhetag (-e) *rest day, holiday*

	das	ruhig *quiet, peaceful*

ruhig   *quiet, peaceful*
das Rührei (-er)   *scrambled egg*
* die Ruine (-n)   *ruin*
rund   *round*
die Rundfahrt (-en)   *tour*
der Rundfunk   *radio (station)*
* russisch   *Russian (adjective)*
* rutschen   *to slip*

SB   *urban railway*
die S-Bahn   *urban railway*
* der Saal (Säle)   *hall*
die Sache (-n)   *thing, affair*
der Saft (¨e)   *juice*
sagen   *to say*
die Sahne   *cream*
die Saison   *season*
der Salat (-e)   *salad, lettuce*
das Salz   *salt*
die Salzkartoffel (-n)   *boiled potato*
sammeln   *to collect*
R die Sammlung (-en)   *collection*
der Samstag   *Saturday*
der Sand (-e)   *sand*
die Sandale (-n)   *sandal*
das Sandwich (-es *or* -s)   *sandwich*
der Sänger (-)   *singer*
satt   *full up, satisfied*
sauber   *clean*
sauber machen   *to clean*
sauer   *sour*
das Sauerkraut   *pickled cabbage*
* das Sauwetter   *awful weather*
* SB-tanken   *self-service (petrol)*
* das Schach   *chess*
die Schachtel (-n)   *box*
schade   *pity*
wie schade!   *what a shame!*
* schaden   *to damage*
das Schaf (-e)   *sheep*
* der Schaffner (-)   *ticket collector*
* der Schal (-e)   *shawl, scarf*
* die Schale (-n)   *bowl*
* schälen   *to peel*
die Schallplatte (-n)   *record*
der Schalter (-)   *counter, box office*
* sich schämen   *to be ashamed*
scharf   *sharp, hot (spicy)*
* der Schatten (-)   *shadow, shade*
schauen   *to see, look*
* der Schauer (-)   *shower*
das Schaufenster (-)   *shop window*
das Schauspiel (-e)   *play*
der Schauspieler (-)   *actor*
der Scheck (-e *or* -s)   *cheque*
das Scheckbuch (¨er)   *cheque book*
die Scheckkarte (-n)   *cheque card*
* die Scheibe (-n)   *slice*
* der Scheibenwischer (-)   *windscreen wiper*
der Schein (-e)   *note*
scheinen   *to seem, appear, shine*
* der Scheinwerfer (-)   *headlight*
schellen   *to ring out, ring the bell*
* die Schenke (-n)   *bar, public house*
schenken   *to give as a present*
schick   *smart*
schicken   *to send*
* schieben   *to push*
* der Schiedsrichter (-)   *referee*
* schief   *crooked*
R schießen   *to shoot*
das Schiff (-e)   *ship*
* die Schildkröte (-n)   *tortoise*

der Schilling (-s)   *shilling*
der Schinken   *ham*
der Schirm (-e)   *umbrella, shade*
der Schlafanzug (¨e)   *pyjamas*
schlafen   *to sleep*
R schlaflos   *sleepless*
der Schlafraum (¨e)   *dormitory*
der Schlafsack (¨e)   *sleeping bag*
* der Schlafwagen (-)   *sleeping car*
das Schlafzimmer (-)   *bedroom*
schlagen   *to hit, strike, beat*
* der Schläger (-)   *racket, bat, stick*
der Schlager (-)   *'hit', pop tune*
die Schlagsahne   *whipped cream*
das Schlagzeug   *drums, percussion*
* die Schlange (-n)   *snake, queue*
Schlange stehen   *to stand in a queue*
schlank   *slim*
schlau   *clever, cunning*
schlecht   *bad*
schlecht gelaunt   *in a bad mood*
schließen   *to close, finish*
das Schließfach (¨er)   *PO box/left luggage locker*
schließlich   *finally, in the end*
schlimm   *bad*
der Schlips (-e)   *tie*
* der Schlittschuh (-e)   *ice skate*
* schlittschuhlaufen (*sep.*)   *to go ice skating*
das Schloß (¨sser)   *castle; lock*
* schlucken   *to swallow*
* der Schluß   *end*
Schluß machen   *to finish*
der Schlüssel (-)   *key*
der Schlüsselring (-e)   *key ring*
der Schlußverkauf   *final sale, closing-down sale*
schmal   *narrow*
schmecken   *to taste (good)*
hat's geschmeckt?   *did you like it?*
Schmerzen (*plural*)   *pain*
* schmerzen   *to hurt*
der Schmuck   *jewellery*
schmutzig   *dirty*
der Schnaps (¨e)   *schnaps, spirits*
der Schnee   *snow*
schneiden   *to cut*
schneien   *to snow*
schnell   *fast*
der Schnellimbiß   *snack*
* die Schnellreinigung   *quick cleaning*
der Schnellzug (¨e)   *express (train)*
das Schnitzel (-)   *cutlet*
* der Schnupfen   *cold*
der Schnurrbart (¨e)   *moustache*
die Schokolade   *chocolate*
schon   *already*
schön   *beautiful*
der Schotte (-n)   *Scotsman, Scot*
die Schottin (-nen)   *Scotswoman, Scot*
schottisch   *Scottish*
Schottland   *Scotland*
der Schrank (¨e)   *cupboard*
schrecklich   *awful*
schreiben   *to write*
* die Schreibmaschine (-n)   *typewriter*
* das Schreibpapier   *writing paper*
der Schreibtisch (-e)   *desk*
die Schreibwaren (*plural*)   *stationery*

* der Schreibwarenhändler (-)   *stationer*
* die Schreibwarenhandlung (-en)   *stationery shop*
schreien   *to shriek, shout*
* schriftlich   *in writing*
* der Schritt (-e)   *step, pace*
H Schritt fahren   *to drive at walking speed*
schüchtern   *shy*
der Schuh (-e)   *shoe*
Schul-   *school . . .*
das Schulbuch (¨er)   *schoolbook*
* schuld sein   *to be guilty*
* schuldig   *guilty*
die Schule (-n)   *school*
der Schüler (-)   *schoolboy*
die Schülerin (-nen)   *schoolgirl*
R schulfrei   *school holiday*
der Schulhof (¨e)   *playground*
das Schuljahr   *school year*
der Schulleiter (-)   *head teacher*
die Schulmappe (-n)   *school bag*
* das Schulsystem (-e)   *school system*
der Schultag   *school day*
* die Schulter (-n)   *shoulder*
die Schuluniform (-en)   *school uniform*
der Schulweg (-e)   *the way to school*
* die Schüssel (-n)   *dish*
schütteln   *to shake*
* schützen   *to protect*
schwach   *weak*
* der Schwager (¨)   *brother-in-law*
* der Schwamm (¨e)   *sponge*
* schwänzen   *play truant*
schwarz   *black*
das Schwarzbrot   *dark bread*
* schweigen   *to be silent*
das Schwein (-e)   *pig*
das Schweinefleisch   *pork*
die Schweiz   *Switzerland*
der Schweizer (-)   *Swiss (man)*
schweizerisch   *Swiss (adjective)*
schwer   *heavy, difficult*
die Schwester (-n)   *sister*
* Schwieger-   *-in-law*
schwierig   *difficult*
* die Schwierigkeit (-en)   *difficulty*
das Schwimmbad (¨er)   *swimming pool*
schwimmen   *to swim*
* schwindlig   *dizzy*
R schwül   *sultry*
der See (-n)   *lake*
die See (-n)   *sea*
seekrank   *seasick*
die Seekrankheit   *seasickness*
* Segel-   *sail . . .*
* das Segelboot (-e)   *sailing boat*
segeln   *to sail*
sehen   *to see*
* sehenswert   *worth seeing*
* die Sehenswürdigkeit (-en)   *attraction, thing worth seeing*
sehr   *very*
sehr geehrte Frau . . .   *Dear Mrs . . .*
sehr geehrte Herren   *Dear Sirs*
sehr geehrter Herr . . .   *Dear Mr . . .*
sehr gut   *very good*
sehr verehrte Herr/Frau   *Dear*

Sir/Madam (more formal)
* die Seide (-n) silk
  die Seife soap
* die Seilbahn (-en) cablecar
  sein his
  sein to be
  seit since (preposition)
  die Seite (-n) page, side
* seitdem since (conjunction)
  der Sekretär (-e) secretary (male)
  die Sekretärin (-nen) secretary (female)
  der Sekt (-e) champagne
  die Sekunde (-n) second
  selber even, oneself
* selbst oneself
* selbständig independent
  die Selbstbedienung self-service (cafeteria, supermarket)
R selbsttanken self-service (petrol station)
* selbstverständlich of course
* selten rare(ly)
* das Semester (-) term (of 6 months)
* die Sendefolge (-n) episode (of series)
* senden to send
* die Sendereihe (-n) series (of broadcasts)
R die Sendung (-en) broadcast, programme
  der Senf (-e) mustard
  der September September
  der Sessel (-) armchair
  sich setzen to sit down
* das Shampoo shampoo
  sicher sure, certain, safe
* die Sicherheit safety
* der Sicherheitsgurt (-e) safety belt
* sichtbar visible
* der Sieg (-e) victory
* siezen to say Sie to someone
* das Silber (no plural) silver
* der Silvester/Sylvester New Year's Eve
  singen to sing
  sinken to sink
  sitzen to sit
* sitzenbleiben (sep.) to remain seated, to repeat a year (school)
* der Ski (-s or -er) ski
* skifahren (sep.) to go skiing
  so so, thus, like this, well
  so viel so much
* sobald as soon as
  die Socke (-n) sock
  das Sofa (-s) sofa
  sofort straight away
  sogleich straight away
* der Sohn (-e) son
* der Soldat (-en) soldier
  sollen to be supposed to, to ought to
  der Sommer summer
  die Sommerferien (plural) summer holidays
R der Sommerschlußverkauf end of summer sale
R das Sonderangebot (-e) special offer
R sondern but
R der Sonderpreis (-e) special price
  die Sonne (-n) sun
* sich sonnen to sunbathe
  die Sonnenbrille (-n) sunglasses

die Sonnencreme suncream
die Sonnenmilch suntan lotion
das Sonnenöl suntan oil
der Sonnenschein sunshine
sonnig sunny
der Sonntag Sunday
R sonst otherwise; once (in the past)
R sonst noch etwas? anything else?
* die Sorge (-n) care, worry
* sorgen to care (for)
  die Sorte (-n) sort, kind
  die Soße (-n) sauce
  das Souvenir (-s) souvenir
  soviel as much, so much
* sowieso anyway, in any case
* sowohl . . . als
  auch . . . both . . . and . . .
  Sozialkunde Social Studies
  Spanien Spain
  der Spanier (-) Spaniard (male)
  die Spanierin (-nen) Spaniard (female)
  spanisch Spanish
  spannend exciting
  sparen to save
  die Sparkasse (-n) savings bank
  der Spaß fun
  viel Spaß! have fun!
  Spaß haben to have fun, enjoy yourself
  spät late
  spazieren to walk
  spazierengehen (sep.) to go for a walk
  der Spaziergang (-e) walk
  die Speisekarte (-n) menu
  der Speisesaal (-äle) dining hall/room
  der Speisewagen (-) restaurant car
R die Sperre (-n) barrier
  die Spezialität (-en) speciality
  der Spiegel (-) mirror
  das Spiegelei (-er) fried egg
  das Spiel (-e) game, match
  spielen to play
  der Spieler (-) player
  der Spielplatz (-e) playground
  das Spielzeug (-e) toy
  die Spitze (-n) summit
  der Sport sport
  der Sportplatz (-e) sports field
  die Sprache (-n) language
* das Sprachlabor (-e or -s) language laboratory
  sprechen to speak
R die Sprechstunde (-n) consulting hours, surgery
  springen to jump
* die Spritze (-n) injection
  der Sprudel (-) mineral water/lemonade
R spucken to spit
  spülen to rinse
* die Spülmaschine (-n) dishwasher
* das Spülmittel (-) washing-up liquid
  der Staat (-en) state
R die Staatsangehörigkeit (-en) nationality
  das Stadion (Stadien) stadium
  die Stadt (-e) town
* der Stadtbummel stroll through town
* die Stadtmauer (-n) town wall

die Stadtmitte (-n) town centre
der Stadtplan (-e) town plan
* der Stadtrand (-er) edge of town, outskirts
* das Stadtteil (-e) part of town, quarter
R das Stadtzentrum (-ren) town centre
  der Stahl steel
* der Stall (-e) stable
R stammen (aus) to come (from)
* der Stammtisch (-e) regulars' table (public house)
  der Stand (-e) stand, stall; level
  stark strong
  starten to start
  die Station (-en) station
* stattfinden (sep.) to take place
R der Stau (-s) traffic jam
* der Staubsauger vacuum cleaner
* die Steckdose (-n) electric socket
  stehen to stand
* die Stehlampe (-n) standard lamp
R stehlen to steal
  steigen to climb
* steil steep
  der Stein (-e) stone
  die Stelle (-n) place, position, job
  stellen to place, put
* sterben to die
  die Stereoanlage (-n) stereo
* der Stern (-e) star
* die Steuer (-n) tax
* das Steuerrad (-er) steering wheel
* der Stiefel (-) boot
  still quiet
  die Stimme (-n) voice
  stimmen to be correct, to tune
* die Stimmung (-en) mood
  der Stock (Stockwerke) floor, storey
  der Stoff (-e) material
* stolz proud
* stören to disturb
* die Strafarbeit (-en) extra work (school)
* die Strafe (-n) fine, punishment
  der Strand (-e) beach
  die Straße (-n) street, road
  die Straßenbahn (-en) tram
  das Streichholz (-er) match
* der Streik (-s) strike
* streiten to quarrel
  streng severe, strict
* stricken to knit
* der Strom river, current; electricity
  der Strumpf (-e) stocking, long sock
  das Stück (-e) piece, play (theatre)
* der Student (-en) student
  studieren to study
  die Studien (plural) studies
  der Stuhl (-e) chair
* stumm silent
  die Stunde (-n) hour, lesson
  der Stundenplan (-e) timetable
  der Sturm (-e) storm
  stürmisch stormy
* stürzen to rush, fall
  suchen to look for
  Süd- south . . .
  der Süd south
  in den Süden to the south
  im Süden in the south
  Super 4-star (petrol)
  der Supermarkt (-e) supermarket
  die Suppe (-n) soup

süß *sweet*
* sympathisch *nice, kind*

das T-Shirt (-s) *T-shirt*
* der Tabak *tobacco*
* das Tablett (-e) *tray*
die Tablette (-n) *tablet*
R die Tafel (-n) *board, blackboard*
der Tag (-e) *day*
die Tageskarte (-n) *day ticket*
R die Tagesschau (-en) *news (TV)*
täglich *daily*
das Tal (¨er) *valley*
* die Talsperre (-n) *dam*
tanken *to fill with petrol*
die Tankstelle (-n) *petrol station*
der Tankwart (-e) *petrol attendant*
R der Tannenbaum (¨e) *fir tree,*
Christmas tree
die Tante (-n) *aunt*
der Tanz (¨e) *dance*
Tanzen *dancing*
tanzen *to dance*
die Tasche (-n) *bag, pocket*
* das Taschenbuch (¨er) *paperback*
book
* der Taschendieb (-e) *pick-pocket*
das Taschengeld *pocket money*
das Taschentuch (¨er) *handkerchief*
die Tasse (-n) *cup*
die Tat *action, deed*
* taub *deaf*
* tauchen *to drive*
das Taxi (-s) *taxi*
der Tee *tea*
die Teekanne (-n) *teapot*
der TEE-Zug (¨e) *Trans-European*
express train
* das Teil (-e) *part*
teilen *to share*
* teilnehmen (sep.) *to take part*
* der Teilnehmer (-) *participant*
* das Telefon *telephone*
der Telefonanruf (-e) *telephone call*
das Telefonbuch *telephone book*
telefonieren *to phone*
telefonisch *on the phone, by*
phone
* die Telefonnummer (-n) *telephone*
number
die Telefonzelle (-n) *telephone box*
* das Telegramm (-e) *telegramme*
der Teller (-) *plate*
R die Temperatur (-en) *temperature*
das Tennis *tennis*
der Tennisplatz (¨e) *tennis court*
der Tennisschläger (-) *tennis*
racquet
* der Teppich (-e) *carpet*
* der Termin (-e) *appointment*
die Terrasse (-n) *terrace*
teuer *expensive*
das Theater (-) *theatre*
* die Theke (-en) *counter*
tief *deep*
H der Tiefdruck *low pressure*
H die Tiefgarage (-n) *underground*
garage
H die Tiefkühltruhe (-n) *deep-freeze*
H die Tiefsttemperatur (-en) *lowest*
temperature
das Tier (-e) *animal*
* der Tierarzt (¨e) *vet*
R der Tiger (-) *tiger*

der Tisch (-e) *table*
* die Tischdecke (-n) *table cloth*
* das Tischtennis *table tennis*
die Tochter (¨) *daughter*
* der Tod (-e) *death*
die Toilette (-n) *toilet*
* das Toilettenpapier *toilet paper*
toll *mad; great*
die Tomate (-n) *tomato*
R das Ton (¨e) *sound*
R das Tonbandgerät (-e) *tape recorder*
R der Topf (¨e) *pot, saucepan*
R das Tor (-e) *gate, goal*
die Torte (-n) *flan, gateau*
* tragbar *portable*
tragen *to carry, wear*
* sich trainieren *to train*
* der Trainingsanzug (¨e) *tracksuit*
* trampen *to hitch-hike*
Transistor- *transistor . . .*
der Traube (-n) *grape*
träumen *to dream*
träume süß! *sweet dreams!*
traurig *sad*
sich treffen *to meet*
* der Treffpunkt *meeting point*
treiben *to do, drift*
die Treppe (-n) *stairs*
das Treppenhaus *staircase*
* treten *to step*
trinken *to drink*
das Trinkgeld (-er) *tip*
das Trinkwasser *drinking water*
kein Trinkwasser *not*
drinking water
trocken *dry*
* trocknen *to dry*
die Trompete (-n) *trumpet*
* trotz *in spite of*
* trüb *gloomy*
Tschüs! *cheerio!*
das Tuch (¨er) *cloth*
tun *to do*
die Tür (-en) *door*
der Turm (¨e) *tower*
turnen *to do gymnastics*
Turnen *Gymnastics*
die Turnhalle (-n) *gymnasium*
die Tüte (-n) *bag*
typisch *typical*

die U-Bahn (-en) *underground*
übel *ill, evil*
* üben *to practise*
über *over, above*
über Köln *via Cologne*
überall *everywhere*
* überfahren *to run over*
die Überfahrt (-en) *crossing*
* überfallen *to attack*
überhaupt *on the whole*
* überhaupt nichts *nothing at all*
* überholen *to overtake*
* überlegen *to think about*
übermorgen *day after tomorrow*
übernachten *to spend the night*
die Übernachtung (-en) *overnight*
stay
* überqueren *to cross*
* überraschen *to surprise*
überrascht *surprised*
* die Überraschung (-en) *surprise*
* übersetzen *to translate*
* übertreiben *to exaggerate*

* überzeugen *to convince*
* übrig *left over*
* übrigens *besides*
die Übung (-en) *exercise*
* das Ufer (-) *river bank*
die Uhr (-en) *clock, time*
die Uhrzeit (-en) *clock time*
um *round, at*
die Umgebung (-en) *surroundings*
der Umkleideraum (¨e) *changing*
room
* umkommen (sep.) *to die*
R die Umleitung (-en) *diversion*
* ums Leben kommen *to die*
* der Umschlag (¨e) *envelope*
* umsonst *in vain, free*
umsteigen (sep.) *to change*
(trains etc.)
R der Umtausch *exchange*
R umtauschen (sep.) *to exchange*
sich umziehen *to change*
(clothes)
unangenehm *unpleasant*
* unbedingt *absolutely*
* unbekannt *unknown*
* unbeschränkt *unlimited*
und *and*
* unentschieden *undecided, a*
draw
* der Unfall (¨e) *accident*
unfit *unfit*
unfreundlich *unfriendly*
* ungeduldig *impatient*
ungefähr *approximately*
* ungenügend *unsatisfactory*
* das Unglück (¨e) *misfortune,*
accident
unglücklich *unfortunate*
unglücklicherweise
unfortunately
* die Uni (-s) *university*
die Uniform (-en) *uniform*
* die Universität (-en) *university*
unmöglich *impossible*
* unrecht haben *to be wrong*
unruhig *restless*
unschuldig *innocent*
unser *our*
der Unsinn *nonsense*
unten *below, downstairs*
unter *under, below*
* das Untergeschoß (-sse) *cellar,*
basement
die Untergrundbahn
(-en) *underground railway*
R sich unterhalten *to chat*
* die Unterkunft (¨e) *accommodation*
R der Unterricht (*no*
plural) *instruction*
der Unterschied (-e) *difference*
* unterschiedlich *variable*
unterschreiben *to sign*
die Unterschrift (-en) *signature*
R untersuchen *to examine*
die Untertasse (-n) *saucer*
die Unterwäsche *underclothes*
unterwegs *on the way*
unwahrscheinlich *improbable*
unzufrieden *dissatisfied*
der Urlaub (-e) *holiday, leave*
der Urlauber (-) *holiday maker*
die Ursache (-n) *cause*

die Vanille *vanilla*

die Vase (-n) *vase*
der Vater (-) *father*
   Vati *dad*
* der Vegetarier (-) *vegetarian (male)*
  die Vegetarierin (-nen) *vegetarian (female)*
H sich verabreden *to make an appointment*
* die Verabredung (-en) *appointment*
* sich verabschieden *to leave*
* die Veranstaltung (-en) *event*
* der Verband (-e) *club*
* verbessern *to improve*
* verbinden *to connect*
* die Verbindung (-en) *connection*
  verboten *forbidden*
  verbringen *to spend (time)*
* verdienen *to earn*
  der Verein (-e) *club*
R die Vereinigten Staaten *USA*
* vergebens *in vain*
  vergessen *to forget*
* der Vergleich (-e) *comparison*
H vergleichen *to compare*
* das Vergnügen (-) *pleasure*
* das Verhältnis (-se) *relationship*
* verheiratet *married*
sich verirren *to lose the way*
R der Verkauf (-e) *sale*
  verkaufen *to sell*
* der Verkäufer (-) *salesman*
* der Verkehr (-) *traffic*
* verkehren *to run (of transport)*
  die Verkehrsampel (-n) *traffic lights*
  das Verkehrsamt (-er) *tourist office*
* die Verkehrsstauung (-en) *traffic jam*
* verlangen *to demand*
  verlassen *to leave*
  sich verlaufen *to lose the way*
  sich verletzen *to get hurt*
  verletzt *injured*
die Verletzung (-en) *injury*
* sich verlieben *to fall in love*
  verlieren *to lose*
* verlobt *engaged*
* der Verlobte (-n) *fiancé*
die Verlobte *fiancée*
* vermeiden *to avoid*
* vernünftig *reasonable*
* verpassen *to miss*
* verreisen *to go away*
* verrenken *to twist*
  verrückt *mad*
* verschieden *different*
* verschließen *to lock*
* verschwinden *to disappear*
* versetzen *to remove, transfer*
* versichern *to insure, assure*
  die Versicherung (-en) *insurance*
  verspätet *delayed*
die Verspätung (-en) *delay*
  versprechen *to promise*
* verständlich *understandable*
  verstehen *to understand*
* die Verstopfung (-en) *constipation*
* der Versuch (-e) *attempt*
  versuchen *to try*
* verteidigen *to defend*
* sich vertragen *to behave*
* verunglücken *to have an accident*
* verunglückt *injured*
* der Verwandte (-n) *relative (male)*

* die Verwandte (-n) *relative (female)*
* verwundet *wounded*
* verzeihen *to excuse*
* die Verzeihung (-en) *excuse*
* verzollen *to declare (customs)*
  der Vetter (-) *cousin (male)*
  Video- *video . . .*
* das Videogerät (-e) *video recorder*
* das Vieh (-er) *cattle*
  viel *much*
  viel Glück *good luck!*
  viel Vergnügen *have a good time!*
  viele *many*
  vielen Dank *many thanks*
  vielleicht *perhaps*
  vielmals *many times*
  vier *four*
  viereckig *square, rectangular*
das Viertel (-) *quarter*
die Viertelstunde (-n) *quarter of an hour*
der Vogel (-) *bird*
  voll *full*
der Volleyball (-e) *volleyball*
* völlig *completely*
* vollkommen *completely*
* Vollkornbrot *wholemeal bread*
die Vollpension *full board*
  volltanken (*sep.*) *to fill up (petrol)*
  vom (von dem) *from the, of the*
  von *from, of*
  von wo *where from*
  von Zeit zu Zeit *from time to time*
  vor *before, in front of*
  vor allem *above all*
  vor kurzem *a short time ago*
  vorbei *past*
  vorbeigehen (*sep.*) *to pass*
  vorbeikommen (*sep.*) *to look in*
  vorbereiten *to prepare*
  Vorder- *front . . .*
R die Vorfahrt *right of way*
  vorgehen (*sep.*) *to go ahead*
  vorgestern *day before yesterday*
  vorhaben (*sep.*) *to plan*
der Vorhang (-e) *curtain*
  vorher *previously*
die Vorhersage (-n) *forecast*
  vorig *last (previous)*
* vorkommen (*sep.*) *to happen*
* vorläufig *provisional(ly)*
der Vormittag (-e) *morning*
  vormittags *in the morning*
der Vorname (-n) *first name*
  vorne *at the front*
der Vorort (-e) *suburb*
* der Vorschlag (-e) *proposal, plan*
* vorschlagen (*sep.*) *to propose*
die Vorsicht (-en) *caution*
  vorsichtig *cautious*
* die Vorspeise (-n) *starter (meal)*
die Vorstadt (-e) *suburb*
* sich vorstellen (*sep.*) *to introduce (oneself)*
die Vorstellung (-en) *introduction, performance*
* der Vorteil (-e) *advantage*
die Vorwahlnummer (-n) *code (telephone)*
* vorwärts *forwards*
* vorzeigen (*sep.*) *to show*
* vorziehen (*sep.*) *to prefer*

R wach *awake*
* wachsen *to grow*
* die Waffe (-n) *weapon*
der Wagen (-) *car*
die Wahl (-en) *choice*
  wählen *to choose*
* das Wahlfach (-er) *optional subject*
  wahr *true*
  während *during, while*
  wahrscheinlich *probable(/y)*
der Wald (-er) *wood (trees)*
  Wales *Wales*
der Waliser (-) *Welshman*
  walisisch *Welsh*
die Wand (-e) *wall*
  wandern *to hike*
die Wanderung (-en) *walk, hike*
  wann *when*
die Ware (-n) *product, goods*
das Warenhaus (-er) *department store*
  warm *warm*
  warnen *to warn*
die Warnung (-en) *warning*
  warten *to wait*
der Warteraum (-e) *waiting room*
der Wartesaal (-ale) *waiting room*
das Wartezimmer (-) *waiting room*
  warum *why*
  was *what*
  was? *what?*
  was fehlt? *what's up?*
  was für? *what sort of?*
  was für ein? *what sort of a?*
  was gibt's? *what is there?*
  was ist . . .? *what is?*
  was ist das? *what is that?*
  was ist los? *what's the matter?*
  was läuft? *what's on?*
* das Waschbecken (-) *wash basin*
die Wäsche *washing, laundry*
  (sich) waschen *to wash*
die Wäscherei (-en) *laundry room*
die Waschmaschine (-n) *washing machine*
* das Waschpulver *washing powder*
der Waschraum (-e) *washroom*
das Wasser *water*
der Wasserball *water polo*
der Wasserfall (-e) *waterfall*
der Wasserhahn (-e) *water tap*
das WC (-s) *WC*
der Wechsel (-) *change*
H der Wechselkurs (-e) *rate of exchange*
  wechseln *to change*
die Wechselstube (-n) *bureau de change*
  wecken *to wake*
der Wecker (-) *alarm clock*
* weder *neither*
* weder . . .
*   noch . . . *neither . . . nor . . .*
der Weg (-e) *way, track*
  weg *away*
* wegen *because of*
  weggehen (*sep.*) *to go away*
* wegnehmen (*sep.*) *to take away*
der Wegweiser (-) *signpost*
* wegwerfen (*sep.*) *to throw away*
  wehtun (*sep.*) *to hurt*
* weiblich *feminine, female*
* weich *soft*

	Weihnachten *Christmas*	
	weil *because*	
die	Weile (-n) *while*	
der	Wein (-e) *wine*	
	weinen *to cry, weep*	
die	Weinkarte (-n) *wine list*	
der	Weinkeller (-) *wine cellar*	
die	Weinliste (-n) *wine list*	
die	Weinprobe (-n) *wine-tasting*	
die	Weinstube (-n) *wine parlour*	
der	Weintraube (-n) *grape*	
* die	Weise (-n) *way*	
	weiß *white*	
* das	Weißbrot *white bread*	
der	Weißwein (-e) *white wine*	
	weit *far*	
	weiter *further*	
	weiterfahren (*sep.*) *drive on*	
	weitergeben (*sep.*) *pass on*	
	weitergehen (*sep.*) *go on*	
*	weiterhin *in future*	
	welcher *which*	
* der	Wellensittich (-e) *budgerigar*	
die	Welt *world*	
* die	Weltmeisterschaft (-en) *world cup*	
*	wem *to whom*	
*	wen *whom*	
	wenig *little*	
	ein wenig *a little*	
	wenige *few*	
	wenigstens *at least*	
	wenn *when, if*	
	wer *who*	
* die	Werbung (-en) *advertising, advertisement*	
	werden *to become*	
	werfen *to throw*	
die	Werkstätte (-n) *workshop*	
R	werktags *weekdays*	
* das	Werkzeug (-e) *tool*	
* der	Wert (-e) *value, worth*	
R	wert *worth*	
*	wertvoll *valuable*	
* die	Wespe (-n) *wasp*	
	West- *west . . .*	
der	West *west*	
	Westen *west*	
	westlich *western*	
das	Wetter *weather*	
* der	Wetterbericht (-e) *weather report*	
* die	Wetterlage (-n) *weather conditions*	
* die	Wettervorhersage (-n) *weather forecast*	
	wichtig *important*	
	wie *how*	
	wie bitte? *I beg your pardon?*	
	wie geht's? *how are you?*	
	wie komme ich am besten . . .? *how do I get . . .?*	
	wie Schade! *what a pity!*	
	wieder *again*	
	wiederholen *to repeat*	
	wiederhören *to hear again*	
	auf Wiederhören *goodbye (telephone)*	
	auf Wiederschauen *goodbye*	
	wiedersehen *to see again*	
	auf Wiedersehen *goodbye*	
*	wiegen *to rock, cradle, weigh*	
	Wien *Vienna*	

das	Wiener Schnitzel (-) *Vienna cutlet*	
die	Wiese (-n) *meadow*	
	wieso? *how do you mean?*	
	wieviel(e)? *how much (many)?*	
	der Wievielte? *what date?*	
* das	Wildleder (-) *buckskin*	
	willkommen *to welcome*	
das	Willkommen (-) *welcome*	
der	Wind (-e) *wind*	
	windig *windy*	
* die	Windschutzscheibe (-n) *windscreen*	
	winken *to wave*	
der	Winter *winter*	
der	Wintersport *winter sport*	
	wirklich *really*	
H die	Wirklichkeit (-en) *reality*	
die	Wirtschaft (-en) *economy; inn*	
das	Wirtshaus (-̈er) *public house, inn*	
	wissen *to know*	
die	Wissenschaften *sciences*	
* die	Witwe (-n) *widow*	
* der	Witwer (-) *widower*	
	wo? *where?*	
	wo . . . her? *where from?*	
die	Woche (-n) *week*	
das	Wochenende (-n) *weekend*	
	wochentags *on weekdays*	
*	wöchentlich *weekly*	
	woher? *where from?*	
	wohin? *where to?*	
	wohl *well, I suppose*	
*	sich wohlfülen (*sep.*) *to feel well*	
der	Wohnblock (-e *or* -s) *block of flats*	
	wohnen *to live*	
der	Wohnort (-e) *domicile*	
die	Wohnung (-en) *flat, home*	
der	Wohnwagen (-) *caravan*	
das	Wohnzimmer (-) *living room*	
die	Wolke (-n) *cloud*	
*	wolkenlos *cloudless*	
	wolkig *cloudy*	
die	Wolle *wool*	
	wollen *to want to*	
das	Wort (-e *or* -̈er) *word*	
das	Wörterbuch (-̈er) *dictionary*	
	wunderbar *wonderful*	
	wunderschön *wonderful*	
der	Wunsch (-̈e) *wish*	
	wünschen *to wish*	
die	Wurst (-̈e) *sausage*	
die	Wurstbude (-n) *sausage stall*	
das	Würstchen (-) *small sausage*	
die	Wut *anger*	
	wütend *angry*	
* die	Zahl (-en) *number*	
	zahlen *to pay*	
	Zählen *to count*	
der	Zahn (-̈e) *tooth*	
	Zahn- *tooth . . .*	
der	Zahnarzt (-̈e) *dentist*	
die	Zahnbürste (-n) *toothbrush*	
das	Zahnpasta *toothpaste*	
die	Zahnschmerzen (*plural*) *toothache*	
* die	Zehe (-n)/der Zeh (-en) *toe*	
	zeichnen *to draw*	
	Zeichnen *drawing (activity)*	
die	Zeichnung (-en) *drawing*	
	zeigen *to show*	
die	Zeit (-en) *time*	

die	Zeitschrift (-en) *magazine*	
die	Zeitung (-en) *newspaper*	
das	Zeitungsgeschäft (-e) *paper shop*	
der	Zeitungskiosk (-e) *paper stall*	
der	Zeitungsstand (-̈e) *paper stand*	
das	Zelt (-e) *tent*	
	zelten *to camp*	
der/das	Zentimeter *centimetre*	
die	Zentralheizung *central heating*	
das	Zentrum (-ren) *centre*	
der	Zettel (-) *note*	
* das	Zeug *thing*	
* der	Zeuge (-n) *witness*	
* das	Zeugnis (-se) *report (school)*	
R	ziehen *to pull*	
das	Ziel (-e) *aim, destination, target*	
	ziemlich *fairly*	
die	Zigarette (-n) *cigarette*	
das	Zimmer (-) *room*	
* der	Zimmernachweis (-e) *room indication*	
die	Zitrone (-n) *lemon*	
*	zittern *to tremble*	
der	Zoll *customs*	
* der	Zollbeamte (-n) *customs official*	
*	zollfrei *duty free*	
* die	Zollkontrolle (-n) *customs control*	
der	Zoo (-s) *zoo*	
	zornig *angry*	
	zu *to*	
	zu Fuß *on foot*	
	zu Mittag essen *to have lunch*	
der	Zucker *sugar*	
	zuerst *at first*	
R die	Zufahrt (-en) *approach (road)*	
	zufrieden *satisfied*	
der	Zug (-̈e) *train*	
H	zugestiegen *got in (bus etc.)*	
	zuhören (*sep.*) *listen*	
* die	Zukunft *future*	
	zum (zu dem) *to the*	
*	zum Wohl! *cheers!*	
	zumachen (*sep.*) *to close*	
	zunächst *at first, next*	
*	zunehmen (*sep.*) *to increase*	
* die	Zunge (-n) *tongue*	
	zur (zu der) *to the*	
	zurück *back*	
	zurück- . . . *back*	
	zurückfahren (*sep.*) *to return*	
*	zurückgeben (*sep.*) *to give back*	
*	zurückkehren (*sep.*) *to return*	
	zurückkommen (*sep.*) *to come back*	
	zusammen *together*	
* der	Zusammenstoß (-̈sse) *crash*	
* der	Zuschauer (-) *spectator*	
* der	Zuschlag (-̈e) *supplement*	
H	zuschlagspflichtig *supplement obligatory*	
*	zuschließen (*sep.*) *to close*	
* der	Zutritt (-e) *access*	
R	Kein Zutritt (-e) *no access*	
*	zuviel *too much*	
	zuviel (e) *too many*	
* der	Zweck (-e) *aim, purpose*	
* der	Zweifel (-) *doubt*	
H	zweifellos *without doubt*	
die	Zwiebel (-n) *onion*	
	zwischen *between*	
	zwo *two*	

ENGLISH–GERMAN VOCABULARY (SELECTIVE)

able: to be able to   *können*
about (= around)   *um* +acc.
about (with time)   *um* +acc.
above   *über* +dat./acc.
abroad (adv.)   *im Ausland*
   to go abroad   *ins Ausland fahren*
address   *die Adresse (-n), die*
   Anschrift (-en)
afraid (adj.)   *ängstlich*
   to be afraid of   *Angst haben vor*
   +dat.
after (prep.)   *nach* +dat.
after (adv.)   *nachher*
after (conj.)   *nachdem*
again (adv.)   *wieder*
against   *gegen* +acc.
ago (adv.)   *vor* +dat.
alarm clock   *der Wecker (-)*
all   *all, alle*
all sorts of   *allerlei*
allowed   *erlaubt*
   to be allowed to   *dürfen*
almost   *fast, beinahe*
alone   *allein*
already   *schon*
although   *obwohl, obgleich*
always   *immer*
among   *unter* +dat.
and   *und*
angry   *böse*
angrily   *zornig, wütend*
to arrive   *ankommen*
as . . . as   *so . . . wie*
as (conj.)   *während, indem*
to ask   *fragen, bitten*
at (prep.) (place) *in, an, bei;* (time)
   um, zu
at last   *endlich*
at least   *wenigstens, mindestens*
aunt   *die Tante (-n)*

bad   *schlecht, schlimm*
bank   *die Bank (-en)*
bathroom   *das Badezimmer (-)*
to be   *sein*
to be situated   *sich befinden*
because (conj.)   *denn, weil*
bed   *das Bett (-en)*
bedroom   *das Schlafzimmer (-)*
before, in front of   *vor* +dat./acc.
to begin   *beginnen, anfangen*
beginning   *der Anfang (-̈e)*
behind (prep.)   *hinter* +acc./dat.
below   *unter* +dat./acc
beside   *neben* +dat./acc.
between   *zwischen* +dat./acc.
big   *groß*

black   *schwarz*
book   *das Buch (-̈er)*
bread   *das Brot (-e* or *-sorten)*
breakfast   *das Frühstück (-e)*
to bring (with)   *(mit)bringen*
brother   *der Bruder (-̈)*
to build   *bauen*
building   *das Gebäude (-)*
bus   *der (Auto)bus (-se)*
to buy   *kaufen*
by (prep.)   *durch* +acc.; *von* +dat.
by train   *mit dem Zug*

café   *das Café (-s)*
to call   *rufen;* (on telephone)   *anrufen*
camera   *die Kamera (-s)*
campsite   *der Lagerplatz (-̈e)*
car   *das Auto (-s), der Wagen (-)*
card   *die Karte (-n)*
to cash (a cheque)   *einlösen*
chair   *der Stuhl (-̈e)*
cheque   *der Scheck (-e* or *-s)*
child   *das Kind (-er)*
Christmas   *Weihnachten*
cinema   *das Kino (-s)*
clean   *sauber*
to clean   *putzen*
clear   *klar*
coast   *die Küste (-n)*
coffee   *der Kaffee*
cold (noun)   *die Kälte;* (=
   illness)   *die Erkältung (-e)*
cold (adj.)   *kalt*
to come   *kommen*
comfortable   *bequem*
counter (shop)   *der Ladentisch (-e);*
   (pub)   *die Theke (-n);* (bank)   *der*
   Kassenschalter (-)
countryside   *das Land*
to cry (= shout)   *schreien;* (= weep)
   weinen
cup   *die Tasse (-n)*
curtain (net)   *die Gardine (-n);*
   (heavy)   *der Vorhang (-̈e)*
to cut   *schneiden*

dad   *Vati*
date (time)   *das Datum (Daten)*
daughter   *die Tochter (-̈)*
day   *der Tag (-e)*
to decide   *beschließen, sich entscheiden*
difficult   *schwer, schwierig*
dining room   *das Eßzimmer (-), das*
   Speisezimmer (-)
dinner   *das Abendessen (-)*
directory (telephone)   *das*
   Telefonbuch (-̈er)

dish   *das Gericht (-e)*
distance   *die Ferne*
   in the distance   *in der Ferne*
to do   *machen, tun*
dog   *der Hund (-e)*
door   *die Tür (-en)*
   back door   *die Hintertür (-en)*
   front door   *die Haustür (-en)*
downstairs: to go downstairs   *nach*
   unten gehen, die Treppe
   hinuntergehen
to drink   *trinken*
to drive   *fahren, führen*
duck   *die Ente (-n)*
during (prep.)   *während* +gen.

Easter   *Ostern*
   at Easter   *zu Ostern*
Easter holidays   *die Osterferien*
to eat   *essen;* (of animals) *fressen*
to eat up   *aufessen, auffressen*
egg   *das Ei (-er)*
elder (adj.)   *älter*
elsewhere   *anderswo*
empty   *leer*
English   *englisch*
enough   *genug*
evening   *der Abend (-e)*
everybody   *jeder*
everything   *alles*
everywhere   *überall*
except   *außer* +dat.
eye   *das Auge (-n)*

face   *das Gesicht (-er)*
family   *die Familie (-n)*
far   *weit, fern, entfernt*
farm   *der Bauernhof (-̈e)*
fat   *dick*
father   *der Vater (-̈)*
favourite   *Lieblings-*
   favourite subject   *das*
   Lieblingsfach (-̈er)
few   *einige, ein paar, wenige*
film   *der Film (-e)*
to find   *finden*
first   *erst*
   at first   *zuerst*
fish   *der Fisch (-e)*
flash: quick as a flash   *blitzschnell*
flat (adj.)   *flach*
flat (noun)   *die Wohnung (-en)*
football   *der Fußball (-̈e)*
for (conj.)   *denn*
for (prep.)   *für* +acc.
to forget   *vergessen*
fork   *die Gabel (-n)*

fortnight *vierzehn Tage*
friend (male) *der Freund (-e);*
  (female) *die Freundin (-nen)*
friendly (adv.) *freundlich*
from (prep.) *von* +dat., *aus* +dat.
front: in front of (prep.) *vor* +dat./
  acc.
furniture *die Möbel* (plural)

garden *der Garten (-)*
gateau *die Torte (-n)*
Germany *(das) Deutschland*
to get (= become) *werden*
to get dressed *sich anziehen*
to get undressed *sich ausziehen*
to get changed *sich umziehen*
to get up/to stand up *aufstehen*
girl *das Mädchen (-)*
girlfriend *die Freundin (-nen)*
to give *geben*
glad *froh*
glass *das Glas (-er)*
to go *gehen, fahren*
to go back *zurückgehen, zurückfahren*
to go for a walk *einen Spaziergang*
  machen
good *gut*
grandmother *die Großmutter (-)*
granny *die Oma (-s)*
grapes *die Weintrauben*

half (adj.) *halb*
half (noun) *die Hälfte (-n)*
half an hour *eine halbe Stunde*
hand *die Hand (-e)*
to have to *müssen*
he *er*
to hear *hören*
to help *helfen* +dat.
her *ihr*
here *hier*
his *sein*
holiday *der Urlaub (-e)*
holidays *die Ferien* (plural)
home: to go home *nach Hause*
  gehen
hope: I hope that, etc. *hoffentlich*
to hope for *hoffen auf* +acc.
hospital *das Krankenhaus (-er)*
hotel *das Hotel (-s)*
hour *die Stunde (-n)*
house *das Hause (-er)*
how *wie*
how much *wieviel*
however *aber*
hungry *hungrig*
  to be hungry *Hunger haben*
husband *der Mann (-er)*

I *ich*
ice *das Eis (-e)*
idea *die Idee (-n)*
if (conj.) *wenn, ob*
ill *krank*
in (into) *in* +dat./acc.
inside *drinnen*
interested: to be interested in *sich*
  interessieren für +acc.
to invite *einladen*
island *die Insel (-n)*
it *es*

jam *die Marmelade (-n)*
juice *der Saft (-e)*

to jump *springen*
just (adv.) *eben*

kitchen *die Küche (-n)*
knife *das Messer (-)*
to knock at *klopfen an* +acc.
to know (a fact) *wissen;* (a
  person) *kennen*

lake *der See (-n)*
large *groß*
last *letzt*
late *spät*
to laugh *lachen*
to learn *lernen*
to leave *verlassen;* (=
  depart) *abfahren*
left *links*
less *weniger*
letter *der Brief (-e)*
to lie *liegen*
light *das Licht (-er)*
to light *anzünden*
to like *gern haben*
to listen *(zu)hören;* (= pay
  attention) *aufpassen*
little *klein*
to live *leben;* (= to dwell) *wohnen*
long *lang*
to look *blicken*
to look for *suchen*
to look (= appear) *aussehen*
to look forward (to) *sich freuen (auf*
  +acc.)
to lose *verlieren*
to lose one's way *sich verlaufen*
a lot *viel, viele*

man *der Mann (-er)*
many *viele*
marvellous *wunderbar*
meal *die Mahlzeit (-en)*
menu *die Speisekarte (-n)*
midday *(der) Mittag (-e)*
minute *die Minute (-n)*
to miss (e.g. a bus) *verpassen*
money *das Geld*
more *mehr*
morning *der Morgen (-)*
mother, mummy *die Mutter (-),*
  Mutti
mountain *der Berg (-e)*
  range of mountains *das Gebirge*
  (-)
much *viel*
my *mein*

near *nahe*
nearly *fast*
to need *brauchen*
new *neu*
newspaper *die Zeitung (-en)*
next *nächst*
nice *nett*
night *die Nacht (-e)*
no *nein*
nothing *nichts*
to notice *bemerken*
now *nun, jetzt*
number *die Nummer (-n)*

of course *natürlich*
old *alt*
on *auf* +dat./acc.

only *nur, erst*
open *offen*
to open *öffnen, aufmachen*
to order *bestellen*
other *ander*
our *unser*
out of *aus* +dat.
outside *draußen*
over there *dort drüben*
own *eigen*

parents *die Eltern* (plural)
park *der Park (-e)*
particularly *besonders*
to pass (of time) *vergehen*
passport *der Paß (Pässe)*
past: to go past *vorbeigehen (an*
  +dat.)
to pay for *bezahlen*
peas *Erbsen*
people *die Leute*
pepper *der Pfeffer*
perhaps *vielleicht*
person *die Person (-en)*
pet *das Haustier (-e)*
piece *das Stück (-e);* (of toast) *die*
  Scheibe (-n)
pipe *die Pfeife (-n)*
plan *der Plan (-e)*
please! *bitte!*
pleased: to be pleased (about) *sich*
  freuen (über +acc.)
poor *arm*
post office *das Postamt (-er), die*
  Post
present *das Geschenk (-e)*
pretty *hübsch*

quality *die Qualität*
quarter *das Viertel (-)*
quick *schnell, rasch*
quickly *schnell, rasch*
quite *ganz*

radio *das Radio (-s)*
railway *die Eisenbahn (-en)*
to reach *erreichen*
to read *lesen*
ready *fertig*
really *wirklich*
reception (desk) *die Rezeption*
  (-en), der Empfang (-e)
to remember *sich erinnern an* +acc.
to repair *reparieren*
to repeat *wiederholen*
to reply *antworten, erwidern*
reply *die Antwort (-en)*
to reserve *reservieren*
restaurant *das Restaurant (-s)*
to return *zurückgehen,*
  zurückkommen
right *recht, rechts*
right (correct) *richtig*
  to be right *recht haben*
to ring *klingeln, läuten*
room (single) *das Einzelzimmer (-)*
room (double) *das Doppelzimmer (-)*
to run *laufen*

sandwich *das Sandwich (-s* or *-es)*
to say *sagen*
scarcely *kaum*
school *die Schule (-n)*
sea *die See (-n), das Meer (-e)*

seaside: at the seaside *an der See*
to see *sehen*
to send *schicken, senden*
she *sie*
to shine *scheinen*
shopping: to go shopping *die Einkäufe machen*
to show *zeigen*
shower *die Dusche (-n)*
since (prep.) *seit* +dat.
since (conj.) *seitdem*
since (adv.) *seither*
single *einzeln;* (unmarried) *ledig*
sister *die Schwester (-n)*
    brothers and sisters *die Geschwister*
to sit, be sitting *sitzen*
to sit down *sich setzen*
slice *die Scheibe (-n)*
slowly *langsam*
small *klein*
to smile *lächeln*
so *so, also*
some *einige, wenige*
somebody *jemand*
something *etwas*
soon *bald*
sorry! *Verzeihung! es tut mir leid*
to speak *sprechen*
to spend (time) *verbringen*
spring *der Frühling (-e)*
stamp *die Briefmarke (-n)*
to starve *verhungern*
station *der Bahnhof (¨e)*
    main station *der Hauptbahnhof (¨e)*
to stay *bleiben, wohnen*
still (adv.) *noch*
to stop *anhalten;* (= to cease) *aufhören*
story *die Geschichte (-n)*
straight away *gleich*
to swim *schwimmen*
sugar *der Zucker (-)*
summer *der Sommer (-)*
sun *die Sonne (-n)*
sure *sicher*

table *der Tisch (-e)*
to take *nehmen*
to talk *sprechen*
tea *der Tee*

telegram *das Telegramm (-e)*
telephone *das Telefon (-e)*
to tell *sagen, erzählen*
tent *das Zelt (-e)*
terrible, terribly *furchtbar, schrecklich*
than (in comparison) *als*
thanks *der Dank* (no plural)
    many thanks *vielen Dank*
their *ihr*
then *dann, denn, damals*
there *da, dort*
thermos flask *die Thermosflasche (-n)*
they *sie*
thin *dünn, mager*
thing *das Ding (-e)*
to think *denken, glauben*
to think about/of *halten von* +dat.
through *durch* +acc.
to throw *werfen*
ticket *die Fahrkarte (-n)*
ticket office *der Schalter (-), der Fahrkartenschalter (-)*
time *die Zeit (-en)*
to (prep.) *an* +dat./acc., *zu* +dat.
toast *der Toast (-e)*
today *heute*
too (adv.) *zu*
too many, too much *zuviel (-e)*
tooth *der Zahn (¨e)*
towards: he came towards me *er kam auf mich zu*
town *die Stadt (¨e)*
town hall *das Rathaus (¨er)*
train *der Zug (¨e)*
    goods train *der Güterzug (¨e)*
    slow train *der Personenzug (¨e)*
    through/fast train *der D-Zug (¨e)*
traveller *der/die Reisende (-n)*
travellers' cheque *der Reisescheck (-e or -s)*
to try *versuchen*

uncle *der Onkel (-)*
under (prep.) *unter* +acc./dat
to understand *verstehen*
until *bis*
upstairs *oben*

vegetable(s) *das Gemüse*
very *sehr*

view *die Aussicht (-en)*
village *das Dorf (¨er)*
vinegar *der Essig*
visit *der Besuch (-e)*
to visit *besuchen*
voice *die Stimme (-n)*

to wait (for) *warten (auf* +acc.*)*
waiter *der Kellner (-), der Ober (-)*
waitress *die Kellnerin (-nen)*
walk: to go for a walk *einen Spaziergang machen, spazierengehen*
to walk *zu Fuß gehen*
to want *wollen*
warden *der Wärter (-)*
to wash (oneself) *(sich) waschen*
washroom *der Waschraum (¨e)*
water *das Wasser*
we *wir*
weather *das Wetter (-)*
week *die Woche (-n)*
well: I am well *es geht mir gut*
when *wann, wenn*
where *wo*
while (conj.) *während*
    after a while *nach einer Weile*
white *weiß*
why *warum*
window *das Fenster (-)*
wish *der Wunsch (¨e)*
to wish *wünschen*
with (prep.) *mit* +dat.
without (prep.) *ohne* +acc.
worry *die Sorge (-n)*
to write *schreiben*

year *das Jahr (-e)*
yellow *gelb*
yes *ja, jawohl*
yesterday *gestern*
yesterday evening *gestern abend*
yet *doch*
you *du, ihr, Sie*
young *jung*
your *dein, Ihr, euer*
youth hostel *die Jugendherberge (-n)*

INDEX